LETTERS

TO AND FROM

CAESAR RODNEY

1756-1784

Member of the STAMP ACT CONGRESS *and the* FIRST
AND SECOND CONTINENTAL CONGRESSES; *Speaker of the*
DELAWARE COLONIAL ASSEMBLY; *President of* THE DELA-
WARE STATE; *Major General of the* DELAWARE MILITIA;
Signer of THE DECLARATION OF INDEPENDENCE

Edited by

GEORGE HERBERT RYDEN, Ph.D.

Professor of History and Political Science
University of Delaware
and
State Archivist of Delaware

Published for the

HISTORICAL SOCIETY OF DELAWARE

BY THE UNIVERSITY OF PENNSYLVANIA PRESS

Philadelphia

1933

MARBLE STATUE OF CAESAR RODNEY
Statuary Hall, Washington, D. C.

PREFACE

THIS collection of the letters of Caesar Rodney comprises all extant letters to or from him which are of genuine historical interest. The basis of the book is the collection which was purchased by the Historical Society of Delaware at the sale of Rodney papers in Philadelphia in 1919. To these letters have been added many more which, as a result of extended search throughout the country, were secured from libraries, historical societies, and private collectors. Such letters and portions of letters as were merely personal have been eliminated. Excisions in the body of letters here reproduced are indicated (. . .). Every effort has been made to secure accuracy. Where the letters themselves were not accessible to the editor, photostatic copies were obtained and, in all cases, the typewritten copy made for the printer has been carefully compared with the originals or the photostats. No attempt has been made to modernize the spelling of certain words or to correct what are obviously misspelled words if, in the opinion of the editor, they could be understood by the reader. Likewise incorrect punctuation marks and irregular capitalizations have been allowed to remain unchanged except in instances where the sense was so obscure as to necessitate corrections.

It is the pleasant duty of the editor to acknowledge the assistance he has received from his associates in the Committee on Publications of the Society, Hon. Richard S. Rodney and Christopher L. Ward, Esq. Judge Rodney has not only contributed important letters out of his rich storehouse of manuscripts, but has also given valuable advice and assistance. Mr. Ward has worked with the editor in the selection of the matter to be published and in the effort to present a correct transcription of the originals. Thanks are due, also, to Col. George A. Elliott, the President of the Society, and to all of its directors for their constant interest in the project and their leadership in providing financial support. To the Library of Congress, the Genealogical Society of Pennsylvania, the Historical Society of Pennsylvania, the New York Public Library, the New York Historical Society, the Public Archives Commission of the State of Delaware, and the other institutions, private collectors, and dealers, who have so generously permitted letters in their possession to be included in this book, and whose individual contributions are specifically indicated in the appendix, the editor makes this acknowledgment of their kindness.

Thankful acknowledgment of their helpful coöperation must also be made to Mr. Henry Clay Reed, Assistant Professor of History at the University of Delaware, and to Mr. Leon deValinger, Jr., Assistant to the State Archivist, both of whom have aided in searching for material in the Delaware Public Archives; to Mrs. Dorothy Sherwood Coy, formerly Curator of the collections of the Historical Society of Delaware, who copied and assisted in checking most of the letters and photostats, and to Miss Anna T. Lincoln, present Curator, Miss Mary McCafferty, and Miss Mary Richardson, for copying and checking later acquisitions. Messrs. Reed and deValinger and Miss McCafferty have also very kindly assisted the editor in reading the proof.

University of Delaware   GEORGE H. RYDEN
Newark, Delaware
February 9, 1933

ERRATUM

The date of letter number 92 on page 99 should be July 22, 1778. It is a duplicate of letter number 276, which appears on page 277 with the correct date.

CONTENTS

ILLUSTRATIONS

INTRODUCTION

CAESAR RODNEY

A Biographical Sketch

CAESAR RODNEY's chief claim to fame in the popular mind has been his dramatic overnight ride from his home near Dover to Philadelphia, where he arrived on July 2, 1776, in time to break the deadlock in Delaware's representation in the Continental Congress and determine the vote of his State for independence. To the historian this event is not so important as the fact that for almost ten years, that is, during the last ten years of his life, Caesar Rodney's career was replete with acts and episodes contributing to Delaware's part in the movement for independence both before and after the Declaration of Independence was adopted. As speaker of the last Delaware colonial assembly, he took a leading part in bringing about the complete separation of the Government of the Three Lower Counties from the British Empire and the Province of Pennsylvania. On June 15, 1776, the Assembly passed its famous resolution effecting the secession, and on the same day gave its delegates in Congress new instructions empowering them to join with the other delegates to vote for independence, to form a national government, and to conclude treaties with foreign states.

As the most active general officer of the Delaware militia before his elevation to the position of President of the Delaware State in 1778, and as a virtual war executive following his election to that office, he was chiefly instrumental in keeping the State faithful to its commitments and loyal to the cause of freedom. Upon this work, and upon his services in the Stamp Act Congress in 1765, in the First Continental Congress of 1774, and in the Second Continental Congress of 1775 onward, rests the larger fame to which Caesar Rodney is entitled.

Caesar Rodney was born on October 7, 1728, on his father's farm in the part of East Dover Hundred, Kent County, near the Delaware River, which, ever since its first settlement by Englishmen, has been called St. Jones Neck. His father, Caesar Rodney, was the youngest son of William Rodeney, the immigrant. His mother, Elizabeth Crawford Rodney, was the eldest daughter of Rev. Thomas Crawford, the first Episcopal missionary sent from England to Dover, Delaware, and its environs by the Society for the Propagation of the Gospel in Foreign Parts. Reared in a cultured home, she was an accomplished woman and early inculcated in her children a taste for reading.

Whatever education young Caesar had as a child he doubtless obtained, as was usual in those days, from itinerant teachers and from his parents. His father having died in 1745 when Caesar was in his seventeenth year, Nicholas

Ridgely, prothonotary and clerk of the peace for Kent County at the time, was appointed his guardian at the first session of the Orphans' Court following the father's death. Being the oldest child, Caesar in all probability remained on his parents' plantation, assisting his mother in directing its cultivation. No letters, however, having been preserved from this period, we must be content with mere conjecture. Whether Caesar went to school after his father's demise is unknown.

Rodney entered public life at the age of twenty-seven with a commission as high sheriff of Kent County in October 1755. This appointment was renewed for the two following years. He served as register of wills for Kent from 1763 to 1778, as deputy recorder of deeds in 1765, and as recorder from 1766 to 1775. From 1767 through the year 1774 he was also clerk of the Orphans' Court and for a year or so, 1770 to 1771, he was clerk of the peace. He was justice of the peace in 1764 and 1766, third justice of the Supreme Court for the Three Lower Counties in 1769, second justice in 1773. He was appointed co-trustee with John Vining of the Kent County Loan Office in 1769, sole trustee in 1775 and 1777, and probably continued in that office until his death.

The House of Assembly of the colonial government, a unicameral body of eighteen delegates, six elected from each county every year in October, met at New Castle from 1704 to 1776. In 1758 Rodney was a delegate from Kent for the first time. Beginning with 1761, with the exception of the year of 1771, he was reelected and served fourteen terms until 1775, the year of the election of the last Assembly of the colonial régime, the final session of which was held in July 1776. In 1769 he was chosen as speaker of the Assembly. In this year he strove unsuccessfully to secure a law prohibiting the importation of slaves into Delaware. He was speaker again in 1773, 1774, 1775, and held that office when the Assembly adjourned *sine die,* to be succeeded by a state legislature consti- tuted in accordance with the first state constitution adopted by the constitu- tional convention in September 1776.

During the colonial period, in the year 1762, he and Thomas McKean were commissioned by the Assembly to collect, revise, and publish the laws of the Government of the Three Lower Counties.

After the organization of The Delaware State, the General Assembly elected him, on February 21, 1777, second justice of the State Supreme Court. He de- clined this appointment, but accepted the office of judge of admiralty and was so commissioned by John McKinly, the first president of the State, on July 17, 1777.

The office of president of the State having become vacant through the cap- ture of McKinly by the British in September 1777, the General Assembly on

March 31, 1778, elected Rodney president for a term of three years, and he held that office until his successor, John Dickinson, succeeded him in 1781.

In 1783 Rodney was elected to his last state office, as a member of the upper house of the General Assembly, then called the Legislative Council and, upon its assembling in October 1783, this body made him speaker.

Rodney's military service began in 1756, when, on the outbreak of the French and Indian War, he joined Col. John Vining's regiment of Kent County militia and was made captain of one of its twelve companies, the one organized in Dover Hundred. He saw no active service, however, this regiment not being sent to the front.

When the news of the battles of Lexington and Concord reached the Three Lower Counties, two regiments of militia had already been organized in New Castle County. Immediately thereafter, on May 25, 1775, two were organized in Kent. Rodney was commissioned colonel of the so-called "Upper Regiment" and John Haslet of the "Lower."

In September 1775 the Council of Safety met in Dover and appointed Rodney brigadier general of the Kent militia, consisting of two battalions, and of the western battalion of Sussex County. Under the new state government he was again commissioned for the same office in 1777 by President McKinly. After McKinly's capture by the British, the acting president, Thomas McKean, made Rodney major general of the state militia, an office which he held until he was made president of the State in 1778.

In the affairs of the revolting colonies Rodney took an active part from the beginning of their revolutionary activities. He was Kent's representative in the Stamp Act Congress which met in New York in 1765. On August 2, 1774, the members of the Assembly, meeting in New Castle as an extra-legal convention, elected him one of three delegates to the First Continental Congress.

In March 1775 he was elected by the Assembly to a similar office in the Second Continental Congress and again in October 1775. In December 1777 the General Assembly of the newly created State appointed him delegate to the Continental Congress then sitting at York, Pennsylvania, but, on account of his many other duties, he was unable to attend its sessions.

In February 1782, and again in February 1783, he was chosen by the General Assembly as a member of the Confederation Congress but, because of illness, never sat in that body.

Having thus briefly summarized Rodney's public activities in general, it remains to consider more in detail his outstanding services to both State and Nation.

When, in company with Thomas McKean, he represented the Three

Lower Counties in the Stamp Act Congress in October 1765, he participated in the drawing up by that body of an address to the King, a memorial to the House of Lords, and a petition to the House of Commons, remonstrating against the Stamp Act and other acts of Parliament and setting forth in thirteen declarations the American theory of the constitutional relationship of the colonies to the mother country.

The Stamp Act having been repealed by Parliament in March 1766, Rodney, McKean, and George Read were appointed by the House of Assembly the following June to prepare an address to the King expressing the loyalty of the Government of the Three Lower Counties to His Majesty and the gratitude of the people in the colony for the repeal of that act.

When the Townshend Act, taxing certain imports into the colonies, was passed in 1767, the House of Assembly, again aroused, adopted in its October session in 1768 a resolution that that act and others, having "a manifest Tendency to deprive the Colonists in America of the exclusive Right of Taxing themselves and thereby to shew their Affection and Loyalty to the best of Kings, are subversive of the natural, constitutional and just Rights and Privileges of the respective Assemblies, and pernicious to American Freedom." The House of Assembly further resolved to send a "humble and dutiful" petition "to our most gracious Sovereign, expressing therein our ardent Affection and Loyalty to his sacred Person," but at the same time "most zealously and firmly, but with the utmost Decency and Submission, to assert our inestimable Rights and Liberties; delivered from God and Nature, handed down from our Ancestors, and confirmed to us by the Constitution; in the most earnest Manner to supplicate Relief against the Said Acts of Parliament, and to implore a Continuance of his Fatherly Care and Tenderness for the Liberties and Happiness of this, and all our Sister Colonies." Thomas McKean, George Read, and Caesar Rodney were designated a Committee of Correspondence and instructed to draw up an address to the King agreeable to the resolutions. The address was transmitted to the Colony's agent in London, Dennys de Berdt, for presentation to the British Government.

After the British Parliament passed the Boston Port Bill in the spring of 1774, closing that port and placing an embargo on all imports and exports as a punishment for the Boston Tea Party, the suffering that ensued in that city, especially among the poorer classes dependent upon work in connection with ship building, shipping, and trade in general, was so acute that appeals were sent out to the other colonies for aid. In Delaware, subscription lists were circulated by county committees of correspondence, and the money collected was sent to the starving Bostonians—or used for the purchase of flour for them. It was furthermore urged by the people of Massachusetts that a general congress be held in Philadelphia in September 1774, to discuss the American grievances in general, and to take some coercive action which might induce the British Parliament to repeal the Boston Port Bill as it had repealed the Stamp Act.

The question of sending delegates to Philadelphia came up in all the thirteen colonies in one way or another. In Delaware it was discussed in three mass meetings held consecutively in New Castle, Dover, and Lewes in June and July 1774. At these three meetings what proved to be almost identical resolutions were drawn up, directing the speaker of the Assembly, Caesar Rodney, to call a special meeting of that body to be held on August 1, 1774. Since only the proprietor or his deputy, the lieutenant governor, in Philadelphia, could call the Assembly together for a special session, Rodney was confronted with a dilemma. If he consented to call the Assembly, his act might be construed by John Penn, the governor, and by the British Government, as unconstitutional and revolutionary, and if he refused he might be dubbed a reactionary by the radical elements. Quickly making up his mind, he sent a circular letter to all the eighteen members of the Assembly. Nearly all the members responded and met in New Castle on the appointed day.

There was no thought at this time of separating from the mother country, but the colonies were thoroughly agreed on seeking redress of their grievances. The meeting in New Castle came to a quick decision. On the second day, August 2, it adopted a set of resolutions, instructing the three members of the body, who were selected to go to Philadelphia, what to do. These members were Rodney, McKean, and Read. Realizing that the meeting of the Assembly was irregular and that it was in reality a convention and not the Assembly (though its membership was that of the Assembly), Rodney signed the instructions to his two colleagues and to himself, not "Caesar Rodney, Speaker," but "Caesar Rodney, Chairman."

The three delegates proceeded to Philadelphia, and met with the delegates from the other colonies on September 5 in Carpenters Hall as the First Continental Congress. Rodney's appearance in Congress is referred to by John Adams in his diary for September 3. "Saturday. . . . This forenoon, Mr. Caesar Rodney of the lower counties on Delaware River, two Mr. Tilghmans from Maryland, were introduced to us. . . . Caesar Rodney is the oddest looking man in the world; he is tall, thin and slender as a reed, pale; his face is not bigger than a large apple, yet there is sense and fire, spirit, wit, and humor in his countenance. He made himself very merry with Ruggles and his pretended scruples and timidities at the last Congress."

The Delaware delegates assisted in drawing up the famous "plan of Association" which forbade the importation of British products into the colonies after December 1, 1774, and the exportation of American products to Great Britain and her other colonies after September 1775, if meanwhile the British Government had not come to terms by repealing the Boston Port Bill as well as other obnoxious measures. Before adjourning, this Congress also agreed to assemble again on May 10, 1775, should the British authorities by that time still refuse to yield.

Of course, the embargo against British imports would have been a flat failure had not Congress called upon all the colonies to see to its enforcement. Consequently, in the Three Lower Counties, immediately after the return of the Delaware delegates from Philadelphia, mass meetings were held to appoint committees of inspection and observation to keep a vigilant eye on all merchants to prevent importation and sale of the proscribed goods after December 1. Rodney was a member of the committee for Kent County. There were bootleggers then as now, and some merchants sought to import, before December 1, large quantities of British goods in order to advance the price later when they became scarce, but when discovered the committees had full authority to deal drastically with such cases.

When the House of Assembly met in an adjourned session in March 1775, it approved the acts of the irregular meeting of August 1774, and approved also the report prepared by the three delegates to the First Continental Congress, Rodney, McKean, and Read. These gentlemen were reëlected on March 29, 1775, to attend the Second Continental Congress, and received a new set of instructions, this time signed by Caesar Rodney as speaker. Although their appointment occurred only three weeks before the Battle of Lexington, the delegates to the Second Continental Congress were to "Avoid, as you have heretofore done, everything disrespectful or offensive to our most gracious Sovereign, or in any measure invasive of his just rights and prerogative." Indicating that the Assembly was in no mood to permit Pennsylvania to deny the right of the Three Lower Counties to act independently in the Congress, the instructions also included the following: "IV. If the Congress, when formed, shall not in every question to be voted by Provinces, allow this government an equal vote with any other province or government on this continent, you are decently but firmly to urge the right of this government in Congress with the other Colonies." That Delaware today is an independent State is partly due to this instruction. The delegates were moreover authorized to treat on behalf of the Government of the Three Lower Counties with any person authorized to speak for His Majesty, the King.

Delaware's three representatives joined with the other delegates in Philadelphia in May 1775 in organizing what was subsequently called the Second Continental Congress, this time meeting in the Pennsylvania State House, later to become known as Independence Hall. George Read, in a letter to his wife dated May 18, 1775, gives a glimpse of a very busy Congress at this time, and also shows himself and Rodney as belonging to the same intimate eating club as Washington and other Virginia gentlemen. He wrote in part: "You too justly hint at my inattention to this kind of correspondence, but the life I lead here will in some measure account for it. I prepare in the morning for the meeting at nine o'clock, and often do not return to my lodgings till that time at night. We sit in Congress generally till half-past three o'clock, and once till five o'clock, and then [I] dine at the City Tavern, where a few of us have established a table for each day in the week, save Saturday, when there is a general dinner. Our daily table is formed by the following persons, at present, to wit: Messrs. Randolph, Lee, Washington, and Harrison of Virginia, Alsop of New York, Chase of Maryland, and Rodney and Read. A dinner is ordered for the number, eight, and whatever is deficient of that number is to be paid for at two shillings and sixpence a head, and each that attends pays only the expense of the day."

As already stated, the Kent County militia officers met in Dover in the same month and elected Rodney as colonel of the Upper County regiment and John Haslet as colonel of the Lower County regiment. Thus in the spring and summer of 1775, when the War of the Revolution broke out, and more than a year before the Declaration of Independence, we find Rodney not only speaker of the House of Assembly in New Castle and a member from Delaware of the Second Continental Congress in Philadelphia, but also actively engaged as a ranking officer of the Kent County militia, and deeply concerned in the military defense of the Government of the Three Lower Counties.

Rodney was in Philadelphia in June when the proposal came up of appointing Washington (a colleague in the same Congress) commander-in-chief of the American forces. Together with Read and McKean, he voted for Washington.

In September 1775, the newly elected members of the Council of Safety, including Rodney, met in Dover to effect an organization and to coordinate the military efforts of the three counties. At this time, three brigadier generals were appointed, Dr. John McKinly for the New Castle militia, Caesar Rodney for Kent County, and John Dagworthy for Sussex County. To prevent any dispute, confusion, or jealousy from developing among the counties, a curious resolution was adopted, the gist of which was as follows: In case Sussex County were invaded and the militia of the two other counties went to that county's aid, the brigadier general, i.e., John Dagworthy, would be the ranking officer. Similarly, if the enemy were operating in Kent County or in New Castle County, the brigadier general of the militia in the county invaded would be the ranking officer. Who should be the ranking officer should all three counties be invaded at once apparently was a problem that did not occur to the minds of the busy members of the Council of Safety. As a matter of fact, when the British in September 1777 actually invaded New Castle County from the direction of Chesapeake Bay, the militia of New Castle County failed to assemble in any appreciable number, and it remained for Rodney, now technically in command of all Delaware militia, since John McKinly had become president, to concentrate the Kent County militia near Noxentown in New Castle County in order to observe, and, if possible, harass the enemy on its southern or right flank. Rodney's correspondence with Washington, whose headquarters were then at Wilmington, clearly shows the Delawarean's earnest, though futile, efforts to be of assistance to Washington, his weakness being due primarily to the failure of the New Castle militia to respond to his or President McKinly's appeals.

But to return to Rodney's activities in the civil branch of government. He remained a member of the Second Continental Congress throughout the year 1775 and during the year 1776 until autumn. He therefore had a part in the work of sending an address to the King, another to the people of Great Britain, and a third to the non-revolting colonies, including Canada. When no concessions were forthcoming from the British Government, and when the radicals in Congress, like John Adams and Samuel Adams, were gaining steadily over conservatives like John Dickinson, Robert Morris, and George Read, Rodney and McKean found themselves more and more in sympathy with the former. This is borne out to some extent by John Adams himself, who, in discussing the question of foreign alliances in his *Autobiography,* wrote as follows: "When I first made these observations in Congress, I never saw a greater impression made upon that assembly or any other. Attention and approbation were marked upon every countenance. Several gentlemen came to me afterwards, to thank me for that speech, particularly, Mr. Caesar Rodney, of Delaware and Mr. Duane, of New York. I remember these two gentlemen in particular, because both of them said that I had considered the subject of foreign connections more maturely than any man they had ever heard in America; that I had perfectly digested the subject, and had removed, Mr. Rodney said, all, and Mr. Duane said, the greatest part of his objections to foreign negotiations. Even Mr. Dickinson said, to gentlemen out of doors, that I had thrown great light on the subject."

Being speaker of the House of Assembly at New Castle, Rodney presided over a session in June 1776 which, as has already been stated, gave new instructions to the delegates in Congress, permitting them to join with the other colonies "in forming such farther compacts between the United Colonies, concluding such treaties with foreign Kingdoms and states, and in adopting such other measures as shall be judged necessary for promoting the liberty, safety, and interests of America, reserving to the people of this Colony the sole and exclusive right of regulating the internal government and police of the same." The second part of the instructions repeated the order of the previous year, namely that the delegates should maintain the right of the colony "to an equal voice in Congress with any other province or government on this Continent, as the inhabitants thereof have their *All* at stake as well as others." This resolution, which was passed by a unanimous vote, virtually empowered the three delegates from Delaware to give their assent to Richard Henry Lee's resolution, which the Virginia delegate had introduced in Congress on June 7, and to the Declaration of Independence. In the light of the Assembly's other resolution of the same day, supplanting the authority of the Crown in the Three Lower Counties, this resolution certainly did not authorize any of the Delaware delegates to vote against the proposal for independence which was then pending in Congress. Moreover, the Assembly followed the advice of Congress expressed in its resolution of May 15, 1776, that all colonies should set up independent governments if they had not already done so. In forwarding a copy of the resolution of Congress to his brother, Thomas, Caesar Rodney had written from Philadelphia: "Inclosed I have sent you the printed Copy of the Resolution of Congress mentioned in my last. Most of those here who are *termed the Cool Considerate men* think it amounts to a declaration of Independence. It Certainly savours of it, but you will see and Judge for Your Self." By passing a simple resolution at this June meeting of the Assembly, therefore, the Three Lower Counties to all intents and purposes declared themselves independent of the British King, for thereafter all officials in the three counties were to consider themselves as officers of the Government of the Three Lower Counties, not of the Crown. Caesar Rodney's hand in effecting all this is clearly seen in the correspondence.

The Assembly adjourned on June 22, whereupon the speaker proceeded to Sussex County at the very time Lee's resolution for separation lay on the table in Independence Hall in Philadelphia. Rodney in all probability knew that the calendar called for its consideration on July 1, but he was so much engrossed as a militia general in investigating a threatened Tory uprising in Sussex County, the news of which appeared even in a London paper later and heartened the British Government, that his return to Philadelphia had to be postponed. He had been to Lewes and other parts of Sussex County, and had returned to his home near Dover, when Lee's resolution was taken off the table early on July 1 and discussed in the Committee of the Whole House. The resolution passed the committee with nine states in favor, Pennsylvania and South Carolina against, Delaware not voting on account of McKean's voting for and Read's against, and the New York delegates remaining neutral, being instructed by their Assembly not to vote either way. The jubilant radicals now pressed for a formal vote by the Congress immediately upon the dissolution of the Committee of the Whole House, but the chairman of the South Carolina delegation pleaded for a postponement of the vote until new instructions could be secured from his State. The radicals conceded the point and allowed a postponement of one day.

In the meantime, McKean, according to a statement by himself, had sent a messenger to Rodney, urging his immediate return to Philadelphia. Rodney must have received McKean's communication in the night of July 1 and 2, because it is known that, after his famous ride, he arrived in time to vote on Lee's resolution in the late afternoon of the second, thus causing Delaware to join the nine states which had voted for the resolution in the committee the day before. Pennsylvania's vote was also cast for the resolution when Robert Morris and John Dickinson stayed away from the session and permitted Benjamin Franklin, John Morton, and James Wilson to outvote two die-hard conservatives, namely Humphreys and Willing. The South Carolina delegation also joined the majority, making the total vote for the resolution twelve states, New York still refraining from voting. The South Carolina people during the night of July 1 and 2 had decided to disregard their instructions to oppose independence. In such a manner was the separation of twelve American colonies from the mother country effected on July 2. New York made the vote unanimous on July 15.

Immediately upon the passage of Lee's resolution, Congress proceeded to consider Jefferson's draft of a declaration of independence, which should announce to the world the act of separation effected on July 2 and at the same time serve as a propaganda document, explaining to the world the reasons for the step already taken, with a view to gaining more adherents at home and in foreign lands, especially in France.

Caesar Rodney was present in Congress during the whole time the declaration was being discussed, i.e., on the second, third, and fourth, and of course voted for its adoption late on the fourth, just as he had voted for Lee's resolution on the second. He briefly tells about his arrival in Philadelphia and his actions in Congress in his famous Fourth of July letter which he sent to his brother, Thomas, in Dover, and which is one of the very few letters written by any of the Congressmen on the day of the adoption of the declaration. (See page 94.)

The summoning of the members of the Delaware Assembly to meet in New Castle on July 22, referred to by Rodney in this letter, was for the purpose of winding up the business of the last colonial assembly, which had been elected in October 1775, and of arranging for the holding of a constitutional convention to frame a state government entirely independent of Pennsylvania, with respect to the executive as well as the legislative and judicial departments. Rodney went to New Castle and presided at this last session from July 22 to July 28. Then the Colonial Assembly adjourned forever. This Assembly passed a resolution calling for the election on August 19 of delegates to the constitutional convention to meet in New Castle on August 27. The resolution reads in full as follows:

The House taking into Consideration the Resolution of Congress of the 15th of May last for suppressing all Authority derived from the Crown of Great-Britain, and for establishing a Government upon the Authority of the People, and the Resolution of this House of the 15th of June last, in Consequence of the said Resolution of Congress, directing all Persons holding Offices Civil or Military to execute the same in the Name of this Government until a new one should be formed; and also the Declaration of the UNITED STATES OF AMERICA, absolving from all Allegiance to the British Crown, and dissolving all Political Connection between them and Great-Britain, lately published and adopted by this Government as one of those States, are of Opinion that some speedy Measures should be taken to form a regular Mode of Civil Polity, and this House not thinking themselves authorized by their Constituents to execute this important Work,
    Do Resolve,
That it be recommended to the good People of the several Counties in this Government to chuse a suitable Number of Deputies to meet in Convention, there to ordain and declare the future Form of Government for this State.
    Resolved also,
That it is the Opinion of this House, That the said Convention consist of the Number of Thirty Persons, that is to say, Ten for the County of New-Castle, Ten for the County of Kent, and Ten for the County of Sussex; and that the Freemen of the said Counties respectively do meet on Monday the nineteenth day of August next, at the usual Places of Election for the County, and then and there proceed to elect the Number of Deputies aforesaid, according to the Directions of several Laws of this Government for regulating Elections of the Members of Assembly, except as to the Choice of Inspectors, which shall be made on the Morning of the Day of Election by the Electors, Inhabitants of the respective Hundreds in each County.
    Resolved also,
That every Elector shall (if required by one or more of the Judges of the Election) take the following Oath or Affirmation, to wit;
I A.B. will to the utmost of my Power support and maintain the Independence of this Government, as declared by the Honorable Continental Congress.
    Resolved also,

That it is the Opinion of this House, that the Deputies when chosen as aforesaid shall meet in Convention in the Town of New-Castle on Tuesday the Twenty-seventh Day of the same Month of August, and immediately proceed to form a government on the Authority of the People of this State, in such Sort as may be best adapted to their Preservation and Happiness.

Thus we see how important a part Caesar Rodney played in bringing about peaceably the political transition from the semi-dependent colonial establishment of the Three Lower Counties on Delaware to the independent status of the State of Delaware. He presided at the demise and burial of the old régime and took a very active part in arranging for the birth of the new régime: first, when, on June 15, as speaker, he presided over the Assembly which passed the resolution for supplanting the authority of the Crown by the authority of the Three Lower Counties; second, when, on July 2, he arrived in Philadelphia in time to vote with Thomas McKean on Richard Henry Lee's resolution, to wit: "That these United Colonies are, and of right ought to be free and independent States . . ."; third, when, on July 4, he voted with Thomas McKean for the adoption of the Declaration of Independence; fourth, when he presided as speaker of the Assembly which passed the resolutions quoted above whereby provision was made for setting up the machinery of a state government; and fifth, when, on August 2, or some time thereafter, he affixed his signature to the parchment copy of the Declaration of Independence despite the fact that at that very time thousands of British soldiers had entered New York harbor on British transports, protected by a fleet of British warships, and that every man who signed the document laid himself open to charges of treason and was liable to be hanged.

Immediately after the adjournment of the Assembly on July 28, and after the campaign had begun for the election of delegates to the approaching Convention, Rodney was confronted by a strong opposition from the conservatives of Kent County. He naturally wanted to be elected a delegate, but as he was kept busily engaged in Philadelphia attending to the affairs of the newly born nation, he could not be on the spot to repair his political fences. His brother Thomas strove to get Caesar elected, but in vain. Consequently, he had no direct part to play in the Constitutional Convention in New Castle in August and September 1776. His correspondence, however, shows him in close touch with the situation. Both the president of the Convention, George Read, and Rodney's other colleague in Congress, Thomas McKean, who had also been elected a deputy to the Convention, wrote to Rodney from New Castle and Rodney wrote to them from Philadelphia.

When the Convention had adjourned and the campaign was begun to elect members to the new state legislature, a bicameral body, the conservatives in

Kent County again prevented Rodney from being elected a member either of the upper house, then called Legislative Council, or of the lower house, then called House of Assembly. He moreover lost out when the time came for this new legislature to elect delegates to Congress for the year 1777. Of the former members only Read was returned, John Dickinson and John Evans being selected in place of McKean and Rodney. Though he refers to ungrateful people in his correspondence, Rodney's patriotic spirit was not dampened. Now he was neither a member of the new State government nor of the Continental Congress in Philadelphia. His freedom from political duties, however, gave him all the more time to devote to military affairs, and in November 1776 he was made chairman of the Kent County branch of the Council of Safety. Then in December 1776, when Washington was being pursued by Howe across New Jersey and only retrieved some of his losses by recrossing the Delaware and capturing the Hessians at Trenton on the day after Christmas, and when Congress had fled from Philadelphia to Baltimore to be out of reach of the British, we find Rodney busily recruiting the militia of Kent County and sending the soldiers forward to aid Washington. His freedom from political duties made it possible also for him to hurry with some of the militia to the scene of hostilities. He was placed in command of the post at Trenton in January 1777, after Washington's main army had taken up its winter quarters at Morristown, New Jersey. As brigadier general, it became his task at Trenton not only to guard the post and the river crossing, which the Hessians had so recently controlled, but also to forward to Washington all the Southern troops which were coming up in response to his call for aid from the states. When the danger was past, he asked Washington to be relieved, a request which was granted with the distinct understanding that he should hold himself in readiness should Washington need his services again.

This was the year when Delaware was invaded by the British and when Rodney, as the most active general officer of the State militia, was keeping in close touch with Washington. It was the year, too, when, after the Battle of the Brandywine on September 11, the British entered Wilmington and captured the first president of the State, Dr. John McKinly. Upon McKean's temporarily taking over the reins of state government, he commissioned Rodney as major general of the militia. Thus Rodney's star again was in the ascendant. In time of danger, it had been discovered that no other man could be depended upon as he. The legislature in December 1777 appointed him as a delegate to Congress again, and in March 1778, when it appeared that McKinly would be kept a prisoner in Philadelphia indefinitely, the Delaware legislature elected Rodney as his successor. He served in the capacity of president the full term of three years and about seven months more, i.e., until November 1781, when the war was virtually over with the surrender of Cornwallis at Yorktown the previous month. Thus we may rightly call Rodney Delaware's war governor. Not only the burden of furnishing Delaware's quota of soldiers for Washington's various campaigns, but also the task of arming and clothing them, and the duty of raising Delaware's quota of provisions (flour and cattle for the most part) and Delaware's quota of money, in addition to securing the Delaware legislature's belated approval of the Articles of Confederation in February 1779, and seeing to it that Delaware's representatives in Congress were adequately reimbursed for their expenses and time—all these and many more tasks were attended to with energy and dispatch, despite the fact that a persistent affliction of asthma and a deadly cancerous growth on his face were steadily breaking down the physical constitution of the man.

Shortly after his relinquishing his office in 1781, he repaired to Philadelphia to seek medical and surgical relief from the serious malady that had constantly been sapping his strength ever since the seventeen-sixties. The first time Rodney had consulted physicians in Philadelphia and submitted to an operation was in 1768. Now in 1781, thirteen years later, he was in desperate straits. Yet his letters from Philadelphia reveal him in a hopeful mood and, although he continued to decline physically until 1784 (the year of his death), his interest in his business affairs appeared as keen as ever, and he even accepted a political honor again when, in the fall of 1783, he was elected a member of the upper house of the legislature, the Legislative Council. This body made him speaker, and he served in this capacity until the following spring.

The minutes of the Legislative Council for April 8, 1784, show that that body "met at the house of the Honorable Caesar Rodney, Esq., the Speaker, he being too much indisposed to attend at the usual place of meeting." The minutes for May 24, 1784, appear as follows: "A sufficient number of the members not having met to form a quorum on that day, they adjourned from day to day until Tuesday, the 15th of June, when all the members met, except the Hon. Caesar Rodney, Esq. Speaker, and Richard Bassett, Esq." This is the last reference in the minutes of the Council to Caesar Rodney in life. He died just eleven days later, on June 26, and was buried on his home farm, Poplar Grove.

His grave remained unmarked for about one hundred years, when a small stone was placed over it by Chief Justice Joseph P. Comegys. In November 1887 an organization known as the Rodney Club was formed for the purposes of removing the remains to the Christ Episcopal Churchyard in Dover and of raising a suitable monument over the new grave. The first purpose of the club was effected in 1888, and with the assembling of the state legislature in January of the next year, this organization, with Mr. Henry Ridgely as its chairman, got that body to appropriate $500 for a monument. The legislative resolution, passed on February 20, constituted the members of the Rodney Club and others as a committee for securing the monument. This committee, with the money appropriated by the State and with $500 additional given to the monument fund by the will of Mrs. Sally Morris of Wilmington, proceeded to the erection of the monument. It was unveiled with appropriate exercises on October 30, 1889. Governor B. T. Biggs presided at the occasion, and the Honorable Thomas F. Bayard delivered the oration.

On July 4, 1923, an equestrian statue of Rodney, showing him riding to Philadelphia to vote for independence, was unveiled in Rodney Square, Wilmington, by the citizens of the state of Delaware. The funds for this memorial were raised by a committee, the chairman of which was General James H. Wilson.

Again, in 1931, the legislature of Delaware decided to honor the memory of Caesar Rodney by appropriating funds for the erection of a marble statue of him to stand in the Hall of Fame in Washington.

In bringing this biographical sketch to a close one cannot better sum up Caesar Rodney's services as an outstanding founder and citizen of the State and the Nation than to quote the concluding lines from Mr. Bayard's oration at the unveiling of the Rodney monument at Dover:

What will be inscribed on this monument I know not, but are there words more fitting than those of Emerson?—

> "Spirit that made these heroes dare
> To die—and leave their children free,
> Bid time and nature gently spare
> The shaft we raise to them and thee."

[*Bibliographical note:* In the preparation of the above biographical sketch the principal primary sources used, in addition to the Caesar Rodney correspondence, have been the following: *Journals of the Continental Congress; Letters of Members of the Continental Congress,* E. C. Burnett, Editor; Kent County deed books, will books, and Orphans' Court books; Governor's Register; *Minutes of the Legislative Council, 1776–1792; Principles and Acts of the Revolution,* by Hezekiah Niles; *Delaware Archives; The Life and Correspondence of George Read of Delaware,* by William T. Read; *Life and Writings of John Dickinson,* by Charles J. Stillé; Reprints of the *Votes and Proceedings of the House of Representatives of the Government of the Counties of New Castle, Kent, and Sussex upon Delaware* for the year 1762 (reprinted 1930) and for the years 1765 to 1770 inclusive (reprinted 1931).]

THOMAS RODNEY

and

CAESAR AUGUSTUS RODNEY

THOMAS RODNEY, the eighth and youngest child of Caesar Rodney the elder and Elizabeth Crawford Rodney, was born June 4, 1744, on his father's farm in St. Jones Neck, Kent County, Delaware. The father died when Thomas was about a year old, and the task of giving the boy an education fell upon the widowed mother, who later married one Thomas Wilson. The boy evinced a bent for mathematics, but, although he made considerable progress in the study of that branch of knowledge, his stronger interest in history caused him to discontinue the former. Later he read books on the laws of nations. When eighteen years of age Thomas left his home to live with his brother Caesar, in order to assist him in managing his various farms. Two years later (1764), he accompanied his brother to Dover when Caesar took up his residence there, and assisted his brother in his several county offices, especially when the elder brother was absent from Dover as the representative of the Three Lower Counties in the Stamp Act Congress in 1765, and when he represented Kent County in the Colonial Assembly at New Castle during many sessions. During these periods, too, Thomas also attended to Caesar's farming business.

On April 8, 1771, Thomas Rodney married Elizabeth Fisher, daughter of Jabez Maud Fisher of Philadelphia, and finding it necessary to enter business for himself in order to make more money than he was getting at Dover, he opened up a shop in Philadelphia sometime in the year 1772, investing money received from his wife and from his brother Caesar, to fill the shelves with merchandise. He evidently was not successful, for he returned to Dover with his family within two years. At another time Thomas entered a partnership in Wilmington, being engaged in the flour exporting business from 1780 to 1782.

Before his marriage, Thomas Rodney in the year 1770 had been appointed one of His Majesty's justices of the peace for Kent County, and in 1774, after his return from Philadelphia, he was reappointed to that position. In 1775 he was elected a member of the Colonial Assembly in New Castle for Kent County, and consequently participated in the deliberations of the last Colonial Assembly which in June 1776 and in July 1776 took the necessary steps which transformed the Three Lower Counties from a colonial establishment to the independent status of a state; for it was this assembly which on June 14, 1776, passed the resolution absolving all crown officials from their allegiance to the

King, and this assembly likewise in the following month definitely fixed the time for the convening of the first state constitutional convention.

Before his election to the last Colonial Assembly and shortly after the Battle of Bunker Hill, Thomas Rodney organized a volunteer militia force and in the same year was elected a member of the Council of Safety for Kent County. He was also a member of the Committee of Observation for the same county.

When Washington's army was retreating across New Jersey toward the Delaware River in November and December 1776, Thomas Rodney in command as captain of a company of Kent County militia led his men away from Dover on December 14 to join the main army. Having reached Bristol by Christmas, the Dover company was brigaded with Philadelphia militia in the division of General Cadwalader. Crossing the Delaware below Trenton, Rodney's men participated in the second Battle of Trenton on January 2 and in the Battle of Princeton the next day. Upon Washington's establishing his winter quarters at Morristown, Rodney's men were encamped there for a few days, but soon returned to Delaware when their terms of enlistment had expired.

Later in the same year (1777), when the British landed at the Head of Elk and invaded Northern Delaware on their march toward Philadelphia, Thomas Rodney acted as his brother's adjutant, Caesar being in command of the Delaware militia at the Noxentown camp in August and September.

In April 1778 Thomas Rodney was elected by the General Assembly as judge of the Admiralty Court, serving in that position until April 1785. He was repeatedly a member of the Confederation Congress from Delaware— being elected February 10, 1781, to serve during the 1781 session, April 8, 1784, for the 1784 session, November 4, 1785, for the 1786 session, October 27, 1786, for the 1787 session, and November 10, 1787, for the 1788 session. Consequently, he was a member of Congress when the Articles of Confederation went into effect, March 1, 1781, and was also a member of that body, although it is improbable that he was in attendance, when it authorized the holding of a Federal Constitutional Convention, when it submitted the work of that body to the several legislatures, and when finally, before it adjourned *sine die,* it set in motion the machinery for the election of the first President under the new Constitution and the convening of the first Congress under that instrument.

Thomas Rodney was elected on October 2, 1786, to be a member of the Delaware House of Assembly from Kent County, and served in the October, January–February, May–June, and August sessions of that body. On October 1, 1787, he was reëlected, serving in the October–November, January–February, and May–June sessions. On October 24, 1787, he was chosen speaker of the House, but served only until November 6, 1787, when Jehu Davis was chosen speaker *pro tempore*.

On December 17, 1802, Thomas Rodney was appointed associate justice of the Supreme Court of Delaware and served until August, 1803, when he resigned to accept an appointment as United States judge for Mississippi Territory. He held this position until his death, January 2, 1811.

Thomas and Elizabeth Rodney had two children that lived to maturity, and one infant boy, who died when only eight days old. The third child was a daughter, Lavinia, who was born in Dover January 16, 1775. Lavinia married John Fisher in 1794, the second United States judge for the District Court of Delaware. The first child was Caesar Augustus Rodney, born in Dover January 4, 1772, before the family removed to Philadelphia. He married Susan Hunn, daughter of Captain John Hunn of Philadelphia, and by her had fifteen children.

After attending an academy in Wilmington, Caesar Augustus Rodney attended and was graduated from the University of Pennsylvania, whereupon he immediately commenced the study of law under Joseph B. McKean. Admitted to the bar in 1793, he early entered politics, being elected member of the Delaware General Assembly from New Castle County for the years 1798 to 1802 inclusive. Defeating James A. Bayard in 1802 for member of Congress from his native state, he served one term. In 1807 President Jefferson appointed him attorney-general of the United States at the same time that he received an appointment as attorney-general of the State of Pennsylvania. He of course accepted the former appointment, and served to the end of Jefferson's second term and for two years of Madison's first term, resigning in 1811. In 1817 he was appointed a commissioner to South America, and in 1820 was elected a member of Congress. In 1822 the Delaware legislature elected him as United States senator, but he did not serve long in this capacity, for in 1823 President Monroe appointed him minister plenipotentiary to the Argentine Republic. His service in the diplomatic corps was short lived, however, for on June 10, 1824, he died at Buenos Aires. His remains being buried in that city, the Government of the Argentine Republic raised a handsome monument over his grave.

LETTERS

LETTERS

to and from

CAESAR RODNEY

I

Commission of Caesar Rodney as Captain of Delaware Militia

BY THE HONOURABLE
ROBERT HUNTER MORRIS, ESQ;

Lieutenant Governor and Commander in Chief of the Province of Pennsylvania and Counties of New Castle, Kent and Sussex on Delaware.

TO CAESAR RODENEY ESQUIRE GREETING

REPOSING especial Trust and Confidence, as well in your Care, Diligence and Circumspection, as in your Loyalty and Courage, I Have Nominated, Constituted and Appointed, and I do by Virtue of the Powers and Authorities unto Me given, hereby Nominate, Constitute and appoint You the said Caesar Rodeney Captain of a Company of Foot Militia raised in the Hundred of Dover in the said County of Kent

You are therefore to take the said Company into Your Charge and Care, as Captain thereof, and duly to Exercise both the Officers and Soldiers of that Company in Arms. And as they are hereby Commanded to obey You as their Captain—So are You likewise to observe and follow such Orders and Directions, from time to time, as You shall receive from the Commander in Chief for the time being, of the said Province, or any other Your Superior Officer or Officers, according to the Rules and Discipline of War, in Pursuance of the Trust Reposed in You. And for Your so doing this shall be Your COMMISSION.

Given under my Hand and Seal at Arms, at Philadelphia, the Ninth Day of April in the Twenty-Ninth year of his Majesty's Reign, Annoque Domini 1756.

By His HONOURS Command,
Richard Peters, Secry.[1]

ROBT. H. MORRIS

[1] Richard Peters had succeeded James Logan as Secretary of the Province of Pennsylvania and of the Government of the Three Lower Counties on Delaware.

2

Commission of Caesar Rodney as Captain in French and Indian War

By the Honourable William Denny Esquire
Lieutenant Governor and Commander in Chief of the Province of Pennsylvania and Counties of New-Castle, Kent and Sussex on Delaware.

To Caesar Rodeney Esquire

Reposing especial Trust and Confidence, as well in your Care, Diligence and Circumspection, as in your Loyalty and Courage, I Have Nominated, Constituted and Appointed, and I do by Virtue of the Powers and Authorities unto Me given, hereby Nominate, Constitute and appoint You the said Caesar Rodeney Captain of a Company of Foot Militia in Dover Hundred in the said County of Kent in the Regiment whereof John Vining Esquire is Colonel.

You are therefore to take the said Company into Your Charge and Care, as Captain thereof, and duly to Exercise both the Officers and Soldiers of that Company in Arms. And as they are hereby Commanded to obey You as their Captain So are You likewise to observe and follow such Orders and Directions, from time to time, as You shall receive from the Commander in Chief for the time being, of the said Province, or any other Your Superior Officer or Officers, according to the Rules and Discipline of War, in Pursuance of the Trust reposed in You. And for Your so doing this shall be Your COMMISSION.

Given under my Hand and Seal at Arms, at Philadelphia, the   Day of
in the Thirtyfirst Year of his Majesty's Reign, Annoque Domini 1757
By His Honours Command.

    RICHARD PETERS
        Secretary   WILLIAM DENNY

3

From Benjamin Wynkoop[1]

Philad^a August 2^d 1765.

I have sent you the Electrical Rod and Mr. Vining has Directions how to put it up. The price is 23/ and I have paid Polly Vining 7/6 as order'd.

The late Account from England are full of a Change in the Ministery which I veryly believe will take place but doubt much whether there will be a total

---

1 Brother of Phoebe Wynkoop, the wife of John Vining and mother of Mary Vining, the famous Delaware beauty. He was also brother of Mary Wynkoop, the first wife of Dr. Charles G. Ridgely, the oldest son of Nicholas Ridgely the elder and half brother of John Vining.

Rout or not. Mr Franklin[1] in his last Letters seems very sanguine as to the Success of his Embassy.

4

From Thomas Rodney[2]

Dover Oct! the 2^d 1765.

Inclosed here, You have a List of the Election. We might have Carried the Whole Ticket, if we had pushed in time, but Lookerman Lead some of our members, so much, in the fore part of the Knight, that, we Did not Immagine he Cou'd be Turned out. Many of your friends were more anctious, than if You'd been present. The other party had Liked to taken the Quakers by a Lie, that Lookerman Reported. That was, that You had Demanded seventy pounds of Trains Estate, for which they had a Receipt, but that was surpresed in time, which turned the Quakers as much the other way. . . . Your Credentials was sent of a Wednessday Morning, by a Gentleman from Maryland sealed up in a Letter, Directed to Philamon Dickerson, who was to Convey them to You, as Quick as possible. . . .

5

To Thomas Rodney

New York, October 7, 1765

I have just rec'd yours with a list of the election but have not time to answer that part. The Congress will not end in less than eight or ten days therefore do not expect to be at home till the Assembly ends at NewCastle. . . .

6

To Thomas Rodney

New York Octo! ye 20th 1765—

When I Wrote you last I Expected the Congress Would have ended in 8, or 10 Days from that time—but Contrary to Expectation We have Not Yet finished—You, and many others, perhaps are Surprised to think We Should Set So long When the business of our Meeting Seemed only to be the Petitioning the King, and Remonstrating to both houses of Parliament—But When you

---

1 Benjamin Franklin was in London as the agent of Pennsylvania Province. He bore a petition from the Assembly requesting that Pennsylvania be changed from a proprietary to a royal province.

2 Caesar Rodney's brother is writing to New York where Caesar, together with Thomas Mc-Kean, is representing Delaware in the Stamp Act Congress

Consider That We are Petitioning & addressing That august Body the great Legislative of the Empire for Redress of Grievances; That in order to point out Those Grievances it Was likewise Necessary to Set forth the Liberty We have, and ought to Enjoy, (as freeborn Englishmen) according to the British Constitution. This We Set about To Do by way of Declaration, in the Nature of Resolves, as a foundation to the Petition, and Addresses; and was one of the most Difficult Tasks I ever yet see Undertaken, as We had Carefully to avoid any Infringment of the prerogative of the Crown, and the Power of Parliament, and Yet in Duty bound fully to Assert the Rights & Privileges of the Colonies—However After arguing, and Debating two weeks on Liberty, privilege, Prerogative &c. &c. in an Assembly of the greatest Ability I ever Yet saw, We happily finished them, and Now have the Petition & Addresses before us, Which We Expect to finish in 3 or 4 Days more at farthest; if so I shall be at New castle Next Sunday, Ready to Set in the house of Assembly on Munday. . . .

7

From John Rodney[1]

Lewes Dec.ʳ 3ᵈ 1765.

. . . I should have been very glad if it had suited my affairs to have spent a day or two with you this fall more particularly at this juncture when you were just returned from the Congress at N.york when I should have Expected to have had my Curiosity Intirely gratified on such a Momentus Occasion, to wit, to see the mode the manner the Arguments & Remonstrances of that most Important Congress, in whose hands we have as it were Intrusted our Liberties. I do not know that Ever I was so desirous of seeing anything of a publick Nature as I have been to see the Petition and Memorial to the King and both houses of Parliament, but have little hopes of seeing it now 'till the same is made publick. . . .

8

From John Rodney

Lewes Feb.ʸ 5ᵗʰ 1766—

I rece.ᵈ the money, by M.ʳ Vandike, and have Inclosed a rec.ᵗ for the same—The favourable Accounts from England in the last papers, with regard to American affairs must give real Pleasure to every well wisher of the Colonies—But to have the joyful News Confirmed of a repeal of the Stamp Act (which we

---

1 John Rodney was a half cousin of Caesar Rodney, being a son of William Rodney, a half brother of Caesar Rodney, the father of the Signer.

may hope our Friends in England do now Enjoy) would be perhaps the best piece of News that Ever America was favoured with—for on the Contrary should the parliament resent the Misbehaviour of the Colonies & take it into their heads to Enforce the Act, however difficult & Injurious it would be to them so to do yet it would certainly terminate in Our Ruin for the Consequence I apprehend would be, Either to submit to that detestable Act, or to be Envolved in an open rebellion, both of which is Shocking even to think of. Remember me kindly to your Brothers & Sisters & all Enquiring Friends.

9

From John Vining[1]

September 8th, 1766

I received your Political Epistle by Doctr. McColl for wch. I thank you. I have wrote to my Brother to stand, in the strongest terms I could devise, but I am afraid it will have no good Effect. I blame him exceedingly for his obstinacy; I would not leave my friends in the lurch on such an important occation for any consideration that could be named. If the Doctr. will decline I must leave it with you to take the man you think will the best answer the end. From some conversation I lat[e]ly had with a friend the taking into the ticket the person talked of between us will not be well relished, however, men are some times oblidged to do that from necessity wch. they would not from Choice; the Consequences that may flow from this Source will probabily be very troublesome hereafter. I can tell you for a truth that B. Franklin has sounded the ministry & Council respecting a Change of Government & that he was informed by the president that if he should be hardy enough to offer the petition for that purpose again it would be taken notice of in a very Different way upon wch. he went to Spain for his health— I shall bring a New Commission of the peace down with me. You should give Mr. Stout a hint perhaps. It may be of service.

Our Gentry need not expect any great matter from a Change of Government it therefore appears that our friend R. H. is upon a cold Drag, quaere if it might not answer his End better not to have any thing to do with the other side the Question.—

I think you ought to send immediately to Mr. McGow & press him to go to

1 Probably written from Philadelphia. John Vining was at one time Chief Justice for the Three Lower Counties on Delaware. He succeeded his stepfather, Nicholas Ridgely, as Prothonotary and Clerk of the Peace for Kent County in 1755, holding both offices until his death in 1770. He also held the office of Recorder of Deeds for the same county from 1754 to 1755 He was elected to serve in every Colonial Assembly of the Three Lower Counties from 1751 to 1770 inclusive, excepting those of 1755, 1759, and 1760.

England in the first ship that sails if his resolution continues of setling amongst us. I am authorized to say that his appointment will be as certain if he will accept as that 2 & 2 make four if he lives. If he has declin'd his intentions then give Mr. Andrews an invitation. All this may be done in a few days. Messrs. Peters & Duche only wait to hear from Mr. McGow when they will write by Capt. Sparkes who will sail in 2 weeks—

10
To Thomas Rodney

Philadelphia June the 7th 1768

The morning after I parted with you I set out from Missrs Wynkoops and drove to New Castle by dinner time, and intended the morning following to have gone to Chester; but when I ordered my horses in the Chariot found the largest horse so ill that we were obliged to Stay that day at New Castle that he might Recruit—but finding he grew worse—I borrowed a Saddle and Bridle of Mr Maurice and set out on the other horse, and left John to take Care of the Chariot, and the sick horse with orders to bring him up as soon as he Should be able to travel—but have Little reason to expect he will live—I got to Philadelphia on Saturday and on Munday applied to the Doctors Concerning the Sore on my Nose, who all upon Examination pronounce it a Cancer, and that it will be necessary I Should go through a Small Cource of Physick, and then to Extract it by a Costick or by Cutting it out, all which (to me) is a Dreadfull undertaking—and will Require so much time—that it is impossible for me now to determine when you may probably Expect to see me in Kent again, If ever—as (no Doubt) it will be attended with Danger—I have a great Many friends and advisers—some advise one thing Some another, Some advise me to the direction and management of one person, Some another, and some to go Imediately to England—however a day or two will determine me—I hope you will not neglect to take the greatest Care of all the business I left you in Charge —and when ever it Shall be necessary with Respect to any business Relative to the Office, That you will apply to Doctor Ridgely who I make No Doubt will Readily lend you his assistance . . .

11
From Thomas Rodney

Dover June 10th 1768,

I Rec'd: your Letter yesterday Evening by Mr Banning and thereby, am not a Little alarmed at the Dangerous Consequences attending or that may attend the Cureing the Cancer on your Nose a matter worthy your serious Consideration as your health and Even your Life May Depend on the treatment thereof therefore Spare not any proper Means of preserving that Life So Valuable to yourself and for the Constant Safety and happyness of which all the Tender ties of a parrent, Brother, and a friend United in you toward me pore in my heart a Thousand Anctious wishes which Inspires me to Advise you to take the most prudent Methods for your own Safety without Setting any Expence whatsoever in Competition with your Life—and further I wou'd beg Leave to Recomend unless this man is Sure he Can Cure you with Safety that you may go to England nor wou'd I have you Let your Business Deter you from going to England if you Shou'd think it best, for I Doubt not but I Can Conduct it in Such a Manner as to Make your Losses there inconsiderable Therefore I wou'd only have you Consult Whether it is best or not in Regard to your Safety—not that I seem the Least Doubtfull of an Intire Cure if the Cancer is properly treated, which wou'd be Vastly More agreable to me Cou'd it be Done in phila but Cannot Consent to your Runing any Resque that may be avoided . . .

12

To Thomas Rodney

Philadelphia June ye 13th 1768—

Yours of the tenth of this Instant, I Received by Mr Cooper, and am pleased to find (by Your Expressions therein) That you have so Just a Sense of Love, Duty and Gratitude, And Do not Doubt (If I am Obliged to go to England) by your diligence and Honest Attention to business, But you Will give me Sufficient proof of What you now only Express—The Governor not only Joyns with the Rest of my friends in pressing Me hard to go Imediately to England But has Assured me That I Shall have Liberty to appoint, (in the mean time) Whom I please to Conduct My offices—upon Which I Informed him that I Should appoint you—The Governor, Mr Allen, My Good friend Mr B. Chew &c Advised me (Previous to my going England) to Consult Governor Hamilton. Accordingly I Waited upon him at Bush Hill. He said it was a Cancer and in a Dangerous place—That he Thought the only Chance I had was to go to England, But by no Means to trust to any person here—However in a few minutes after, he told me he had a verry particular Respect for me, That he had brought over Some of the Medicines that were applied to his nose with direction for applying them—That I should have What I wanted of them to be applied under the direction of any Doctor I thought proper, And that he would Visit me every day, during the operation, That he might be Able to inform me Whether it opperated in the Same manner as it Did with him. Perhaps you will think this a greater mark of friendship, than I had any Right

to Expect from M͟r Hamilton. However it is even So—And this day The operation is to be begun under the Care of Doct͟r Tho͟s Bond—If this fails of Making
a Cure, and does not put me in a Worse Scituation than I now am I Shall go
to England in two or three Weeks—I am Quite prepared for the Voige, Except
that I must first Return to Kent to Settle a few Matters, and Make Regulations, Which I Should not Chuse to leave undone—I Still Retain my usual
Spirits, But My Case is truly dangerous, and What will be the Event, God only
knows. Make my Complm͟ts M͟r and Miss͟rs Vining, Tell Miss͟rs Vining I Still
hope That this Cloud, (tho: now dark and dismall) will one Day disperse—
and I shall have the pleasure to Carry Polly to Dover . . .

13

To Thomas Rodney

Philadelphia June 23d 1768

The inclosed is the Letter I mentioned to you in my last, and desire You'l
deliver it Accordingly—My last Letter to you was dated last munday Since
When the Doct͟r has Extracted the hard Crusted Matter which had risen so
high—And it has Left a hole I believe Quite to the Bone, and Extends for
Length from the Corner of my Eye above half way down my Nose—Such a
Sore must take some Considerable time to Cure up—if ever it does; However
Since it has been Extracted, I am perfectly easy as to any pain—And M͟r
Hamilton (Who Continues to See me every day) is of Opinion as well as the
Doct͟r that a Cure will be perfected—Give my Complim͟ts to Doct͟r Ridgely.
Tell him, that on Tuesday last his Apprentice (M͟r Tilton) Exhibited at the
College, and that ye Physicians Give him a great Carrector. Doct͟r T. Bond told
me, he was a Young fellow of great merit, that in sort he was a verry Cleaver
fellow, and did Credit to the man under Whom he Studied . . .

14

From Thomas Rodney

Dover June 25th 1768—

Your Letter Dated the 13th Came Safely Conducted to Me by M͟r Hogson,
wherein I was inform'd of your Resolutions Concerning the Cancer, Which
Seems to be the most prudent that Cou'd have been Dictated to you in those
Circumstances, and I am Exceeding Glad to hear that you are (Thereby)
Likely to git Clear of So much Trouble and Expence, as otherwise Might have
Insued; it also gives Me great Satisfaction to hear of Your being Treated with
so much Kind[n]ess and Humility by all your friends in Philadelphia, and in

particular I am Charm'd with the Candid, Sincere and jenerous behaviour and advise of M.̣ Penn and M.̣ Hamilton, Who's Hearts Seem's warm'd with a feeling Sence of true and Virtuous friendship, which Speaks Them worthy of more praise than My pen Dare Venture to Express; Instead of which May they Long Injoy the gratful Rewards of that bounty they Show to other's—I Let M.̣ṣ Vining know that you Still hope to have the pleasure of bringing her Daughter Down to Dover; Which (as well as for your happy Discharge from the present Danger) Shee Ernesly wishes May be Soon—The paper You Desired Me to give Doct.̣ Ridgely I Deliver'd to him, and also Let him know what you said about the Lot, upon which he Replyed that he was not fully Determined But he thaught he cou'd not Sute himself better than in buying Yours, Downtown—I also Recd: your Letter by M.̣ Pryor Dated the 20th for which I only waited before I wrote to know what Success was Discover'd by the applycation of M.̣ Guy's Medicines to your Cancer; which to my great Satisfaction, is thereby Expressed to have (as far as was then tryed) the Same Effect, and opperate in the Same manner they Did with M.̣ Hamilton, which is a favourable promise of an Intire Cure, the progress whereof I Shall be glad to hear by Every Opertunity, In Return for which I Shall not Neglect to write to you as often as I Can—

15

From Thomas Rodney

Dover July 11.̣ 1768.

In your Letter Dated the [?]th of June (which Recd: by M.̣ṣ Nancy Richardson) you have Given Me a particular account of the then Stage of your Cancer; which I am Glad to hear, has Such favourable Simtoms of an Intire Cure, which I make no Doubt will Soon be perfected by the Carefull attention of Doctor Bond; together with the friendly advise and Directions of M.̣ Hamilton; who has already expirienced a Simelar operation in that of his own, whereby he was Enabled to be of Singular Servise to you, and therein, he has Surpassed your highest wishes with his Grateful favours; wherein he has forever Merrited your Sincerest Gratitude and Esteem— . . .

16

From Thomas Rodney

Dover Oct.̣ 26th 1769

We have heard from Newcastle that you was Chose Speaker[1] but not any thing more—M.̣ Vining Continues up Stairs yett and therefore will not be

---

1 Speaker of the Assembly.

with you—The Doct<u>r</u> is not in Town or perhaps he wou'd write for he was Enquireing an Oppertunity. [Wi]lly Rodney has Declined Sitt<u>g</u> up for the Sher<u>f</u>: office Which he Declar'd to me just now and is for Sett<u>g</u> up Crawford Rees Who is Very anctious about it and only weits to see the members before makeing a positive Diclaration—how he may Succeed I Know not—but the project appears Very absurd to me

17

From John Rodney

Lewes, March 3<u>rd</u>, 1770.

I Presume there will be Sundry petitions preferred to the House of Assembly in March next, signed by a great Number of the Inhabitants of Sussex, in order to have the Court House &c fixed at the Cross Roads[1] vizt. at John Clowes's—It is really surprizing to see what disturbances a few Ambitious designing Men may Effect—they seem Determined at all Events, to *Oppose* whatsoever is *Proposed* by some other, who are not of their party, although it be for the good of the publick in general; and Even for some of them in Particular—For let it be right or wrong, they will immediately cry out their Liberties are sinking.—They are alarmed at such proceedings; they are oppressed &c—so that they make some people believe that Ruin is even at the door, by which means the more Ignorant sort will sign Petitions or do any thing that these great Patriots shall advise them to—But to return to the Case of the Court House; They say that the Cross Roads are the most Central place in Sussex and therefore most Convenient for the Major part of the Inhabitants. That the Cross Roads are Central I deny, for it is thirteen miles from Lewes to the Cross Roads; and about 5 or 6 Miles from thence to the Line, which now divides Sussex from Worcester; therefore admitting that the Cross Roads are near midway from the upper to the lower End of Sussex, yet it is Evident they are about 4 miles westerly of the Center.—Lewes Town is as near the middle of the County with respect to the upper & lower End, but only it lays on one side of it—and I think there is a place about 5 miles from Lewes that is full as Central and more advantageous and Convenient for the Inhabitants in general, than the Cross Roads—I have not heard, nor am I able to Concieve, one Reason that can be offer<u>d</u> Except that of the Centre being most Convenient for the Majority of the County, But I apprehend many Reasons may

1 The Cross Roads was at the head of navigation of Broadkill River, at or near the present site of Milton A bill for the removal of the county seat to that place was defeated in the Assembly, sitting at New Castle, on March 24, 1770. The removal to Georgetown took place twenty-one years later.

be given to obviate that, or any other they can advance,—If the publick buildings should be removed to the Cross Roads, they will be fixed in a very poor
part of the County, and of Consequence among the poorer sort of the Inhabitants. If they should be fixed near the Centre, they must be somewhere on
the Broad Kill Creek, which is so bad that Shallops often lay from Change to
full, and from full to Change again before they can get out.—On the other
hand Lewes Town is the most Suitable place I apprehend in this County for
the Publick buildings; we have opportunitys almost every Week for nine
months of the year to send for necessaries to Philadelphia. There are many
able farmers near Lewes, who can Supply the Town with other necessaries;
besides the advantage of the fishery—neither of which is the Case at the Cross
Roads—Lewes is pleasantly Situated and Esteemed a very healthy place, & the
Land is good in and about the Town for five miles round:—It was laid out
for a Town 95 years ago as appears by the antient Records; and many Laws
have been made directing the Courts and Offices to be kept there—The publick buildings have remained there without one Attempt being made before,
that I know of, to remove them—The Inhabitants in and near the Town
& their predecessors purchased their Lands at a high rate, under Faith & Confidence that it would remain a Town from generation to generation—And
shall their prospects of future advantages be at once frustrated to answer the
private Interest, or party Schemes of a few Men or even the Convenience of
two thirds of the County, to save them a few miles riding at most not above
Eight miles once or twice a year? for the other one third part bears the Chief
of the burden of the Courts, of Jurymen &c—besides those two thirds, for that
is full as many as would any ways be advantaged by a removal of the Court,
are in the same Condition now that they have Ever been in—they seldom serve
in publick business, and indeed very few of them are fit for it. They do Exceed us in number if we come to count Noses but notwithstanding, I think
that those who live most convenient to Lewes, together with those that may
be reckoned Indifferent as to their Situation, (who would not receive any advantage by a removal worth mentioning) are nearly Equal in number, & pay
the greatest share of the publick Tax.—If the Publick buildings should be
Removed the Consequence would be very bad to a great many people both in,
& near Lewes, their Lands & Improvements would be Reduced to less than
half their present Value, nay some will not sell for more than ¼ part—I knew
a Man who was offered £400—for his houses and Lotts a few years since,
which he refused—But if the Court house should be removed I believe no one
would give more than £100 for the same premesses. And would it not be
Extreemly hard that one half of the Landed Interest of a great number of
Persons should be sunk (at least without an adequate Satisfaction was made)

And that, that very Interest, should as it were be taken from them, & added to others—more Especially if we consider that the former had no reason at the time of purchase to apprehend such a Revolution; and that the latter at the time of Purchasing their Lands, could not have had any reason to expect such an addition to be made to their Estates.

The above I concieve is no Exaggerated state of the Case; many more Ilconveniences might be Enumerated, which I make no doubt will be naturally suggested to the House of Assembly should they enter into a Debate on this subject.—If it should happen that a Majority of the House is like to be in favour of their Scheme (which however I flatter myself will not be the Case) Y[et] if it should be so I hope you will think it Reasonable to use your influence to prevent it . . .

18

From John Penn[1]

Philadelphia, March 5th 1770

I am of necessity obliged to remain in Town some days after the Meeting of your House of Assembly and as I imagine you will not have any Bills immediately ready for my Consideration, I hope my not being with you at the beginning of the Session will not be attended with any inconvenience.

If you will be kind enough to inform me when it will be necessary for me to be at New Castle I will wait upon you with pleasure. At all events I intended to have been with you the beginning of next week.

19

From Charles Ridgely[2]

Dover, March 12, 1770.

I must remind you of a short act for confining the Voters of this Government to the respective Counties wherein they reside—in the same act I think it would be very well to say in so many precise words, what a Freehold is: with

1 The last proprietary of the Province of Pennsylvania and the last colonial governor of the Government of the Three Lower Counties on Delaware. He was a grandson of William Penn.

2 Son of Nicholas Ridgely, the guardian of Caesar Rodney. Charles Ridgely was a physician. He was also treasurer of Kent County from 1769 to 1774; member of the Colonial Assembly in the years beginning October 1765 to 1768 inclusive and in the years beginning October 1770 to 1774 inclusive; delegate to the first State Constitutional Convention in August–September 1776; member of the House of Assembly (lower branch of General Assembly) for the years beginning October 1776, 1777, 1779, and 1782. He was born in 1737 and died in 1785.

me indeed there is no doubt—but many of our Construers of Laws, & the bulk of the people, are certainly quite at a loss in that matter.—But I think if any explanatory Clause should be made, that every real Estate producing £5 per ann clear of charges, should make its owner a Freeholder—and no monied Estate should do it, because in that there is too much uncertainty—

But if a Law, from want of Time, or other Causes, cannot now be had, for confining the Voters to their own Counties—at least a Vote of the House, might be obtained, which probably would for the present answer the End— as few I believe would venture to act against it—

You promised me to introduce to the House a short Act, for altering the Trials of Slaves—at present the method is certainly unconstitutional—& if the Justices were to issue their Venire for the Freeholders, who should find the fact—& let it be other wise conducted on its present Plan, the mode of Trial would be more agreeable to our Constitution, & might be as cheap and expeditious—My Brother still continues much indisposed, & unless the Weather becomes much better, will not, I think, be able to attend the House, this Sessions—

Matters here are in Statu quo, as you left them—pray will you adjourn again, or do all your business now . . .

20

To Thomas Rodney

Newcastle March 14th. 1770

I Recd your Letter this day by Crawford Rees arrived here a Little before Dark with The Books unhurt—And now Set down (between ten and Eleven oClock, with as bad Pen, Ink, and paper, as any private Gentleman would Ever Wish to Write with) to Scribble a few Lines Relative to the Transactions of the Regislative* Body now at Newcastle.—

Since I wrote you last Some progress has been made in Sundry Bills, but (as Yet) none brought into the house Except the fee Bill, Which was laid this day before the Governor for his Concurrance—

The Petitions from Kent for the better Regulation of the poor of that County had their first Reading on Fryday last—were Read a Second time on Munday. Upon the Same days Were Read Petitions from Sussex Respecting The poor of Sussex County praying the *Act* for the Regulation of the poor of Newcastle County (Which directs the poor to be maintain[ed] by the Several hundreds to which they belong) Might be Extended to the County of Sussex.—On Reading those Petitions the Matter was debated Some time, and then ordered for further Consideration to the next day—on Tuesday the Petitions from Kent were first brought on—M! Killen after the Matter was Introduced Rose in favour of the Petitions (Which were for the Building & Regulating an Hospital) and Was Supported in his Motion verry Warmly by M! Read—M! Mc-Kean was also with him—However after much argument for, and Verry Little against the Petitions, the Question (Whether a Committee should be appointed to bring in a Bill for the Building & Regulating an Hospital &c.) was put, and (Contrary to my Expectation,) Carried in the Negative—upon this, M! Collins Demanded the Yea,s & Nay,s Should be Entered—M! Clark was the only Member from Kent in the opposition—The Rest were for Such a Bill and were Joined in Vote by Mess!ˢ Read, McKean, and Kollock—It was then Moved that Kent Should be included in a General Law With Newcastle & Sussex. M! Killen then grew furious, and Kent Was Excluded—

There is a Committee appointed to bring in a Bill for Supporting and keeping in Repair all the Kings Roads, Landing Roads &c. throughout the Whole Government by Tax—

You Mentioned Something of Hessy Kollock, Sally Armitage &ᶜ—In Answer to Which I tell You I have been So Engaged that I have not even Seen Sally Armitage, and Should have had as Much to Say for Hessy had I not dined & Supp,d at M! Read,s on Sunday last—By The Next oppertunity, I may perhaps be able to tell you more about Them—

I am verry Sorry to hear M! Vining Continues poorly, pray Remember me to him & Tell him I Should have been most pleased if he had Wrote to me—make my Compliments to the Doct!, Communicate to him as Much of This Letter as Relates to politicks, and Tell him I Would have answered his, But that there is no better paper than this in New castle and of this but Six or Seven Sheets—

With Respect to my business at Home I Cannot go into particulars, Must Request Generally that you Will take Care of every part of my property in My absence—

Remember me kindly to Sally—tell her I have bought a verry fine Riding Chair, and if Sally Armitage Chuses to Go down Will offer her a Seat—

I have five [hundred?] things to say to M! Vining and the [?] and to hear as many from them—But [for?] Want of time and paper Can only say That in my humble Opinion, The Kent Seats Do not appear Quite so formidable now as I have known them—

P.S. The Govern! Came this day, and with him Major Fell, M! Secratary, M! And^w Hamilton and M! Hockley—M! Chew is Expect^d Fryday or Saturday, and M! Tillman the beginning of Next Week—

* Expression frequently used by Some members, for want of Something better to say—

21

From Thomas Rodney[1]

Philada. Septr. 19th 1771

Mathew Manlove inform'd me that you Lost you[r] Election in Murder-kill Hundred, and that there is Some Reason, for a Suspicion of fraud at the General Election—I was at Mr. Wynkoops this morning, and in the Course of Conversation Communicated it to him, upon which we Consulted about a Remedy, and Conclu[d]ed that the best thing you Can Do (to have a fair Election) is to make the Sher: have a Seperate Box for each Inspector, so to have all the Votes of Each Hundred in a box by its self—And as they are Red out, not Tare them, but string them or put them into another Box, in the same manner—And this is the practice here in Philada. and no Doubt must insure a fair Election, or at Least if any fraud is Commited you'l find the author—However you'l act as you think best—this I wou'd not have mentiond (as Comg. from me) to anybody Except the Doctor, Least in my present situation it might prejudice you

22

From Thomas Rodney

Philada: Septr: 22d 1772.

The capn. All, & Ozbourn are arrived from London, but they bring little inteligence that is new, however have sent you this paper whereby you will be better inform'd—I think (notwithstanding the great warlike preparations) there is no likelyhood of war, between England, and France or Spain; for the present situation of Europe rather require their uniting, to support that ballance of Power, which is so politically necessary, to be maintained: And which at this time seems to be threaten'd with a dreadful shock, from those three great contenental powers that are forming an overthrow and division of the Kingdom of Poland; which must of consequence create a combination too popular for the general good of Europe—It is said the French Ambassador has remonstrated on this head to the court of Great Britain. How our minister may manage this affair is yet uncertain: but he seems to be a great politician, and from his past conduct I shou'd suppose that he foresaw those rising storms that have disturbed and are now like to disturb the good order & quiet of Europe.—

I suppose you are acquainted with our difensive preperations by building a

1 Thomas Rodney kept a shop in Philadelphia from the autumn of 1771 until the summer of 1773.

Fort, on one of Mr. Galloways Islands near red bank, which is Just now emerging above the surface of the mud, and will be Finished perhaps in two or three years, So that if any hoistile invaders shou'd attempt the navigation of Dalawar, after that time, we shall (barring high Tides inundatıons & storms) be able to give them a warm reception,—All Electıon matters are quite still here, tho there is many discontented spirits, about the high duty of 4ᵈ· a gallⁿ continued on rum; And also about a late act concerning leather—Your important day draws near, and I hope wıll end to your satisfaction—I understand by the shaloopmen that many people are displeased with L. . . .s conduct with respect to the lıttle Election—but I suspect his success has been too popular in some parts, to "Auger well" &c. . . .

23
To the Speaker of the House of Burgesses, Williamsburg, Va.

Sɪʀ,   Newcastle on Delaware October 25ᵗʰ 1773.

I am ordered by the House of Representatives of this Government to acknowledge the receipt of your Letter of the 19ᵗʰ of March last, addressed to the Speaker of the late Assembly here, inclosing a Copy of the Resolves entered into by the House of Burgesses of your Colony,¹ and to inform you that the same were laid before this House the first time they met after receiving them; and I now have the pleasure of transmitting to you a Copy of their Minutes and Proceedings on this occasion, which are so expressive of their Sentiments of the measures adopted and recommended by your House, that nothing need be added thereto—²

In the Name and by the Order of the House
I am with great respect
Your most obedient Servᵗ
Caesar Rodney Speaker

24
From New Castle County Committee

Sɪʀ   Newcastle July 11ᵗʰ 1774.

The Committee appointed at the general County meeting on the 29ᵗʰ of

1 The "resolves" forwarded by Peyton Randolph, Speaker of the Vırgınıa House of Burgesses, provıded for the organızatıon of a Commıttee of Correspondence to communıcate wıth all other colonıes relatıve to recent ıllegal acts by the Brıtısh Parlıament.

2 The Assembly decıded on October 23 to organıze a Committee of Correspondence, as the Vırgınıa body had done, and elected Caesar Rodney, George Read, Thomas McKean, John Mc-Kınly, and Thomas Robinson as members.

June last,[1] having met here this day, and taking into their consideration the 4th Resolution as to the convening the Representatives of this Government for the purpose of appointing persons to attend a Congress proposed for the Colonies in general, are of opinion that such a convention of the Representatives should be as soon as conveniently may, and beg leave to propose the first day of August next for that purpose, and Newcastle as the place of meeting, and hope that it will have your approbation; and in full confidence thereof request the favor of you as Speaker to write circular Letters to the Representatives of the people of this Government to meet at that day and place, or on such other short day as you may think will be more convenient.

Convinced of your Zeal for American Liberty we rest assured that you will comply with the earnest wishes of the Inhabitants of this County to procure an appointment of a Committee to represent the whole Government at the general Congress whenever they may meet.

We inclose with this divers Letters addressed to you as Speaker, and to the Committee of Correspondence, which the Committee opened agreeable to your request. Those from Boston were answered by the Committee of Correspondence, a copy of which answer we send you with 40 printed Subscription Papers for your County and Sussex, part of which we beg the favor of you to transmit to that County speedily,[2]—and are

Your most obedient
Humble Servants

Jno McKinly
Jas Latimer
Geo: Read
Alex. Porter
Saml Patterson
Nichs Van Dyke
Tho Cooch
Geo: Monro
Rd Cantwell

Caesar Rodney Esquire.—

1 All three counties held mass meetings (those in Kent and Sussex counties being held in July) for the purpose of calling upon the Assemblymen to meet in New Castle, August 1, to decide upon sending delegates to the First Continental Congress in Philadelphia, September 5, 1774.

2 Subscription lists were circulated in the three counties to afford aid to the poor in Boston, who were suffering from unemployment due to the closing of that port by the act of parliament known as the Boston Port Bill.

25

From George Read[1]

New Castle, July 13th 1774.

This will be deliver'd to you by Express together with a Letter addressed to you as Speaker requesting a call of the members of Assembly in Consequence of the 4th resolution of the people here—I was at Wilmington yesterday and got 40 blank Subscription Papers struck off for the Use of your county and that of Sussex—I also send you such publick Letters as have been rec'ed since I saw you last. We did not think it necessary to write answers to any other than those from Boston until Deputies for the Congress shou'd be appointed—A Copy of which was drawn yesterday to be sent to you but by accident I imagine I left it at Wilmington with Doctor McKinly but as it Contains nothing particular I hope you will overlook the omission—I wrote to you on the Evening of the 29th of June last inclosing a copy of our resolves with a Letter of the like import to Mr Robinson of Sussex and intrusted them to Thos Skillington Innkeeper at the Cross Roads in your County and hope they were safely delivered in time—I now inclose you also two Printed Copies of our resolves least any accident shou'd have happened to the Written Copies and rely on your sending one of the Printed resolves to Sussex with such part of the Printed subscription Papers as you may think fit—the Messenger that brings you this will wait for your Letters of Call to the members of this County and they shall be delivered—As we only got our printed subscription papers yesterday they have not been offered yet to the People—I am informed by Private Letter from Philada. of the 9th Instant, that a Proclamation was published in the York Paper—which has been issued by Gen. Gage wherein he forewarns all people in his Government from Signing any Agreement for the non importation of British Goods as they will answer it at their Peril, he undertakes to call all such agreements traiterous, hostile & rebellious and strictly injoins and Commands all civil magistrates Sheriffs &c. to apprehend any and all such People who may have Signed any such agreement and to confine them in order that they may be tried for it—I do not recollect any other matter worth Communication —our Committee adjourned till Monday next when they will expect from you. [P.S.] Don't omit to bring up the publick Letters sent you.

1 George Read, together with Caesar Rodney and Thomas McKean, signed the Declaration of Independence for Delaware two years later.

26

*To John McKinly, James Latimer, George Read, Alexander Porter, Samuel
Patterson, Nicholas Van Dyke, Thomas Cooch, George Monro, and
Richard Cantwell*[1]

Dover July 15th 1774

I Received you[r] letter requesting me as Speaker to write circular letters to
the Representatives of the people of this Government to meet &c. This mode
for the appointment of proper persons to represent this Government at the
general Congress I verry much approve of—And Shall I do assure you Most
Chearfully Comply with your request—But cannot help thinking it may be
done with more propriety imediately after the intended meeting of the people
of this County, which is on Wednesday next. I hope and indeed Expect the
people here will adopt the same mode that you have. Therefore must beg leave
to defer writing the Circular letters till the day after the meeting of the people
here, least it Should give offence to some who wou'd wish To have a hand in
Every good Work, and thereby injure the Cause—Gent. n you may Expect to
hear from me by Express as soon (after our meeting) as letters can be wrote
and the Express get there which I apprehend will be time Enough for the first
of August—for I would by no means retard a business of so great importance
—I shall send an Express to Sussex this day, and endeavour to know by him
what they are about to do—In short you may be assured I Shall do every thing
in my power to have a Convention of the Representatives on the first day of
August next at Newcastle

27

To George Read

Dover July the 21st 1774

Yesterday We had a verry full meeting of this County, Upward of Seven
hundred inhabitants, some think more than Eight; with this (agreable to
promise), I have sent you a packet inclosing a Letter from the Committee of
this County to the Committee of Your's, as also A Copy of our Resolves, and
a letter to Bradford the printer inclosing another copy of them for the press
which hope you will forward to him as quick as possible: Some people were
much displeased with your haveing appointed New castle as the place of Meeting, and it was not without some difficulty that Some others Reconciled the
people to the place, More of this another time; The meeting of the people of

1 Written in answer to the letter from these persons, dated July 11, requesting that Rodney
issue a call for the members of the Assembly to meet in convention to appoint delegates to the
First Continental Congress.

Sussex County is to be on Saturday next, and there is a Report prevails here, that they are so offended at your fixing the mode and place, but more especially the place That they are determined not to fall in With your Plans But that the people at their meeting, Shall or Will Chuse one Deputy for that County. However I shall dispatch an Express early tomorrow morning to Thomas Robinson with a verry pressing letter from the Committee here, to adopt your measures, and that if they should not, they will defeat the whole business—the Express will have Orders to be there before the meeting of the people, and to wait for a full accot of What they shall do—I shall write a private letter to Robinson enjoining him to use his endeavour to have the plans of the other two Counties adopted—I have sent circular letters to all the Members of Your County. You'l be pleased to have them delivered; I have also writ circular letters to the Members of this County Who desired me to inform you that they would be in New castle ready to enter upon business by ten of the Clock on the first of August, and hope your Members will give their attendance by that hour—further with Respect to Sussex, I have prevailed on Clarke to ride to Crapper's to persuade him to use his Interest in bringing about the before mentioned Measures and also have got Jacob Stout Esqr to Write to Wiltbank. I Do most sincerely wish the worthy members of Sussex may be prevailed on to adopt the Measures proposed. I expect to hear from them by Sunday Evening, and if I find it will avail will Call them in due time for the Convention

28

To Charles Ridgely[1]

SIR   Dover 21st July 1774

In compliance with a Request of the Committee of Correspondence for the County of Kent you are hereby desired to give your attendance as a Repre-

1 This letter supplies an important link in the chain of events leading to Delaware's joining the other colonies in severing the constitutional tie with the British Empire. Although Caesar Rodney, the Speaker of the Colonial Assembly, wrote similar letters to the other five members of the Assembly from Kent County and to the six members from each of the other two counties, New Castle and Sussex, this letter is the only one known to be extant at the date of publication of the Rodney correspondence. Mass meetings had been held in New Castle, Dover, and Lewes in June and July for the purpose of considering the proposal of holding a convention in New Castle to consider the matter of sending delegates to the First Continental Congress, scheduled to meet in Philadelphia on September 5. Each mass meeting had decided that the members of the Colonial Assembly should constitute the convention, which should meet in New Castle on August 1. Moreover, each mass meeting had appointed a Committee of Correspondence for its own county to communicate to the speaker of the Assembly the resolves of the mass meeting In this particular letter Rodney is officially informing Dr Charles G. Ridgely of Dover of the action of the Kent County mass meeting The whole procedure was, of course, radical and revolutionary, as under the colonial government only the proprietary governor, in this case John Penn, enjoyed the right to call a special session of the Assembly.

sentative of this Government at the Court house in the Town of New Castle on the first day of August next, Then and there together, with the other Representatives of the Government, to take into your most serious Consideration the verry alarming situation of the American Colonies, and to appoint deputies to attend at a general Congress at such time and place as shall be generally agreed on

Caesar Rodney Speaker

To Charles Ridgely Esq.

29

Instructions to Caesar Rodney, Thomas McKean, and George Read, delegates to the First Continental Congress at Philadelphia, adopted at New Castle, Delaware, August 2, 1774

At the meeting of the Convention of the Representatives of the freemen of the Government of the counties of Newcastle, Kent and Sussex on Delaware, on the 2d day of August 1774 A.M. it was unanimously Resolved to instruct the Deputies then appointed in behalf of the people of the said Government to attend the General Congress, that they do endeavour to prevail with the Deputies of the other Colonies and Provinces at the said General Congress to adopt the following or similar Resolutions.

1. In the first place, That we most solemnly and sincerely acknowledge and declare, that we do and will bear faith and true allegiance to His most sacred Majesty King George the Third, our most gracious Sovereign and rightful liege Lord: that we will, upon true revolution principles, and to the utmost of our power, support and defend the protestant succession, as established in the illustrious House of Hanover; and it is our most earnest desire that the connexion, which subsists between Great-Britain and her Colonies, whereby they are made one people, may continue to the latest period of time.

2. That the subjects of His Majesty in the British American Colonies have had, and of right ought to have and enjoy all the liberties, privileges and immunities of free and natural born subjects within any of His Majesty's Dominions, as fully and amply as if they and every of them were born within the realm of England—that they have a property in their own estates, and are to be taxed by their own consent only, given in person or by their representatives, and are not to be asseised of their liberties and free customs, sentenced or condemned, but by lawful judgment of their peers.

3. That the only lawful representatives of the freemen in the several Colonies are persons they elect to serve as Members of the General Assembly thereof; and that it is the just right and privilege of the said freemen to be

governed by laws made by their General Assembly in the article of taxation and internal police.

4.   That all trials for treason, misprision of treason, or for any felony or crime whatsoever, committed and done in the said Colonies ought of right to be had and conducted in His Majesty's courts held within the same, according to the fixed and known course of proceeding; and that the seizing any person or persons suspected of any crime whatsoever committed in them, and sending such person or persons to places beyond the Seas to be tried, is highly derogatory of the rights of British subjects, as thereby the inestimable privilege of being tried by a jury from the vicinage, as well as the liberty of summoning and producing Witnesses on such trial, will be taken away from the party accused.

5.   That all Acts and Proceedings of the British Parliament, for prohibiting and restraining American manufactures; imposing taxes on the British Colonies; extending the powers of custom-house officers, and admiralty courts here beyond their ancient limits; and seizing and sending persons suspected of committing treason or misprision of treason in these Colonies to England for trial, are unwarrantable assumptions of power, unconstitutional and destructive of British liberty.

6.   That the successive Acts of Parliament, made in the last Session, for the inflicting pains and penalties on the town of Boston, by shutting up their Port and blocking up their Harbour; for altering the administration of justice in certain criminal cases within the province of Massachusetts Bay; and for new-modelling the constitution of that province, established by royal charter, are in the highest degree arbitrary in their principles, unparalelled in their rigor, oppressive in their operation and subversive of every Idea of justice and freedom.

7.   That it is the indispensible duty of all the colonies not only to alleviate the unexampled distresses of our brethren of Massachusetts Bay, who are suffering in the common cause of America, but to assist them by all lawful means in removing their grievances, and for the re-establishing their constitutional right, as well as those of all America, on a solid and permanent foundation.

8.   That it is our fixed, determined and unalterable resolution, by all lawful ways and means in our power, to maintain, defend and preserve our before-mentioned rights and liberties, and that we will transmit them entire and inviolate to our posterity; and further, that we will adopt and faithfully carry into execution all and singular such peaceable and constitutional measures as have been agreed on by this Congress.

9.   That we are unfeignedly thankful to those truly noble, honorable and patriotic Advocates in Great-Britain, who have so generously and powerfully, tho' unsuccessfully, espoused and defended the cause of America, both in and

out of Parliament; that we still feel that warmest affection for our brethren in the parent state; and that it is our opinion, as it is our hope, that the cool and dispassionate among our fellow-subjects in Great-Britain will applaud our measures, and co-operate with us, in every manly struggle for the preservation of those our rights, with which their own are so intimately connected.

And further, we do earnestly recommend it to our said Deputies to use their utmost endeavours to prevail with the Deputies from the other Colonies to frame decent and becoming Petitions to His most gracious Majesty and both Houses of Parliament for the redress of all our grievances, and to agree to a non-importation of goods from, and exportation to Great-Britain, until relief shall be obtained.

Notwithstanding any thing herein before mentioned, it is not our meaning, that by these instructions our said Deputies should be restrained from agreeing to any measures that shall be approved by the Congress.

Signed by the unanimous order of the Convention,

Caesar Rodney Chairman[1]

30

To Thomas Rodney

Philadelphia Sepr 9th 1774—

On Thursday the 1st of this month after a verry warm disagreable Ride I arrived in Town together with some of the Virginia Gentlemen—by Sunday evening last the delegates from all the diffirent Colonies (Except North Carolina & Georgia) Came to Town and on Munday they met at Carpenters Hall, When the Hon. Peyton Randolph was unanimously Elected to the Chair by the name of President—Charles Thompson was Chose Secretary and two Door keepers and Mesengers was also appointed. The Congress then proceeded to business and have set every day since—I doubt their Rising before some time in October Perhaps the Middle—All the seven delegates appointed for Virginia are here, & more sensible fine fellows you'd never wish to see, in short it is the greatest assembly (in proportion to the number) that ever was Collected in America—And the Bostonians who (we know) have been condemned by many for their Violence, are moderate men, when Compared to Virginia,

---

1 Although the body of delegates consisted only of members of the Assembly, it was an extra-legal meeting since it was not an adjourned session nor a special session called by the governor. Hence Caesar Rodney, who was Speaker of the Assembly at this time, wrote the title "Chairman" after his signature instead of the title "Speaker."

South Carolina and Rode Island, in short all the Colonies seem to be hearty in the Cause—and have the greatest Respect paid them by all the first people here—A Letter to Mr Cushing by Express from Boston informs that all is Quiet as Yet, That their Superior Court had met under the act of Parliament for altering their Government, but that it Could not proceed for want of Jury men who would not attend, That allmost all the Judges appointed under that act had waited on the Governor with Resignations—Captain Inglis is arrived with some dry Goods from London, George Emlens Ship is Expected every day Quite full, there is an accot. of her Sailing, All & Fortner are also Expected soon—I have been Verry poorly ever since I Came to town, but hope shall get better . . . The Congress meets at nine, therefore have not more time than to say

31
From Thomas Rodney

Dover Sept: 11th 1774.

I have not had an opertunity of writing before (except Lockerman who's going I did not know) nor have we heard from you since you went away—On Fryday last we recd: the account of the onsett at Boston, as related in Halls paper of wednesday last; but wait with great anxiety to hear a more full and explicit account, as well, as what steps the congress will take upon such an Occation; as we judg all the colonies will look up to that grand council, for their direction in case of a general rupture—And untill the peace of England and the colonies may be settled on a permanant foundation.

Our Vicars (as the doctr calls them) seem put to silence by the above mentd account of the hoistile invasion of Boston, perhaps judging it impolitic longer to oppose the popular opinion against such unhear'd of oppression—However before this, their junto of domestic police, had formed the Attempt to exclude you from their political favour & ticket, but were defeated in this by your warm friends in their council, viz C—K. C—ls & P—B. together with the popular warmth for you out of doors—However your good friend Doctr R— has layed a trap with his Old Machine L—mn which he no doubt thinks may gain his purpose of throwinge you off the assembly—but your friends ar apprized of this and will not omit to lower his Turban at this election; and the voice of the people is increasing greatly against him. L—mn was also prevaild on to git his son to sett up fore sherriff, but his best friends would not agree to carry him upon which he declined—So much of domestic policy & opinion which stands favourable at present; and I am now more anxious that nothing may thwart the united wisdom and virtue of the congress, in which we trust the fate of the colonies (under providence) is now reposed.

I shall be very glad to hear from you the first opertunity—and shall be glad you would procure and send me all, Dunlaps–Halls, and Bradfords papers that have come out since you left home, as I have [not] got any of them . . .

32

To Thomas Rodney

Philadelphia Munday Sepr 12th 1774

With this You have inclosed the Pensylvania Packet of this day, as also another Letter intended to have been sent by Mr McFarson who intends going to Lewis adjourned Court, but finding he did not purpose being at Dover before Saturday next, and Seeing Mr William Gray in Town by whom it might get a Quicker Conveyance Gave it him with this—Mr McPherson will give you the New York paper of Thursday last, I Gave it him for that purpose— You'l find in that paper a Speech of the Bishop of St Asaph intended to have been Spoken in the house of Lords—and is now printed here in pamphlets— it is one of the Best peices I ever Read—I Continue in a Verry poor State of health not so bad but that I have given my constant attendance in the Congress. The Congress does not now Sit in form haveing appointed two Committees one Consisting of 24 the other of 12 Members I am one of the 24 Who are to report the Rights of the Colonies, the infringments of those Rights, and the means of Relief—What Shall be done after this appointm.^t of the Committee the Congress has injoined every member to keep a Secret till the Whole business is done, when the whole of their proceedings will be published to avoid needless disputations out of Doors; This is much to the disappointment of the Curious; We do not Expect to rise till some time in October—There are more Strangers in Town now (Exclusive of the Gentlemen of the Congress) than ever was known at any one time—George Emblins Ship Capt.ⁿ Miller is arrived from London as full as She Can Swim with dry Goods, All is looked for every day, and it is Supposed Fortner will not be Long behind him—An Irish Ship is just Come to town Who Landed her passengers at Newcastle and says that in puting them on Shore a Small Boat with 22 of them with their Effects was overset 19 of whom Lost their lives between the Ship and the Warff—I beg you'l write me by the first oppertunity Giving a State of Affairs below both public and private, and if any thing accurs out of the Common Road I Shall take Care to advise you of it . . . The gentlemen of the City are entertaining the Gentle men of Congress every day by parcels—and on Fryday next the

Citizens in General are to entertain the Whole Congress at the Statehouse, it is intended to be the greatest intertainment that ever was made in this City, the Expence of which is Computed to a Thousand pounds at least—

33

To Thomas Rodney

Philadelphia. Saturday Sep[r] 17th 1774

By Express which arrived here Yesterday from the Committee of the Town of Boston to the general Continental Congress, We are Informed the County of Suffolk of which the Town of Boston is the Capital, had entered into Certain Resolutions, a Copy of which was inclosed us, Generally to the purport of not Suffering the Commander in Chief to Execute the act of Parliament changing their Government by Persuading, protecting and Compelling officers under the new Regulation to Resign and by a Refusal in jurymen to Serve &c, That they have ordered all those able to bear arms to keep in Readiness to defend their inherent rights—Even with Loss of Blood & Treasure; That they are determined not Injure the General or any of the Kings Troops, Unless Compelled thereto by an Attack made by the Troops on them—

They Complain of the General's seizing the Powder at Cambridge which they say was private property: and also that he is now fortifying the only pass that leads from the Town of Boston into the Country from whence the inhabitants of the Town are daily Supplied, This pass is a narrow neck of Land about 120 Yards wide at which he has placed a number of Troops and 28 Canon, That the Country people passing and Repassing this place are Suffered to be insulted by the Soldiery—And that the inhabitants feared (from those movements of the General) he had designs of apprehending and sending to England those persons who have Stood foremost in the great Cause of Liberty —That in Consequence of his Conduct, and these their suspitions the inhabitants of Suffolk sent (by a Committee appointed for that purpose) An address to the General, enquiring the Cause of his Stopping up and fortifying the pass, Seizing and securing the magazine's &c. & their disaprobation of his Conduct —and that they had no Intention to assault either him or his Soldiers—But that if he Continued to block up the pass, and thereby prevent them of the only means of Supplying the Town with necessaries—They Should Look upon it as a Commencement of Hostilities—Upon the whole they sent an Express to the General Congress here, for their Instructions as to their future Conduct—The Congress mett on that business this day and have Resolved thereon—Which you will see in the Packet of Munday being ordered imediately to be printed, as well that the General, as the people might know what they thought of the matter—If Morris or Henry Stays till Munday I will send you the Mondays paper—Mr Richard Penn has got Hockley office—about £1200 a Year—

Your Acco⸍ of Polltick's in Kent as Set forth in Your Letter by Butler, places them in that State I Expected they would be—However do not °Doubt but a great Majority of the people will Shew Such a firm Attachment to the Cause in which I am embarked as (with the assi[s]tance of my Real friends) Will defeat their little Low Ungreatefull Schemes—If the Shallops go before Munday I Shall Inclose you the New York paper of thursday in this—if not Shall inclose the Mundays paper with it in another Cover—Let me here every thing, by Every oppertunity. V. Loockerman will give you acco⸍ of the Entertainment of Yesterday—by Whom I wrote Several days ago—Remember me Kindly to all friends—and next to Relations, to Doct⸍ McCall who did not forget me—

34

To Thomas Rodney

Philadelphia Munday Sep⸍ the 19th 1774—

I wrote you on Saturday by John Morris the St Jones's Creek Shallopman, Who was to leave town that Night; With him Also I directed another paper inclosing the New-York newspaper of Thursday last; With this Letter Which will go by Matthew Henry's Shallop I shall inclose you the Pensylvania-Packet of this day;—

Some time ago, I do not doubt that you were all much allarmed on a Report that the Kings Ships were fireing on the town of Boston. When that News came to this City, the Bells were Muffled, and kept Ringing all that day; However in a few days after, that news was contradicted here, and hope by this time it is so With you—By Some late verry Authentick accounts from Boston Government to the Gentlemen of that place now at the Congress, We are informed that, there was about three days, between this Report's passing through the Massachusets & Connecticut Governments, and its being Contradicted. That When the Expresses Went to Contradict this false Report they found in these two Governments, in different parties upward of fifty thousand men Well armed, Actually on their March to Boston for the Relief of the inhabitants: and That every farmer Who had a Cart or Waggon (and not able to boro arms) were with them loaded with Provisions, Amunition and Baggage &^c all headed by Experienced officers Who had Served in the late American War—And that Vast numbers more were prepar.g to March. Upon the news being Contradicted, they Returned peaceably to their Several places of Abode, but not till they had Sent some of their officers from the different parties to Boston to know the real Scituation of Affairs there, and to direct them What principal officers in the different parts of the Country they Should hereafter Send Expresses to in Case they Should Stand in Need of their Assistance—It is Supposed by Some of the friends of Liberty at Boston that the alarm was set on foot by some of the friends to the Ministerial plan, in order try Whether there was that True Vallour in the people—if this was the Case, I suppose you will think with me That by this time they Can have no doubts remaining—Indeed I think it is proved by the General's own Conduct, for, ever since that, he has been fortifying himself, Which I imagin is more for his own security, than to attack the Inhabitants—Yesterday Afternoon Captain All from London, Came up to town, But no news that he may have brought has as Yet Transpired Except that friends to the American Cause are daily increasing on the other Side the Water—

35

From Thomas Rodney

Dover Septr: 20th 1774

I recd your two letters and the paper by Mr. Gray (on my way down to Mispillion election) and your other by Lockerman since—but have not heard that you have recd. mine sent by Andw. Butler—wherein I hinted at some thing of our domestic police; but matters seems somthing changed since then —I had a long conversation with Cook last night, as he came chiefly to know what part I should act, the Doctr. being suspicious that I would not favour him—I told him, that the Doctrs. conduct in publick measures had deprived him of my assistance; that we had found a strong party (without candidates) to carry a ticket made up of men selected from both parties; that five of those men so carried must (beyond all doubt) be on the return, & that the other at this time appear'd to stand a fairer chance of being on than the Doctr.—Cook prest my carrying the Doctr. & said he apprehend[d] If I did not that he would declare off—I told him my sentiments were fixt & I should not change them— Locker[n]. a[s] I hint[d]. had been in tow with the Doctr. and had sett out against you but finds. the rapid progress of our third party scheme (and he being one of our men) has tackt about & is violent against the Doctr. who I think will undoubtdly be left off—I have inclosed you all the tickets whereby youl see Baning is carried on both sides as well as by us but never the less it is apprenhended youl be much the highest on the return. Cook says the Doctr. has declared that he will carry you this year, let you[r] friends act as they will; but perhaps my sentiment may change his mind: however let it be as it may you stand safe.

Court
Caesar Rodney
Charles Ridgely
Thomas Collins
Jacob Stout
John Clark
John Baning
————————— Cook & Barret

Middle Ticket
Caesar Rodney
John Hazlett
Thomas Collins
William Killen
John Baning
Vinct. Lockerman
————————— Cook & Barrot—some Gray

Country
William Killen
John Hazlet
Vinct. Lockerman
John Baning
Thomas Hanson
Powell Cox
Cook & Gray

36

From Thomas Rodney

Cross Roads[1] 22d Sep: 1774

This comes by an express sent you upon political affairs—a State of which I wrote by Palmer but he will not be up perhaps by this—Suffice it to say a number of us have declared (independent of parties) to Carry, Caesar Rodney, Thomas Collins, Will: Killen John Hazlett, John Baning & Vincent Lockerman—This I declared to the Sherf who was sent to know from the Doctrs upon which has happen'd great comotion among some of your party—and Tom is sent to know if you are not at the bottom—Or to git something from under your hand which may be turned to your disadvantage—therefore write

1 Now Smyrna, Delaware.

few words, & cautious; that is that you have not advised anything to me, and
are not acquainted with what I may do—or to that purpose, if you write any
thing—My conduct will be consistant with your interest which is united with
the publick good. Collins Cook & Barret will be firm—you will run high—and
the Doctr. is in danger of falling which makes this great strugle—I have not
hinted any thing private against the Doctr. his publick conduct I have disap-
proved—but he will certainly be agt. you privately if not publickly.

37
To Thomas Rodney

Philadelphia Sepr 24th 1774, Saturday

There is little or nothing new since I wrote you last; I think I wrote you of
Mr Hawkley's death and that Mr Richard Penn has got his office—I have now
the pleasure to tell you of a Truith that in this the Governor has the whole and
Sole Merit, and that it has brought about an entire Reconsiliation, Mr Penn
has (since) been to see the Governor and the Governor him, their wives have
also Visited. I shall tell you more of this matter if I live to see you. Mr R. Penn
is a great friend to the Cause of Liberty and has Treated the Gentlemen delegates with the greatest Respect. More or less of them dine with him every day
and his brother wishes his Station would admit of his acting the same part;
All these matters are for your own private Speculation, and not for Public
View, by this you may See that some people with you are mistaken in their
Politics, and you may also take for granted every Body here are not well
pleased with the coalition of the two Brothers—

Since I wrote last Fortner and Allen two London ships Quite full Came to
town and are now nearly discharged, there are three or four more Expected
verry soon, in Short every Body say half the Quantity of Dry Goods never was
before imported as now are, and likely to be this fall, So that it will not be
necessary for you to Come up for the purpose of purchasing till after the Election—You may tell those whom it may Concern that Missrs Charlton who used
to take in Some of our Kent Ladies to Lodge, was buried the day before
Yesterday from whence they will (no Doubt) Readily Suppose She is dead—

This Letter is intended to Come by Allen McClain by whom I shall Send
you the Last Wednesday's paper which will furnish you with the news up to
that time—This day the post Came in by whom we have the Boston News,
Wherein is inserted General Gages's answer to the Committee for the County
of Suffolk whoes address to him you had in the last paper I sent you. His answer is to the following purport—

Gentmn.

I have no intention to Stop up the pass between the Town and the Country, but that the people Shall pass and repass as usual without molestation; I have no intention to disturb the peace and Quiet of the inhabitants of the Town; But as I find the people of the Masachusets Bay are determined not to Submit to the Several Acts of Parliament, Shall Write to his Majesty for further instructions &c. or to this Effect—from this you Will readily Suppose the General is about to Act a prudent part—Query, was he not friten'd into that prudence by the manly prudent opposition of the inhabitants of that Government —I have never Recd but one Letter from you Since I Came up, and Can say of a Truith I never wanted to have one from you much more than at present, —therefore live in hopes every day that Some Chance hand will throw one in my way—I Expected one of the Shallops Would have been here by this time but Can neither see or hear any thing of them—Tell Betsey and Sally that I have not got well Yet, and that I have verry little Expectation that I Shall while I am under the necessaty of Spending all those that ought to be my Leisure Hours, in Feasting or be thought to neglect those who kindly invite; However Remember me kindly to them both, and tell Casar that I will send his *Fiddle* by the first Shallop—

P.S. I have inclosed you a Request from the Congress to the Merchants, that [they] might know in time what they may Expect.

38

From Thomas Rodney

Dover Septr. 28th 1774—

I have recd: from you 4 letters one by Morris—one by Henry—one by Lockerman and one by McClane—have wrote two—My last by Palmer—My sentiments to the Sherr. mentioned in my last occationed great rage and fury in the Doctr. at a meeting held the next evening. He determined to send express to you next day to know if you were not concerned in my conduct, tho I had fully assured the Sher. & sundry persons sent by him to me, that you were not. However his passion cooled before morning & he dropt the scheme of sending & it seems determined to carry you and also dropt Baning & put in Robert Holliday—Baning told me, that Lockerman informed him about three weeks ago that the Doctr. offer'd to carry him (Lockerman) if he would strike at you and we had this further evidence that Lockerman had begun the business —However this is a secret known to few therefore let go no further—Except the above alteration, matters stand now as stated in my last—& the middle

ticket has gaind greatly and made much noise—Cook—Barret & Collins in
the midst of the Doctr₅ rage declared they wou'd carry you through thick &
thin; and you will run generally on all sides, except a few persons—But I expect it will be a crooked election, for it seems very probable that the doctr.
will be left unless he can still prevail with Lockerman, to favour him which is
yet susspectd. However I can tell you more when I come up which I expect
will be on Munday next—and in the mean time let these particulars remain
with your self.

P.S. This Maenuverer in politics is looked on with pleasure by the other party
who expect it will occation a seperation between you and the doctr. which
[I by] no means intend—But to convince him that the good of his country, &
real friendship should never be subservient to the gross passions of pride &
envie which was probably the rule of his conduct on this occation.—

39

From Thomas Rodney

Dover March 19th 1775—

We have received the good Tidings of the favourable reception the Congress
Petition has met with at the Throne; and the favourable turn the American
affairs seems in general to have lately taken over the wa[ter.]

This news I apprehend will greatly tend to silence that Spirit of op[po]sition
(which has hitherto existed in a few factious bosoms) to the united and patriotic measures of the colonies—Perhaps indeed it may work the same effect
on those factious discontented spirits here, which it is said to have done on
those of the same stamp in England, who are said to be now striving (since
there adverse designs faild) to take the lead in patriotic measures—So be it,
for I can rejoice to see them made proselites to virtue upon this principle—
Let america be free, and I care not how many pretending patriots it makes.

Doctᵣ McCall is transported with the glad tidings above mentioned; and has
grown so elate that he has formed a few questions and answers, and sent them
up to be published; which (if they can git admittance) perhaps you may see
in Tomorrows paper—But in the midst of this he has recd: a long letter from
his Son Mark, who informs him "that the last letter sent by the Comₜₑₑ of
correspondₑ for Kent, to the Comₜₑₑ of correspondₑ at Philadₐ is very ill received by the latter—That they call it a mixt medly of nonsence; and that they
were drawn into a scrape by the first letter: and left in the lurch by the last—
And further that they do not hisitate to call the Kent Comₜₑₑ very harsh names
such as D——d R——s S——s &ᶜ"—And this has made the doctᵣ very uneasy;

supposing that the letter was unfairly dealt with, after it was ordered to be copied by the comtᵉᵉ—But this is too rash a supposition to have any weight— For if there be any truth in Marks letter I must rather think that some imprudent representations of the Doctᵣ or his son (in a too heated pursute of the cause) has occationed such language in some of the inconsiderate ones in the Philadᵃ Comtᵉᵉ—For the Doctᵣ tells me he wrote to Mark; "that Mᵣ K——n made a formula of a letter which breathed Tar & Feathers: That Doctᵣ R—— drew another which requested all further pursute or serch to be stoped—That the latter was rejected; and the former (with some alterations) adopted" This you will recollect was not the case—but that the alterations was made in the latter; by expunging the part mentioned as well as what else was most disagreeable, and ading what was thought necessary—And from this misrepresentation it is very likely other imprudencies have arose*—but I should be sorry to see them go so far as to stir up divisions among the real friends of Liberty. I shall say no more at present on this head, but leave the sequel to your own sugestions—

We have read the proceedings of the Pensylvania Assembly, and think they have Acted wisely—And we are glad to hear Our House has followed there example, in approving of the works of the last Congress, and appointing Delegates for the next—I understand that the Doctᵣ has informed his wife that the House Acts with great unanimety and friendship.

* Mark informs the doctᵣ that he is waited on very often by the Comtᵉᵉ of Philadᵃ and that they have permitted him to be acquainted with all their proceedings &ᶜ

40

Instructions to Caesar Rodney, Thomas McKean, and George Read, delegates to Second Continental Congress[1]

Lower Counties on Delaware,

In Assembly.

Friday, March 17ᵗʰ 1775. A. M.

On Motion,
    Ordered,
        That Messᵣˢ Evans, Ridgely, McKinly, Hall and Rench, be a Com-

1 On March 15, the Delaware Colonial Assembly approved the proceedings of the Convention at New Castle, which, on August 2, 1774, had appointed Caesar Rodney, Thomas McKean, and George Read as delegates to the First Continental Congress called to meet in Philadelphia on September 5 following. The Assembly also approved the proceedings of that Congress and of the conduct of the Delaware delegates. The same gentlemen were elected on March 16 to serve as delegates to the Second Continental Congress called to meet in Philadelphia, May 10, 1775.

mittee to prepare Instructions for the Gentlemen appointed to represent this Government at an American Congress proposed to be held at Philadelphia in May next.

Friday, March 24th P. M.

The Committee appointed to prepare a draught of Instructions for the Delegates appointed to represent this Government at the American Congress proposed to be held at Philadelphia in May next, did report, that they had essayed a draught of the same, which they laid upon the table for the inspection of the House.

On Motion,
  By Order,
   The same was read the first time.

Wednesday, March 29th P. M.

The draught of instructions to the Delegates appointed to represent this Government at the Congress proposed to be held at Philadelphia in May next, was read the second time, paragraph by paragraph, and after some amendments, agreed to, and follow in these words, to wit.

  Instructions to the Deputies appointed by this Government to meet in General Congress on the tenth of May next.

1.   That in every act to be done in Congress you studiously avoid, as you have heretofore done, every thing disrespectful or offensive to our most gracious Sovereign, or in any measure invasive of his just rights and prerogative.

2.   That you do adhere to those claims and resolutions made and agreed upon at the last meeting of the Congress, yet for the restoration of that harmony with the parent state which is so essential to the security and happiness of the whole British empire, and which is so ardently wished for by this House, you may on our parts yield such contested claims of right as do not apparently belong to the Colonists, or are not essentially necessary to their well being.

3.   That if His Majesty should be pleased graciously to appoint any person or persons to treat with the Colonies on the present unhappy disputes subsisting between them and the Parent state, you, or any of you the Congress shall nominate, may treat with such person or persons on behalf of the inhabitants of this Government.

4.   If the Congress when formed shall not in every question to be voted by Provinces, allow this Government an equal vote with any other Province or Government, on this Continent, you are decently but firmly to urge the right

of this Government to an equal Voice in Congress with the other Governments.

I do certify the above to be a true copy of the Minutes of Assembly.

DAVID THOMPSON, Clk to the Assembly.[1]

41
To Thomas Rodney

New Castle May the 8th 1775.

I arrived here yesterday afternoon & soon after waited on Col. Bland one of the delegates from Virginia, who is since gone up to town in the stage & says the other delegates from his colony, (he believes) might have got as far as Chester last night. Mr. Hall, Mr. Johnson & Mr. Tilghman of Maryland set out from here this day soon after dinner & about the same time, a brig from South Carolina passed by with the delegates from that colony. Mr. Chaise of Maryland went through this town yesterday. Mr. Read & I are to set out to-morrow morning attended by the Militia of this town at the instance & request of the Company. The Province Assembly who are now setting have added Dr. Benjamin Franklin & Mr. James Wilson of York Co. to the Congress. The Comm'ee. of New-Castle Co. have given & published as their opinion that one shilling & six pence in the pound upon the rate of assessment should be immediately collected from the inhabitants of the Co. The Comm'ee have set about to collect & the people pay it with more cheerfulness than they have been known to pay any tax heretofore as I am informed. Thus ends the news for the present. I sent your letter to Wilmington this morning. Mr. Adams had none of those exercises. But I have rec'd as a present of the gentlemen here twenty-four of them which I have sent you & desire you will furnish each company in Kent with one of them as a present from me. When I get to town, you shall hear from me again.

N.B. The money raised by the New-Castle Committees order is for purchasing arms, ammunition &c.

42
From Thomas Rodney

Dover May 10th 1775

I recd: yours and the manual exercise—There is Ten Companies already inroll'd—and we expect all the rest will be inrolled this week—have inclosed a

1 Caesar Rodney was Speaker of the Assembly.

list of the officers already Chose—The people go so fully into it that I expect we shall form Twenty Companies—

Yesterday Robert Holliday was examined before the Committee and has render'd satisfaction as they informed—but I have not yet seen what it was.—Richd. Smith also has sent twice for me, and yesterday I went to see him, upon which he sent a letter to the Com. declaring "that he never had any thing in view but a reconciliation between England and the colonies upon the full establishment of all the American rights and priviliges, which he is determined to defend (with his life and fortune) against all invasions whatsoever" but the Com. it seems has not said any thing on that head. . . .

If you Can spare the money shall be glad you'l send us a drum, Coul's. &c. by this vessel—

43

To Thomas Rodney

Philadª May the 11th 1775—

I have verry little news (as yet) to write you, more than what the printers (who are verry apt to get the whip-hand of their neighbors in that way) have set forth in their papers, Which you will get by Post—Billy Rodney[1] will give you a discription of the public entry of the Bostonian deligates into this City yesterday, it was verry grand and Intended to Shew their approbation of the Conduct of the good people of that Government, in the distressing Scituation of affairs there—I believe from the best accounts, that General Gage was forced upon the plan of Sending Troops to Concord by the other officers of note, together with ye tory party in Boston, Mandamus Councellors &c—Alledging that the people would address Resolve and threaten, but would not fight—The general tho over-ruled it seems was not Convinced there fore Sent a Second Brigade—The purpose of the Expidition was to destroy the amunition, arms, provisions and Bridges, and some say to take Hancock and the other delegates who they know to be in that part of the Country. Mr Hancock told me he had been to see that Small Company at Lexington Exercise, and had not left them more ten minutes when the Troops Came up, and that they had no Suspision of any—Last Evening I See a verry intelligent man from Massachusets Government who was in the engagement, and got him to relate the Story—He says they fired on the people at Lexington as related, and killed seven on the Spot, they dispersed without returning the fire, that the Troops went on to Concord distroyed much flower & pork, threw a Quantaty of Ball in the River, Broke two Cannon and did other damage, That by this time one

1 William Rodney, a brother of Caesar and Thomas.

hundred and fifty Provincials had Collected near the Bridge, that the Troops fired on them and killed three, that the provincials for the first time Returned the fire, which they Continued and encreasing in their number drove the Troops back as far as Lexington—where, when Joined by the second Brigade they made some Stand but Soon Retired again, which they Continue without makeing any Stop till they got to Charles-Town. He says they retreated at the rate of near six miles an Hour—That there never was more than four hundred Provincials who see them till they got to Buncar's Hill at the Edge of Charles-Town, that there were better than two Thousand provincials who had way-laid them but were on the wrong Road, and about two thousand more who followed verry fast but Could not Come up till at Buncar's Hill—That the Provincials had thirty Six Killed, That he Cannot tell how ma[n]y Regulars were Killed, but that the provincials buried one hundred and three of them which they found dead on the Road from Concord to Charles-Town— . . .

There is such a martial Spirit prevails in the province, That I Can't get you a Drum & Colours in less than two weeks by which time Fleeson says they Shall be ready—The packet I desired Mr Maurice to Call at my house for, I have since found in my Trunk—The Congress met Yesterday Chose Peyton Raldolp[1] president, & Charles Thomson[2] Secray, Franklin, Willson & Thos Willing[3] are added. The Congress will be opened this day with prayers by Mr Duchee,[4] and then proceed to business—

44
Instructions to Caesar Rodney, Thomas McKean, and George Read, delegates to Congress[5]

In Assembly at NewCastle Wednesday 7th June 1775

The House being informed by the delegates, appointed to represent this colony in the Grand Continental Congress now held at Philadelphia in the province of Pennsylvania, that the said Congress are unanimously of opinion, that it is absolutely necessary for the preservation of the lives, liberties and properties of the good people of the twelve united Colonies and of the parish of St Johns in Georgia, to have an armed force at their general Expence, suffi-

1 Peyton Randolph was a delegate from Virginia.
2 Charles Thomson, the secretary of the Continental and Confederation Congresses from 1774 to 1789, was secretary of the Newark (Del.) Academy Board of Trustees in 1773.
3 Benjamin Franklin, James Wilson, and Thomas Willing were delegates from Pennsylvania.
4 Rev. Jacob Duché.
5 After the instructions of March 29, to the Delaware delegates, occurred the battles of Lexington and Concord, April 19. George Washington, a member of Congress from Virginia, was chosen unanimously by that body on June 15, as Commander-in-chief of the Army of the United Colonies.

cient for repelling and defeating all hostile attempts by arms to deprive them of the same, took the matter into their most serious consideration, and approved of the measure.

Resolved nemine contradicente

That the Inhabitants of this Government be chargeable and charged with their Quota or share of said Expence, to be ascertained by the Congress, & that this House will provide for the same by all ways and means in their power.

Resolved nemine contradicente

That the sum of five hundred pounds be drawn for by the Speaker upon the trustees of the several Loan Offices of this Government, according to the proportion Act, to be paid to Mr. Speaker,[1] Thomas McKean and George Read, Esquires towards the share of this Colony of the Expence aforesaid, and that the same be hereafter replaced in the said Offices by the Assembly.

Extract from the minutes of the House—

JOHN MACPHERSON, Clk of Assembly

45
To Thomas Rodney

Philad^a June ye 20th 1775—

In full expectation that You would be in Town for a Considerable time past, I have neglected to Write to you, however as you have now put every Expectation of that sort aside, have taken an Oppertunity by Doct^r Tilton of sending you this . . . Your Drum went by Morris's Veshell the last Time & Suppose you have got it. The Colours are not yet Ready—I Can now let you into a part of our proceedings in Congress—We have ordered Two Millions of Dollars to be Struck here as a Continental paper Currency, for the defraying the Expences of Defending our Constitution Rights and priviledges, the money is to be Sunk by all the twelve Colonies in Seven Years according to their Quotas which are Settled in proportion to the number of Inhabitants in Each Colony. We have appointd Coll. George Whashington General & Commander in Chief of all the Colony forces. General Ward (now with the army before Boston) to be Major General, & Second in Command, General Lee, a Major General & Third in Command, Coll. Skıler [Schuyler] a Major General & fourth in Command, and Coll. Putnam a Major General & fifth in Command—All the Brigadeer Generals, Coll^s, Lieut^t Coll^s Majors &c are

---

1 Caesar Rodney.

Confirmed according to their appointments by the Colonies where the Troops they Command were Raised—General Washington Viewed the militia of this place today, and sets out for Boston Camp next day after tomorrow. General Lee will go with him & they will have a large Escort from this City as far as T[r]entown at least—

I am much pleased to hear you have Sold the Sloop and as times have but a verry Gloomy appearance I wish both the other Veshells were Sold, provided they were *well* sold—however you neglected to let me know what You are to get for the Sloop—I am Glad to hear that there is like to be a good Crop of Wheat & Hay, the Hay we know how to dispose of, but God knows what we shall do with the Wheat—There is little or no reason to Expect the Congress will Rise; Rather think they will Set the whole of this season, but am in hopes that a week or fortnight hence the most material Business will be so settled as that I shall obtain leave of Absence for two weeks, about two weeks hence you may Expect me down—Your Coat is Calculated for the light Infantry of the first Battallion, The Uniform of the Second Battalion is to be Brown, & White facings, and their infantry Blue, & white faceings—Lieut! Coll! of the first Battalion is to have an Epelet on the Right Shoulder and a Strap on the left, the Major an Epelet on the Left, and a Strap on the Right, of Gold Lace—I heard this after noon by Express from Rode Island that a part of the Troops Expected at Boston, from Ireland are arrived and Landed at Boston, and That the Remainder are looked for Every day as they Sailed together, I mean the first mentioned four Regiments with the Horse. Some of the Horse are also Come and landed; the above news I Believe is true and believe after they have had a few days to recruit from their Voige we may Expect warm work, and warm it will be I dare say, for we Just had an Express from our provintial Camp Who informs of a Truith that we have there Eighteen Thousand men ready to Receive the Regulars and indeed wishing they may Come out—provided they intend to persist in their oppression; I wish our new Generals were at the Camp—

46

To Thomas Rodney

Philad? June 29th 1775

Since I wrote you last there has been a Verry Considerable Engagement between our Troops and the Regulars upon Bunckers Hill a little Back of Charles town, an accot. of which you'l have in Yesterdays paper as full as we have had it as Yet—But Expect further Accounts of it Every day—I have sent You by Cap? Henry Bell a Book, for your further improvement in the military art.

A Gun for Caesar and for Betsey, Sally and their friends 16 or 17 fine Pine-apples—I Expect without fail to Set out for Kent next Tuesday morning, Should have Set out Saturday afternoon but M: Read prevailed on me to let him go home this Week on promise to Return by next Munday Dinner. He is then to attend till I Return which is to be in two weeks from the time I leave this—

P.S. We have Just heard that the Company of Light Horse belonging to this City are gone on with the General to the Camp near Boston

47

To George Washington

SIR,   Philadelphia June 29th 1775—

The Bearer hereof M: John Parke has taken his degrees of Bachelor and Master of Arts in the College in this City and studied the law under one of us (M: M:Kean) for almost four years. He is an Ensign in the 2d Battalion of the Militia here, and is desirous of serving his country as a Volunteer under you. He has frequently drawn his *pen* and is now resolved to draw his *sword* in support of the American cause. We therefore beg leave to recommend him particularly to your countenance and favor, and hope you will distinguish him agreeable to his merit as soon as an oppertunity of promotion presents.

We wish you health, success, happiness and every blessing Heaven can be-stow, and are; Sir,

Your most obedient humble servants
Caesar Rodney
Tho McKean

To George Washington Esquire, Commander in chief of the forces of the united Colonies in North America—[at Cambridge, Mass.]

48

To Thomas Rodney

Philadelphia, Monday, July 3d, 1775

I wrote by Captn. Bell that I should set out for Dover as of tomorrow morn-ing. I now have to tell you that the business of the Congress will not admit of my going till Sunday morning, therefore if alive and well you may expect me at Dover on the afternoon of Munday next. Since I wrote you last we have had some further accts. of the Battel at Bunckers Hill in a letter signed by one

Burr, who is a man much to be confided in, this letter is published in this days paper which I have inclosed you. By private intelligence received the day before yesterday, General How about three days after the engagement died in Boston of his wounds received at Bunckers Hill.[1] The nine companies of riflemen for Pennsylvania are nearly compleated and are to be headed by Capn. Thompson as Coll. and you may tell Mr. Magaw that his Brother is appointed and going Major. They will be ready to march for the camp near Boston by the latter end of this week.

49
To Thomas Rodney

Philadelphia, July 27th, 1775.

. . .

It will be some time before the Standard Colours are done, they are now in hand and you may assure Mr. Loockerman they will be ellegant and cleaver.—

By a Vessel arrived about an hour ago from Bristol, we have a London paper informing us of the arrival of the Vessel that went Express from the people of Boston to London giving them an account of the Battle at Lexington —upon the spreading of this news there, the Ministry (it seems) published in the papers that they had recd no accounts from America, by this many people were led to discredit the accounts brought by the Massachusetts Express— However Arthur Lee (now an alderman) publishes imediately in the papers that all those who doubted the truth of the news—Might Repair to the Mantion House, Where the Depositions taken Relative to the Lexington Affair were deposited for their perusal and satisfaction; When the Ship left Bristol the news was generally Credited. However she left there too soon to know much of the effect it had on that side the Water—We shall know more of this Matter before long, till when I am Convinced the Congress will not Rise— Whether they may then or not I cannot now pretend to say—However I do know that they are heartily tired—and so am I.

50
To Thomas Rodney

Philadelphia, Sept. 13th, 1775.

I have had no letter from you Since you Returned Home, Expected one by Robert the Post but am dispointted—I am verry little if any better than when I wrote you last. Yet able to attend the Congress and in hopes of getting better

1 A false rumor.

before long—Wheat is now Selling tho verry Slowly at 3/6 per buss[ll]. much
more offered to sale than bought as none buy Except a few Who want for their
own Use—Corn is 1/6 the highest—So soon were the Markets Cut up—Mr.
McGarmant Will tell you about Lockermans money—and the Colours will be
down by the next Post—Get the ballance of the Bill for the Colours from
Lockerman. He paid me ten pounds Which you will deduct out of it. I have
had private Conversation with Nat. Fortner who is just from London. He tells
me he is Convinced that our differences will be Soon Settled, on our own
terms—and Says it is more than two to one that there is before this day an
entire change in the Ministry.

51
From Thomas Rodney

Dover Septr. 17th 1775

. . . The Council of Safety have been sitting all the week & adjourned last
night—They have formed Regulations for the Military—have Confirmed the
officer appointed (a few Tories excepted) and have appointed Brigadier Generals Viz McKinley your self and Dagworthy—without any preference to
either—but when ever together each has the preference in his own County—
    The resentment of the people has been high against the Doctr. I suppose
from his giting in the council—and information was made against him—but
he was acquited by the Committee—he, Stout & Holladay has declined &
Collins proposed to join the Ticket & they agreed upon five men—Your self,
Collins, Hazlet, Killen, Baning, & Doctr. Tilton, or Cook or Clark mintioned
for the 6th but neither could be fully fixt on—And for the means of quiting
(much against my own Interests and inclynation) I was prevai[l]d on to be
mention as the sixth man—but Clark has declared to Stand alone which ham-
per Barrot on his Acct. but he is going with the advisce of Collins to try to
quit him—What may be the consique[nce] I dont know—

52
To Thomas Rodney

Philadelphia Sep[r]. 27th 1775—

    By your last letter I imagined matters in the Political Channels would have
gone on Smoothly; But am unexpectedly informed by a letter from a gentleman of that County that, You are all like to be in the Utmost Confusion—This
gives me much Concern, more Especially when our public affairs require the
greatest unaminity, for our union is our strength.

One Circumstance relative to your politic's gives me infinite Concern—it is this (as related to me) That you intend to leave Mr Barrett out of your Ticket as Sher. and that Some person in your interest had told Barrett that he had no business to put *me* in his Ticket. You are to Consider Mr Barrett as an honest man, a man who has been long in persuit of the Sheriff's office, and with a verry general approbation of the people of that County, That he has a large family to maintain, and has applied a large part of his property to the obtaining the office of Sheriff—When these things are taken into Consideration, party will no doubt give way to Common Justice—Mr Barrett has much at Stake and I believe an honest man, therefore hope that you and your friends will Carry him Steadily—Perhaps you and your friends have proposed a Ticket which Barrett (from former obligations to some one or two individuals) Cannot Carry throughout—and therefore Ye have declared against him—I hope such Reasons will never determine you to Act against such a man—I wish you would agree to Carry him and let him know that you will—Because a man in his scituation who has so much at Staqe [stake] must be verry uneasy—It is a little Extraordinary that one or more of those who are said to be your friends, or rather, your Party Should Tell Barrett that he had no business to put me in his Ticket, that it was only to grace his Ticket, and therefore forbid his doing it &c. I say this is so Extraordinary that whoever they were who told Barrett so, I pronounce was no friend to either you or me—

When I saw in your Letter the names which were to fill the Ticket I made no Doubt but that Collins, Cook and Barrett had been present and Consenting to the formation of it and that of Course there would have been an intire Harmony—This I must say (when the times so much Require) gave me great pleasure—However this seems not to have been the Case And therefore fear there will be much disturbance at Your Election, and perhaps events brought about in Consequence of it that neither you or I would wish—Unless you use your endeavour to be more Explicit with some men who both you and I would wish to be in friendship with—I would have you weigh and Consider those matters as fully as the Short Space of time between the Receipt of this Letter and the Election will permit . . .

53

To Thomas Rodney

Philadelphia Monday Oct. 9th 1775

I Received your letter by Mr. Barrett dated the 2d of Oct., but rather suppose it was dated the 3d—Wherein you inclosed me a list of the Poles, which gives me an opportunity to Congratulate you on your safe arrival uppon the Stage of

Honor, Trouble, Expense and Abuse.[1] Therefore would advise you to be Carefull to deserve as much of the first Article your Station affords, and to be equally careful not to seek or deserve either of the latter: for, they will come, when they will come—and let me tell you that it is Honorable for a man to be punctual in the discharge of every public trust. Therefore I expect to see all the Representatives for Kent, at Newcastle on the 20th of this instant, and not be dropping in for a week following the day they ought to have met:—

As it is a very great disadvantage to me to be so much from my private Concerns, I hope therefore you will, between this, and your Coming to Newcastle, put all my business as well as your own upon the best footing you possibly can, or else when both are away we shall doubly suffer—

I am sorry Circumstances turned out so Contrary to your Good intentions toward John Bullen. But your carrying Sipple so near him as to put it in the power of the others to shoot him ahead certainly broke your scheme with respect to him—for it was just and right that Bullen (according to your party agreement) should have the Commission. Yet as those maneuvers of party are, and ought to be unknown to a Governor, and as it is a Just Rule of Conduct in him to give the Commission to the highest in Vote, I could not serve Bullen unless I had asked as a favour, Which (I dare say you will be of opinion with me) would have been paying too dear for a Commission of no more importance than that of a Coroner. You may perhaps have it in your power to take better care of him another time—But we shall talk more of this another time—

On Friday about eleven Oclock at night Doct. Bearsly[2] of this City was seized by Order of the Committee of Observation, for having wrote Letters to England injurious & distructive to us in the American Contnt, and wicked with respect to this City, and is now Confined in Goal I gather with one Brooks who came here with Governor Sheen.[3] Mr. Carter, an apothecary, who was in partnership with Speakman, and one Mr. Snowden, all of whom were aiding the Doct. in his plan—You must know Bearsly has been a Considerable time since marked out as a thorough-power Torry, for which, together with his having insulted the people he was (since I came to Town last) carted through the streets.—But the offense for which he is now confined is this circumstance; On Wednesday last a ship sailed out of this Port for London, in which Mr. Carter was going pasenger. A few days before she sailed Young Dewees, son of the Sheriff, went to pay Doct. Bearsley some money and com-

1 Refers to Thomas Rodney's election as a delegate from Kent County to the House of Assembly for the Government of the Three Lower Counties.

2 In *American Archives,* Force, 4th Series, vol. III, p. 985, where this letter is reproduced in part, the editor interprets Bearsly to be Kearsley.

3 In *American Archives* the editor interprets it Skene.

ing suddenly in his Room found him and Carter together, with a bundle of Papers before them, which they gathered up in seeming confusion. This, with Bearsley's Torry Carrictor gave Dewees suspition, and he accordingly informed a few of the Committee who kept the matter secret, let the ship sail, and the passengers go down to Chester by Land to go on Board. On Thursday evening which was the day the passengers went, a small party was sent down to Chester. They stayed there that night in Cogg [incognito] and saw the passengers go on Board next morning. They then immediately pushed on board, seized and examined Mr. Carter who in a little time told them that there were several Letters from Doct. Bearsly & Mr. Brooks and one from Mr. Snowden, that he had the charge of them [the letters] and was concerned with them in the plan they had concocted, But that the Letters were then in the Custody of a woman down in the Cabin and that she had then [them] concealed in a pocket sewed to the inside of her Shifty-Tails. Where in fact they soon after found them and came back to town, (leaving Carter as they had promised upon his making a discovery of the Whole Matter on a peth [an oath?] before Mr. Graham at Chester) and then seized the authors. The letters were to Lord Dartmouth and other Ministers of State. But under cover to Mrs. McCawley [Macaulay]. The purpose and design was proposing their sending to Philadelphia five thousand Regulars, on which condition they would engage five thousand more here to join them, provided the Royal Standard should be also sent in, and, Bearsly appointed to *bear* it, for that Great numbers of those who now wear Cockades and Uniforms were hearty in the Ministerial Cause— That the Post were a pack of Cowards for that he (Bearsley) had made above five thousand of them run by snapping a single pistol at them, etc.—They had with them for the use of the Ministry one of Joshua Fisher's plans of Delaware Bay & River, whereon they had described the place where the Che.vaux [chevaux-de-frise] Defense's were fixed; Besides these and many more villinous Contrivences—They were taking home the out-lines for a print to be struck off in London shewing Bearsley's late Exhibition in the Cart, going through the streets of Philadelphia with the mob, many of whom he undertakes particularly to describe, to wit: Beadford,[1] etc. etc. many of whom were actually not there, and how he now and then by snapping his pistols made them run, etc. etc. His abuse of the Congress Committees, etc. (in his letters) is intolerable, such as Rebels, villians etc.—After the Committee of Safety had examined them and the Contents of the Letters, they sent a Pilot Boat down the River to overtake the Ship, to bring up Carter, and to seize the Box of Letters and to bring all of them that they supposed to be from, or to suspicious persons. This Boat returned that very afternoon, brought Carter and put him

---

1 In *American Archives* the editor interprets this name to be Bradford.

in Goal, and also brought a number of letters belonging to and wrote by other persons; The Committee of Safety has been sitting on these affairs all this Day —But I have been so closely confined to Congress today that I don't yet know what they have done—or what others are accused.

It is now near eight at night and Mr. John David the bearer of this sets out tomorrow morning therefore shall only tell you that I am tolerable well and desire my love to our families, and conclude . . .

54

To Thomas Rodney

November the 27th 1775

After a very cold disagreeable ride, I am in town; and have had since I came a smart fit of the astma; Soon after I parted with you, the evening before I left home, I began to be strongly impressed with the thoughts of taking lodge-ings as soon as I should arrive in town, and these thoughts being accom-panied with many weighty reasons, (which I will communicate to you, when I can do it by means of my tongue, instead of my pen, & thereby save the trouble of writing so much) I went to lodgeings the night I got to town, with a certain Widow Dewer opposite John Cadwallader's in Second Street; This place was recommended to me by a friend of mine (one Mr. Milligan) and from what I have yet seen she is a verry genteel, well behaved kind Body, her house is fully and genteely furnished, She has no lodger but me. I have a good lodgeing Room and Parlour to myself—her own family consists of three Chil-dren to wit, two girls and one boy, and one servant Girl—She keeps a good Table and is verry oblidgeing, therefore you may Suppose I am so far verry happy—I am to pay her 30/ a week for my self, and 10/ a week for my Servant, and am to find my own Wine, Spirits and fire-wood, I have already laid in my Wine, Spirits and one cord of wood—and pray remember the three Cord we were planning to be brought up in the New Schooner, and remember also that I would have the destination of it altered—that is I would have it brought to my Lodgeings where I hope to see you when you come up. I would by no means have the wood to go where we first intended—More of this when I see you—

While poor David Beverige was at Lewis his Brigg came in loaded with Sugars, Molasses and Coffee. She has since run upon the Chevaux De Frise, and imediately sunk in five-fatham-water,—no part insured—one or two river boats have struck and been sunk by them the moment they touched—I men-tion this that you may give strict orders to your people to be careful in passing them with the New-Schooner—for if She touches them She is shorely lost, with all her Cargo—

Missrs. Washington, Missrs. Gates, Coll. Custis & his Lady and one Mr. Lewis all of Virginia set out from here this morning for the Camp at Cambridge accompanied by all the military officers, the three Companies of light-infantry and the Company of light-horse—As they come up General McKinly with forty or fifty of his Battalion attended them to Schuylkill-ferry—

We have certain inteligence that there are 2500 or at least 2000 troops landed at Boston from Ireland and it is thought by many, that with this reinforcement they will make a push to get out, by attacking our lines—If they should attempt it, I hope our brave American Boys (who have been hitherto fortunate) will give us a good account of them—

Wednesday Novr 29th 1775.

You will find in this days paper an account of the surrender of Montreal to General Montgomery on the thirteenth instant; The Congress has (as yet) received no Express, but expect one every hour as the account is generally believed, Mr. Livingston being a man of Carrector, Brother to a member of the Congress and brother-in-law to General Montgomery . . .

P.S. Remember to bring up one of Caesar's frocks that I may have his Uniform made, and as you come by Land I desire you would inform yourself what State our Money printing is in, I shall want to know—

55
From George Read

[New Castle, Del.] Jan. 19, 1776

I have just rec'd Letters from Messrs Andw Allen & Wm Hooper requesting your attendance and mine immediately at Congress as there is business of the last importance depending, particularly a motion the general Tener of which is to declare the Principles on which America has hitherto acted and those which they are disposed still to proceed on, they are extremely pressing and I totally unprovided as to my business here have determined to be at Philada this Evening and should be glad you wou'd come up immediately. I last Evening got a Verbal Accot which may be depended upon that Genl Montgomery stormed Quebec ye 28th or 29th of Decr and after passing the 2d Entrenchmt and Attempting ye 3d & last was killed with our frd McPherson, that happen'd at the upper Town. Arnold attacked the lower Town, in the onset had his leg broke, and was carried off but upon Montgomery's falling, Donald Campbell ye Quar Master took the Command with his rank of Colo & retreated with that part of the Army without interruption as Carleton immediately proceeded with his whole force to the lower Town and then surrounded and took Prisoners most if not all Arnold's Men, an unlucky stroke. Montgomery & McPherson were buried with Honours of War and Carlton treats the Prisoners well, but there are great doubts whether we shall retain our Situation in Canada. Some extraordinary Exertions are necessary, fail not to come up immediately & bring some Gold with you.

56

From Thomas Rodney

Dover Feb.ʳ 3.ᵈ 1776—

M.ʳ Collins was at Town to day and informs that they are about half done sining the money, they have divided what is done & Manlove is gone home with the Sussex Share, suppose Collins has ours in charge 'Till you come— they are to return the week after next to finish—The Council is to meet on Tuesday next to determine with respect to one part of M.ʳ Bevriges Terms Viz. that the Counsil should risk a proportional part of the vessel, which I believe they wont do, as they have an offer of better terms at Wilmington by a Vessel just going—but if M.ʳ Bevirige does not insist on their risking the vessel I believe they will prefer sending by his vessel; and the Comm. for that purpose will send him an answer next week—and it seems likely that I shall be obliged to go to Wilmington to Contract for the flower as Collins can't go up till the week after.—

Col: Hazlets Comm.ⁿ is come to my hands to be forwarded to him. We understand that the two Companies in Sussex are very near full, & those in this County are also nearly full neither of them wanting more than 10 or 15 men—we also hear, by Collins, that Smiths in the lower end of New Castle is full, and I make no doubt they will all be full in two weeks more—

A motion was made in our Comm. by T. Skillington to have it Disolved but not seconded—It now stands adjourned to the first day of March . . .

57

To Thomas Rodney

Phil.ᵃ Sunday. Feb. the 4.ᵗʰ 1776.

The letter you wrote to Collins & the copy of the Council's order I delivered, & conversed with him on the subject—Mr. Collins was of opinion with me, that it would be more prudent to employ some person in Phil.ᵃ who had been accustomed to that kind of trade than to join with the New-Castle Co. people in the expedition they then had on foot. The applying to a proper person here was lost to me before this, as soon as I got to town, I spoke to David Beveridge, who immediately told me he would undertake it provided he & the contractors could agree, which he had no doubt of & on Tuesday last, I provided an express to go to Collins at Wilmington & return on the next day, which he did—By this express Beveridge wrote Collins the out-lines of the bargain but that they might confer more particularly desired Collins would meet him as on Thursday last at Chester. When the express returned, he showed me Collins' answer which was that he was obliged to set out on that day for Kent—that he should be up again in 10 or 12 days—would then endeavor to fix the matter & that from the appearance of the weather, he thought it would then be time enough. This is all I now know of the matter except that several other very good hands have since been with me to get the contract—so that you & Collins or either of you may have a contract whenever you set about it. The night before last Capt. Nason (who went to France in the service of the Congress) came to town. He says he came in a brig commanded by Capt. Craig. That they had 7 weeks passage from Bell-isle to the coast off Egg-Harbor—that he then came on shore & crossed the Jersey[s] to town—That the brig stood for our Capes, that she has on board, on account of the Congress 15 tons of gunpowder, 60 tons of salt-petre & 1300 stand of excellent fire-arms—& he supposes she is now safe within the Capes. Gen. Arnold is likely to recover—He expects to be fit to do duty in 3 weeks from the date of his letter which was the 5th of Jan. & troops are now on their march for Canada from all the Colonies as far south as Penna Gen. Woosters sent Arnold 120 men immediately—We are determined (God willing) to have Quebec before the frost breaks up. I intend to set out for Dover on Sunday next—But what Col. Collins will do with the money (which I hear he has carried down) in the meantime I can not say. I hope it will be made safe some-where.

I understand that the Commee of Inspection & Observation from this city & county have tho't themselves elected but for 6 months & that accordingly, they directed a new election. I therefore suppose your Commee have ordered a new choice & hope that you & your friends will endeavor to recommend the choice of such persons as will prudently but firmly support the cause. This is a critical period & you all well know how much depends on the County Committee.

58
To George Read and Thomas McKean

New Castle, March 6th 1776

I am ordered by the House, to require your immediate Attendance, unless

Business of the first Importance should make your Stay in Congress necessary
—if so, you are immediately to let the House know it.

59
From George Read

[Philadelphia, March 6, 1776]

The state of the publick business in Congress has been such that I cou'd not
leave this place with Propriety for these two days past tho' truly little has been
done in them particularly the Marine Committee is so wanting in Attending
Members that for 2 Evenings past we could not procure a sufficient Number to
proceed to business, it is proposed to supply some vacancies this day if Congress shall be prevailed on to attend to it, and I firmly resolve on leaving this
place on the morrow to attend our House of Assembly to whom I beg you to
excuse me, whether Mr McKean will go down I know not he has not given
me his Answer. We have nothing new here save that the Assembly of this
Province yesterday voted 2 Battalions of 1500 men in the whole to be raised
for the particular defense of the Province.

60
To Caesar Rodney, Thomas McKean, and George Read, delegates
to Congress[1]

In the House of Representatives for the Counties of New Castle, Kent and
Sussex, upon Delaware, at NewCastle,

Friday, March 22d 1776, P. M.

Instructions to the Deputies appointed by this Government to meet in
General Congress.

1st That You embrace every favourable Opportunity to effect a Reconciliation
with Great-Britain, on such Principles as may secure to your Constituents
a full and lasting Enjoyment of all their just Rights and Privileges. And as
the most probable Means of obtaining such desirable Ends You are to cul-
tivate with the greatest Care that Union and Harmony which so happily
prevails throughout the United Colonies; and consequently to avoid and
discourage any separate Treaty.

2d Notwithstanding our earnest Desire of Peace with Great-Britain upon the
Terms aforesaid, You are nevertheless to join with the other Colonies in

1 These gentlemen had been reappointed delegates to the Continental Congress by the Delaware Colonial Assembly on October 21, 1775.

all such Military Operations as may be judged proper and necessary for the Common Defence, until such a Peace can be happily obtained.

3ᵈ On every necessary Occasion You are decently but firmly to urge the Right of this Government to an equal Voice in Congress with any other Province or Government on this Continent, as the Inhabitants thereof have their All at Stake as well as others.

Extract from the Minutes,

Jᴀꜱ Booᴛʜ Clk of Assembly¹

61
From Thomas Rodney

Dover Aprill 26th 1776—

Mʳ John Gordon Understanding that there is to be a paymaster appointed for the Delaware Batalion, takes this Opertunity to apply for your interest in his favour—He says he can give suffitient Security for his true performance of that trust, and as you are as fully Acquainted with his fitness as I am, I need not say any thing on that head, nor add further more than, that I wish him to obtain the appointment, if it be not engaged before he arrives—

He has a letter from Doctʳ Ridgely to Mʳ Read in his favʳ and a few lines from Mʳ Killen & my self to Col: Hazlett—& also to Col: MᶜKean who we have refer'd to you for better information— . . .

P.S. A number of the Officers I am informed not knowing of Mʳ Gordons Applycation has recommended Mʳ Millan at Cantwells Bridge but should be remmember'd that Mʳ Gordons Property & Connections are suffitient reasons perhaps to give him the preference to a Young man who in other respects may be equally fit—

62
To Thomas Rodney

Philadᵃ May the 1ˢᵗ 1776

I have obtained and sent you here with a Commission for Mʳ Thomas Holland the Adjutant, appointing him a second Lieutenant in the Delaware Battalion; And also a Commission for Mʳ John Corse appointing him an Ensign, vacant by the promotion of Mʳ Holland. Be pleased to deliver them (with my Complimᵗˢ) to those Gentlemen—

Your Mention of Mʳ Gordon with my knowledge of and long acquaintance with the man—will induce me to make use of my influence to Serve him,

1 Caesar Rodney was Speaker of the Assembly.

whenever I Can do it with propriety, as in this Case—and Should have verry little doubt of Obtaining it for him, But am apt to think no paymaster will be appointed: as there is no instance of the like to any other of the Battalions, Unless when Joined the Army—Where there is a pay-master-General— . . .

No news Except that Yesterday a Court of Admiralty was held on the Tender Prize when She with her Tackle &c &c was Condemned—And that this day is like to produce as warm if not the warmest Election that ever was held in this City—The Terms for the parties are Whigg & Tory—dependance & Independence—

63
From Thomas Rodney

Dover May 5th 1776

I recd. your letter & post with Holland & Corse's Com! which deliver'd—Manlove has not been up yet for the money but I expect M! Collins will Take it tomorrow

Yesterday your Batalion was reviewed by the Lieut: Colonel It Consisted of near 800 under Arms, and the whole went thro' the manual ex[er]cise and manoevers usual at Reviews with more dexterity than I imagine they would have done. If the morning had not been wett I apprehend we should have had a 1000 men under arms—there was But five of my Company (consisting of 68 private) absent: four of whom were sick & the other a broad on business—this is the fruits of our Malitia Law, join'd to the Spirited Zeal of the True friends of America—Nevertheless there is much pains taken by some particular politicians (presuming on the assistance of Quakers) to render the makers of it Obnoxous—But I trust that the people are & will be so fully convinced of its usefulness, propriety & Equality that such endeavou[r]s will be but vain.— . . .

We here, by report, that there is four Men of War at the Cape; & that a party from Dunmore has Lande[d] near Poak a Moke—that Col: Simms & Col: Watson are gone to oppose them—You no doubt are informed if this be true—

64
From John Haslet[1]

[Cantwells Bridge,[2] Del., May 7th 1776]

Two Hours after my arrival at Dover Yesterday, I received an Express from

---

1 Commanding officer of the First Delaware Militia Regiment.
2 Now Odessa, Delaware.

Col. Cantwell, with Information, that three Men of War were in sight of Port Penn, that they expected an Immediate Attack, praying Immediate Assistance —Another brought Intelligence, that the Roe Buck was fixt on one of the Thorowfare Shoals; to Ascertain this Capt. Rodney with Lt. Learmonth set out in the night to reconnoitre with Certainty, & meet such troops as we cou'd Arm at the Cross Roads—the Lt. did meet us, the Roebuck had gone off—Capt Caldwell marched with one hundred & thirty men well armed, paraded at 4 O'Clock in the morning at Cantwells Bridge found Capt. Rodney, the Men of War are gone up to Newcastle, or rather to the Chevaux-de-frise, I shall return with the Captain, & Order Capt Caldwell to continue his March, Col: Bedford to take command of the Detachment—the Post brings us the Irish Intelligence, forty thousand Men divided into five Parties, tho' they were all Commissioners, will do very well, if we can get arms, I flatter myself we shall give a good account of our proportional Debarkation—

65

To Thomas Rodney

Philadelphia May the 8th 1776.

I am much pleased to hear that my Battalion beheaved so Well, both as to their assembling and the discharge of their Duty when Met—as to those turbulent Spirits Who would endeavour to render the instruments of those wise and Necessary Regulations obnoxious to the people, and would Even Sacrafise the Most Virtuous Cause any Body of men ever were Engaged in, to gratifie themselves with a seat in the House—I Detest them and their wicked designs—And make no doubt but you and all real friends to Liberty will take the hint in time, and by an active persevering part disappoint them, and Save Your Country from the government of all such Courtly Tyrants—If you set about the work and are Industrious, I make no doubt of your Success— . . .

Yesterday afternoon We were informed by letter from General McKinly that the Rhobuck and Nautilus Men of War then lay at Newcastle—and at 3 oClock the same afternoon all the Gondola's left the fort and went down to attack them, Especially if they can get them Seperate—I have Sent down to Sally a pound of What is recommended to me for the best Green-Tea in the City, it Comes at 35/ beside the Canister—Tell Betsey to taste it, and if she likes it, I will Send her a pound by the next post—I shall Procure ten or twelve pounds if not more Good Bohea Tea—but must wait an opportunity by Water to send that down—I should be glad to know how Your family and Mine are now Circumstanced as to that article—

I have no News of importance Except what you will find in the papers, by which you will see that our (Much talk'd of) Comissioners are turned into Men of War and foreign troops.

66
From George Read[1]

Wilmington Friday May 10th 1776

The enclosed letter came to hand this evening, by the person employed to take the two hundred pounds of lead to Lewestown, sent by brigadier M'Kinly, upon the requisition of Colonel Moore, which you have seen.

The Committee of safety have thought it highly necessary that you should be acquainted with the situation of the magazine at Lewestown, to exert your influence for an immediate supply of powder and lead; which, I suppose, must be by land, as the Roebuck and Liverpool will probably continue as high up the river as Reedy Island; this morning they are in the bite below New Castle, and though the row-gallies have proceeded down, from the Christiana Creek's mouth about two hours ago, I am apprehensive the high wind now blowing will not permit their acting to advantage in that cove.

We have had warm cannonading between the ships and gallies these two days past, all within our view. Great intrepidity was shown on the part of our people, who compelled the two ships to retire, not much to their credit; but it appeared to me the ships were afraid the gallies would get below them. Young Captain Houston led the van. As to other particulars, I must refer you to some of the very many spectators from your city, who will have returned before this . time.

I suppose it will be thought that too much powder and shot have been expended by the gallies in these attacks, but I am well satisfied they have produced a very happy effect upon the multitudes of spectators on each side of the river; and in that part of the Colonies where the relation shall be known, British ships of war will not be thought so formidable. A few long boats drove, and apparently injured, those sized ships that seemed best calculated to distress us. The committee of safety are going this morning to New Castle, and downwards, to see what may be necessary to advise for the protections of the shore below. Truly the people at large have shown great alacrity and willingness on this occasion. I know not when I shall be with you, as I may be of some little use here. I shall stay till there is some alteration in the appearance of things. Excuse this scroll.

1 To Caesar Rodney and Thomas McKean.

67

From Thomas Rodney

Dover May 12th 1776—

. . . From the great success of our Gallies I hope our River will soon be cleared of the Brittish Pirates that the shallop may git up again—No news here—but we hear by report from the City that 12,000 Hissians are arrived as the first of the Hopeful Commiss.ᵗˢ of Peace—That M.ʳ Dickerson has become an Independent &c—I Trust that this Subject will not be disputed much longer—the worst of Tories must now Confess the black design of Administration—And that Independance is the only Guardian of freedom in America. Our Comm. is adjourned to the 7th of June. If you advise any thing to be done before the House meets either by the Comm. or the people by Petitin &c we shall be glad to know it—
N.B. The Tea is very good

68

From John Haslet

[Dover, May 13ᵗʰ 1776.]

We are much distressed here on receiving an Order of Congress, inclosed by the Council at Newcastle to exchange L.ᵗ Ball for a Certain Capt. Budden of the City of Philadelphia; Our Uneasiness does by no means arise from opinion, that to exchange an officer of the Roe-Buck for·the master of a Merchantman employed in Private Business, is unequal; but from our apprehensions of Danger to the Community; if the Lieut. is permitted to go on Board, while his ship continues in our Bay; You, Sir, well know the Humanity with which he has been treated at Dover, the General Acquaintance which he has Contracted, & the Particular Correspondence he has held with Persons, who have discovered very little Zeal in Defe[n]ce of American Liberty, he has been heard to express great Satisfaction on finding so many true Subjects to his Majesty in the Circle of his Acquaintance: he knows our Naked & defenceless Situation; he knows, it is in his power with 150 men well armed to desolate great part of this Seemingly Devoted County. Popes Company is armed by us for the Defence of Lewes. Cap.ᵗ Caldwell marched a Detachment of 150 men completed for the Field by my Orders, as soon as Intelligence was had of the Men of War going up the River, which leaves us without a Sufficient Number of Guns to mount a Sergeants Guard—all this is known to M.ʳ Ball—

Have not Congress been hurried into this Resolve by the Weight of Cap.ᵗ Buddens Influence in the City, & the Inclination of the Wilmingtonians to Ingratiate themselves with the Commander of the Roebuck. I can't help thinking, in the Spirit of a freeman, but with absolute Submission to the Decisions of [Congress, had] the Matter, appeared in its true light [to] them, the Order had not issued. The armed Vessels are expected down every hour. The Council here have called on me for their Arms, & I shall order Capt. Caldwell to march his Detachment back here forthwith, if the L.ᵗ is sent on Board. In all this I flatter myself with receiving the Approbation of Congress—as the future Danger, if any, before a Reinforcement, will be in the two Lower Counties—perhaps before the L.ᵗ can march from here, & be sent on Board, we may be happy enough to hear from you—this shall go by Express—hope you will be able to collect my meaning from this Hasty unrevised scroll, & shall leave it without other apology, to depend on y.ʳ Good sense to give it weight by your Representation.

P.S. I have this Instant been informed by the President of the Council now siting, that their Sense of the Matter will be sent up with the Prisoners to Newcastle to morrow—

69

From John Haslet

Dover 14th May 1776

Mr. Killen yesterday Evening conjured up Several Difficulties, about the Payment of the Continental Money, it Originated from this—Mr. Bail recd. from me last week One thousand Dollars to pay off the Subsistence of the Troops at Dover, & on my going down to my own House, the Gentleman set out for Newcastle, & has left the accompts unsettled—he had no leave of Absence; will his Receipt be a Sufficient Voucher for me to Congress? Will the Receipts of the Capts on the Back of their Pay rolls be so also, in Case any of them should Embezzle the Soldiers Money, after it is paid to them—I have hitherto paid the Capts only & the Staff Officers, according to the Rule of the Brittish Army. I was extremely wanting to my Self, in not taking the leave of Congress on this Matter while in town as the Circumstances of Some of the Capts are narrow, I find myself much Embarrassed—You will lay me under Infinite obligations by sending me as Early as convenient Your Instructions on this Head

70

To Thomas Rodney

[May 15ᵗʰ 1776]

I have sent you inclosed, Extracts from the Journals of the Congress Relative

to the Capture and Condemnation of Prizes—and the fitting out Privateers;
Also the Art of makeing Common Salt—

71

To John Haslet [?][1]

Philadelphia May the 17th 1776—

I am much oblidged by the Letter received from you since your departure,
I happened to be dining at Mr Hancocks in a large Company when it came to
hand Who were all much pleased to find such Attention paid by the Troops
and people in General there to the movements of the enemy—

You will find published in the next paper of tomorrow a matter of such importance as ought and no doubt will, Command your serious Attention—It
is No less than a Resolution of Congress Recommending it to the Assemblys
or Conventions of all those Colonies (Who have not already done it) to Assume Regular Government. That the several Colonies may be Competent to
the opposition now making, And which may tend to the good Order and Well
being of the people; in Short, the Absurdity of Governor and Magistrates holding their Authority under our principal Enemy, must be Evident to every
one.—

The Reasons, if duly weighed, must inforce the Necessaty of immediately
laying the foundation of a new Government, (Which may be with us) similar
at present to the one we now have. Except as to the derivation of author[it]y.
Nothing will tend more to Ensure Success in the prosecution of the War; because there is nothing so conducive to vigour, Expedition, secrecy, and every
thing advantagious in War, as a well Regulated Government. Much inconvenience and detriment have been already Sustained, from the want of a
proper distribution of the Civil powers—Confusion and perplexity accom-
pany us, in almost every department; which is hurtfull to us in general, but
particularly injurious to our Warlike operations. We Stand in need of a Good
Executive, and may Expect our undertakings will go on much more prosper-
ously, if we Speedily provide One—

It is impossible to tell how long the War may last; And no prudent man would
choose to Trust himself long, without the Security of a Regular Established
Government. The Civil and Municipal Laws, for want of proper Authority
to Execute them, will grow into disuse and Contempt—All the Evils of

1 Probably Colonel Haslet, since the first paragraph seems to refer to Haslet's letter of May
7 from Cantwell's Bridge. See also Haslet's letter to Rodney, "May 1776," page 86, and Thomas
Rodney's letter to Caesar, May 26.

Anarchy may then prevail, and the most Wanton depredations be Committed. To Correct these Mischiefs, and for Want of Laws and Magistrates, Whose Authority is Acknowledged and Respected, recourse may be had to Military power; fatal, perhaps, to the Liberty and Safety of the people. When the people are accustomed to irregular Government, it is Exceedingly difficult to recover them to the love of order, and obedience to those Laws which are the Essential bonds of Society. Bad habits in the political, as well as the Natural Body, are Verry Easy to be acquired and verry hard to be Eradicated.

Many Arbitrary Exertions of Authority are every day to be seen among us, which tho Justified by the present Necessaty, are Nevertheless much to be Regretted, so far as they tend to Exhibit bad precedents, and to introduce a disorderly Spirit in the State. These things to men of penetration Wear a Serious aspect, and Seem Urgently to demand a Speedy remedy, which is only to be found in the Establishment of a Regular Constitution. The Continuing to Swear Allegiance to the power that is Cutting our throats, and attesting jurors to keep the Secrets and Try offenders against the peace of our Sovereign Lord the King &c is Certainly absurd—However as I know all these things to be familiar to you, Shall dwell no longer on the Utility of the Measure—and Turn my thoughts a little to what may (perhaps) be necessary to bring it about.—In the first place will not the Assembly to whom this Recommendation is [made], be apt to say at their next meeting, We ought to know the Sence of our Constituants? if so, would it not be best the people Should make known their desire by petitions to the house Signed by them previous to the Sessions of Assembly to prevent delay which in this case is dangerous? Will it not be better that the Petition be fully drawn, and prefaced with the Recommend[at]ion of Congress? Will it not be Expedient for proper persons who are friends to the Cause, To set about that work as soon as the Recommendation appears in the public papers least those Who are unfriendly should give opposition by the Same mode? Will not Doctr. Tilton who we know to be an Active patriot be One of those proper persons? I leave all those things to your Mature Consideration, but think it would be improper for those Who are presently members of the Assembly to be openly Active in the Matter; and for this Reason as I am a Member of both Congress and Assembly, hope you will not Communicate this to any—Except my brother Tommy, Mr. Killen and Doctr. Tilton, or Such other person in whom you may have the fullest Confidence, not to mention it.—

The Resolution before mentioned has Actually passed Congress, and as it is a Matter of the first importance think it would not be Amiss for you, Mr. Killen, Tommy & the Doctr. Tilton to have a Short private Council Composed of your four Selves only, held soon on the Occasion—Else The weaker part of mankind may be led astray by the designing—Therefore it is that I Give you this timely Notice—Tho, Nothing Relative to your plans ought to Transpire or be put in Execution till you See the Resolution published in the Newspaper; However your usual prudence Will dictate to you those and many more things—

The Colony of Rhode-Island has passed an Act, Repealing an Act (which had been long Since passed) Securing to the King the Allegieance of the people of that Colony. Massachusetts has done the Same—

Coll. I Mifflin Came to Town last night from New-York. We have no, News that I think verry Matterial, out of the line of News-papers—but when there is any worth your attention it Shall be Carefully Communicated

72

To Thomas Rodney

Phila May 17, 1776

Enclosed I have sent you the printed Copy of the Resolution of Congress mentioned in my last. Most of those here who are *termed the Cool Considerate men* think it amounts to a declaration of Independence. It Certainly savours of it, but you will see and Judge for Your Self. . . .

73

To Thomas Rodney

Philada Saturday, May the 18th 1776.

This day's post brings no[. of] letters from our Commissioners at Montreal in Canada by which we are informed of the following disagreeable intelligence. That 2 men of war, 2 frigates & (I think) one sloop of war had arrived at Quebec—that the Samson [garrison ?] under the command of Gen. Charlton a thousand in number sallied out against our troops who then happened to be dispersed in small parties. Compelled them to retreat, with the loss of a few killed, all their artillery, 500 small arms & all their sick in the hospitals &c. Gen. Arnold upon hearing it, marched from Montreal with his forces to meet them & make a stand in case the enemy should be reinforced so as to pursue— Our last 10 Battalions had not crossed the lake.
P.S. The letter from the Commissioners [of] Congress was dated the 10th of May at Montreal.

74
From Thomas Rodney

Dover May 19th 1776—

I recd: your Letter & Betsy her Tea per post; as I was walking Down Town
with Mr John Dickerson when I recd: it I mentioned to him the Resolution of
Congress; and he answer'd it was made before he Left there; upon which I
observed to him many advantages that would follow our assuming Government to which he agreed & observed many others "And that it would not pre-
"vent but perhaps promote a more speedy reconciliation, because the longer
"they let Government exist before they offer Terms the more firm that Gov-
"ernment would be, & therefore the more difficult to effect a reconciliation."
I should apprehend from the above sentiments that Mr D—— has some glim-
mering hopes of reconciliation yet, or that he ment thereby, to flater those who
have such hopes, to acquiese in the resolution of Congress—Peace, and reconciliation will henceforth be my ardent wish but never to mix our Government
with Britains any more—It is known here that the resolution is published—
but the news only arrived last night; Torism is dum, and many suspected
persons give it there approbation, I believe it will meet with no opposition in
this County—

75
To Thomas Rodney

Philadelphia May 22d 1776—

I find by your Letter of the 19th Instant, my Last letters to you, with which
I inclosed you the Resolution of Congress to which is a Long preamble leading
you to the design of the Resolution—had not then Come to hand—I sent them
by Mr William Gray who I believe did not leave this Town till Sunday morning last—
You don't say whether you had seen Coll. Haslet's letter to which I had Refered you—By the next post Shall be glad to hear your opinions on the *Mode*
best to be adopted for Effecting the Change—The people in this City I think
have Acted rather unwisely—They have Called a Town-meeting—by which
they have determined to apply to the Committees of Inspection of the Several
Counties throughout the province, to depute a Certain number of each of those
Committees, to meet together at Philadelphia—And there agree on, and order
what numbers of members shall be Elected by the people in Each County
within the province—to meet in Convention at Philadelphia—The Whole

number for the Province to be One hundred—This Convention is to be Chose for the Special purpose of Laying the plan of Government—and when that is Done, and an Assembly Chose and Returned agreable to Such plan—The Convention is to be disolved—This mode for Establishing a Government appears to be, and really is verry fair—Yet I think they are unwise—Because we are Certain that a verry powerfull force is Expected from England against us, some are Come, the rest will undoubtedly arrive before midsummer. We shall be oblidged to Exert every Nerve at every point, and we well know how necessary Regular Government is to this End—and by their mode it will be impossible for them to have any Government for three months to Come, and during that time much Confusion—If the present assembly Should take order in the matter, the work would be done in one Quarter of the time—However many of the Citizens seem to have little or no Confidence in the Assembly—

With us below I hardly know what Step will be best—in our County a new Choice Could not mend the Ticket, but might make it worse—In the other Counties there is verry little probability of an Alteration for the better—I want to have the opinion of your Set Concerning it, by next Post— . . .

One of our Rifle-men that Travelled across the Country with Arnold, and taken prisoner while on Centry at Quebec, was sent to England: a few days after he landed, he was sent to London and put in Bridawell in Irons—Sawbridge (the Lord Mayor) went to him, Examined him and had him imediately discharged & sent down to Bristol, where a number Gent? procured him a passage to Hallifax. He left Bristol the 24th of March, arrived in this City the day before Yesterday—And tho searched at Hallifax two or three times, brought undiscovered a number of Letters and newspapers to the Congress, by which we are possessed of all their plans for the distruction of America—*No Commissioners*—Capt? Craige who was appointed to make the Exchange of prisonners with the Roebuck—has returned to Chester with Capt? Budden, L? Ball and all the rest of them—They say (for I have seen Budden & Craige) that the men of War are gone off to Sea, that they Stood after them 12 Leagues without the Capes, then lost sight of them and Returned—

76

From Thomas Rodney

Dover May 26th 1776

I recd: your letters per M? Gray; & that of the 22? per post—and am extremely glad to hear that the Congress has got good information of the designs of our enemies—for this is of great consiquence in making a proper opposition—

Col. Hazlet shew'd us your letter and we conclude it was best to present petitions to the Assembly, but as there seems some impropriety in a petition—we have changed the mode into Instructions to the Members for this County to Comply with the recommendation of Congress—And if that is refused by the assembly to git them to direct the appointment of a Convention of 90 members; and if this is refused, to withdraw and disolve the assembly—the follow^g Clause is in the instructions if they should Comply as afs^d Viz. "Always saving to the freemen and inhabitants of this Colony, the full enjoy-"ment of their just Rights and Liberties agreeable to The Constitution, Laws, "Customs and Usages of the same"*

It was offered to my Company yesterday & twenty six of them signed it, the rest Chose to have it under Consideration Till next muster day but many of them say they are now ready to sign—Loukerman appear'd & Charged his son not sign—he's frightened almost out of his wits & seems half at least on the other side of the question—his late conduct has been so particularly penurious that he is abused by almost every body—There was much fun with him last night but it is too long to tell—We are all perfectly of your sentiments with respect to leaving the Change to the House of Assembly for the reasons you mention, unless they should refuse &c—

We fear that the contest in Pensylvania may injure the cause, but hope that it may be otherwise—The assembly is not to be trusted; a Convention is inconvenient— . . .

P.S. I will not presume to charge the wisdom of Congress in any case with doing what is wrong or Omitting to do what is right, but it appears to me that a paymaster is an officer absolutely necessary in every Batalion especially when seperated from the army. The consequence of not having one in the Delaware Batalion is, that the privates are constantly grumbling about their pay, and "Saying that they will rub out this campain but will not inlist again" The fact is, that want of such an Officer whose particular business it would be to attend to paying them of, The money, tho' perhaps [not?] always, yet having to go thro so many hands at present, that it is not regularly paid away—And as the officers have suffitient to imploy them in their own departments, it is a pitty but they were relieved from this task—I do not mean hereby to throw blame of any body—but wish the Ill consiquences may be prevented.

* "So far as they are not injurous, or destructive to the union, general safety and happyness of the united Colonies"

77

To Thomas Rodney

Philadelphia May the 29th 1776

You tell me you are proceeding on the Recommendation of Congress by way of Instruction to the members of the House for that county.[1] I fully approve the methods and hope you will proceed in the business Deliberately, Coolly and persuasively, but diligently—I don't doubt the Assembly will Act prudently, if otherwise, it will then be time enough for the people to take the matter up in another way—The Recommendation of Congress was certainly meant to go to the Assemblies, where there were such who had authority to Set: and the people of this province[2] haveing Taken the matter up upon other Grounds have occationed verry great disturbance, such as I would not wish to see in our Government—The Colonies of North-Carolina and Virginia have both by their Conventions declared for Independence by a unanimus Vote; and have Instructed their members to move and Vote for it in Congress reserving to Each Colony the exclusive right to frame government for it's Self—the Convention of North-Carolina has appointed a Committee (of its own Body) to draw up and Report to them a plan of Government—South-Carolina and all the New-England Colonies have declared of some time since—When these things are known to the people they will no doubt have great weight with them—I have not seen this day's paper yet, but imagine You'l have the doings of one or more of those Colonies published there—However whether in the paper or not, you may depend on the whole of the above relation to be matter of fact—Col! Dickinson's, Col! Robertdoe's, Col! Cadwallader's, Col! McKean's and Col! Matlock's Battallions, three companies of Artillery & the Light-horse of the militia; and Col! Shee's and Col! Magaw's Battalion's of the Continental Troops were all Reviewed the day before Yesterday, on the Common, by the Congress, General Washington, Gates and Mifflin, accompanied by a great number of other officers, most of the Assembly, the Presbeterian Clergy who were here at the Sinod—and 21 Indians of the Six Nations who gave the Congress a War-dance Yesterday— . . .

Mr Ball the Lieut! is now fixed at Germantown. Since the return of the Liverpool into our Capes, there has been another attempt of the Committee of Safety here, to have Ball Exchanged for Capt? Budden, but Totally rejected by Congress— . . .

Perhaps I may be able to get down for our Assembly which sets next Munday week—

1 Kent County.   2 Pennsylvania.

Would docr: Tilton Think himself oblidged, by an appointment (in his way) of forty dollars per month in Virginia, or toward Canada? these things have frequently happened of late, and wou'd probably be in the power of a friend to Serve him—

Mr Jourdan informs me, that McLain has lost the Letter I sent by him to Col! Haslet—I don't Recollect any thing verry material in it—But that Evans the Contractor, had an application made to Congress to have the Troops Quartered at some two places in the Government that he might the more Conveniently provide for them. otherwise he must decline the Contract—Which Congress absolutely Refused—for that it would be interfering with the business of the Col!, That they never will interfer with his duty but when it shall Evidently appear to them for the greater security and protection of the Government—I took the Liberty to tell Col! Haslet, that I did not doubt he would Study Mr Evans Convenience (especially as his providing for them would be a saveing to the public) whenever he Should think the Safety of the Government wou'd not be Endangered by it—I also mentioned to him (as my opinion) that if he Should Send all the Troops out of Kent—the Committee of *Safety* there would Call upon him for the Arms lent, and put them into the hands of the Militia for the imediate protection of that County—I am asstonished that McLane should have Lost the Letter—but if it should Contain any matter of politics (which I do not recollect it did) shall be verry angry, and Even Suspect some Unfair play.

78

From John Haslet

[May, 1776]

I sit down in the utmost Haste to acknowledge yours 23rd May just come to hand, & also your two preceeding favors. Mr. Evans applied to me some three weeks ago, & received for answer, that as soon as the Clothing cou'd be got from the Tradesmen, five Companies shou'd march to Wilmington, three to be stationed at Lewes. By order of Congress, he left Dover abruptly, & I saw him no more. Wednesday Week I attended on the Troops at Lewes, and find Mr. Evans has furnished almost nothing there but flower; they draw flower from him, and meat from the Council in Great Confusion. I ordered the Quartermaster to settle the Subsistence Accompts up to the 8th May, When the Contract took place. The people are clamorous for the Subsistence Money due since that time; Uncertain whether Congress wou'd allow us any after the Commencement of the Contract, have refused to pay, & refered them to the Contractor, which is by no means pleasing to them, shou'd most thankfully receive your Instructions on that head. Two of the Companies are now at Wilmington, & three others under Marching Orders, the Council of New-castle refused to arm any of their Men, & Capt. Smith on his way to Lewes recd his arms here. Doubtless the Council will soon demand them, as the County is now ungaurded, & a large tract of Marsh covered with stock from one end of it to the other is Open to the Depredations of the Enemy! Ought not an officers Guard to be mounted some where in Little Creek; & another in the Bottom of Mispillion, is not the Property of this County as Valuable as other peoples? should not proper persons be employed to provide for such guards at the One Place and the other, if Mr. Evans will not supply them, if this Battalion is continued here, Would not the Government be better served in this Way, & the Community equally well; that Part of the Independent Company Stationed at Lewes have no Direction from the Council, no Orders from the Capt. of the Company, & appear as Useless Expenses to our Little Dominion—

Capt. Rodney, Counsellor Killen, &c met on the Receipt of yours, the Barris-ter promised to essay a Petition, but on my return two days after cou'd do nothing in it, was not apt to take the Lead; 'twas not his business to Collect the Sense of the People &c—on all this you will Imagine, I left him with Looks of Indignation—Our first essay was a Petition, which on second thoughts was turned into Instructions to the Representatives of Kent, enjoining Compliance with the Recommendation of Congress; or if that cou'd not be carried in as-sembly to withdraw in a Body & dissolve the House—[1]

A vast Majority in Sussex are against, all here who endeavored to stiffle the Opposition at first are straining every Nerve to divide, the Poisonous Example of Maryland gives Energy to their Efforts, what the fate of our Application here will be, I cannot with certainty yet inform you: But fear Congress must either disarm a large Part of Kent & Sussex, or see their Recommendation treated with Contempt. Col. Polk's Battalion, 'tis said, will lay down their arms, the Shallopman Oliver brought down from Philadelphia Printed Copies of Petitions agst. a Change of Govermt. most Industriously handed about by Beaucham & others of the Committee—I thank you for your speedy & effectual Interposition in Mr. Baals affair. Every Body sees it now in the true light, tho' Our Privy Council, without Vigour, when you are from among them, would neither write themselves nor keep their Prisoner till the Effect of the Letter to you should be known.

1 The Continental Congress on May 15, 1776, recommended that the colonies set up State governments. The Assembly of the Three Lower Counties complied on June 15, 1776, by passing a resolution suppressing all authority derived from the Crown and establishing a government upon the authority of the people.

I propose to follow the troops up to Wilmington next week, & hope the pleasure of meeting you in Assembly.

79
From Thomas Rodney

Dover June 2ᵈ 1776.—

. . . The Tories are circulating a petitⁿ agⁿ Complying with the resolution of Congress—I have not got a sight of it yet, they keep from the view of the Dover Whigs—but are exerting themselves as making there last attempt which I hope it will be—all the officers & principle persons in my Company signed our instructions yesterday, a few of the inconsiderable ignorant ones declined it—but I hope we shall obtain suffitient, upon which to ground a Complyance with the resolution of Congress—

80
To Thomas Rodney

Philadelphia, June 5th, 1776.

. . . The Petition of the Lord Mayor and City of London to the King, and his answer will convince those people (who have opposed the Resolution of Congress) of their error; if they be open to conviction, it certainly will. You will have it in this day's paper.

81
From John Haslet

Longfield, Wednesday June 5ᵗʰ 3 P.M. [1776]

the Inclosed Testimonies &c came to me by Express not two Hours ago. I thought it my Duty to forward them to Congress with all possible Expedition. I should have considered this Business as the unmeaning Effusion of Drunkenness at a Vendue, Had I not good Reason to apprehend, that something Similar is on foot in this hundred. Jos. Oliver one of our Committee brought down lately certain printed Petitions from Philadelphia against Independence as tis said, which have been handed about with great assiduity by others of the Committee. At the Mispillion Muster last Saturday these papers were produced. Squire Clark with others clamorous for them, a scene of confusion ensued, some wou'd muster not [at] all, others, once a fortnight, & they broke up in disorder. I have by the Express, who brought the Inclosed Letters from Col. Hall & Major McDonough, wrote the Latter Orders to secure all the Ammunition & arms at Lewes, & put himself in the best posture of Defence, to call in the Guard from the false Cape; and if the matter assumes a still more serious appearance, to seize the most suspected of the Ring Leaders as Hostages for the good Behaviour of their Dependents. I have recommended to the Major to pay much Regard to the Opinion of Col. Hall & Mr. Fisher, & to conduct this whole business in a manner as little Offensive to the Inhabitants as possible. Arnolds House, it seems was burnt by Accident, which is made a complaint against the Soldiery. I can't help thinking, tho' very probably mistaken, something of vigorous Exertion necessary in both Counties—A word however to the wise, & yr. Consummate acquaintance in Both renders it needless to say more, the source of corruption & Direction is at Dover, an Hint from thence, pervades the Lower Part of the County in a trice. Clark Swordin, Beauchamp Cullen &c. tis said, keep up the Circulation. & all the Dirty September(?) machinery of Church & Presbyterian is hackneyed thro' the Hundred, & thickened as it goes. How matters stand in the upper District, you will better learn from Captain Rodney; that Nest of Hornets, the Congress is sufficiently cursed below—

Have I been too Precipitate in the Orders to Major McDonough Or how shall I conduct myself. Sorry I am, the troops are at Wilmington, still more that we are not completely armed. The subsistence Accompts of the Battalion will take up my time till Saturday at Dover—then I propose to March towards the Borough, unless some Emergence shou'd call me back to Sussex—the Ammunition Ordered there by Congress, when I was in town, is not yet arrived—

82
From James Sykes

Dover, June 13th 1776.

I have the pleasure to inform you that Mr. John Chew with a party of the Light Horse set off early yesterday to Sussex in order to obtain a perfect Account of the matters contained in Col. Rhodes's Letter to Col. Collins and as the inclosed papers will shew the intention of those people in Sussex who were said to have collected for the purpose of Assisting the people of the men of war against their Country, any comment of mine on the ocasion will be unnecessary—I thought it highly necessary after the express that was sent yesterday that the inclosed intelligince should be immediately transmitted to the House of Assembly.

Several of the Companies of the upper Battalion who had not reached further than Dover last night are returned home and those that marched from Dover yesterday I suppose are on their return—

P.S. Mr. Chew informs me that on these papers being signed the Militia of Sussex imediately dispersed. He desires you would keep the papers as he is under promise to return them—

83

From Thomas Collins[1]

June 14th, [1776]

By an Express from Collo Rhoad[2] Dated June ye 12th Instant 12 O'clock at Night, in Consequence of which our Battalion Assembled by Orders I had issued to the Several Capts.—Capt Popes Company, & Light Infintry, marchd from Dover about Eleven O'clock Wensday Morning, about 3 O'clock the Light horse followed. About 5 O'clock, Capt. Skillington Capt Gordon proceeded on the march, which Companies I march'd with and left orders with the Major to Dispatch the Other Companys as soon as they could be Acquipt. Thursday Morning the two Companies I was with were joined about brake of Day by Cap. Blacks & Capt. Stout, we proceeded on our march and about two Miles before we came to the Mispillion Church, on the Rhoad to Lewis, we met a Company and said they were Discharged by Col. Rhoad, and before we reach the Church we met three other Companies all giving us information of the Difference mad[e] up in Sussex, we proceeded to the Church afsd and there we met Coll—Rhodes with the residue of his Battalion from three Runs, and from the information of Mr. Rhodes who sd he was assured it was settled, we concluded to return, (but must let you know the Residue of our Battalion Marched from Dover thursday Morning Early) and this Instant Recd a Copy of a Letter from Col. Dagsworthy to Coll Rhodes which I inclosed you, and as the Assembly is now seting you will mention it to them and if they think proper will take order, you are in possession of the proceedings of the Council of Safety of Sussex on the former Occation as I am inform'd by Mr. Sykes—I shall send Express Immediately to ye Council of Safety of Sussex and in the meantime to warn Our Battalion to be in rediness to march at a Minute Warning.

1 Colonel of 1st Battalion of Kent County militia. On the reverse side of the letter there is a note stating that it refers to an insurrection in Sussex County in June 1776 and that it was addressed to General Rodney then at New Castle.

2 Colonel Rhodes, Commanding officer of the 2d Battalion of Kent County militia.

84

Resolutions of Delaware Assembly

In the House of Representatives for the counties of New-Castle, Kent, and Sussex, upon Delaware, at New-Castle.

Friday, June 14, 1776. A.M.

Mr. M'Kean delivered in at the Chair a certified copy of a Resolution of Congress, of the fifteenth of May last, which was by order read and is in the words following, to wit,

"In Congress, May 15, 1776.

Whereas his Britannic Majesty, in conjunction with the Lords and Commons of Great-Britain, has by a late act of Parliament excluded the inhabitants of these United Colonies from the protection of his crown. And whereas no answer whatever to the humble petitions of the Colonies, for redress of grievances and reconciliation with Great-Britain, has been or is likely to be given, but the whole force of that kingdom, aided by foreign mercenaries, is to be exerted for the destruction of the good people of these Colonies; and whereas it appears absolutely irreconcileable to reason and good conscience, for the people of these Colonies now to take the oaths and affirmations necessary for the support of any government under the crown of Great-Britain, and it is necessary that the exercise of every kind of authority under the said crown should be totally suppressed, and all the powers of government exerted under the authority of the people of the Colonies, for the preservation of internal peace, virtue and good order, as well as for the defence of their lives, liberties and properties, against the hostile invasions and cruel depredations of their enemies, therefore

Resolved, That it be recommended to the respective Assemblies and Conventions of the United Colonies, where no government sufficient to the exigencies of their affairs has been hitherto established, to adopt such government as shall in the opinion of the representatives of the people best conduce to the happiness and safety of their constituents in particular and America in general.

Extracts from the minutes,
Charles Thomson, Secretary."

By special order the same was read a second time, and, On Motion, Resolved unanimously, That this House do approve of the said Resolution of Congress.

Saturday, June 15th, P.M.

Whereas it is become absolutely necessary for the safety, protection, and happiness of the good people of this colony, forthwith to establish some authority adequate to the exigencies of their affairs, until a new government can be formed; and whereas the representatives of the people, in this Assembly met, alone can, and ought at this time, to establish such temporary authority.

Resolved unanimously. That all persons holding any office, civil or military, in this colony on the thirteenth day of June instant, may and shall continue to execute the same, in the name of the government of the counties of New Castle, Kent, and Sussex, upon Delaware, as they used legally to exercise it in the name of the King, until a new government shall be formed, agreeable to the Resolution of Congress of the fifteenth of May last. Extract from the minutes,

James Booth, Clerk of Assembly.

INSTRUCTIONS to the Deputies[1] appointed by this Government to meet in General Congress, which were unanimously approved of.

FIRST, That you concur with the other Delegates in Congress, in forming such farther compacts between the United Colonies, concluding such treaties with foreign Kingdoms and states, and in adopting such other measures as shall be judged necessary for promoting the liberty, safety, and interests of America, reserving to the people of this Colony, the sole and exclusive right of regulating the internal government and police of the same.

Second, On every necessary occassion, you are firmly to urge the right of this government to an equal voice in Congress with any other province or government on this Continent, as the inhabitants thereof have their ALL at stake as well as others. Extracts from the minutes,

James Booth, Clerk of Assembly.[2]

85

From George Read, John McKinly, James Latimer, and James Rench

New Castle June y[e] 25th 1776

We have just rec'ed your Letter[3] addressed to G: Read and much approve of your intention to stay a few days in Sussex to compleat the business you have

---

1 Caesar Rodney, Thomas McKean, and George Read.

2 Caesar Rodney was Speaker of the Assembly.

3 The letter alluded to has not been found. The letter here printed was addressed to Caesar Rodney and John Evans.

begun—but submit to your Consideration the apparent Necessity of the House of Assembly's Meeting on some day this Week and if that be on Saturday morning it may answer a good End particularly as to the Quota of Militia demanded by Congress from this Government and devising some ways & Means of supplying or procuring a restitution of the arms taken by Congress lately imported, for the use of a part of that Quota of men to be furnished from hence—this ought to be acted upon before we[1] return to Congress—as to the making up of a house if Co! Moore returns, which he promised to' do, it may be accomplished—The Speaker upon recollection must know that the several parts of the business referred by Congress to ye 1st of July may take up a length of time that the Delegates of this government cannot say when they can attend another meeting of the house, what I[2] allude to particularly is the articles of Confederation[3] therefore we hope the members below will attend you up—this is our opinion which we submit to them and you

[P.S.] If you sh.d have left Lewis before this reaches you—Send Notice to Co! Moore.

86

From John Haslet

Kent 30th June 1776.

I have the Pleasure to inform you, that the Evening after your Departure,[4] a Party of officers from Snowhill brought up Job Ingram Prisoner to Lewis,

---

1 George Read and Caesar Rodney.

2 This letter was written by George Read, the other signatures being secured by him as endorsing his views.

3 A committee headed by John Dickinson (at this time a representative of Pennsylvania) had been appointed by Congress to prepare a frame of government. At about the same time a committee headed by Thomas Jefferson of Virginia had been appointed to prepare a declaration of independence. It seems that Read of Delaware, like Dickinson, was more interested in the former as a necessary prelude to a formal declaration of independence at this time.

4 There has long been a tradition that Caesar Rodney was at Lewes when he started on his famous ride to Philadelphia to cast his vote for independence. This letter proves conclusively that he had left that town some days before June 30. The fact that he had been in Sussex County so recently, however, no doubt made it appear to the popular mind that he had ridden directly to Philadelphia from Lewes Having attended the opening of the Assembly as Speaker on June 11, and having had a great deal to do with that body's adopting on June 15, a resolution (in pursuance of the resolution of Congress of May 15) creating a *de facto* government for Delaware, independent of the British Crown and of the Province of Pennsylvania, an adjournment of the Assembly had been agreed to so as to enable the Speaker (now the ranking officer in the government, John Penn no longer being a colonial governor) to hurry to Sussex County to investigate the reported Tory uprising The receipt of the letter from George Read, dated June 25, had evidently hastened Rodney's departure from Sussex County.

where he is now confined, mighty Innocent as he says. Berkley Townsend yesterday morning also surrendered himself & is in Safe Keeping. A small Detachment of Delawares & Riflemen went in Quest of the General Boar but returned with non inventus est—Capt Overlin & others have signed the Declaration, & been disarmed—

Yesterday recd an Order of Congress dated 25th June to furnish a Guard for the Powder Waggon to Virginia, which was immediately obeyed. At the Same time another dated 18th Inst to station two Companies of the Battalion under my Command at Cape May, to replace two Companies formerly there, now ordered to Canada. You well know, Sir, from the Pecular Circumstances of the Battalion this Order is to me extremely embarassing; it appears to me very probable the Commissary, now absent, will not supply those two Companies with Provisions at such a Distance; you also know, that we have no arms fit to be depended on but the Militia Arms of Kent, & that my Reputation is engaged to the Council of Safety, not to Order them out of the Government, & to return them when called for. You will lay me under great Obligations, by stating this matter to Congress,[1] or by Directions in what Manner to conduct myself. Only furnish us with Arms, & Command us where you please. To send Over two Companies of unarmed men wou'd by no means answer the Intentions of Congress.

87

To Thomas Rodney

Philadᵃ July the 4th 1776—

I have inclosed you a Summons directed to the Sheriff to Summon the Member[s] for our County to meet in Assembly at Newcastle on the 22d day of this Instant which I hope you will have put into his hands as soon as possible after it Comes to Yours[2]—I arrived in Congress (tho detained by Thunder and Rain) time Enough to give my Voice in the matter of Independence[3]—It

1 Colonel Haslet in all probability wrote this letter from some point in lower Kent County, perhaps in the vicinity of his home, if not at his home, near what is now the town of Milford, and Rodney had evidently seen him there while he was on his way to Philadelphia via his home near Dover.

2 A special session of the Assembly was being called by Caesar Rodney, the Speaker, to determine the question of framing a constitution for the State. When the Assembly met, it decided, on July 27, that a convention be held for that purpose on August 27, and made arrangements for the election of delegates to the same to be held on August 19.

3 Rodney had not returned from Sussex County in time to go to New Castle by "Saturday morning," June 29, to continue the sessions of the Assembly as requested by Read in his letter of June 25. Read had then proceeded to Philadelphia in order to be present in Congress on Monday,

BRONZE EQUESTRIAN STATUE OF CAESAR RODNEY

Rodney Square, Wilmington, Delaware

is determined by the Thirteen United Colonies with out even one decenting Colony.[1] We have now Got through with the Whole of the declaration and Ordered it to be printed, so that you will soon have the pleasure of seeing it[2] —Hand-bills of it will be printed and sent to the Armies, Cities, County Towns &c To be published or rather proclamed in form— . . .

88

From John Haslet

Lewes 6th July 1776

I did myself the favor to write you by Mr Bell, how much I was embarrassed by the Order of Congress directing two Companies to Cape May,[3] hope to receive your answer by this days Post—

July 1, when Richard Henry Lee's resolution for independence was to be taken off the table and debated. On that day, after a long and spirited debate between the conservatives, led by John Dickinson, and the radicals, led by John Adams, Congress, sitting as a Committee of the Whole House, passed the resolution with nine states favoring it, two states (Pennsylvania and South Carolina) opposing it, and with Delaware's vote not cast due to Read's opposing the resolution and McKean's favoring it and Rodney's being absent. That Rodney did not foresee such a quick decision is quite probable. That he had left Sussex County several days before with a view to going to Philadelphia and had seen Colonel Haslet in lower Kent County while on his way north is certain. He had probably stopped at his home near Dover for a day or two of rest and for the purpose of looking after his personal affairs when McKean's message reached him, perhaps in the night of July 1–2. In this connection it is necessary to state that we have only McKean's word for it that he sent an "express" to Rodney, as there is no reference by the latter to this fact in any of his known letters. It is quite certain that Rodney reached Philadelphia on July 2 (probably late in the afternoon) and that he joined McKean in placing Delaware with the majority when Lee's resolution was voted for in a formal manner upon its being referred from the Committee of the Whole House. Since Pennsylvania and South Carolina also joined the majority on the second, the vote for the resolution on that day was twelve states, New York's delegation remaining silent as on the day before. What Rodney means in this letter is, that he arrived in time to vote for Lee's resolution on the second. This is proven by the curious fact that when John Hancock, the President of Congress, put the motion on the second, he made a tally-sheet on the back of Lee's original resolution, and indicated Delaware's vote as in the affirmative. This tally-sheet may be seen in the manuscript division of the Library of Congress.

1 Rodney was mistaken, as New York did not adhere to Lee's resolution and to the Declaration of Independence until some ten days after this letter was written.

2 Immediately after the passing of Lee's resolution on July 2 had made the United States independent of the Mother Country, Congress proceeded to discuss Jefferson's draft for a declaration of independence which was to serve as an explanation to the world of the act of July 2. The draft was debated paragraph by paragraph, the tedious work not being completed by the Committee of the Whole House until late on the fourth. Then the Declaration, as we now know it, was adopted by the same twelve states as voted for Lee's resolution on the second. The formal signing of the Declaration did not begin until August 2. Then Read joined Rodney and McKean and made Delaware's vote unanimous.

3 Refers to his letter dated "Kent 30th June 1776."

Last Thursday Evening[1] arrived here Gen! Dagworthy, Jones & a Band of
Patriots from Broad-Creek, who depose & say, that an open Correspondence
is carried on for the purpose of trade with Lord Dunmore, that he daily recruits his shattered Bands among them. That the Tories seem rather Irritated
than reformed. A copy of their Depositions is inclosed by the Council to the
Presid! On their Request I have ordered down One Company of the Delawares; & on my Request they ordered down their Fragment of Independants.
A Copy of my Orders to the officer, who commands the Detachment is inclosed
to you; & hope (from the Patriotism of the Council for Kent) my sending
their Arms so much farther will be pardoned, as 'tis still within the Government. I wou'd fondly hope, my Tardiness in obeying the Cape May Order,
will not be supposed to Originate in any other Principle, than mentioned in
my last to you. For Gods Sake, let us have arms, May we not have those saved
by Cap! Barry from the Brig? will it not be in your power to engage for us
Rifles to complete One Company, now Pensylvania is supplied.

I congratulate you, Sir, on the Important Day, which restores to Every
American his Birthright—a day which Every Freeman will record with Gratitude, & the Millions of Posterity read with Rapture.

Ens: Wilson arrived here last night,[2] a fine Turtle Feast at Dover antici-
pated & announced the Declaration of Congress, Even the Barrister himself
laid aside his Airs of Reserve, mighty happy. I must beg Pardon for having
taken up so much of your time with small matters.

89

From John Miller[3]

Near Dover, July 8, 1776.

Your late tour into Sussex to enquire into ye grounds & reasons of ye late
Insurrection there, has doubtless given you a much better idea of ye Spirit &
conduct of that people than any of us can have here—But as there now Seems
to be a prevailing apprehension that Some in this county were connected with
that conspiracy, & had no small hand in promoting it, tis thot an Enquiry into
that matter as Soon as possible, would produce Some good consequences, at
least to this Government—

If a number among us, have ye Same Influence, in Affairs of Government,
they had, but a month or two ago, when their counter petitions were circulat-

---

1 Haslet's letter was written on a Saturday. The previous Thursday fell on July 4.

2 Ensign Wilson arrived in Lewes on Friday evening, the fifth, bringing the news of the
adoption of the Declaration of Independence the day before.

3 Minister of Presbyterian Church at Dover.

ing & Signing here,[1] you may easily judge which way ye majority will probably go at ye anniversary Election.[2]

The Result of that Enquiry, could it be Soon made, wou'd no doubt open many peoples Eyes here, & prevent their being misled at a time, when the friends of Liberty should have their whole Strength collected to a point of the greatest Importance to this Government.

You will therefore probably think with me, that if a few days could be redeemed for that purpose, as soon as you could leave ye Congress & before ye Assembly sits, it would answer much better than to defer it, till ye next Session is ended, as ye Session may be long, & time afterwards may be wanting, to give a large class of men a just Idea of their Duty & Interest. Excuse my freedom in Suggesting these thoughts

Honble Caesar Rodney, Esqr.

90

From John Haslet

Lewes, July 9th 1776

I am to acknowledge the Receipt of your favours of the 4th & 5th Inst.[3] Soon after arrived an Express with Orders to station a single Company here, & March the others to Wilmington, I have by Express represented the State of the Battalion, &c which you will see—I am preparing to obey, if Congress do not reverse the Order in Part—but cannot think of Carrying the Militia Arms up there from Kent—tho if the 8 Ships of War now at the Cape move up the Bay, I shall be puzzled what to do—

Another Insurrection is talked of here as a very Probable Event, on the Removal of the Troops—

91

To Thomas Rodney

Philadelphia, July the 10th, 1776.

You mention in your last that Mr. Wells is discharged the Service. Coll.

1 Refers to time when opposition developed in Kent County against the resolution of Congress of May 15 calling upon the colonies to set up independent governments. The counter petitions opposed action by the Assembly at New Castle, but were ignored by the Assembly when on June 15 it passed the resolution separating the Government of the Three Lower Counties from England

2 Refers to the October elections for the Assembly. As a matter of fact Miller's fears proved well founded, for not only was Rodney not elected a delegate to the Constitutional Convention at the election on August 19, but was defeated by the conservatives for the first legislature under the State constitution in October 1776 and was left off, together with McKean, the State's delegation to the Continental Congress in November 1776

3 These letters have not been found.

Haslet has not as yet reported that matter to Congress. When he does I shall attend to what you have said on that head.

With respect to the other matters you sent me,[1] I am of opinion that any good effect which might flow from them must be local, I mean that it would be confined principally to the inhabitants of that County,—and on the other hand, at a time of such eminent danger, when powerful Armies are actually knocking at our gates, and the serious attention of every friend to American Liberty is employed in giving that manly opposition to those vile invaders of their just rights, privaledges and property, whether it would be prudent to hold out to the World such numbers of internal enemies—especially as by the manly and determined spirit prevailing in the Congress their wings must and will be clipped. The Declaration has laid the foundation, and will be followed by laws fixing the degree of offence and punishment suitable. Some people have done things, which if done in future nothing less than life will be sufficient to attone for. These enemies to our righteous cause will (I apprehend) be less on their guard if they are not held up in that public way, than if they are, and will undoubtedly meet their due reward, provided you persue steadily your line of Patriotism, and at the same time keep a watchfull eye toward their conduct in the pollitics of your County. These things must and will be enquired into. But, Sir—now is the time and season that our open and avowed enemies are pressing hard. They call forth the attention and utmost vigilance of the Congress to that point. They well know they have internal enemies in disguise, and whenever, by the blessing of God, their virtuous efforts shall be crowned with success, they will immediately turn their thoughts toward those sappers of the rights of mankind. It is also the business of every Government so soon as formed to take in hand that business, South Carolina has already set them a good example.

I have sent you a pamphlet called Observations on the Nature of Civil Liberty &c., wrote by Doctor Price in England. It is an excellent piece, and don't doubt (properly used), will tend to strengthen your patriotic or in other words independent party. I have also directed one to Doctor McCall as present.

The Militia of Pensylvania are beginning their march this day toward New York and I do suppose that by the last of this week General Washington will be thirty thousand strong at least. Coll. Haslet's Battalion (except one company which to stay at Lewis) is ordered up to Wilmington, as a security to Philadelphia, in the absence of their Militia, as well as to the Lower Counties, and hopes for this reason the Committee of Safety will permit them to retain (while thus employed) the Militia Arms belonging to the public. . . .

1 Thomas Rodney's letter has not been found, but he evidently had requested advice relative to holding an inquiry in Kent County to ascertain whether and how much the conservatives or Tories of that county were implicated in the Sussex County insurrection of the previous month.

92

To Captain Carson

Dover July 22. 1776

As the English Armed Vessels have all now left the Delaware, & as a power-ful French fleet is lying off our coast, the inhabitants of this state, do not, in my opinion, appear to be in that danger from an invasion of the Enemy, so justly apprehended by the General Assembly, when they Entered into the resolution for Establishing the independent Company you command in this county. I do, therefore, in virtue of the powers given by the General Assembly, hereby dis-band the above mentioned independent Company; You are therefore immedi-ately to discharge the officers & privates thereof from further service. You are also, so soon as it may be convenient, to make me a regular return of those who may have been Engaged, & done duty in said Company.

N.B. The Newcastle & Sussex Companies were ordered to be disbanded on the 11th instant.

93

To Thomas Rodney

Philadᵃ August the 3d 1776

I recd yours of the 30th of July and Shall endeavour to Answer it—Captⁿ Gordon might have had the place you mentioned But on Talking with me Verry prudently declined it—The History of your Manuvurs, procession &c please me and the more so, as I had heard of the Choice without knowing the principal on which it was made—

With respect to the return made me by the field officers, They have neglected to send me the dates of their Commissions or appointments in the Militia. I have therefore wrote to them to return me the dates before Commissions Can be made out—as to the Subalterns, these being placed with an older or younger Captain does not affect their Rank as that will be preserved by the Commission made out for them—and as that will be the Case it is better they should be fixed in such Companies as best please them—I showed Captain Gordon the return made me by the Field-Officers shewing the order in which they Chose to be placed with respect to the Companies—Which Mr Gordon said was agreable to their desire so far as he had knowledge in it. That he was shure it was right as to Caldwell's Company—

With Respect to the Choice of a Convention, I would Submit it to you and Your friends Whether (when you have fixed on such Ticket as meets with your approbation) it would not be best to persue and Endeavour to impress the Utility of such Choice being made by the people (Especially at a time when the Establishing their Rights and priviledges as freemen depends on such Choice) upon Your former plan, I mean of true Whiggism, True patriotism—This plan if pursued with diligence and such Cool argument & reasoning as the Cause will point out & justify—I think must Carry with it Persuation and Conviction. It certainly will with all such as are not Governed by a party Spirit—If any person or persons be proposed in oposition to Your Ticket who have heretofore been unfriendly to the Cause—point out to the people their former Conduct, and Submit to them the propriety of Trusting to such men, at such an Important Crisis. Your Scheme ought to hold out to the people more of the Patriot, than of party-man—I will again Submit as before—Whether the Enquiry & Examination proposed to be had before the Committee will not Tend so to irritate as to occassion many people by taking Sides in that matter to loose sight of the Cause, their true interest—For if they are lead to believe that you and your friends are Governed more by party Spirit than by the True Interest of America, they will hold you in the Light of all other party-men and deal with you accordingly—You say the Committee are about to make this Enquiry—Are there a sufficient number of Patriots in that Committe to answer Your Expectation? Are there a Considerable majority of them that wish the Enquiry should be had? Will they (if matters turn out as you Expect) publish their opinions to the County so that the friends to Liberty may benefit by it? It is an Enquiry that ought to have been made but it is an Enquiry that ought to be made by men of understanding only—Do such make a Majority of the Committee tho: good men? By what authority do they take it up? Are not many of the members principals in the matter of Enquiry? All these things I Submit to the Good Sence and prudence of You and Your friends—Tho you Seem to have determined on the measure (by Your Letter) before my opinion was asked. In Short it is difficult for me to give an opinion in this Case as I am a Stranger to the present Complection of the Committee—However as this Convention is undoubtedly the most important assembly that Ever was chose in that Government would advise the avoiding Every kind of Violence and on the other hand the u[t]most diligence and persuation to procure as many friends to Liberty on the return as possible. By this means men who have been known to be heretofore unfriendly to Liberty (if properly pointed out) Cannot prevail. The people when uniritated Generally hearken to reason and make prudent Choices—But you may be able to let me know more about these things by the next Post.

Yesterday Came to Town a Ship belonging to the Congress from France with ten Tunns of Powder, about forty Tunns of Lead, one thousand Stand of Arms, &c. &c. And the Same day an Armed Veshell taken by Captain Barry at Sea—

94

To Thomas Rodney

Philad? August 3d 1776

Since I finished my other Letter have been up at Congress where We Recd Inteligence by letter from Capt? Weeks in the Congress ship, the Reprisal, That he has at Sea on the 13th of July taken two prizes, a Ship and a Schooner bound for Liverpool Loaded with Cotten, Sugar Rum &c. The Letter Came by the Prize Schooner which arrived in an Inlet near Egg Harbour—and the Ship Prize has been Seen off the Capes of Delaware and Supposed by this time got in—This days Post is not yet Come in from New-York—It is past his usual time of Coming and therefore Imagined there will be Something important which delayed him—I wish it may be Good—The Delaware Came to Town this morning—and then passed an Order of Congress Yesterday morning for Captain Darby and his Company now at Lewis—To Come up and join the Battalion—or at least to follow them—for as the Congress have now Got arms I imagine they will not Stay long here—Let not the Contents of my other letters be seen by any, unless a friend in whom you Can Confide—

95

From Thomas Rodney[1]

Dover Aug? 5th 1776

I recd: your two letters yesterday Capt? Gordon—am glad to hear of Our great Success by Sea,—The Tories here are exerting them selves to git in convention—there Ticket now is C. R, J. C, R. B, T. C, J. Cook, T. Tilton, T. W, J. Clark, J. S, J. Sykes—leaving you out—but they seem at a loss how to contrive it for they have put out several Tickets to see I believe how they would be relished—I wrote the above to send by last post but had not time to finish—Their Ticket I believe is now fixed thus—C. Ridgily, Rich? Basset, T. Collins, J. Cook, S. West, J. Clark, J. Stout, Tho? White, J. Sykes & R. Lockwood. Whether they will keep Lockwood in as he declares he will not push either Ticket but will vote for part of both & they sent him to us to propose a Junction but it would not take—they seem much Out of Heart at present—Our ticket was finally fixed yesterday a great number of our principle friends present as

1 This letter refers to the conservative and radical tickets (called Tories and Whigs) for the Kent County delegation to the first State Constitutional Convention in New Castle, called for August 27. At the election on August 19, the conservative ticket was elected as follows: Charles Ridgely, Richard Bassett, Thomas Collins, John Cook, Samuel West, John Clarke, Jacob Stout, Thomas White, James Sykes, and Richard Lockwood.

well as most of the members—C. Rodney, W. Killen, Thos Rodney, J. Carty, S. Snow, J. Baning, V. Lockerman, Powell, Cox, Frans Many—J. Revell,— from the present disposition of the Whigs it appears we shall carry the Ellection—The Comm. yesterday unanamusly Resolved to enquire into the insurrection on Tuesday next, and have Order'd summonses for that purpose—the Tories are abashed at this—Doct! R. declares he will not concern in the Election—I believe he will only act behind the Curtain—Cook & Collins are the Heroes of their Tickets—

96

To Thomas Rodney

Philada August 8th 1776—

The Delaware Battalion[1] is under marching order for Amboy subject to General Washingtons further orders—They are compleatly armed as [?] Guns as you could wish to see.

Haveing a few idle minutes I have inclosed you a paper containing a few Queries and submit to you whether that, or something like it taken or Copied in an unknown hand and secretly distributed so as to become public at this time might not be of use, by drawing the serious attention of the people at this important Crisis—But as I know but verry little, or rather nothing of the present Politics, or the disposion of the people at this time, wholely submit the matter to you and wish the people may consider their true interest.

Mr. McKean is yet in the Jerseys, and not likely soon to return—The terms of Confederation[2] now before the Congress and our Colony not represented without Read and me both, therefore cannot expect to see you in Kent verry soon—

97

From Caesar Rodney and Thomas McKean

To all whom it may Concern

I beg leave to recomm[end] Allen McLane[3] (who is inclined to the Camp at Amboy) as a warm friend to American Liberty

Caesar Rodney

---

1 Colonel John Haslet's regiment.   2 Articles of Confederation.

3 Allan McLane gained fame later in the captures of Paulus Hook and Stony Point. His son, Louis, distinguished himself in Jackson's administration as Minister to Great Britain, Secretary of State, and Secretary of the Treasury. His grandson, Robert Milligan McLane, became a Commissioner to China and later Minister to France.

Philadª Aug
13d 1776
Perth Amboy—Head Quarters August 15ᵗʰ 1776

I do join in the above Certificate of Brigadier General Rodney, one of the Delegates for the Delaware Government and request all whom it may concern to permit Mr Allen M, Clane to pass and repass unmolested to the City of New York or elsewhere.

Tho McKean Col. 4ᵗʰ Batt.
Philª Associators

98

To Thomas Rodney

Philadelphia, August 14, 1776.

. . . By your letter, I stand informed as to the names of your antagonists in the ensuing election; and am pleased to find you hope to succeed. But are you not too sanguine in your expectation? I wish your ticket may be supported by the freemen of the County, because I believe those men wish to have the great work in which we are now engaged finished in such a manner as to afford to the community at large that personal safety, security of property, free enjoyment of religious persuasion, and that equal and easy distribution of justice, which they have a right to expect, and without which they cannot be happy.

I did not expect to be carried in the other ticket, because I see some names there who I believe are too far gone in personal prejudice and private emolument to do justice to merit, or to consider the rights and privileges of the people at large their interest. But if the people cannot or will not see these things, though glaring, they must and will suffer.

The time is now big with importance, as to Continental as well as Governmental matters. The armies at New-York are like to come to blows in a few days. One hundred and some odd transports, with Hessians, arrived at the Hook the day before yesterday. The English Army is supposed to be upwards of twenty thousand strong; ours better than thirty thousand, in high spirits, and eager for action, &c. I shall be able perhaps to write you more on that head in a few days.

99

From Thomas Rodney

Dover Augt 19th 1776

I am very Porely with the yellow Jaundice and have been some days therefore send but a few lines—The Ellection[1] is going against us their lowest man at this time is 150 vote ahead of you who are the highest our side—shall write you ful next opertunity—Major Hodgson has an Order of the House on you for £200,—which he is pressing to have paid—I let him have £40. out of £43"10"0 which I recd: of Jonoth. Hunn for you on bond as he said—please to send an answer by the Post about the order—

100

To Thomas Rodney

Philadelphia, August 21, 1776.

Last night, by the post, I received an account of your defeat in the election, and in which I was not disappointed, being convinced you continued to be sanguine in your expectations without taking the necessary steps to carry a point of that sort; added to all the rest of your bad policy, you suffered Caldwell's company to march away just before the election, when there was no necessity for it, as the other companies were not half full in any of the Counties. Parke tells me the conduct of your Light-Infantry heretofore had drawn down the resentment of the people, which put it in the power of that party who were opposed to you to make this use of it.

As to the orders which Hodgson has on me, he can't stand in need of the money; for, knowing that I could not be down, and that Mr. McWilliam had not the wherewithal to satisfy his order, the Delegates procured of Congress three thousand dollars for the purpose of advancing a month's pay to the soldiers and contingent expenses, fifteen hundred of which have been sent down to Colonel Patterson. However, as you have paid him forty odd pounds in part, it is so far well. I hope you have taken his receipt, but cannot tell how you ascertained Hume's debt, as you had not the bond.

As Mr. Read will go to the Convention, and our Colony requires two Delegates to make a representation, I shall come home next week if possible; but if I should not be down time enough, pray attend to the Orphan's Court. The present Convention is solely for the purpose of framing Government, and will not be allowed to go out of that line, except it be so far as is necessary to supply the Flying-Camp with such things as may be heretofore omitted. The people may perhaps think better of this matter the next time they choose.

P.S. One Woodcock, at Wilmington, has been speaking to me about a privateer he was applied to to build by Captain Pope. He says he has a parcel of

---

1 Refers to election on same day of delegates from Kent County to the first Delaware Constitutional Convention, which assembled at New Castle on August 27.

carpenters sent to him and cannot go on for want of the iron-work, rum, &c. Some person among you ought to go immediately and enter into a contract with him and find the means of supplying him.

101

To Thomas Rodney

Philadª Augˢᵗ the 28th 1776

. . . I intended to Come down but have been prevailed on by the other delegates to Stay and attend Congress during their absence, the business in Congress being important to each Colony (Especially ours). They proposed that the Convention[1] Should Give the power of Voteing for the Colony to one delegate to prevent our Colony suffering while they were imployed on other business—This I Consented to, being determined that the folly and ingratitude of the people Shall not divert my attention from the public Good—I have Seen Independence declared, and when I See this Campaign Well Ended (as I hope it will) and Regular Government Established, Then I intend to leave the public, and take the private paths of Life—future Generations will Honor those names, that are neglected by the present Race.[2]

As soon as I Recd the accounts from Kent and Newcastle of the Elections I wrote to Mr McKean at Amboy and desired he would give imediate attendance at the Convention. He got my Letter and in Consequence thereof Came to Philadelphia on Sunday Night last, and set out Yesterday morning verry Early to Newcastle[3]—While he was here I mentioned to him the Circumstance of Vesting the power of Voteing (in Congress) in one delegate. He liked much to have the power in one, But was so aversed to and determined against the Convention takeing upon them, or Concerning with, the least Iota Except the barely frameing a plan of Government that he was of opinion he should never Consent to their appointing delegates, or even altering their power, least they should afterward be inclined to hold it out as a president for their takeing upon them some other matters which he thinks they would willingly be at—He say that for his part he is tired of attending the Congress, but is determined *they* shall turn him nor no one Else out—That if they are determine

1 The State Constitutional Convention at New Castle.

2 Caesar Rodney here betrays chagrin and disgust at not being elected a delegate to the State Constitutional Convention at New Castle, a convention which he had worked for in July as Speaker of the Assembly.

3 On Tuesday, August 27, 1776, Thomas McKean went to New Castle to attend the Constitutional Convention. He had been elected a delegate for New Castle County. He represented the radical elements, being a Whig.

to do these things by the Strength of their Majority, He will Try the Strength of the County with *them* Even at the risk of the Court House—

In the opinion of many people the Convention of this province are makeing such Strides as will Effectually knock up both them and their plan—

When our Delegates Return I am to go home for the Remainder the fall—

I am (by promise) to hear by Every opertunity how they go on at Newcastle—About Ten Thousand of the Enemy are Landed on Long Island they have been Schirmishing Every day since and we are Constantly looking for Something important—Washington is in high Spirits; says they have over Stayed their time, That he is now Ready for them—the sooner the Better—Putnam Commands on Long-Island and has with him Major Gen! Sullivan, Brig! Gen! Lord Sterling and three other Briga!s

P.S. I wrote to Coll Haslet since the Battalion went to New-York But have not Yet got an answer—Therefore don't know How they are there—

102

From James Tilton[1]

Long Island 29 Aug!t 1776.

Before I left Dover, Capt: Rodney was kind enough to read me a paragraph in your Letter to him, enquiring, if I would accept of a place in my own way, of forty Dollars per m°? I apprehended it was a Birth in the General Hospital; but as I was then unacquainted with the Constitution of the Hospital, I could only judge of your proposal by the fee. I am now better acquainted with the Hospital & therefore troubel you on this occassion. I find the Director has four assistant Surgeons, and under them a number of mates. If you can procure me a Surgeon's birth I shall be much obliged to you: but I will not accept of a mate's place. I don't know the fees annexed to these offices, but judge of them by the Rank & Condition they enjoy. I have every Reason to think, the number of Hospital surgeons must be encr[e]assed immediately, I am well informed, an American Diploma or Degree in medicine, was an ample Recommendation of my Collegiate D! Potts to a Director Generalship. I hope this may likewise serve me in procuring a surgeons place. Besides, as to my abilities to serve, I appeal to the medical professiors, one of whom is now a member of Congress.—

I will not trouble you with an acc! of our missfortunes on Long Island as you will have it from better hands—I shall only add that I stand the Soldiers Life as well as any of my fellows

1 Dr. Tilton was a surgeon from Delaware in the Revolutionary Army. In the War of 1812 he held the post of Surgeon-General of the United States Army.

103
From Thomas Rodney

Dover Aug.! 30th 1776—

I recd: your letters by last post & the one preceeding & one ment.d in that— I am pleased with your resolution, ment.d in your last, as I should be sorry to hear that the unsteady passions which Govern the people, should at [any time?] give the least shock to that Virtue which hath so long & [?] supported American Liberty—Tho' the people in a popula[r] [Govt?] often put away good men for bad ones, & tho' such a Cha[nge] could not be more dangerous at any time than the pres[ent], [yet?] I look on the present change with us as an example wh[ich] favours Liberty—If the people will not continually s[upport] those men who have served them faithfully at all Hazard[s] [it] cannot be supposed that they will long support those men who in opposition to the publick weal have pursued their own private interest only—these men by a violent exertion of the influence of the Majistracy; and decending to assert the most base, low & infamous falshoods; have succeeded for once, because the people were blinded that they could not see their true interests—But be assured they that set them up will pull them down again

After devoting ten years to the service of your country and publick business, to the great prejudice of your own private interests you certainly deserve to [en]joy the sweets of Retirement, which is the happyest life in this State, and you'l have this reflection th.! after the time you mention that you have accomplished the establishment of American liberty; and that you could not do any thing that would ad to the Honour already acquired—but I believe the people will not let you execute this design—They will soon be tired of those who they have now set up—and will begin to call again upon those men whose virtue hath been proved to the utmost—When the great matters which you ment.d are compleated I shall be content—nor shall desire to have any hand in politics, unless at any time liberty be incroached upon—nothing but the great cause of Liberty which we have been imbarked in could have induced me (who have an increasing famaly & so little for them) to have spent so much of my time & money in publick servises— . . .

104
From George Read[1]

Co.! Patterson has ordered Major Neill to call upon you for the 1500 dollars for which you have M.r Treas.r Hillegas's Note which you will please to procure

1 At this time George Read, a delegate for New Castle County, was President of the State Constitutional Convention at New Castle.

and deliver to the Major taking his receipt for the same—Col Patterson tells
me he deld your order as Speaker for £200—to Lt Col Hudson part of which
to wit abot £40 hath been paid by Mr Thos Rodney, he now desires that the
residue of this order or such part thereof as you can spare may be paid to
Major Neill and for this purpose the Col will direct Hudson to deliver the
order to Major Neill—he also wishes that a further advance cou'd be procured
from Congress—he talks of Marching all the Companies on Wednesday—
The Convention have passed a Vote of Credit for £600 to be paid into the
Cols hands for the purchase of Blankets Bayonets & paymt of Quarters—this
with some other provisions for hastening the March of the Battalion is all that
has been done here as yet—The dispute as to the Sussex representation in Convention took up all our time 'till Friday Noon—the forming rules—Tests &c
was not finished till the Noon of this day and we are now sitting by candle
Light—Inclose you a recommendatn of Will: Millan for paymaster which you
may make in Congress when you think proper

    Mr McKean has been absent since yesterday Noon his Son being sick at Mr
Thompson's.—Your Hble Servt is in the Chair which he wants size as well as
Capacity to fill—We have nothing new here but are impatiently waiting to
hear the particulars of the late Loss on Long Island—

105

From John Haslet

Camp at New York, August 31st 1776

    I recd yours with pleasure because it was yours, all the Rest was Indigna-
tion—We went over to Long Island, a Genl. Engagement ensued, the Southern Troops[1] i. e., Ld. Sterlings Battalion bore the Violence of the attack & repulsed the Enemy but were outnumbered at least three to one, & obliged to
retire; the Delaware Battallion have been complimented as the finest in the
Service, they stood unmoved in firm array four Hours exposed to the fire of
the Enemy, nor attempted to retire till they received Orders from the Genl.—,
then effected a most Noble Retreat up to the Middle thru a Marsh of Mud &
brought off with them 23 Prisoners[2]—I fear we shall be out numbered, expect
every moment Orders to March off to King's Bridge, to prevent the Enemy
Crossing the East River & confining us on another Nook. What the Event will

    1 Including the Delaware troops.
    2 Neither Colonel Haslet nor Lieutenant-Colonel Gunning Bedford was in command at the
Battle of Long Island since both had been ordered to attend a court-martial on Manhattan Island
that day. Major Thomas McDonough, future father of the naval hero in the War of 1812, was in
immediate command during the engagement.

be, God knows. Lt. Stewart & Harney with 25 Privates fell in our Regiment—
Ld. Sterling & Genl. Sullivan, Prisoners. Miles & Allee, the lame Piper killed
—250 of Smallmans[1] missing Atl[e]es[2] Cut to pieces—I fear Genl. Washington has too heavy a task, Assisted mostly by Beardless Boys—if the Enemy can
Coop us up in N.York by Intrenching from River to River, horrid will be the
Consequence from their Command of the Rivers—

Between five & Six Thousand Dollars of Continental Money remain in my
hands. Unknowing what to do with it, I have entrusted it to the care of Dr.
Rogers & Chaplain Montgomery—if I fall, please to take Order in the Matter
—I have not time to say one Word more, tis the first letter I have had time to
write. Please to mention to some of your Friends below that I am well, by
whose means it may reach Mrs. Haslet—

106
To George Read

Philad? Sept? the 4th 1776

Inclosed you have a Resolution of Congress, one of those papers was delivered to the Delegates of each Colony to be by them transmitted to their
several Assemblies or Conventions, that Order might be taken therein.

I mentioned in my last the arrival of General Sullivan,[3] and then hinted the
business of his Comeing; The day I Wrote you last he was admitted in Congress and informed them That he had been on bord the Eagle, and then had
private Conversation with Lord Howe. The Substance of Which Was, that his
Lordship declared he had Ample power (together with the General)[4] to settle
matters between Great Britain and the Colonies in Such manner as Should be
for the True Interest and benefit of both—and to make such Settlement permanent, That he wished for nothing more than to Converse with General Washington or some one or more Members of Congress on that Head, but that there
was a difficulty in the way which prevent it, for that his Rank & Scituation was
attended with that kind of delicacy, That he Could not Treat with the Congress as Such, and had no doubt that the Congress from their Scituation lay
under the same difficulty—therefore proposed his haveing Conversation of an
Hour or two with Some of the Members as private Gentlemen. That he would

1 Evidently means William Smallwood, colonel of Maryland regiment.

2 Samuel John Atlee was colonel of the Pennsylvania Musket battalion.

3 General Sullivan, having been taken prisoner by the British at the Battle of Long Island, was
used as an intermediary to bring about a conference looking toward the ending of hostilities. A
Committee of Congress met Lord Howe at his headquarters at Staten Island, but with no results.

4 Lord Howe commanded the British fleet in New York harbor. His brother, William Howe,
commanded the British army.

meet them in that Carrector also Where ever they pleased. That he did not
doubt by this Step Matters might be put in a train of Accommodation—if not
that it would only be so much time Lost. That his Lordship further said he
had stayed in England two months after he was otherwise Ready to Come, on
purpose to obtain those ample Powers before mentioned, by Which means the
Declaration of Independency had taken place before his Arrival;—There was
other Conversation Such as that his Lordship thought this a fine Country,
That he had many friends & Acquaintance here, and that he Should be pleased
Much to have an opportunity to Ride thought [through?] the Country to
See them &c &c—You Sir may be desirous to know what Congress think of
this Message delivered by Sullivan at the request of Lord Howe—To Satisfie
your desire I think I may Venture to say that a verry great Majority of the
Members look in it as an Insult, And believe a Resolution will pass that no pro-
posals for the future be Received, Unless Reduced to Writing and Signed Some
person Who has Authority to Treat with the Congress as an Assembly of the
United Independent State of America, or to that Effect—

From Certain inteligence Rec'd. Since I Wrote last, Col! Haslet, Col! Smallwood and Col! Bedford were Setting on a Court-Martial in York at the time
the Delawares and Marylanders were Engaged With the Enemy—That those
two Battalions fought as Bravely as Men Could possibly Do—That the Marylanders lost 259 Men Missing Many of Whom were Killed. That it was owing
Chiefly to their being Seperated by which Means the Enemy got between
them and Oblidged them to fight in Small parties. The Delawares being well
trained Kept and fought in a Compact Body the Whole time, and When
Oblidged to retreat Kept their Ranks and Entered the lines in that Order,
frequently while Retreating Obliged to fight their way through Bodies of
the Enemy, Who had before made an Attack on our lines, Where they were
repulsed and were also retreating and Met each other. The Delawares in this
retreat lost four or five Men, one or two Killed and two or three drowned in
Crossing a Creek. This would have been all their Loss, but unfortunately about
the be[ginn]ing of the Engagement had placed a Small party of Observation
at Some Distance with Whom they Could never again Join (the Enemy haveing Got between them) tho frequently attempted & Greatest part of those
were lost, either Killed or taken prisoners, but supposed Chiefly Killed—Upon
the Whole the Delaware Battalion has now Missing Thirty one including two
Officers to wit Lt. Stuart, and Lt. Harney, the Major had a Slight wound on
the Knee. This is the Whole of the damage the[y] have Sustained—Captain
Adams of Kent after fighting bravely a Considerable time was Seized with a
Most Violent Collick. He was sent off the Ground. & a Soldier with him to
Conduct him to our lines, in his way he had to Cross a deep Marsh in which

when the Battalion Crossed they found him Just Expiring. They Carried him over on boards, Got him in the lines, and he is now well.

Our old friend Billey Livingston is appointed Governor of the Jersey—Hoggden Chief Justice, the other appointments not Yet Come to hand—P.S. You'l Communicate the matter Relative to Sullivan's Message, to Mͬ McKean.

107
From Thomas Rodney

Wilmington Septͬ 4th 1776

I came up from home yesterday with Mesͬͬ Killen & Baning to New Castle yesterday evening—but as we saw none of the whigs there (they being out of Town) we learnt nothing the proceedings of our T—y [Tory] Convention—Doctͬ Rigly is Gone home—Mͬ Baning and myself came to Wilmington this morning partly to git rid my self by [?], of the Jaundice & he of the fever & Ague—and partly to hear & see if any thing serious was done about a Privateer which Captͥ Pope wrote about but find that it was declined & nothing further is to be done in it. we shall leave here tomorrow for home again—I left all well at home except my little daughter who had the fever & ague very bad—We hear a thousand lies every day about the proceedings at York—every thing is said by the Tories to magnify the streng[t]h of the enemy and to lessen ours—and added to this that Gen. Sullivan is sent by How[e] to offer proper terms of reconciliation &ͨ I found Abraham Winkoop ful of this at Cantwell bridge jus recd: from Doctͬ R——y—&ͨ I have no news from below worth relating—But shall be glad to have a good acco[u]nt of matters at New York if you have time by Post—This comes by a Gentleman from Virginia with whom I dined & is sͩ to be Mͬ R. H. Lee member of Congress.[1]

108
From John Haslet

Camp at Kings-Bridge, Sept. 4th 1776

Not having it in my Power to write you one word worth your attention, I have troubled you but once. here are we on the Heights above Kings Bridge, exposed to wind, Weather & the Enemy, who appear to have it nearly as much in their Power to cut off our Communication as ever. Our Army has been once

1 The same Lee who introduced the resolution in Congress on June 7, 1776, for separation from England, which was passed on July 2, 1776.

already deranged—Immensity of Labor & Expence thrown away in fortifying L. Island at once abandoned, & N. York soon to be in the Same Situation. from the Superior Number of the British Troops, & the Advantages of their Fleet the City is Indefensible, (you know, Sir, I speak only my own opinions to those in whom I confide) their throwing men across any part of N.York Island, easily in their power some where to effect in one night, & diging up a slight Intrenchment, effectually, reduces the City, & all within their Line, to the Dire Necessity of fighting at vast Disadvantage, or Surrendering att Discretion Dreadfull Alternative! Had Long Island been rendered Useless to the Enemy, N.York laid in Ashes, when we were ordered to L. Island, & the Heights between this & Connecticut Properly Occupied, the Enemy must have attacked at disadvantage; or we at Liberty to fight when we pleased, & if Worsted wou'd have had it in our power to retire to the next Adjacent Hill, & obstinately disputed every Inch in their Progression. 'tis true this kind of Devastation may be condemned as Cruel, but Provinces e'er now have been sacrificed with applause to the Safety of a Kingdom, & what ought not to be done for the Safety of a Continent. The Gen! I revere,[1] his Character for Disinterestedness Patience & fortitude will be had in Everlasting Remembrances; but the Vast Burthen appears much too much his own. Beardless Youth, & Inexperience Regimentated are too much about him. the original scheme for the Disposition of the Army appears to have been on too narrow a scale, & every thing almost sacrificed, or Indangered for the Preservation of N.York & its Invirons, all which deserve from every Honest American [Political] D-nation. We have alarm upon alarm—Orders now issue, & the next moment reversed. W! to Heaven Gen! Lee were here is the Language of Officers & men. I had the honor to mention to you in my last, that the Delaware Battalion is in high Reputation. In Consequence of L! Sterlings Captivity, a new arrangement has been made of the Troops, all the Pensylvanians & Delawares are here in Gen! Mifflin's Brigade, who complimented me yesterday on the Behavior of our Troops. Shall thank you for a Line to him in our favor, when you write him next. Col! Smallwood wou'd also been with us, I'm told, but for a Dispute of Rank between him & me, & which when brought before the Gen! was decided in our favor—

To your Last you will before now have received a short & dry answer—how cou'd it be otherwise? Human patience cannot bear it—However from the Choice of N.Castle Mess! McKean & Reed [Read] will be continued most certainly & nobody to vie with you but D! Ridgely, whose Attachment to his Interest will certainly induce him to decline; if so, all is well, as we say in Camp

I request you to make my Compliment to the Barrister & Cap! Rodney I

1 General Washington.

condole with them mightily in their present State of Dejecting Dereliction, & beseech them to inform Mrs Haslet I am well—

We expect every moment Something Important here, & hope in our next to fight on more equal terms, & give you a more pleasing Account

109
To George Read

Philadelphia Sep^t 7th 1776

Since I wrote last three Letters directed to you have come to my hands. I imagine they are from New York and have sent them with this by the New-castle Stage—

In My last Letter I gave you the Substance of Sullivans Message, and What I then thought would be the Determination of Congress thereon. However the Matter (after three days debate) has in Some measure received a different determination; The Congress have refused sending any of their members to Confer as private Gentlemen, but with a view to satisfie some disturbed minds out of Door's, Rather than an Expectation of its bringing about Peace, They have appointed a Committee of Congress to repair to New York with powers to Confer with Lord Howe, to know the Extent of his powers, and the Terms he Shall propose—Gen! Sullivan was furnished With a Copy of this Resolution Certified, and Returned to Lord Howe Yesterday. You will See by this that if Lord Howe Receives the Committee thus sent, he Acknowledges the Congress, and of Course the Independency of the States, Which I am Convinced he will not do. Yet it may tend to Convince the people at large that we are desirous of peace Whenever it Can be had upon those principals—

There is no Material Change in affairs at New York—Except that a Great part of our Army are gone up to Kings-Bridge, among others the Delaware Battalion, and that Captain Wallace is gone up the East River with his Ship. She was fired on by the fort, but not much if any hurt. She proceeded up till She got to a place Called Blackwells Island and Anchored. Our people there with two twelve pounders Oblidge her to Slip her Cable and get behind the Island—

P.S. how goes on your Convention?

110
To Thomas Rodney

Philadelphia Sept! 11th 1776

I have no letter from you by this post, and indead but seldom have from whence I Conclude you have either verry little to say for your selves or become verry Idle. As to one M⸗ Killen (a former Acquaintance of mine) I have never heard but once of him since the late Storm which happened in your part of the Country.[1] That Blasted the Whig interest and laid prostrate many of the patriots; If he too be fallen tell him he nobly fell in defence of his Country's rights, and for his Comfort, Virtue it self hath it's days of Tryal—The Israelites (the Chosen people of God) met with Crosses and disappointments in their Journey from the Land [of] Bondage to that of Liberty, But by a steady perseverence and divine assistance they at length possessed the promised Land—So that That God, who Vieweth & Judgeth all Things with Unerring Wisdom, Seeing the Rightiousness of his Cause (Tho he permitteth Temporary Obstructions) will one day (with a firm Reliance on him) Crown his Virtuous Endeavours with Success and Cause the modern Pharoah's with their Hosts to be buried in the Sea of their Toryism, as he did the antient Pharoah in the Red Sea. The Bulk of the people have been lead astray from a Virtuous persuit by the Art and Cunning of Wicked and designing men among You. He must undeceive and put them again in the right path—They are naturally honest and mean well, but are weak and Credulous and by so much as wicked and designing men are more industrious than the Honest and Virtuous, are they lead to do that which is Evil and to leave undone that which they ought to Do.

I have Recd two Letters from our friend Col⸗ Haslet since the Engagement on Long-Island, the last is dated at the heights near Kings-Bridge where his Battalion and about 9000 others now are—he is Well and desires to be kindly Remembered to you and M⸗ Killen, who he terms the Barrister, and says "I Condole with them mightily in their present State of dejecting Dereliction"— It is a long letter in which he Concludes with saying "We Expect every moment something Important here, and hope in our next fight to be on more Equal terms, and to give you a more pleasing account.—It Seems Jack behaved Well and brought off his Colours like a Hero— . . .

From what I can learn of the Convention at Newcastle—They will attempt nothing but Barely the framing a plan of Government Except what may be necessary for the dispatching the flying Camp Battalion. M⸗ Read lets me know that matters go on Sloely, and that the members of Kent & Sussex grow uneasy to get home—This is (I know) as it used to be with them.

I suppose you have heard that General Sullivan has been with Congress on a Message from Lord Howe and as it has occationed Various reports suppose you wou'd be glad to know as of a Truith the Sum and Substance of it—It is this—That Lord Howe told General Sullivan in Conversation, that he and his

---

1 Rodney refers to the defeat of the Whig candidates in Kent County for delegates to the Constitutional Convention at New Castle.

brother the General had full power to Treat, That he had Stayed in England near two months after he was otherwise ready to come, for the purpose of Obtaining Such ample powers—That he Wished to Converse with General Washing[ton], or rather in preference to that, with the members of Congress on that head by which he thought Peace Interesting to both England and America might be had—but to bring about this Conference there was a difficulty—for that his Scituation was attended with that kind of delicacy he could not in the first instance acknowledge the Congress, and on the other hand he had no doubt they were in the like Scituation—Therefore desired That some of the members might meet him where they Chose, as private Gentlemen, and that he on his part would meet them as Such—That if they Should Agree on Terms of accommodation, that then the Congress must be acknowledged or the work Could not be Confirmed—Congress taking this matter into Consideration Think little or nothing is to be Expected from it—but thinking it might Create a division among the people, by the influence of the unfriendly to the Cause, thought it necesssary to take the matter up, and determine on it in such manner as might prevent the Scheme of his Lord-ship takeing Effect —Therefore the Congress in the first place determined that it was Contrary to both their power and opinion to send members to Confer as private Gentlemen—They then proceeded to appoint a Committee of Congress to go and Confer with Lord Howe on the Term of peace, who are to report to Congress —Now you will see by this method the Congress hold out to the people their willingness to put an End to the war, whenever it Can be done on principles of Liberty and Safety—and by this you will find that if Lord Howe will Treat with them (which none of the Congress Expect) it is acknowledgeing the Congress in their independent State, and if that is done the sooner the Better —I would just observe that this Stroke seems already to have baffled the Tories here—the Committee of three Set out the day before Yesterday. The proceedings of Congress Relative to these matters I believe will soon be published, till when let it remain with you, and your friends—

III

To John Haslet

Philadelphia Sep: 12th 1776—

I have been favoured with two Letters from you, one dated at New York, the other at Kings-Bridge, in both of which you desired I would Communicate to my friends Your Situation after the Engagement from Whom Miss:s Haslet might hear it—Imagining it might be a Considerable time before the news wou'd Get to her in that way, and that in the mean time She would be verry uneasy, therefore Wrote a Letter to her imediately on the Rect of your first in which I Let her know the whole affair and Sent it by a Safe hand—I am happy that I have it in my power to Congratulate you on the Bravery your Battalion has Shown in the late Action, and the great Honor the Officers and Men have Acquired by it—They are much Spoken of here and I have been often Complimented in behalf of the Government on their account—They deserve much of their Country, and (as an Individual) have my most hearty Thanks—I am Extreemly Sorry for poor Stuart, and the other brave Lads that fell, tho in the Bed of Honor—Must Confess I don't like your present Situation, Yet hope the best, The Justice of our Cause, and the bravery of our Troops may do Wonders.

In Your last Letter you seem to Show some uneasiness least there should be Some Change in the delegates, I believe you may be easy on that head, In the first place I imagine They would not venture to Risque the making Such an Uproar in the Government, as the turning me out probably wou'd make; and in the next the undesigning Patriotick part are determined to protest against their doing any thing but that of framing a plan of Government—In Mr. Reads last letter to me is the following paragraff "Our business has been delayed in Convention by the death of Mrs. Thompson, the sister of Mr. McKean, Who was burried this day, Mr McKean's Eldest Son lies dangerously ill at Mr. Thompson's house, and I know not when he can attend—A Committee of ten is Employed in the Drafting a declaration of Rights, The rest of the Members from Kent & Sussex are Gitting impatient, Doct. Ridgely is Returned Home Sick, Such is the Situation of matters—Here"—When Mr. Read went to Newcastle he prevailed on me to Stay in Congress, and that he would get the Convention to give a power to one Member to Act, so that our Government might be Represented by me alone till the Convention Should Rise—I mentioned this to Mr. McKean who directly declared they Should make no appointment of Delegates, nor even alter the powers Given them, least they (meaning the Convention) Should plead that as a president [precedent] for going into some other appointments—Which they were not Authorised to do by their Choice—Therefore Upon the Whole I don't imagine they will Attempt any Change—But sir whether they do or not, I do not purpose Continuing here longer than till the other Gentlemen Return; I have made a verry Great Sacrefise of my property to the Cause, Government never paid me above half what I have necessarily Expended even When my friends were at the Helm—What may I Expect from these? They would see me Serve without a Shilling, You know they wou'd, because you know they like not either me or the Cause—General Dagworthy, Mr. Clowes and Mr Peery were here, and Say the Tory plan for leaveing me out of the Convention was, first to put me at the head of their Ticket to Show their approbation of me, after which they put another person in my Stead, and assigned as a Reason for it, That it was now a Critical time, That it was absolutely Necessary We Should keep up our Representation in the Congress, That they wished I might not be laid under the necessaty of leaving the Congress at a time so Interesting, Which I must Do if Chose in Convention &c—These Gentlemen then said that the Inhabitants of Newcastle County had not Considered to the Matter in that light, for they had Chose both their delegates.[1] In Answer to this; it was said, they, the people of Newcastle had done verry Wrong &c. By Such little Cunning are the people to be Cajoled—I Saw a Man from Mispillion Who left there a day or two before my letter Could have reached it, Who told me that yours and Captain Adams's families were well, but they were in Much distress for the Delawares who (from all accots they had Received) were at least two thirds Cut off—That almost all the Officers were killed particularly you. He told me the people were Generally distressed, haveing most of them some friend or Relation in the Battalion—My letter I am sure has set that Matter Right.

I wrote above a Week ago to Mr Montgomery the Chaplain, not knowing then whether you was among the Dead or living Should be Glad to know whether the letter got Safe hand—be pleased to Enquire of him an let me know in your next which I hope will be soon—

112
To George Read

Philadelphia, September 13th, 1776.

The whole of your time must certainly be engaged in the affairs of the Convention or I should have heard from you more frequently. I have wrote you three letters since you went to New Castle, but whether you have received more than one of them I cannot say. However, this letter is a proof I am not discouraged as yet.

The people here have been for several days fully employed in forming conjectures with respect to the conference between the commissioners of Congress and Lord Howe.[2] They have been various: some, Lord Howe has full powers, and if we have not peace it is the fault of Congress; others, there is

1 George Read and Thomas McKean, though members of Congress, had been elected delegates to the State Constitutional Convention by the New Castle County voters.

2 The Congressional Commissioners were Benjamin Franklin, John Adams, and Edward Rutledge.

no doubt but they will finally settle matters, and the army be disbanded; others again are cursed if they believe he has any powers at all. However, this business is put an end to by the return of the committee, who report that having sent a letter to Lord Howe, by express, to acquaint him of their coming, they proceeded to Amboy, where they arrived on Tuesday evening, and there the same evening received a letter from Lord Howe in answer to theirs, letting them know that he would meet them, on Wednesday, at a house on Staten Island, opposite Amboy, that his lordship the next day sent his boat for them, with a flag, and met them himself at the water-side, and in a very polite manner conducted them up to the house, where he had a dinner and plenty of good wine for them, and that after dinner they had a conference, which, with the time they were dining, was about three hours. Upon the whole, it seems his lordship has no power to make a peace, or even to order a cessation of arms; that he had a power to confer with any person or persons whatsoever to hear what they had to offer, and report to his Majesty, but that previous to anything else we must return to and acknowledge obedience to his Majesty. This being done, he did not doubt, on his representing matters home, but that the several acts of Parliament and instructions might and would be revised and many of our grievances removed. The whole proceedings of the committee, Sullivan's message, and everything relating to it, will be published on Monday or Tuesday.

One Mr. Duff, a young man, called on me for a commission as a doctor's assistant in our battalion of the 'flying camp.' Should be glad you would let me know immediately when and how he was appointed, and whether he ought to have a commission. They are to march on Tuesday, if possible, and if there be propriety in giving him a commission I could wish he had it, as it would be of great service in case of his being a prisoner.

We have letters dated in July last, from our Connecticut friend in Paris. There's a change of ministry in France; and he is the greatest man in the world except Lord North, and has as great a levee as he has. This is a secret.

113

From Thomas Rodney

Dover Sep.r 14th 1776—

I recd a letter by last Post from you. I wrote you one by Liut.t Thomas Parke some time ago—my last was from Wilmington by M.r R. H. Lee from Virginia —Shall in future Number my letters that you may know whether you receive them or not—But have so little to inform you of that I am hardly able to compose a letter Just now—I was informed By letter from Collins last Sunday that Congress had required three Battalions of Malitia from this State to go to York &c He sent for a State of the Publick arms & the private Arms in my Company—which I sent him—it seems the Convention is not like to grant the requisition on pretence that there is not arms—I am pursuaded there is a thousand Arms in this County fit for use saving Bayonets—

Brown informs me that small vessels are much wanted Philad?—Stockly says he was Offered £350 for his; My sloop worth a great deal more than his, & if what he says be true perhaps she may sell for £400—She Carries about 1200 bu? is 2 years old, very sound & well found, sails & Riging all good—If you should hear any enquiry for such a one, please to sell her & I will send her up immediately—At any rate shall send her up soon to sell her as she is of little use at present . . .

114
From George Read

NCastle ye Sept ye 17th 1776

I admit your censure for not keeping up that correspondence which you were justly intitled to from me but it really proceeded from a desire I had to give you some satisfactory accot of the business we have been more particularly engaged in to wit ye Declaration of Rights and the plan of Governmt—as to the first it has been completed some days past but there being nothing particular in it—I did not think it an object of much curiosity, it is made out of ye Pensilyania & Maryland Draughts—A Committee appointed for preparing ye Plan of Govt, had drawn up one, but it has undergone such daily amendmts yt it cou'd have been little satisfactory to have known ye 1st State of it—The Genl heads of it at present are that ye Legislature is to consist of 2 branches—A Council & Assembly, The 1st of 9 members 3 for each County—ye lowest in Vote to go out after ye 1st Year & so of ye rest—but may be rechosen—ye 2d branch of 7 members chosen annually[1]—A President to be chosen by joint ballot of both houses for 3 Yrs and ineligible for ye 3 next years to have ye Executive powers of Govt & in Case of death &c. ye speaker of ye Council to act in his stead—to Embody ye militia with ye Consent of ye Council & then have ye Sole Command—Delegates to Congress to be chosen by joint ballot of both Houses—3 Judges of ye Supr Cot to be chosen by Presidt & 2 Houses by joint ballot during good behaviour & hold no other office—Judge of admiralty to be chosen by the same—4 or 5 Justices of ye Comon Pleas & Orphs Cot to be

---

1 That is, seven from each county.

chosen by Presid! & Council during good behaviour & excluded from other office—Secretary Att.ny Gen! Register for Probates of Wills y.e Register in Chancery—Clks of Comon Pleas, Orph! Co!s & of y.e Peace by y.e Presid! & Council for 7. years if of good behaviour—House of Assembly to nominate 24 persons for Justices of y.e Peace whereof Presid! & Council to appoint 12 during Pleasure—y.e members of Council to be Justices of y.e Peace thro' y.e whole state—Just. of Common Pleas Conservators thereof in their Counties—Co! of Chancery as heretofore 'till future Provision of y.e Legislature—Shffs & Coroners as formerly—President to appoint one of ye 2 Candidates—Co! of Appeal to Consist of President for time being & 6 others during good behaviour 3 of which to be named by each house—Clk of Sup.e Co! to be Appointed by Ch: Justice & recorder of Deeds by Justices of Comon Pleas for 7 years good behaviour—Persons *ineligible* to either House of Gen! Assembly, Justices of Supreme & Comon Pleas Co!s Secretary, Trustees of Loan offices & Prothonotaries, officers of Army & Navy of y.e united States—officers of Army & Navy of this State & all other officers before ment.d accepting such offices to Vacate their Seats & new Election ordered—Gen! Assembly to appoint officers of Army & Navy—Members of y.e Legislature or person in office to Swear or Affirm Allegiance to y.e State & a submission to its Constitution & its Laws—No Importation of Slaves from Affrica & none to be bro! into y.e State from Elsewhere for Sale—General Elections at time & place as heretofore except as to y.e first one not fixed as to time as yet—these are y.e principal heads of which the Members who are now all around me are trans[c]ribing for report & discussion—there is as yet great appearance of harmony I hope it will Continue—I do not discover any thing that ought or probably will interrupt it except y.e common one of hurrying to get home—as to y.e Surgeon's mate M.r Duff it was y.e opinion of y.e Gentlemen composing y.e Convention that y.e Surgeon shou'd have y.e appointm! of him so that he may be commissioned—You have a Letter for Co! Patterson which I opened—We have heard nothing since of Mitchell or his Comp.a—I shall write to Co! Patterson y.e 1.st leisure moment—excuse me to him Cap! Dunn will hear from me also—he has taken up an opinion y! y.e Independent Company commanded by Cap! Latimer ought not to take y.e first rank in y.e battalion—tho y.e last are y.e regular Troops of this State y.e other the Militia—I must brake off Cap! Latimer's messenger is impatiently waiting—

P.S. as I have forgot to mention a word of business which occasioned the begin.g of this Lre until I had finished I hope you will not commit y.e like mistake —Cap! Latimer has Co! Collins's Draught on you for £500 which you must procure for him immediately without excuse if so much private or publick monies in y.e hands of Whig or Tory in Philad.a. City—

To Thomas Rodney

Philadelphia Sep: the 17th 1776

Knowing that Small Veshells were in great demand here at present, and knowing also That the Sloop Could not be so interesting to keep as to sell at such a time, had determined to write you (previous to the Rect: of Your Letter) to send her up here imediately for the purpose of haveing her Sold— Am Glad to find you are in the Same mind with me and therefore that you would not delay a Single moment in Sending her after the Rect of this, because it is uncertain how long this demand will Continue, however am Convinced from the reason of the things Ariseing from Certain Circumstances, the demand cannot hold Long—John Bell has Sold both his for more than a hundred pounds more than he Ever thought of Asking—in short more than they Cost him at first—Therefore don't neglect to Send her imediately— . . .

Our Committee have returned, have seen and Conversed with Lord Howe, have found out that he had no more or other powers than at first Contained in his declaration—This Jaunt was only to prove what they knew before, purely for the Satisfaction of the Tories—Shall forward John's letter to Kings-Bridge —No news from Camp that is important but Expect some Every moment— What will you Do now for want of a Post rider?

To George Read and Thomas McKean

Philadelphia Sep: 18th 1776

I have sent my Servant to you with the following disagreable inteligence; By Letters from General Washington to Congress, we are informed, That General Howe with About 6 or 7 thousand of his Troops took possession of New York on Sunday last. We are not so Much Astonished That he Should get possession of New York (because we have Expected it for Some time past) as at the Scandelous behaviour of our Troops that were placed to defend the post Where the enemy Landed, Who run away from their lines & breastwork, in a most dastardly manner when not more than Sixty were Landed to oppose them—You must know That the Main Body of the Enemy have been for time past placed on the long-Island side opposite the mouth of Harlem Creek or River, and had Erected Several Batteries there, That played on ours at Hornshook on the New York Island Side of the Harlem; a part of this main Body of the Enemy had also taken possession of Montisure's [Montresor's] Island situate at the mouth of Harlem and is divided from Morriseny [Morrisania] on the East Side of Harlem, and Harlem point on the West Side, by a Water not so Wide as Schuylkill ferry—at one or both of these places it was and is Expected they would attempt a Landing—General Whashington therefore fixed his Head Quarters on the Heights of Harlem (as they are Called) on the York Island Side of the Creek, and posted Generals Miflin with his Brigade consisting of Shee's, Magaw's, Haslets and Some other Battalions, On the heights of Morriseny—He had also placed on the Heights near Kings-Bridge five or Six thousand to Support either the main army or Mifflins detachment as the Case might Require—The General finding that two forty Gun Ships, two Frigates and one twenty, had Come up the East River, and Come to an Anchor opposite Turtle Bay, which is four Miles above the City, and three miles or thereabout below head Quarters, placed Brigadeer General Parsons with his Brigade and Some Connecticut Militia in the Whole near three Thousand there, to defend that post, at least till they Could be Supported by the Main Body or a detachment from it—General Putnam With about Three Thousand Were left in the City to defend it in the best manner he Could till the Stores Should all be Removed in Which had been Employ[ed] for Several days before—and Would have Compleated in one more.

From all I Can collect This was the Scituation of Affairs on Sunday morning. When the Ships before mentioned began a verry heavy Fireing at Turtle-Bay, to Scour the Country previous to their landing the troops, but hurt no Body that I Can hear of—When the Fireing ceased their Troops began to Land and ours to Run as if the Devil was in them in Spite of all the Gene! Could do. They never fired one Gun—General Whashington haveing discovered their intention to Land at that place, and haveing properly disposed of his troops in case of an Attempt in either or both the other places, ordered a Reinforcement and set out there himself. However before he Got to the place, met our people runing in Every direction. He Endeavoured by persuasion, Threats &c to get them back, but all to no purpose, in Short they Run till they left the General to Shift for himself—General Putnam Who was in New-York with his people, hearing What had happened made the best of his Way for head Quarters least he Should be kooped up—, fought his way Through the Enemy's lines, brought his men to Camp With ye Loss of only three or four as said—It Seems not one of the men who Run from the place of the Enemy's landing Was from this Side the North River—all New-England men —General Washington Writes he is advantageously scituated at present, and if attacked Should be more than a match for the Enemy if their numbers were even More than they are provided his Men would fight, which is more to be Wished than Expected—I have Wrote on this Subject till I am in an Ill

Humour and My only Compfort is that by the time you have read it You'l be
as Angry as I am—

I have inclosed M⟨r⟩ McKean's order on the Trustees of Newcastle thinking
it might be Wanting—

117
From Thomas McKean

Newcastle Septemr. 19th 1776

Your favor of the 10th instant was delivered to Mr. Read by your boy, and
the order in my favor I received. The news gave infinite concern to some of
the Convention, but I cannot describe the effect it had on some others. Poor
General Washington, how I feel for him—Oh the Poltroons, that run away,
three thousand from sixty—The glory of the American arms is stained and
the cause, in my opinion, will suffer greatly by it—However I am determined
to die hard.—Great is the struggle, but God will yet support us.—

You must ere this have heard sufficient to appologize for my not writing to
you agreeable to promise—The death of a sister, and an expectation for a fortnight of the death of an eldest son, with many other untoward circumstances
will (I flatter myself) excuse me with you.

The Convention have agreed on a declaration of rights & fundamental rules
for this State; they have also agreed to all the articles of the new Constitution
(which consists of thirty) except the three last, in reading one of which after
nine o'clock last night we got into great heats. Indeed their making the President of the new Government, who, by my draught, approved of by the Committee, was a discreet, modest & respectable Magistrate and useful member of
Society, is now a very powerful & dangerous Man; you would have sworn he
was named, and a prodigious favorite; together with their fixing the new
Election on the 21st day of October next (tho' Mr. Basset moved for it to be on
the first day of October and was seconded by Doct Ridgely) had displeased me,
and some others who had no private selfish views, very much. All the arguments drawn from Colonel Hazlet & Patterson, with their two Battalions,
being absent, and thereby, tho' exposing their lives for their country, loosing
the chance of any compliments or distinction from it, or opportunity to serve
it, for seven years to come, in the civil department, had no effect; I might as
well have harangued the walls—The matter had been settled out of doors,
and the new elections, and the loaves and fishes, were to be secured at all
events. I can almost name you every officer in the new Government, and will
venture it when I see you. I say, all these things had greatly displeased me,

when Mr. Basset moved, that the new General Assembly should meet on the 20th of October at Dover, and was immediately seconded by Doctor Ridgely —This was to please the poor Gals of Kent, and to increase their popularity in that county before the grand election. I answered the Gentlemen, that the Seats of Justice in each county, and the seat of Government for the colony, were fixed by acts of Assembly, and that we might as well remove the one as the other, and indeed repeal any other law or make any new one we thought proper—that we were not vested with the legislative power, being expressly chosen for the purpose of "ordaining and declaring the future form of government for this State," which being a special purpose excluded an Idea of any other being delegated, as no other was mentioned—that the Sovereign power of the state resided in the people collectively, and they had delegated a certain portion of it to us, which if we exceeded we were usurpers & tyrants—However the matter had been determined out of doors as usual, and no reply was made (for truly none could be made) but the question was called for, tho' Colo. Cantwell and Messrs. Porter & Lea of this county were absent, two of whom had gone home after night and were to return this morning. Mr. Evans moved, as it was late and many members absent, that the question might be postponed 'till the morning; this was refused; upon which I moved the previous question which was put & carried agst me 14 to 11 all the members for Kent & Sussex (except Messrs Moore, Wiltbank and Kollock) voted for it. Upon this I told the President that I could not with honor, nor in conscience, sit any longer in such an Assembly, and took my hat and withdrew, being followed by Van-Dike, Jones, Robinson &c. but before Mr. Thompson and Mr. Evans came away, the other Gentlemen moved to adjourn, which was done whilst there were twenty (including the Presid.) which was just a quorum, in the House.—

What will be done next, I can't say, but am ready for anything. Your Kent members had determined to choose new Delegates, Council of Safety, and in short to do anything & everything, as I have been informed; Doctor Ridgely was to be in your place, this is a fact; but I think it will not do, and I suppose the stealing an election in October may postpone any alterations until then.—

As I write this scrawl, while facts are recent & fresh in my memory, please to preserve it until I see you, which will be in a day or two.—

118

From Thomas Rodney

Dover Sept: 19th 1776—

Under Care of M: Tho: Wilds & Tho: Kirkly is sent from here Zackry Bailey of Capt: Caldwells Company Dalawares, & Elias Flowers, John Mer-

rick, Levin Lecat, & Williams Evans of Woodgate Company Flying Camp—
W<u>m</u> Ho[r]sey is Sick & will be sent by my Vessel—Please to direct these men
what they must do with the deserters Afs<u>d</u>—My Vessels will be up soon as
possible, and if you have no objections, the Schooner too may be sold as I can
git another built against the Spring here if necessary as these men are in a
Hurry I can say no more at Present

119

To Thomas Rodney

Philad<u>a</u> Sep<u>r</u> 22d 1776

I am glad you are Sending the Sloop up to Sell, and hope you'l not delay
doing it least some of the men of War now at New York Should be thought
no longer necessary there, and be sent to our Capes, A Circumstance of this
Sort would inevitably knock up the Sale of all kind of Veshells, for it is the
Trade they are now pushing that keeps up the demand for them, and the men
of War Comeing to the Cape would put an Emd [end] to that Trade—Superfine Flower is now at 18/ Shillings and Rising as brown Tells me—Tho' when
I Sold Could Get no more than 13/6—it is what they Call light packed or
seven Quarter that brings this price—I should have no objection to Your Send-
ing the Schooner also—But am Doubtfull Shee is too Flat and therefore would
not answer the purpose of foreign trade and of Course not sell well—If the
Sloop is not Come away before you Get this Letter, would advise you to get
John Bell to Come in her. He has been dealing in that way and would be of
Great [use] to me in Selling her here—But if Shee is Come away and You
Should Conclude to Send the Schooner pray Get him to Come in her—I had
some Convention [conversation] with Bell while in Town, and he promised
to Call on You Concerning the Sale of them—I don't know what you do for
News now since your Post has fell Through—I have Recd no Letter from
Conolel Haslet for eight or ten days past, But Received one from a worthy
Gentleman of my Acquaintance dated the 16th Instant, Wherein he says—
"Yesterday a most Inglorious day! The British Troops Landed on New York
Island, from Long Island, at a place Called Turtle Bay about five miles above
New York City, when the Appearance of only a few of them made two or
three Regiments of Americans Retreat—Retreat did I say, it ought to be *Run
away* notwithstanding all the Solicitations, prayers and I might Say Tears of
General Washington—These were not Southern Troops—Our people had a
few Hours before, Evacuated New York. The Enemy then Took possession of
it, and all the Lower End of the Island—A line was immediately Thrown up,

about eight miles from New York Across from East to North River, the Enemy possessing the West and We the East part up to Kings-Bridge, and the Pensylvanians and Delaware Encampment is on the East side of the Bridge, under the Command of General Mifflin—This far for Bad news—This morning I was Spectator to a most Glorious Scene—The Enemy advanced to an Eminence, about a mile from our Lines. The Maryland and Virginia Troops were Ordered by General Washington to disposses them, and with undaunted Bravery they Marched up, when a Smart Engagement Ensued, Fresh Troops were Poured in upon both Sides, The Contest Obstinate and Long—Finely our Heroes Forced them From three different Grounds, at which they Retreated leaveing behind Them Three Field-peices, and many Slain; In the number of our Killed, which does not amount to ten, We Count Some officers of distinction, Particularly one Colonel Knoulton of Connecticut Who Commanded and who had Infinitely more than Roman Bravery. As I was there only Accidentally and came away as soon as the action was over Can't give you particulars—The Delaware Battalion were not Engaged—Col! Haslet has been for some time and Still is Unwell. Some of the other officers have Laboured under what the New England men Call the *Camp Difficulty,* but are Getting Better.—"

Our people are not yet Returnd from Newcastle. I shall Come home in a Short time after their Return whether appointed a Delegate or not—in short Shall stay no longer than these Veshells if they Come up may detain me—

120

From Thomas Rodney

Dover Sept! 22ᵈ 1776—

I have Sent by Brown, under the Care of Simon Bullen, North and Dawson —Sixteen deserters; 14 of whom say that they belong to Capt! Watkins Independant Company from Maryland and the other two to Capt! Woodgates from Sussex—the former Complain & say that they deserted on Acc! of the Severity & Ill usage from their Capt!—The Latter say that all their officers declared they would lay down their Com? & that they would not go to the Camp—Our people are now in pursute of sixteen more who passed by here last night & the night before—It appears to me that there must be some unaccountable missmanagement in the officers, that occations so many deserters; & I am Surprized, that such bodies of them should git this distance without being Taken up—Would it not be prudent for Congress to Station proper officers at all the ferries to Examine & prevent deserters passing?—And to publish a general reward for every deserter that shall be taken up and Carried to Camp or Philad?—For those people who are likelyest to take them up not knowing whether they shall git any thing for it or not, let them pass without examination. I fear if Congress does not find some remidy for this growing disorder that their Troops will be much thined—12 of these now returned have their Muskets on their Shoulders & Many of them their knapsacks and Catooch boxes, yet say they passed the ferries of Schook-Killn [Schuylkill] and Christiana; came through the Town of New Castle and were exam⁴ by some of the members of Our Convention, and were not Stoped.

It is necessary that the persons concerned in taking and carrying these deserters up should be paid for their Trouble & expences—

N.B. I expect the sloop from Egg-Harbour every day & shall send her up immediately—I wrote in my last to sell the schooner too if you choose & can git a good price—Brown has no Objection; & he has not p⁴ any thing towards her yet—If it will be any advantage you may purchase his part before you sell

121

From Thomas Rodney

Dover Sept! 23ᵈ 1776

I wrote of yesterday by the schooner on board of which is 16 deserters—This will come by the Hands of Fardinand Carson (brother to John) who has undertaken to ride as post in the room of Parke—he is the best that we can git I cannot say that I know much of him as he has not been long in this place; However he has rode post some time into Maryland and M! Baning says he is very Sober & he believes very Honest; & he also offers good Security for the performance of this trust, and as he is a young fellow & has nothing else to do I am apt to think he may do very well; at least better than any other person that we can git at present—I believe I shall be safe with my debtor, Parke; but it appears by Lockermans book that his Diposition is wide of the Truth; for it appears there that the settlement they made is of their other acc!ˢ & not the rent—& as that settlement is on the same day Parke mentions, this Circumstance is against him.

As game is very Plenty about the plantations I have sent by Simon for 2ʷ of Powder & 8ʷ of Shot, and shall be glad if you know—that you may advise him where he may git—

We had a report this week that the British Army Stormed or attempted Our lines on Tuesday last, whereby they lost 3000, slain & 2000, Taken prisoners but I fear this news is rather good tha[n] true:—That we lost 1000, with Gen!

Putnam slaın &ᷝ—A Copy of your letter To McKean & Read was brought down here by Doctᵣ R. and from thence a general resentment raised against the new England Troops—the bad conduct of a few is applyed to the whole &ᐧ prejudices of this sort are not easily erased, & nothing could please Tories better than a Circumstance of that sort, as they lay hold of every pretext to abuse that people—everything that raises popular resentments which tend to divisions among ourselves pleases them, because they know that is the only thing that can promote the interest with effect which they wish to succeed— The Greatest men sometimes do weak & foolish things and Currage is not always the same; Viterans in many instances in History have acted like errant Cowards—Currage & Cowardice are often Governed by attendant Circum-stances—Edward & Henry but the days before the Battles of Agin Court & Poictiers would have surrender'd up all the Laurels they had won in so many Glorious Campains, for the bare permission of Marching out of France un-molested—This being denied, dispair accomplished for them what currage never thought of—I cannot be the least discurraged in a cause like ours for the misconduct or even the actual cowardice of a few Troops; but I look with more regret on the resentment & distrust that may arise among the colonies on such accᵗ—In a Contest so universal we must expect to meet with many difficulties & miscariges—But these instead of discurraging should Stimulate us with a more Active Vigilence in surmounting them all—These are Senti-ments unecessary to impose on those who already feel the same; but I don't know whether I have not run on thus, for want of some thing else to say—We have nothing new here political or entertaining. We are all pretty well at present except Livinia who is still very poorly, but is somthing better—Mᵣ Killen is very Ill wᵗʰ the Boilious fever, tho not dangerous, yet he [is] so frightened that he has not the Spirit of a mouse—It never was more sickly here tho few have died—

122

From Thomas Rodney

Dover Septᵣ 24th 1776

Mᵣ Collins informs me to day that the Convention has appointed James Sykes Esqᵉ To Sign the £4500, now in your Office and requested that I would let him have it—I informed him that I had given you the Key when last at New Castle, and he desired me to inform you of this—but do not know how will send the key unless you receive this before Simon leaves Town as I appre-hend you would not Chuse to trust it with anny other person—I tolld Collins of the dificulty of gitting it down, & he seemd to apprehend that as Read &

McKean would both be in Congress soon that you w.d come home—However if this Should not be the Case, I have some expectations of being up the first or Midle of Next Week as the sloop is now in the Creek & will go of immediately to Philad.a it will occation my going up as I have money to pay there & shall Chuse if the Vesels are Sold to Apply at least a part thereof to that purpose—

This will Come by Capt.n Gordon who is bound with M. McCall & J. Carson to the Camp—as he has no acquaintance there or that way but among the Dalawares it is likely he may stand in need of some pass or letters—but probably he may be too modest to ask this, and may therefore Suffer inconveniences at least unless you should think to give such as you may think necessary.—

The Convention it seems has order'd the raising of 400 men & have appoint.d West Col: Latimer L. Col: & Ben: Caton Major & left the other officers to be such as will offer, or be afterwards appointed by the Council—The field officers are such together with the plan that I belive they will hardly git a Battalion—I am pursuaded (as I have heard many already refuse) that among those who are fittest for it hardly an officer will accept under this mode tho they unanimusly expected (& were willing) to go when they heard of the requ[i]sition of Congress for the Malitia to be sent as Malitia—and even now an independant Company of 100 men might be raised in ten days; if they Could be admitted as such into pay—

123

To Thomas Rodney

Philadelphia, September 25, 1776

That the New-England men placed to defend the landing-place, behaved in a most dastardly, cowardly, scandalous manner, is most certain; but that courage is not always to be found the same, even in the same person, is equally true, and verified in the very same men; for some of them the day following were in the other engagement, and behaved with great bravery, as did the whole body engaged. You have some account of the skirmish in the papers; therefore I shall refer you to them and a letter I wrote by Wilds and Bickley. I saw Carson, but not till this morning, when he told me that some person by the name of Jones, from Mifflin's Cross-Roads, had set out from below since he did, and having got here before him, with subscription papers signed by some people below, went to the several printing offices before he did and engaged the packets to carry down as a post in the place of Parke. After I saw Bradford the last, and telling him what accounts I had from below, and what Carson himself had said, they said they would let Carson have the papers for

the gentlemen of Dover and elsewhere, except those who subscribed to the
other. I suppose the subscribers will settle the matter between them when they
go down. I doubt whether you will get any powder and shot. The schooner is
not arrived as I know of; and you have made no mention of the sloop, but sent
the schooner before you heard what my opinion was about selling her. I wrote
you concerning them both by the Bickley. My pen is confounded bad, and I
am too blind to mend it, and Captain Papley, who mends and makes them
for me, is gone out; therefore must bid you farewell.
P.S. The Convention is dissolved; made a plan of Government it seems, and
ordered an election at a short day. Quere: Do their late opponents intend
calmly to submit, or try again to rally? I am sorry for Mr. Killon's illness.

124

From Samuel Patterson[1]

Head Quarters Amboy Septr. 27th 1776

Agreeable to promise to write you, now in part have set down, haveing this
oppurtunity by way of a Journaliseing—

I arrivd. here last monday morning with 6 Comps. my battalion. General
Mercer here, and General Dickinson. Both have been Exceeding polite to me
since here, and admire our Battalion much. This has added much to my
Pride., also the General has Chosen our light Infantry for his body Guard—

The Evening before last I was officer of the day about sun down a Boat of
Hessians came over to our Shore, opposite a large marsh above the mill Guard
and Stuck Stakes there with a number Bills which was taken down, enclosd.
is a Coppy of each Sort the general had the rest deliverd him.

This morning a flag was sent over to the Island with Capt. Hambleton and
a Lady Mrs McMontys Daughter and Child opposite my door. They ordered
them not to come near, which our people not beating the parley by Drum so
soon they Hessians were near firing on our flag for want. They sent a boat of,
would not let ours land—Since I have been here they have been fortifying
opposite to us by Batteries and small lines all maskd. with Bushes as also the
same done to their Tents which were open here when I came. It is the oppinion here the are affraid of us. I hope we shall make them so on Tryall.—The
Battal. is kept busy on duty about 50 sick owing principally to the water, but

---

1 Colonel Samuel Patterson, a miller from Christiana Bridge, commanded a battalion of Delaware militia which was quickly organized at the request of Congress to serve until December 1,
together with forces from Pennsylvania and New Jersey, in the so-called "Flying-Camp" for the
purpose of protecting Philadelphia and the Delaware River valley region in general from invasion
during the time Washington's army was engaged on the Hudson.

are somewhat mending. I sepose about 4000 men here. I am happy in my Situation and hopes to Continue here if I can. Fine Quarters and Great plenty oysters Fish &c. No ladies to be seen, God help us. I hope for better Times Soon please to let Mr. Read know I am well and any part of this. and for Gods sake dont let the people choose the officers in Coln. Wests Batt. if so a poor figure.

125

To Thomas Rodney

Philadelphia, October 2, 1776.

I received your letter yesterday about three o'clock in the afternoon, by post. Lake, who set out from the creek's mouth on Monday morning arrived here yesterday afternoon about one o'clock; but did not call on me until the evening. However, this could be no fault of his, unless it had pleased God to have endowed him more understanding, for I really believe (as he says) that he had been hunting from the minute he came, and could not find me or the house where I lodged. If he had been lucky enough to have blundered on the house he would have found me, as I happened to be at home all that afternoon. This turned out to be the case at last; for stalking along the street he saw Monsieur standing in my door, which relieved him. I shall sell the vessel as soon, and as for as good a price, as possible. Mr. Read is not yet come up. However, I shall set out for Kent on Saturday or Sunday at farthest, whether he comes or not. Yesterday I received a letter from Doctor Tilton. The officers are in pretty good health, except Colonel Haslett, who has been unwell with the flux for a considerable time past, but getting better. One paragraph in the old man's letter is very full of the great honour obtained by the Delaware battalion, in the affair at Long-Island, from the unparalleled bravery they showed in view of all the Generals and troops within the lines, who alternately praised and pitied them. By General Howe's return of the prisoners to Congress, Lieutenant Stewart and Lieutenant Harvey are both alive and well.

General Mifflin came to town the day before yesterday. He brought letters from General Washington informing Congress that Mr. Moylan, the Quartermaster-General, had resigned his commission, as unable to conduct the business of so many troops. That in consequence thereof, the General says he had prevailed on General Mifflin to accept, confident that there was not another man in the army who could carry on the business upon the present large plan. Under these circumstances, Mifflin has with reluctance accepted. General Mifflin says our army is numerous; mending fast as to their sickness; in high spirits; well fortified, and wish for nothing more than a general engagement. There is seldom a day but some prize or some French trading vessel comes into this port—some days two or three. . . .

126

From John Haslet

Camp near Mount Washington 5th Oct.ʳ 1776

Your favor 12th Sept.ʳ is now before me, for which you have my most hearty thanks. Your attention to M.ʳˢ Haslets Peace of mind, & Industry to preserve it, are infinitely obliging. Your Congratulations in behalf of the Regiment are thankfully rec.ᵈ & I have the pleasure to assure you are seconded by the whole Army here. Our Continual Movment from place to place, with constant Fatigue prevented my writing you the first month as oft as my inclination prompted; & since have been nearly a month confined by the Dysentery, from our Exposure on Long Island to cold & damp Lying on the Ground, have been so emaciated & exhausted as almost to bid Farewell to every thing, just begin to recover.

I did feel some uneasiness with respect to a Change of the Delegates at first, but on Second thought pronounced it groundless—but find it recur on your proposing to retire & quit your Station. I acknowledge the Justice of your Reasoning, & the Ingratitude of the people, as well as the Malignity of their present leaders; the Venal Sycophantic Race do not deserve the Consideration of Men of Wisdom & Virtue for anything in themselves—I know, you have already sacrificed a large share of Private Property to the Evil & unthankfull, in this you resemble the Supreme manager, who makes his Sun to Shine on the Evil & the Good—& bad as times are, you have a few freinds still of the Latter Character. And my Dear Sir, who can better afford it, Providence has blessed you with a fortune to your prudence Inexhaustible, by which you are enabled to live where you please, & to keep the first Company where you do live, & all this with few Drawbacks upon it. how then can you lay out a part of it to more Noble purposes, than in Serving your Country, guarding her Rights & Priviledges & forcing Wretches to be happy, even ag.ˢᵗ their Will. In this you will act as Vicegerent of the Soverign Goodness, & cooperate with Heaven to save a Wretched Race; & tho' you may not effect the Righteous purpose, the Testimony of an Approving Conscience, the Applause of Conscious Virtue, & the approbation of all Good Beings, will more than Ballance the Sacrifice—a 1000 things might be urged to the same purpose, but a Word to the Wise

I'm not all surprized at the Tory Strategem to leave you out of the Convention Ticket, 'tis like the Rest of their doings, Dark Low, dirty, illiberal. What a Wretched struggle must they have had in Convention their Consciences drawing one Way, & the influence of Congress another. I'm told they have done as little as possible, & modelled their new government as like the old as maybe. Dr Ridgely going home sick, is only the Old Stale Trick over again. I'm told their influence in N.Castle is much on the Decline, & an Entire Revolution in favor of Whigs expected next Election; wou'd to Heaven Kent wou'd open her Eyes, & go & do likewise—

As to Military matters, have little to write; On the Brave Ld Stirlings being made a Prisoner, We, with the Pensylvanians, went into Gen! Mifflins Brigade, & encamp on the Lines by the Gen!^s House—you will have heard before this can reach you, of the Skirmish on the 16th ult. in which the Enemy were repulsed with spirit, & fled with so much precipitation, as to leave three fine field peic[e]s behind them, (We lost but five on L.Island), Loss on our side a Brave Col Knoulton, a Capt. & 4 or 5 privates, about 30 wounded—a few Days ago a foraging Party 2000 strong under Gen! Putnam advanced with 100 Waggons to forrage on Harlemplains in the Intermediate Space between their Lines & ours, & brought off their waggons loaded with Wheat unmolested—the Enemy at first struk their tents expecting an Attack but seeing our Intention, looked quietly on. Putnam had much mind to salute them, but a Peremptory Order from Gen! Washington commanded the Party back with the Forrage—You see, they have so great appetite for fighting. Our lines from the East to the North River with Harlem River in the Rear, are now so strong, that 'tis thought they will not attempt them if they attack at all, 'tis expected farther up the East River at Morrisania, to get between us & the Country, or on the Jersey Side—Many think they have reached their Ne plus ultra for this Campaign—

Col. Moylan thinking himself unequal to the Task of Q. Master Genl has resigned. Gen! Mifflin appointed to that office protempore Col. Shee has [?] resigned his Regiment—am obliged to break off here. high time say you—I shall be happy to hear you are well, & whatever you communicate of men & things will highly oblige

127

To John Haslet

Philad^a Octr the 6th 1776—

It is now a long time Since my Eyes have been blest with the Sight of one of your Letters, I hear you have been Ill of Flux, fever &c for which I am Extreemly Sorry, but hope not so bad as to have been the Cause of your not Writeing—I believe You are under some difficulty by the Irregularity of the Post—However hope you will soon mend, both of your Illness and disposition to Write me—

If Health and Weather permits, I Set out This day for Kent, and don't Intend to return to Congress soon again, at least not in the present Reign.[1] My Domestick business will Employ me all the remaining part of this fall, let matters turn out hereafter as they may—On weighing and duely Considering the matter I thought it best and safest for your Interest (in Case any accident Should happen to you) to keep in my Custody the Vouchers and other papers you left with me Rather than place them in the Treasury, unless They Could have been passed and filed imediately, which Could not be done without you —I shall Carry them home with me, Where they Shall be Secure and Subject to your Order, or in Case of Your Death (Which God forbid) to the order of Such person or persons as You Shall intrust with Your Affairs—They are now printing in the papers of this City the plan of the Delaware Government, therefore if you are fortunate Enough Ever to Get those papers you'l be blest with a Sight of the Plans and will have an oppertunity to pass your opinion of it—but whether you like it or not You are bound to Swallow it—for they have Ordered an Election to be held on the 21st day of this Month for the filling it up with men, and for Your further Comfort will have it in their power (I Dare say) with Such men as they Shall Think proper to point out—In this State, in the Counties of Chester, Bucks & one other they have held Elections for Assemblymen, Sheriffs, Coroners &c. and Signd Returns Regularly to the Governor as usual. The Sheriff of Chester Came up here with his return but the Committee of Safety hearing of it apprehended him, and he is now (as the Quakers say) under deallings—I Suppose by this time you have seen the plan published by Congress for Establishing an Army, By this Plan You'l find a bounty of twenty Dollars and one hundred acres of Land to Each Soldier that will Enter. There is also a Bounty in Land to the officers—You will no doubt wonder that the Congress have not Raised the pay of the Officers. I Confess it is Strange that they have not—But depend on it (between you and I) their pay will be raised verry soon, and verry Considerably too. This for your private Satisfaction therefore not to be mentioned Yet.—Your private Satisfaction: Did I say? in this I may be wrong not knowing whether you may find yourself disposed to Enter the List during the War; or whether if you Were so inclined, as the Congress Have left it to the Several Assemblies

---

1 This was Rodney's last day in the Continental Congress. Although he was elected to that body on December 17, 1777, he never attended on account of his military duties and his election as President (Governor) of Delaware in March 1778.

to appoint all the officers Except General officers, You'd have any Chance in the nomination Even if you deserved it ten times as much more as I think you Do. However time will inform us more of These Matters—The Whigs of our Government Seem to have given up all pretentions by their Conduct, They are not satisfied with Great numbers of them having necessarily gone to the Camp, but many others have wantonly Gone, as if for no good Reason but to be out of the way—They are Such as might be of Service at Home, and Cannot possibly be of any there—I mean Mark McCall, Gordon, Vandike, Griffin &c. who I Suppose you have by this time seen. They did Tell me they wou'd be back by the fair, whether they will or not I Can't Say—Pray make my Compliments to the officers of your Battalion.

P.S. Don't Suppose from what I have said, they have left me out of Congress. they have not—[1]

128
From Samuel Patterson

Head-Quarters, Amboy, October 6, 1776.

Your three favours came to hand last evening. For answer, I am extremely sorry for your situation, and fear your disorder. As soon as I received yours, went about the inquiry for the root. There is so few of the inhabitants in town, that it was some time in the night before I got to hear of such. At last found an old lady who I gave money to, to send off this morning for some. As yet she has not arrived, or should have sent it by this hand, Doctor Spencer, of New-Castle. She says it is never got till November, and then used to be brought into town to sell; used as a tea; and to her knowledge has cured many that came here on purpose. I shall not fail of forwarding it to-day to Woodbridge; to go by post.

As to the other parts of your letters, have not full time to answer, As to Mr. Watson, have not seen him. Shall let him know the answer to his; but believes he does not want to resign, as he begins to know, like all the rest, that money can be made in that way; and if so, believes he will acquiesce in small bluffs. [?]

Captain Caldwell's company and Colonel Hodgson arrived here about the 1st instant. They are all here now but what Captain Mitchell's men are to follow him.

I received a letter from the Hon. George Read, acquainting me another

1 Rodney means that the Convention at New Castle did not oust him from the delegation to Congress. Nevertheless the first State legislature under the new constitution failed to re-elect Rodney and McKean on November 8, 1776, when it re-elected George Read as a delegate to the national body.

battalion is to be raised with us. I cannot see the propriety of such an attempt, when mine is not near full and full officered, to save expenses. I should thought, as we are not more than four hundred and fifty men, officers included, instead of six hundred, and at this season, so far advanced, is, in my humble opinion, hurting the intention. If any such should come, they must be mostly of the Militia kind; and half a month will cure them for ever going again, and persuade others not, if you should be ordered to raise one in the spring. They can only say they go up the hill and down, at this season, as the time is so short.

We left Captain Mitchell's drum at the maker's, by accident. I can sell all our drums and I believe colours, at the end of our campaign, if ordered. This you can consult, and let me know.

[P.S.] Captain Woodgate is sick. Three men dead in our battalion, from below. about seventy now sick.

129

From George Read

Wilmington Oct! ye 9th 1776.

I had a Letter from Co! Bedford of the first Instant in which he mentions the State of the Delaware Battalion to wit abo! 70 men wanting to Compleat the regiment—100 sick who suffer much for want of Medicines & many other things that upon the whole it has been a hard & discouraging Campaign—that he himself had been unwell from time to time but had lost no duty—that Co! Haslet & Major McDonough are both unwell—the Co! in the country 5 miles distance these 3 wks past—that he, Co! Bedford, is confined to ye Camp otherwise he shou'd have come down to provide winter cloathing & Blankets, of the last they want near 200—having reced this account I thought it necessary to be transmitted to you that your Branch of the Council of Safety with the Committee of Inspection might use their Endeavours to collect Blankets and every species of Cloathing within their Circuit that every encouragement may be given to the Soldiers in ye delaware Battalion to continue in the Service—New Castle County having furnished the most of those Blankets which that & Patterson's Battalion took with them—they are become scarce, however I have hopes that some will be collected—I think it of more immediate importance to get a speedy supply for those in Service than to persevere in a fruitless Attempt to send more to encrease the wants of such as are there—I have wrote a line on this Subject to Co! Collins and wou'd recommend to you to call the Council of Safety together—

130

From John Haslet

[October 10, 1776]

I did myself the Honor to write you a day, or two ago, have got into the vein of Scribbling, & shall pester you without Mercy, while that humor lasts. Yesterday Morning, the Roebuck the Phoenix, & the Repulse, (which had lain in in the N, River with two others at the end of the Enemies lines) moved up the River with all the Ease & Unconcern Imaginable, & passed the Chevaux amidst the Thunder of our Artillery from Mount Washington, & Constitution, a very Furious canonade was continued for upwards of two Hours. Our Men all upon the Lines expecting an Immediate Attack, but nothing of the kind happened, they saw no Enemy, scarcely any body was seen on Board the ships, nor did they fire a single Gun, except two broadsides at fort Washington—'tis said, they recd. some shot; By this movement Our Communication with the Country by Water is cut off, a very considerable Loss to us; there was a good deal of firing up the River; & tis sd two gondolas & two small traders of ours taken—two Millions Feet of Plank necessary to Barrack the Army, We have not half of one; down the N. River, the Easiest Way to have got them, now impassible. it wou'd be a joke if it had not too much melancholy in it. The Phoenix & Rose passed down in August, thro' the Only Gap in the Chevaux, which has been left open even untill now; the ships moved up to them at a Gentle Rate, then stood in close to the Shore, passed the Open, then stood out, to avoid one sunk a little below close on shore; Such is their Intelligence of Every Motion & neglect of ours—the Prisoners mentioned in my last, informed the Genl on Oath, that the Common Conversation with them was, let the Rebels build Barracks, then we shall attack & carry their Lines, & the Lodgement will serve us for the winter; that they are in want of fresh Provisions, but healthy & a large Number of Transports sent to Ireland for Provisions.

I had the Honor to wait on B. G. Ld. Sterling[1] just returned to camp; to congratulate his safety & Reappointment to Command of his old Friends in Brigade; Q. M. Mifflin last night arrived; the Flag with his Ldship, brought me Letters from Poor Stewart, has he been politely treated by the Capt. of the Ld. Rockford, but writes in the most Languishing plaintive, Pitious terms of his Captivity, & begs in very moving strains yr. generous Interposition for his Exchange. He knows yr. Influence in Congress—he desires his compliments to Miss Wilson & Nixon. In my late Illness recd most Cordial Sympathy &

1 Lord Sterling was captured in the Battle of Long Island. The Delaware regiment was in his brigade.

many favours from Lt. Col. Cadwallader. But am I right in my head, to ramble at this rate & to you, yet can assure you tis but little past 10 o'clock P.M. therefore it must be Delirium, which yr. Goodness will forgive.

In my last forgot to mention the State of Popes Company; Himself has done almost no Duty since he left Philadelphia; Wells Cashiered, Stewart a Prisoner; & Mr. Wilson not well this fortnight, his step, like mine, too Quick —there is Mr. Benjamin Hazel, a volunteer, fled from the Tories for Better Company—wd. not be disagreeable to the officers nor to me, tho' I have no acquaintance; if he has your Approbation, shou'd be glad, you wou'd have his commission sent up as soon as may be; or if Mr. John Ball is better liked, he had something like a promise from me; it will be a means of introducing either of them to a Company on the New Establishment. I believe it will give no Offence to Messrs Stewart & Wilson; because the former wishes only to serve in capacity of surgeon if at all; the Latter purposes going to sea at ye end of this Campaign—Your Sentiments soon will oblige. also what you think of the Regular Regiment. Commissioners have been here, from the Convention of Pennsylvania to know, who will serve, who not.

Five Boats full of Eastern Troops, were sent in a Dark Night to force Montresores Island, Only one landed, 4 ran away; Major Henley a Brave Officer, killed. Had another Boat supported him, the Island had been their own, his men repulsed with Loss; a Capt. made the Scape Goat of the Party, tried by Ct. Martial, Ordered to be Cashiered, the Genl. offended, that it wanted Capital, ordered them to reconsider the Matter; the Court sent him a Letter with Peremptory Refusal; they had decided by the Articles of War, the testimony & their Own Consciences, Reconsideration needless—so far the Matter is gone—a Virginia Majr. Wounded in the Skirmish on the Sixteenth, since Dead of his Wounds, the Eldest Capt. of the same Regiment appointed to succeed him, the Capts. of two other Regiments Elder than the Gentleman promoted, wasted on the Gen'l with a Remonstrance agst it as Injury to them couched in very strong terms.

Some officers have poured much contempt upon the Eastern Troops, & great Animosity subsists just now among them—'tis true, they are not like the Children of the South, this however between Ourselves 'tis even got among the Soldiery, whose Officers, I think much to blame, who have sown the seeds of Discord, & have used my small Influence to discourage it, for two Reasons, One 'tis directly Contrary to the spirit & resolves of Congress. 2d. that 'tis likely to have most Dangerous Consequences. By this time, Sir, you think at least, the Man has certainly lost his Senses, truly tis something like it, . . .

[P.S.] Have wrote Nicol. Vn Dyke a most flaming Letter, runing O'er with Patriotism, praying him not to let the People attend Noxtown fair rather than ye Election & sell their Birthright for a piece of Ginger Bread—Dr. Tilton writes Capt. Clark on ye Same head on back of letter.

131
From John Haslet

Camp at Fort Washington, Oct. 13th 1776

I think I mentioned in a former Letter my apprehensions, the Enemy w'd pass by Our Works, & land farther up the Country[1]—yesterday one hundred Sail ships of War & Transports sailed up to [Fr]og's point—[. . .] 8 miles from Harlem, & debarked 'tis sd. between [—— and?] ten thousand Men. A Great Number of Vessels we just hear, went up last night—[a des]erter who came Over yesterday, informs, that Genl. How has divided his whole [force] into three Divisions, that Fifteen thousand are to land at the place above men-[tioned] the same Number to come up the North River, & attack on that Side —that two [brig]ades are left on York Island to Defend their Lines, com-manded by Genl. Grant—[Troop]s, flanked on Right & Left by two Battalions of Hessians—to oppose this Body [we] have to the North of Harlem River 5000 Men from Massachusetts & N. Hampshire just arrived [. . . ,] McDou-gals, Clintons, Parson's & two other Brigades, amounting to more than [. . .] more, this Accompt I had yesterday from Ld. Stirling—On a few days now seems to hang the Fate of the Campaign, & the American Army; if we are able to repulse them, I think nothing farther will be attempted—if they succeed, & can draw a line behind us from River to River, We are completely Surrounded, & the utmost exertions of desparate Valor alone must cut a way thro them to the Country—I have already given you my sentiments of the Arrangement, & derangements of the Army, need not repeat them. Genl. Washington gave it in Orders yesterday, that he now thinks himself sufficiently strong, & is de-termined to defend his Post to the last Extremity. One of the two deserters, who came over yestereday, says Ld. George Lennox Br. to the Duke of Richmd lately Arrived, & brought with him 20,000 Men, 3,000 from Gibralter, 2000 from [. . .] the rest Hessians & Hannoverians—This is certainly Ex-aggeration—I have heard from Genl. Sterling that Lennox is arrived with 12 sail, & no more—if I survive the Conflict you shall hear from me Our fate as soon as possible Adieu

1 In his letter of October 10, Haslet wrote about the British war vessels passing up the North (Hudson) River past Fort Washington. In this letter he tells of Howe's movement up the East River with a view to turning Washington's left wing. The British forces embarked from Man-hattan Island opposite the south end of Blackwell's Island and passing Hell Gate, reached Frog's Neck, now Throgg's Neck, New York, at about 10 o'clock in the morning.

132

To George Read

Dover Oct.ʳ 14th 1776

We have bought all the Cloths we have been able to lay our hands on, Shall fall on the method you proposed to secure what Blankets we can, all for the purposes you mentioned—and Shall be glad you'd write me by next Post, when you think we shall get the money to pay for the Cloths & blankets, Whether we are to look to the Congress or to this Government in the first Instance—

The printed Copies you desired I would see forwarded to Sussex, Upon Inquiry I found were left by the Post at the Cross Roads and are there yet. I asked the Post why he left them there and he gave me for answer that there came on so hard a Rain He could not possibly bring them further without Spoiling them.

133

From George Read

Wilmington Oct.ʳ yᵉ 16ᵗʰ 1776.

I have yours of the 14ᵗʰ wherein you query where money is to be had for payment of yᵉ Cloths & Blankets to be procured for the Delaware Battalion— I presume it may be obtained from Congress as soon as one or more of the Officers shall be sent from Camp upon this Errand—It seems it was given out in orders before Parson Montgomery left Camp that 2 officers from each regiment shou'd be sent for this purpose and as Col: Haslet is recov.ʳᵈ tho not Join'd the regiment yet, when he does, probably Bedford will be one—however at all events the House of Assembly when they meet on Application will make some immediate Provission—At a meeting of our Council of Safety on Monday last we issued a recommendation to the members of the Committee of Inspection in each Hundred of this County to contract for and collect all the blankets Linnen & Wollens fit for soldiers use and that the Council of Safety wou'd use the most speady means to provide for the payment—but as we are so near Philad.ᵃ, this County is overun with a number of Hucsters who are perpetually prowling among us picking up every article of the sort—In a Letter from Col. Patterson of yᵉ 12ᵗʰ Instant is the following Paragraph—"I wrote you the other day per Hu: McCracken of Xteen with a Letter for Mr Rodney and a small bundle of Medicine for his Eye do forward it by a special hand, if gone home; I shall send him more to your Care to morrow" now I have neither seen or heard of McCracken but shall leave a note for the Post to inquire for him as he passes Xteen to morrow—I hear nothing new, this day's paper you will have as soon as this—I have not seen it as yet—

I go for Philad? to morrow morning if the weather permits—

134

To George Read

Dover Oct! the 25th 1776

Since I came to Kent I have purchased and paid for Corse Cloths to the Amount of near two hundred pounds. They come verry dear, but What is Worse, I have little or no Expectation That many more can be Got—The Shops throughout this County seem to be Intirely drained. Part of those I have are Home-made—Be pleased to let me know whether You would propose that the House should take Such Order in the Matter as to Enable one to Raise an Amount against this State for these Articles procured for the Delaware Battalion, or Whether I must look Elsewhere to be reimbursed. Dear as the Clothes are, They will now sell for Considerably more than I gave—

The Last papers Anounce the Almost Total Defeat of our Fleet under General Arnold. Tho' I greatly feel for the Loss the Continent hath Sustained, and the Many disadvantages we may Labour Under in consequence of it, Yet I cannot but be much pleased with [the] behaviour of that Brave officer and his men—They are certainly a parcel of fine fellows, and Will, While they Shew Such Bravery, Convince their Opponents That America is not to be Subdued but by Americans—Yet the Uneasiness and discontent Which too Generally prevails among the Common people, partly occasioned by the Scarcity and Intolerable Price of necessary Articles, is much to be Lamented—as it tends more to the injury of the Cause than any thing I know—The disaffected by painting the distresses of the people in Strong Colours, Will Create such a general discontent As that I fear the more Unthinking among them Will in a little time, Wish to Submit even at Discression Rather than Contend—For this Approaching Evil, We must find a Remedy—Government must Exert itself—But what can Government Do with Men Who, having it in their power, Are Base enough to Ingross these Necessaries of Life in a time of general distress, When Every Nerve should be Strained in the prosecution of the Cause, with a view to Accumulate fortunes Even at the Expense of their dearest Rights and priviledges—To Submit now is, undoubtedly, to be Slaves—However I know You have turned your thoughts for a Considerable time past to these Things, and your more fruitfull Invention will Contrive, if possible, a Remedy—

I Read a Letter from Col! Patterson a few days ago & No News, but says Watson the Quarter-master, has, as all Quarter-masters do, discovered a profit in the business, and therefore intends to Continue in the Service—

135
From John Miller, Junior[1]

November 10th 1776.

If a detachment of the militia should be ordered from this state, I have resolved to act in some character in it; but as I would prefer an appointment in which I could act with most credit and usefulness, I shall consider it as a mark of your favor if you use your influence in giving me the office of Surgeon—

However if any person acting on the same principle with myself should be esteemed more suitable, I shall still think it a happiness that I am able to act in a less dignified, tho' not less noble station—

136
From John Haslet

November 12, 1776.

I received his Excellency's[2] orders to take possession of the hill [Chatterton's Hill] beyond our lines, and the command of the Militia regiments there posted; which was done. We had not been many minutes on the ground, when the cannonade began, and the second shot wounded a militia-man in the thigh, upon which the whole regiment broke and fled immediately, and were not rallied without much difficulty. Soon after General McDougall's brigade took post behind us. Some of our officers expressed much apprehension from the fire of our friends so posted. On my application to the General, he ordered us to the right, formed his own brigade on the left, and ordered Brooks's Massachusetts Militia still farther to the right, behind a stone fence.

The troops being thus disposed, I went up to the top of the hill, in front of our troops, accompanied by Major McDonough, to reconnoitre the enemy. I plainly perceived them marching to the White-Plain, in eight columns, and stop in the wheat-fields a considerable time. I saw their General Officers on horse back assemble in council, and soon their whole body face about, and in one continued column, march to the hill opposite to our right. I then applied to General McDougall again to vary his disposition, and advised him to order

1 Dr. John Miller, son of Rev. John Miller of Dover.
2 General Washington.

my regiment farther onward, and replace it with Colonel Smallwood's, or
order the Colonel forward, for there was no dependence to be placed on the
Militia. The latter measure was adopted. On my seeing the enemy's March to
the creek begin in a column of their main body, and urging the necessity of
bringing our field-pieces immediately forward to bear upon them, the General ordered one, and that so poorly appointed, that myself was forced to assist
in dragging it along the rear of the regiment. While so employed, a cannon-
ball struck the carriage, and scattered the shot about, a wad of tow blazing in
the middle. The artillerymen fled. One alone was prevailed upon to tread out
the blaze and collect the shot. The few that returned made not more than two
discharges, when they retreated with the field-piece. At this time the Maryland battalion was warmly engaged, and the enemy ascending the hill. The
cannonade from twelve or fifteen pieces, well served, kept up a continual peal
of reiterated thunder. The Militia regiment behind the fence fled in confusion,
without more than a random, scattering fire. Colonel Smallwood in a quarter
of an hour afterwards, gave way also. The rest of General McDougall's brigade
never came up to the scene of action. Part of the first three Delaware companies also retreated in disorder, but not till after several were wounded and
killed. The left of the regiment took post behind a fence on the top of the hill
with most of the officers, and twice repulsed the Light Troops and Horse of
the enemy; but seeing ourselves deserted on all hands, and the continued
column of the enemy advancing, we also retired. Covering the retreat of our
party, and forming at the foot of the hill, we marched into camp in the rear
of the body sent to reinforce us.[1]

137

To George Read

November the 17th 1776

At the Request of the Members of the Council and Assembly, Delivered me
by Mr Collins, I Sent to the care of Thomas McKean Esqr, in Philadelphia by
John Palmer, Shallopman, Sixty Blankets and all the Cloths of any kind What-
soever, that I could procure here Suitable for the Delaware Battalion. They
Were Packed in three Hogsheads and accompanied with a Letter to Mr Mc-
Kean—But as the Collectors of those Articles had not then made me their Re-
turns in proper Order, Could not Send him the Invoice and Account of them—
I have Now inclosed you a General Account of them and the charges thereon,

1 Colonel Haslet here describes the only action, aside from cannonading, in what has been
termed the Battle of White Plains, October 28, 1776.

All Which I have presently Charged to this State as directed by Mr Collins.—
On Munday the fourth of this month One George Gibson who says he is a
Captain in the first Virginia Regiment, Was Sent by the State of Virginia and
General Lee, on an Expedition to New-Orleans, and was passing through here
With Letters from the Governor of that place to Congress, applied to me to
assist him with Horses and a Small Matter of Cash. I procured Horses to send
him a part of the way, let him have Six pounds, which was all he asked, and
have inclosed you his Rect. for it—As the money was advanced for the public
Service Should be Oblidged to you to procure it again for me. Before I let him
have the money he Shewed me his Credentials signed by Mr Pendleton and
many other Gentlemen of Note in Virginia—Yesterday and the day before I
Received two Letters from General McKinly by Express, with Copies of
other Letters inclosed, Informing that a Great number of Veshells had Sailed
from New-York, That it was Expected they Intended up Delaware to pay
Philadelphia a Visit. On the Rect. of this Peice of Inteligence Imediately
Issued and sent Orders to all the field-officers in this and Sussex County to See
that their Several Battalions were imediately prepared with their Arms, Accoutrements &c to march When and Where they Should Receive orders for
that purpose. This I did in discharge of my duty as Commanding Officer, But
between you and I, I no more Believe they are comeing at this Season of the
Year to Attack Philadelphia, Than I believe they Intend Beseiging the Moon
—I am much pleased to find by the Postscript of Mr Hancock's letter that
General Charlton[1] with all his forces have Retreated—Whenever you have any
thing Either publick or private Worth while, and proper to Communicate to
me, and Should be fortunate Enough to Stear Clear of those Violent Lazy fits
That some times Seise you, Should be Much obliged to you to let me have it—

138

Minutes of Kent County Branch of Council of Safety

November the 30th 1776

A Quorum of That branch of the Council of Safety belonging to Kent
County appointed by the General Assembly of this State at their last sitting
met. Present

> Genl Caesar Rodney, Esquire
> Richard Bassett, Esquire
> John Banning, Esquire
> James Sykes, Esquire

1 General Carleton of Canada.

The Council went into a choice of a Chairman and Gen! Rodney was chosen Nem. Con.[1]

The Council taking into their consideration the great scarcity of Salt within this County and the distress that must be occassioned to the Inhabitants thereof unless a speedy supply of that necessary article be obtained—

1. Resolved

That this Council will apply to the Committee of Safety of the State of Pennsylvania for as much salt as can be obtained from them for the Inhabitants of the County

2. Resolved that the Chairman of this Council write a Letter to the said Committee of Safety of Pennsylvania for that purpose and inclose therein a Copy of these Resolutions—

3ᵈ Resolved that the Trustee of the General Loan Office for the County of Kent pay the amount of the Salt that may be obtained as afsᵈ on the draught of the Chairman of Committee of Safety of Pennsylvania

4ᵗʰ Resolved

That the same salt when obtained shall be distributed among the Inhabitants of this County who are not already provided in equal portions according to the quantity obtained the portions to be assertained by the Council when the whole quantity is known. Every person to whom such portion is delivered paying the money at the time of delivery and that no more Than the prime Cost shall be demanded except the necessary expence arising thereon, to be also assertained by Council

Resolved/

That Mʳ John Banning Major French Battell and Mʳ John Pryor be and they are hereby appointed a Committee to deliver out in equal portions said Salt among the Inhabitants afs. according to the number in their respective families on the payment of the money for the quantity delivered—

To this Board was exhibited an account of Major French Batt[ell?] for money by him paid for casting Balls and making Catredges amo[unting?] to £2.18—

Ordered that the Military Treasurer pay the same—

In Council of Safety December the Seventh 1776—

The Council having Certain Information that a Great Number of the In-

1 Since the first State legislature, meeting in October, failed to elect a president (governor) of the State as required by the Constitution, but entrusted, until its next session, the executive power to the Council of Safety, it is interesting to note that Caesar Rodney, as chairman of the Kent County branch, was a sort of *de facto* or military executive of that county. This situation continued until the election of McKinly as president in February 1777.

habitants of this State, in this time of General distress and in Open Violation of the Recommendation of Congress Have got into, and are Carrying on in this County the Vile and indecent practices of Horse-racing and Cock-fiting Therefore Resolved That in the opinion of this Council all such practices ought imediately to be Suppressed, and that all Judges, Justices & other peace officers, as allso all other True friends to the Glorious Cause in Which we are Engaged, ought to be aiding and Assisting in discountenancing and Suppress[ing] the Same, by Apprehending the persons Concerned Therein, or Otherwise as the Case may require—

139
To John Haslet

Dover Dec: the 14th 1776

As my Brother Tommy is the bearer from whom you may know all that you want to hear & that I know, I shall make this letter verry Short[1]—Imediately on the Rect of your Last I wrote as usual to Miss:: Haslet, and have to tell you that M: Bell at whose House She was the Other day Informs me She is verry Hearty but much troubled about your ReEntering the Service[2]—in this She and I differ verry much being greatly pleased when I was assured you wou'd Continue—There is a part of Your last letter puzzles me greatly: You say you intend to Consult L. Sterling[3] About Showing my last letter to the General[4]— As I did not keep a Copy of it, have been trying to no purpose to recollect what it Contained, And Should have been verry uneasy was I not Convinced of your understanding, prudence and friendship, which wou'd lead you to do nothing Tending to my disadvantage and therefore perfectly Easy—but am Anctious to know what it was you intended to Show—be pleased to inform me—

140
From Thomas Rodney

Chester Tuesday dec: 1776

I have inclosed all the prints that I have got—There is a hand bill of Con-

1 Captain Thomas Rodney's company of militia from Dover Hundred left Dover on December 14 to join Washington's army. It is very doubtful if this letter was delivered, since Rodney's company did not reach Trenton until the second battle at that place on January 2 and Haslet was killed at Princeton on the third.

2 Although the time of service of Haslet's regiment expired on January 1, 1777, the Colonel personally continued in the service in command of troops under General Mercer of the Continental Line.

3 Lord Stirling.   4 George Washington.

gress exciting the people in the Warmes[t] terms to Turn out and defend their Country—There is a bounty of 7 dollars to Ten givers by the assembly of pensylvania to all the Malitia that will Turn out—I have a great number of officers from Camp no Two of which Tell the same Story about any one fact—I have heard that Lee has found Washington—again that Washington has Crossed into Jersy—again that none of these things have hapened—again that Lee has given the Enemy a drubing—again that Lee is Taken prissoner—and again that the enemy has retreated before him &ᶜ—And the news of this day is that Lee is actually Taken—I had this information from Col: Price & Two other Maryland officers this afternoon vizᵗ That Genl. C. Lee heard 4000 Hessians were Comming to attack him—that he took 11 men & went 4 miles from his Camp to reconiter them & puts up at the House of a Tory who Gave the Enemy word of his Situation—That How immediately Sent off 70 Light Horse Who Took him Prisoner & rode of with him with out giving him time to git his Hat That Genl. Washington rec'd this accᵗ from Genl. Sullivan by Express—That Col. Stone had this from Washington & these officers from him—But I believe none of all this—nor any thing I have heard since I left Kent—no body knows any thing about the designs or actions of the Generals & yet every body seems to know every thing—It was reported as a fact at New Castle that I was taken very sick at Cross Roads & Turned back—& a few Hours before we arrived at Wilmington it was affirmed that all the Company had got discurraged & gone home again—Judge of the rest by this—We are all at Chester now in very good Health and the highest Spirits—and we have had the pleasure on our way of receivᵍ the prayers & blessings of men women & Children—the Whigs Sincere & the tories desembling—& the Country seems inspired with new Spirit as we Come—New Castle County is rousing fast. Three Companies have marched already—and many more will in a few days—Pensylvania is marching in by 100dreds & by 1000's—The Best Judgment I can form of the Situation of the Army—Is that Lee has about Ten thousand men (this upon the information of Genl: Mifflin to a Lady in this Town who Told me she had from him the day before yesterday) and is well posted about 25 miles from the Enemy—That Genl: Washington has about 16000 men extending from opposite Trent Town Several miles up the River —That the Enemy Continue from Trent Town to Prince Town &ᶜ—That Genl: Gates is at or over the North River bringᵍ up 3,000 Regulars & 8000 Malitia to Reinforce Genl: Lee &ᶜ—They took 12 Light Horse which were carrᵈ into Philadᵃ last Saturday—We met the Philadᵃ Tories and other Prisoners under Guard to day going to Baltimore—I could go on a half Hour longer but cut the ball of my fore finger with handle of a knife and it prevents my being able to hold the pen any longer for this time but hope by the first opertunity after Tomorrow to give some information that you may rely on—but this for the present. I think Philad: is and will be safe this Campain[1]

[p.s.] Genl: Putnam Commands in Philad:—

141

To Thomas Rodney

Dover, December the 23d, 1776.

I have but little news, little paper, and therefore very little to write. I received both your letters, the last yesterday, and am much pleased that your company meet with applause. As they know how, I hope they will continue to deserve it. You say you feel better for the little campaigning you have had. If you will take care to expose yourself no more than the good of the service and your duty require, I do not doubt it will continue. I am pleased to hear that the people of New-Castle County, by a sense of their duty, are rousing from their former slumber. There are some anxious spirits in this County, but fear they will not be able to produce another company in time. I am very sorry that Mr. J. Dickinson, and the other gent[n]. you mentioned, should have discovered sentiments inimical to the freedom and independence of the American States. I both hoped and believed they were of a different sentiment from that in this great interesting cause. . . .

From present appearances, I think this campaign must soon end. God send it may, for this is a most inclement season for the poor soldiers. Nothing but the importance of the cause could support them in such a day of trial.

Remember me to Johnny. Tell him I am pleased that he has entered the service, and that I hope he will set about the business of war with firmness, and make it his study to acquire knowledge in that way. Don't forget to write by every opportunity.

1 In response to Washington's appeal for more troops during his retreat across New Jersey, Caesar Rodney began to recruit Delaware militia, which, about January 18, he brought on to Trenton, i e, about two weeks after the Battle of Princeton. Meanwhile, Thomas Rodney, Captain of the Dover Hundred Militia, had been sent forward, and, when this company reached Philadelphia, it was sent on to Bristol by General Putnam There it was brigaded with the forces under General Cadwalader, who had received orders from Washington to cross the Delaware to Burlington, N.J., and march northward with a view to striking the Hessian commander, Count Donop, at Bordentown This movement was to take place simultaneously with two others, one division under General Ewing to cross the river below Trenton and the other division under General Washington to cross the river above that place Both Cadwalader and Ewing failed to cross on account of the ice (For a more detailed account of Captain Thomas Rodney's experiences at this time see his diary as printed in *Papers of Historical Society of Delaware,* or the original manuscript in the Library of Congress.)

P.S. I cannot tell what has become of the shallop, or how she is to be got down, and am afraid she may be lost by ice. I wish she could be contrived down.

142

To Thomas Rodney

Dover Dec.ʳ the 29th 1776

This is intended by M.ʳ. Burtle Shee who [pur]poses to Set out for the Camp to Morrow Morning. We still Continue here to be in the most anxious uneasy scituation you can possible Conceive. Seldom a day passes but we have some inteligence both of our Army, and that of the English, and nothing we hear to be depended upon. By some accounts Howe is Retreating and General Washington about to Repass the Delaware. Again it is roundly asserted that there Can be no Doubt but Howe will keep his Ground in the Jersey till the Spring, when he Will be Strengthened by a large fleet up the Delaware. Thus the Mind Anxious for the Salvation of America is held in Suspence. I Think it absolutely necessary that Howe Should be Routed from the Jersey this Winter, and the soo[ner] it is done the better. But am afraid our General has not yet got Force enough to do it. Ever since you left [?] I have been doing every thing in my power to draw [?] the Militia of this County to Join the Army, But to verry [?] as yet. Some days ago I proposed Marching mys[elf] with such as Should be willing, and have appoin[ted] Such as are to meet prepared for that purpose [?] on Thursday next. What Effect this may have that day will determine. However be that as it may I Shall be in Readiness, or at least as much so, as so Short time will admit of. Some people are of opinion that many will turn out, some others that they will not. M.ʳ Collins is determined it seems to March with me. The Major talks of it. It would have given me much pleasure to Receive from you a letter dated some few days after your arrival at the Camp because I suppose you would in that time be able to form Some tolerable Judgement of the Real si[tua]tion of Affairs there—I am Just now, while [?] made happy by a Peice of news which is repor[ted] a fact and to be depended upon—That General Was[hing]ton has Regained possession of Trenton. That [?] killed and wounded many, and Taken a Great [?] Number of prisoners with ten or eleven Brass Field-peices and a verry Considerable Quantity of Stores, and that He is in a fair way to Drive the English Army before him,—God of his Infinite Mercy Grant it may be true—If our people turn out I shall be with you Quo General, if not Quo private Gentlemen. My present determination is to Come at all Events—Our families are both well, and I beleive Betsey will write by this oppertunity—The Interesting Scituation of our public Affairs will point out to you the propriety of

Writeing me by every oppertunity in Stronger terms than any other arguments I Can make Use of—Therefore hope you will not neglect to do it—

By a letter from Lieutenant McCall to his father, I am Informed that your
Company is Stationed at the House of Mr Andrew Allen,[1] Where Mrs Allen
Continues to reside with her Children, and that She Applied to you as Commanding Officer of the Company for protection & Civil Usage—This, I am
Much pleased to hear, you readily engaged to Afford her, so far as was Consistant with your Duty—I am Verry Sorry Mr Allen has taken a Part so Unfriendly, or Rather in direct opposition to that Cause in which all the Freemen of America are so deeply Interested, and for Which all who Think as I
do Would sooner spill the last Drop of their Blood Than Even Stand Nuter—
But as Mrs Allen has allways Supported, and I am Convinced Verry deservedly
the Charector of a Most Amiable Good Woman, And as her Scituation at this
time must be Extreemly Dilicate, It Will be Unnecessary to Recommend to
you the Treating her with all The Tenderness and decent Respect due to her
Charector and in your Power Consistant with a proper discharge of your
Duty—So far as I am acquainted with your people, I am persuaded they Will
be disposed to Treat her Rather with Complisance than the least degree of
Rudeness—

143
From Thomas Rodney

Allen's Town, in Jersey, twelve miles from Princeton,
twenty do. from Brunswick, Dec. 30th, 1776.

I wrote you a long letter on the 24th, which I had no opportunity of sending,
and left it in my trunk at Mr. Coxe's, two miles from Bristol; it contains the
news to that time, which I cannot repeat here. On the 25th instant, in the evening, we received orders to be at Shamony Ferry as soon as possible. We were
there, according to orders, in two hours, and met the Riflemen, who were the
first from Bristol; we were ordered from thence to Dunk's Ferry, on the Delaware, and the whole Army of about two thousand men followed, as soon as the
artillery got up. The three companies of Philadelphia Infantry and mine were
formed into a body, under the command of Captain Henry, (myself second in
command,) which were embarked immediately to cover the landing of the
other troops. We landed with great difficulty through the ice, and formed on
the ferry shore, about two hundred yards from the river. It was as severe a
night as ever I saw, and after two battalions were landed the storm increased

1 The Allens were among the most prominent Tories in Pennsylvania.

so much and the river was so full of ice that it was impossible to get the artillery over, for we had to walk one hundred yards on the ice to get on shore. General Cadwalader, therefore, ordered the whole to retreat again, and we had to stand at least six hours under arms—first, to cover the landing and till all the rest had retreated again; and by this time, the storm of wind, hail, rain, and snow, with the ice, was so bad, that some of the Infantry could not get back till next day. This design was to have surprised the enemy at Black Horse and Mount-Holley, at the same time that Washington surprised them at Trenton; and had we succeeded in getting over, we should have finished all our troubles. Washington took nine hundred and ten prisoners, with six pieces of fine artillery, and all their baggage in Trenton. The next night I received orders to be in Bristol before day; we were there accordingly, and about nine o'clock began to embark one mile above Bristol, and about three o'clock in the afternoon got all our troops and artillery over, consisting of about three thousand men, and began our march to Burlington—the Infantry, flanked by the Riflemen, making the advanced guard. We got there about nine o'clock, and took possession of the town, but found the enemy had made precipitate retreat the day before, bad as the weather was, in a great panick. The whole Infantry and Riflemen were then ordered to set out that night and make a forced march to Bordentown, (which was about eleven miles,) which they did, and took possession of the town about nine o'clock, with a large quantity of the enemy's stores, which they had not time to carry off. We stayed there till the Army came up; and the General finding the enemy were but a few miles ahead, ordered the Infantry to proceed to a town called Crosswick's, four miles from Bordentown, and they were followed by one of the Philadelphia and one of the New-England battalions. We got there about eight o'clock, and at about ten, (after we were all in our quarters,) were informed that the enemy's baggage was about sixteen miles from us, under a guard of three hundred men. Some of the Militia Colonels applied to the Infantry to make a forced march that night and overhaul them. We had then been on duty four nights and days, making forced marches, without six hours' sleep in the whole time; whereupon the Infantry officers of all the companies unanimously declared it was madness to attempt, for that it would knock up all our brave men, not one of whom had yet gave out, but every one will suppose were much fatigued. They then sent off a party who were fresh, but they knocked up before they got up with them, and came back and met us at this town next morning. They surrounded a house where there was six Tories; took three of them; one got off; and one who run and would not stop, was shot dead. They gave him warning, first by calling, and at last shot two bullets over his head, but he still persisted; and the next two shot, one bullet went through his arm and one through his heart. The enemy have fled before us in the greatest panick that ever was known; we heard this moment that they have fled from Princeton, and that they were hard pressed by Washington. Never were men in higher spirits than our whole Army is; none are sick, and all are determined to extirpate them from the Jersey, but I believe the enemy's fears will do it before we get up with them. The Hessians, from the General to the common soldier, curse and imprecate the war, and swear they were sent here to be slaughtered; that they never will leave New-York again till they sail for Europe. Jersey will be the most Whiggish Colony on the Continent: the very Quakers declare for taking up arms. You cannot imagine the distress of this country. They have stripped every body almost, without distinction—even of all their clothes, and have beat and abused men, women, and children, in the most cruel manner ever heard of. We have taken a number of prisoners in our route, Hessians and British, to the amount of about twenty. It seems likely, through the blessing of Providence, that we shall retake Jersey again without the loss of a man, except one General Washington lost at Trenton. The enemy seem to be bending their way to Amboy with all speed, but I hope we shall come up with the Princeton baggage yet, and also get a share of their large stores at Brunswick. I hope, if I live, to see the conquest of Jersey, and set off home again in two weeks. Some of my men have complained a little, but not to say sick; they are all now well here.

144

From John Haslet

[No date][1]

When I last wrote you, God knows, I do not; this I can affirm, that I have received no answer.

After a long retreat from a full conviction of the enemy's superior numbers, but performed in order, with a firm determined countenance, we at last stopt on ye banks of Delaware—there we were stationed—thank you says Gen! Rodney—

On Christmas at 3 oClock we repassed the river—a party of Virginians formed the van Guard & did the most of the fighting—Lord Stirlings Brigade had the honor of fighting 1000 Hessians to a surrender—We should have gone

---

1 The letter was written probably on New Year's Day 1777 at Trenton. Colonel Haslet was killed at the Battle of Princeton on January 3. This was, therefore, his last letter to Rodney.

on, & panic struck they would have fled before us, but the inclemency of the weather rendered it impossible—We repassed the river, rested one day & then were ordered back—I'm sorry to inform the Gen! that Capt. Holland, Ensign Wilson, D! Gilder¹ & myself are all who have followed the american cause to Trenton, two privates excepted—On Gen! Washingtons being informed of this, he declared his intention of having officers & men bound neck and heel and brought back as an example to the army—I told the Gen! the truth but not the whole truth—the last I reserved for you, and you will blush with me— Seven Philada light horse, yesterday brought in nine light horse men, with one horse, who were sent to impress waggons—We just now hear, that the bridge on this side of Princeton is cut down and the enemy retiring—[A] sufficient number of troops are ready to drive them out of the Jersey—We hope to greet you well—on our victorious retu[r]n from Trenton. I fell into the Delaware at 3 OClock in the mor[n]ing, up to my middle—have had the piles and swelled legs ever since—but no matter, if we drive them to New York—

If I return it will be to salute you, if not we shall meet in Heaven—Your Goodness will give M!ˢ Haslet such news as you think proper—I have Gen! Washington's leave to return and superintend the recruiting service at home— but cannot go for a few days longer—Hope soon to lay myself at your feet, and am wt. great esteem & sincerity

your John Haslet

N.B. the four Allens, we hear, are with Gen! Howe, Galloway &c. the former fled his B! the Gen! in pursuit—M! Tilghman informed the Gen! in my Hearing, that the Dover light Horse were coming up—is it so—I shall believe like Thomas, when I see it—Gen! Washington is dictator I mentioned to Lord Stirling t'other day, that I thought myself dismissed from the Service, on Col! Smallwoods being prefered before me—what made the Case in point was the dispute of Rank between us, determined by the General himself in my favour —the preference was as in Gen! Woosters Case a modest Hint to retire—they both remonstrated. I shall not take my Resolution till I see you, nor can give the Reasoning p[r]o & Con at large—I hope you recd my last—it was a s[or]t of Journal closed at Brunswick one Day with God b[le]ss you—we shall certainly drive them off the Hand of Ishmael was here, meaning Dr. Miller, a very important part of the Delaware Regiment at present—Gilder is sick, he i[s] to serve with me at the Head of Lord Stirlings Brigade—& insists [on] his Compliments to Misses Wilson, Nixon, Miller & the General himself, if he pleases to accept them

1 Dr. Reuben Gilder, a surgeon in Haslet's regiment, who later joined Hall's regiment.

145

From Thomas Rodney

Morris Town New Jersey Jan.ʸ 14th 1776 [1777][1]

I wrote you last from Allen Town, & since To Betsy from this Place By M.ʳ Rotherford—In & since the Battell at Prince Town we have Taken at least 400 Prisoners—Also a goodeal of Baggage & Provisions. Gen.ˡ Maxwell Took 120 Prisoners at Eliz.ᵃ Town with 30 waggons & one schooner Loaded with Stores & Provisions—Our Out parties are Cutting them of every day & night, & they have been so Cooped up & Harrassed that we have Certain intelligence this evening that they have Evacuated Brunswick after Burning a part of the Town—Gen.ˡ Heath is at Congress Bridg. Gen.ˡ Washington here, Gen.ˡ Maxwell at Eliz.ᵃ Town, Gen.ˡ Putnam at Cross[w]icks and every Department increasing Hourly—& Considerable Betts are layd here that we shall be in possession of the whole of Jersy or New York in ten days—500 of the Germain Troops at Wood Bridge being ordered to Brunswick Clubed their Muskets, declared they would not fight & marched down to Amboy. The whole of them are sick of the war & say they were brought here to be slaughtered. How himself is Pannic Struck at the Masterly Strokes of Gen.ˡ Washington—

Yesterday we Buried Col: Ford of the Jersy Militiar (and owner of the House where we are & an Elegant one it is) with the Honours of War—and To day we Buried the Brave Col: Hitchcocks who Command.ᵈ a New England Brigade Raised immediately after the Battel of Lexington—The Infantry performed the firings at both—and I Command[ed] at the last, he being a Continental officer—yesterday I put the younger officers to do the Service, as I have had the Command of the Light Infantry Battalion since the Battle of Prince Town being the Eldest Capt.ⁿ—Gen.ˡ Mercer is like to recover tho' we had numbered him among the dead—

My Company has Stained those Glorious Lorrels which they gained in a four weeks Severe duty—Most of them were in the Hottest of the Battle at Prince Town without receiving a wound or loosing one life—But on the tenth of this Instant their Time Expired & they determined to go home yet on the Gen.ˡˢ addressing them they determined to Stay longer But this morning all of them But Tilton M.ᶜGermet (& Bullen & M.ᶜKnot who are sick) set of Home, I could not prevail on them to Stay longer—When I shall be at Home is Uncertain But hope to see the enemy evacuate Jersy first, the period which from

---

1 When Thomas Rodney wrote this letter he was not aware that his brother had already left or was leaving Delaware with the new militia contingents.

the first expected to Stay & see, & I think I shall not go before If I Can be of any valuable use in Staying, & the Gen! Has requested Me not to leave him notwithstand⸆ my men being gone.

I saw Gen! Dickerson to day who says you are well—But I must Press my advise upon not to Come into the field Your Present State of Health is not fit to Encounter the Severity & Difficulties of a winters Campain—all that you'l git to Come from Kent will be but few & may be Command⸆ by Collins—Your Servises will be more beneficial to the Cause by Stay⸆ at Home—But if Collins will set out I think you may push a great many out after him but if you Come away there is no one left To incurrage the Tardy one to Turn out —But if you should not be able to git any out, I thank God that the American Cause is now Safe—And You may rely that the Pensylvania Malitia now Here have sent a spirited Letter to their Council of Safety insisting that they shall make every man Turn out that is able to bare arms (except those who pretend Concience) under pain of Confiscation and Bannishment,—that they make such the fate of all Tories and the Malitia will Support them in it—

The Enemy are only in possession of that little spot between the Rariton & sound from A[m]boy to Brunswick—

I have but this sheet of paper therefore Cant write to Betsy Give my love to her & the Children, Billey, Sally, Johnny, Doct! Moleston &⸆—I sent all the way from here t[o] M! Copes for my Cloaths & Horse & Johnny [had brought?] My Horse Home—If I could git Him by any [?] means it would Oblige me for when I Came to [this place?] my feet was near wore out but are now re[covered?]. 180 miles home is a long march—If Jacob [?] Could be Spaired he knows the Roads I wish h[im to?] be sent with my horse let him Come on [to?] me

146

Caesar Rodney's Orderly Book

(Trenton, N. J., January—February, 1777)

On the following pages, 156 to 168 inclusive, are reproduced the contents of Caesar Rodney's Orderly Book, dated from January 16 to February 19, 1777. Having hurried up to Philadelphia from Dover after receiving the news of the battles of Trenton and Princeton, General Lord Stirling appointed him as commander of the post at Trenton while the main army under Washington went into winter quarters at Morristown. Rodney's principal work was the forwarding of troops to Major General Israel Putnam at Princeton, to Brigadier General Philemon Dickinson on the Raritan, and to General Washington.

*   *   *   *   *   *   *

Dr. Sir   Philada: Jany 16th 1777

I have Directed the ninth Virginia Regiment, the Twelfth of Pensylvania, the Malitia of this and the Delaware State to proceed to Trenton to which Place I must also desire you will repair & take the Command of the whole there—I have informed Genl. Washington thereof and he will either send to you or me instructions for your further motions—If they come to my hand I shall immediately Communicate them to you—in the mean time I must request that you will immediately endeavour to send out a Number of Scouting Parties toward Brunswick or Wherever the Enemy May be Stationed in order to have them closely watched and to obtain the most early intilegence of their movements—Captn. Hugg of the Pensylvania Artilery is at NewTon with some Brass Artilery, I believe five pieces in all—You will give him Directions to join you immediately. Captn. Lee with the first Squadron of Virginia Horse are to proceed immediately to Genl. Washingtons Camp by the way of Penny Town, Flemingtown—Chambers Mill—Veal Town and so on To Morris Town—

I am sir your most
Hum. Servt.
STIRLING[1]

*   *   *   *   *   *   *

Colonel Cook's Battalion of Continental Troops, now in this town, as also the Delaware and Pensylvania are to proceed from hence to Trenton—

CAESAR RODNEY
Bristol, Jany. 18, 1777   B. G. Militia
Counter Sign Delaware

*   *   *   *   *   *   *

Ordered that the Captain or Commanding Officer in Each Company of both Continental and Militia Troops now in town Immediately Return the Number and State of their Companies,—the Whole to Parrade at Ten OClock. The Guard to be then Relieved, and then all the Troops to Draw three days Rations Except Rum of which they are to draw for one day. Ordered also that the Captain or Commanding officer of Each Company See that his Men

---

1 This letter is copied in the handwriting of Thomas Rodney in Caesar Rodney's Orderly Book.

have good Quarters, keep Selves Clean and Sober and See that the[y] do no Injury to any of the Inhabitants—

Trenton Jany 19th 1777—

CAESAR RODNEY
B. G. Militia

* * * * * * *

Ordered, that Lt. Coll. Murray's two Companies of Pensylvania Militia March Imediately & Join the Army under Major General Putnam at Princetown—

Trenton Jany 19th 1777—

CAESAR RODNEY
B. G.——

* * * * * * *

Ordered that Captain Fisher and Captain Creek with their Companies March Imediately and Join the Army under Major General Putnam at Princetown—

Trenton Jany 19th 1777

CAESAR RODNEY
B. General

* * * * * * *

Sir

You are to March the Regiment under your Command for Princetown to Morrow Morning by Nine OClock and there Join the Army under Major General Putnam, and for this purpose you are to Cause the Rations drawn for Your Regiment to be Cooked this Evening—

Trenton Jany 19th 1777

CAESAR RODNEY
B. General—

To Coll. Cook, or the Commandg Officer of his Regimt.

* * * * * * *

Ordered that Every Captain when the assemble is beat Imediately appear with his Company on Parade. He is to take Care that Every Man in his Company have the Rations that are ordered to him. He is to See that the Sergeants of his Company Do their Duty in Every Respect—These orders being necessary it is Expected Each Captain will Strickly obey them as he will be answerable for the Neglect—

Trenton Jany 19th 1777.

CAESAR RODNEY
B. General

Officer of the Day ⎫
Lt Coll. Rhodes ⎭

Counter Sign ⎫
Trenton— ⎭

Sir

You are to be prepared to March with Your Battalion of Delaware Militia by Ten OClock to Morrow Morning for Princetown, and there Join the Army under Major General Putnam—

                                               CAESAR RODNEY

Trenton Jany 20th. 1777—   B. General
    To Coll. Collins—

*   *   *   *   *   *   *

Sir, You are to March to morrow Morning by Ten OClock with Your Company of Pensylvania Militia to Princetown. and there Join the Forces under Major General Putnam—

                                               CAESAR RODNEY—

Trenton Jany 20th 1777—   B. General—
    To Capt. William Parker Esq.
This order Countermanded—

*   *   *   *   *   *   *

Sir You are to March to Morrow Morning by Ten OClock with Your Company of Pensylvania Militia to Princetown and there Join the Forces Under Major General Putnam

                                               CAESAR RODNEY

Trenton Jany 20th 1777   B. General
To Captn. William McAlvoy Esqr.
This order Countermanded
Officer of the day ⎱   Counter Sign ⎱
  Benjm. Hazell ⎰   Crosswicks ⎰

*   *   *   *   *   *   *

Sir You are to Draw to morrow Morning two days Rations for all your Officers and Men and be Ready to March by Eleven OClock in the Morning of the Same day to Princetown and there Join the Army under Major General Putnam—

                                               CAESAR RODNEY

Trenton Jany 21st 1777   B. General
To Colonel Stroud of
the Pensylvania Militia—

*   *   *   *   *   *   *

Ordered that the Guard Be Strengthened with a Captn. & twenty four Men
to be furnished from all the Troops now in Town in proportion to their
Numbers

CAESAR RODNEY

Trent Town Jan.y 21st 1777—   .   B. General

*   *   *   *   *   *   *

Instructions for the officer of the Guard. You are to Direct your Centinels to
Let no person pass them after Nine OClock unless they be going Express,
have a pass or give the Counter sign

CAESAR RODNEY

Trenton Jay. 22. 1777—   B. General
Countersign (Brunswick)

*   *   *   *   *   *   *

Sir/
You are to March with your Company at Eleven OClock this Morning for
Princetown and there Join your Regiment in the Army under the Command
of Major General Putnam

CAESAR RODNEY

Trenton Jany 22. 1777—   B. General
To Captn. Brady of Col. Cooks Regiment

*   *   *   *   *   *   *

Ordered that Captn. Parker and Captn. McAlvey draw this Morning two
days Rations for their Companies

CAESAR RODNEY

Head Quarters Trenton   B. General
Jan.y 22d. 1777—
Countersign (York)

*   *   *   *   *   *   *

Ordered that the four Companies of Col. Watts Battalion Pensylvania now in
Town draw three days Rations, that Captn. Parker & Captn. McAlevys Com-
panies draw two days Rations, and that they all hold themselves in readiness
To March to Morrow Morning at Ten OClock

CAESAR RODNEY

Trenton Jany. 23d 1777—   B. General
   Countersign (Independance)

*   *   *   *   *   *   *

Sir

You are immediately To March the three Companies of Your Batalion, to Prince Town and there Join the Army under Major General Putnam—

CAESAR RODNEY
B. General

Trenton Jany 25th 1777
To Col: Watt or the Commandg. officer of his Batt.

* * * * * * *

Guards fixed as Usual—
    Countersign—Hattenfield—
  General Orders

Ordered that all the Troops now in Trenton Except Captain Rankin's Company of Delaware Militia and the Artillery Company, March at Eleven OClock to Princetown, and there Join the Army Under the Command of Major General Putnam—

CAESAR RODNEY
B. General

Trenton Jany 26th 1777—

* * * * * * *

Sir/

You are to morrow Morning by Ten OClock to March with Your Company, and the three Brass Field pieces now in this Town to Princetown. You are to take with you the Amunition belonging to them, and that part of Captain Hamiltons Company now Stationed on the other Side the River, near the Upper Ferry—
Trenton Jany 26th 1777—

CAESAR RODNEY
B. General

To Captain Hugg, of the Artillery

* * * * * * *

Sir, I am Informed that there is a barrell of Flints on the other Side the River near the upper Ferry. If they are there, You are to have them brought to this Town—
Trenton Jany 26th 1777—

CAESAR RODNEY—
B. General—

To Captain Saml. Hugg
of the Artillery—

* * * * * * *

Guards fixed as Usual—
    Counter Sign—Frankford—

* * * * * * *

Ordered that all the Troops in this Town draw Three days Rations, have their Provision Cooked if Possible this Evening—and that they all hold themselves in Readiness to March to Morrow Morning—and wait orders for that purpose—

Trenton Jany 27th 1777—

CAESAR RODNEY
B. General

* * * * * * *

Guards as usual
    Countersign. (Newark)

* * * * * * *

Ordered that Coll. Watt with the four Companies of his Battalion now here, March to morrow at Ten OClock for Princetown and there Join the Army under the Command of General Putnam

Trenton Jany 28th. 1777—

CAESAR RODNEY
B. General

* * * * * * *

Ordered that all the Troops now in this Town (Except four Companies of Coll. Watt's Battalion) March to morrow morning at Ten OClock from hence by Penny Town, Fleming Town, Chambers Mill, Veal Town to Morris Town and There Take Their further Orders from his Excellency General Washington—

Trenton Jany 28th. 1777—

CAESAR RODNEY
B. General—

* * * * * * *

Guards as Usual
    Countersign (Boston)

* * * * * * *

Guards as Usual
    Countersign (Liberty)
Jany. 29th
  1777—

* * * * * * *

Sir

You are Imediately to March with Your three Companies from hence to Princetown, and there Join the Army Under the Command of Major General Putnam

Trenton Jany 30th 1777—

                                                      CAESAR RODNEY

To Major Boggs of Coll. Blane's Battn.   B. General
     of Pensylvns. Militia—

                    *   *   *   *   *   *   *

Ordered that Captn. James Crouch Imediately draw for his Company Three days Rations, have as much thereof Cooked as May be Necessary—Be prepared to March to Morrow Morning, and wait my further orders for that purpose—

                                                      CAESAR RODNEY

Trenton Jany 30th 1777—   B. General—

                    *   *   *   *   *   *   *

     Guards as Usual—
          Countersign. Newport

                    *   *   *   *   *   *   *

Jany 31st. Guards as Usual—
          Countersign Congress—

                    *   *   *   *   *   *   *

Feby 1st. 1777—
     Guards as Usual
          Countersign—Putnam—

                    *   *   *   *   *   *   *

Ordered that Major Ellmer with Three Companies of Coll. Seeley's Battalion of Jersey Militia Imediately March to Princetown and there Join the Army under the Command of Major General Putnam—

                                                      CAESAR RODNEY

Trenton Feby 2d 1777—   B. General

                    *   *   *   *   *   *   *

Ordered Captain Crouch of Coll. Cox's Battalion draw one days Rations More for his Company and March them as Early to Morrow Morning as possible from hence to Princetown and there Join the Army Under the Command of Major General Putnam

                                                        CAESAR RODNEY
Trenton Feby 2d 1777—   B. General

              *   *   *   *   *   *   *

Ordered That a Guard Consisting of twenty four men with one Subaltern Officer, one Sergeant and one Corporal be fixed for this Night, and that the Guard be furnished by the officer Commanding Battalions or Companies, out of and in proportion to the Number of Troops they have now in Town—

                                                        CAESAR RODNEY
Trenton Feby 2d 1777—   B. General

              *   *   *   *   *   *   *

Countersign
    HANCOCK

              *   *   *   *   *   *   *

Ordered that Coll. Thomas Mayberry with the four Companies of his Battalion now here Imediately March from hence to Princetown and there Join the Army under the Command of Major General Putnam

                                                        CAESAR RODNEY
Trenton Feby 3d 1777   B. General

              *   *   *   *   *   *   *

John Emery a Soldier in Captain Chambers's Company of the Congress Regiment having been in this town Ever since the Seventh of Jany by order of his Captn. and in that time has drawn No Rations—Ordered that the Commissy of Provisions furnish him with Rations from that time till this day—

                                                        CAESAR RODNEY
Trenton Feby 4th 1777—   B. General

              *   *   *   *   *   *   *

Guards as Usual

Countersign (Washington)

* * * * * * *

Feby the 5th 1777—Guards as Usual   Countersign

* * * * * * *

Ordered that Coll. Reeds Battalion of Jersey Militia March Imediately from Hence to Princetown and there Join the Army Under the Command of Major General Putnam—

CAESAR RODNEY

Trenton Feby, 6th 1777—   B. General

* * * * * * *

Ordered that Coll. McCoy with his Regiment of Continental Troops March to morrow Morning By 9 OClock from Hence to Princetown and there Join the Army Under the Command of General Putnam and wait his further orders—

CAESAR RODNEY

Trenton Feby, 6th 1777—   B. General

* * * * * * *

Guards as Usual
Countersign
DUBLIN

* * * * * * *

Ordered that William Tucker Continue to Act as A.D.Q.M in this Town—

CAESAR RODNEY

Trenton Feby 7th 1777—   B. General

* * * * * * *

Sir/

You are, as Waggon Master, to Attend to the Orders and Requisitions

Made, from time to time, by William Tucker as A. D. Q. master in this Town
Untill further Orders.—

CAESAR RODNEY

Trenton Feby. 7th 1777—   B. General

*   *   *   *   *   *   *

Guards as Usual
   Countersign
      Addams

*   *   *   *   *   *   *

Ordered That a Guard of Twenty four men, With One Lieutt. one Sargeant
and one Corporal be Mounted This Evening—And that the men be furnished
from the Several Companies now in Town, In proportion to their Strength—

CAESAR RODNEY

Trenton February   B. General
8th 1777—

Instruction to the officer of the above Guard—Your Sentinels are to let no
person pass them after nine OClock at night (Unless he be Coming Express to
the General, or be one of the Physns. of the Town) Without the Countersign.
   The Countersign
      —SALEM—

*   *   *   *   *   *   *

Ordered That Smith Snead Captain of a Company in Coll. Fleming Regiment
of Virginia Continental Troops—Who has been after deserters—Immediately
March from Hence to Princetown, There Report to Major General Putnam
and take his further Orders—

CAESAR RODNEY

Trenton, Feby 9th   B. General
   1777—

*   *   *   *   *   *   *

Ordered that Lieutn. Coll. Baity with five Companies of Militia belonging to General Johnson's Brigade take the Rout directed in Philadelphia to
head Quarters and that the Mr. Sullivan, the A.D.Q.M. Imediately furnish

him with one good waggon for the purpose of Transporting his Baggage to Curryells Ferry.

CAESAR RODNEY

Trenton Feby. 9th. 1777—   B. General

* * * * * * *

The Lieutenant of the Guard made his Report which is filed—

* * * * * * *

Ordered that a Guard of Twenty four be mounted with a Lieutenant, Sergeant and Corporal

CAESAR RODNEY

Trenton Feby 9th.   B. General
1777—

Instruction for the Officer of the Guard Your Centinels are to Let no person pass after nine OClock at night, Unless he be Coming Express to the General, or be a Physn. of the Town, Without the Countersign—
    Countersign
    MARYLAND

* * * * * * *

Sir,
    You are Imediately to March the two Companies of Pensylvania Militia under your Command to Princetown, There Join the Army Under the Command of Major General Putnam, and take his further Orders.

CAESAR RODNEY

Trenton Feby   B. General
10th 1777—
    To Major Latchen—

* * * * * * *

Sir
    You are Imediately to March with the three Companies Under Your Command from Hence by the most direct Road to Join the Forces Under the Command of Brigr. General Dickinson on the Raraton—

CAESAR RODNEY

Trenton Feby 10th 1777   B. General
    To Coll. Hillmer—

* * * * * * *

Sir

You are to draw two days Rations of Rum for Your Company. if to be had, And to March with them to Morrow Morning by Nine OClock from Hence to Princetown and there take the further Orders of Major General Putnam— The Quarter Master of this Town is Hereby Ordered to Supply you with one waggon, and four Horses—

                                                        CAESAR RODNEY
Trenton Feby 10th 1777—   B. General
    To Captain Yates

*   *   *   *   *   *   *

Guards as before—Instructions to the Guards as before—
    Countersign
        Honesty—

*   *   *   *   *   *   *

Ordered That Lieutenant Colonel Homes with Jersey Militia Now under his Command, March from Hence by Nine OClock to morrow Morning by way of Princetown, and Join the Forces on the Raraton Under the Command of Brigd. General Dickinson—

                                                        CAESAR RODNEY
Trenton Feby   B. General
11th 1777—

*   *   *   *   *   *   *

Guards as before—Instructions as before—
    Countersign
        CONSTITUTION

*   *   *   *   *   *   *

Ordered That Captain William Price of Jersey Militia Imediately March with Company from Hence, by the way of Princetown to the Raraton & there Join the Forces Under the Command of Bridg. General Dickinson—

                                                        CAESAR RODNEY
Trenton Feby 12th 1777—   B. General

*   *   *   *   *   *   *

Ordered that Captain Black of Coll. Dill's Battalion of Pensylvania Militia Imediately March from Hence to Princetown and there Join the Army Under

the Command of Major General Putnam—ordered that the Quarter Master
Imediately furnish the Captain with a Waggon to Princetown

                                                      CAESAR RODNEY
Trenton Feby 12th 1777—   B. General

*   *   *   *   *   *   *

Ordered that Coll. Taylor of the Jersey Militia with the Troops Under his
Command Imediately March from Hence, by way of Princetown, to the
Raraton, and there Join the Forces under the Command of Brigd. General
Dickinson

                                                      CAESAR RODNEY
Trenton Feby 12th 1777—   B. General

*   *   *   *   *   *   *

Sir,
    You are Imediately to March with your detachment of Coll. McCoy's Regi-
ment from Hence to Baskin Ridge and there Join Your Regiment under the
Command of Brigd. General Lord Stirling—

                                                      CAESAR RODNEY
Trenton Feby 13th 1777—   B. General
    To Lieut Richardson

*   *   *   *   *   *   *

Sir,
    You are Imediately to March with the Company under Command belong-
ing to Coll. Martin's Regiment of Continental Troops from Hence to Princetown and there take your further orders from Major General Putnam.

                                                      CAESAR RODNEY
Trenton Feby. 19th 1777—   B. General
    To Lieut. Mitchell—

*   *   *   *   *   *   *

Trentown 3d. Feby 1777
                          A report of ye. main Guard
Parrole — — — — — — — — — —
    Countersign — — — — Hancock
Guard Consisting of one Lieut., 1 Sergt. one Corporal & 24 Privates, one Sentry
by day & 6 by Night
                          Nothing Extrordinary
                                                      JAMES FORBES[1]

1 On a loose sheet of paper in Caesar Rodney's Orderly Book.

147

To Thomas Collins

You are to be prepared to march with Your Battalion of Delaware Militia by ten OClock tomorrow Morning, for Princetown and there Join the Army under the Command of Major General Putnam—

Caesar Rodney
B. G. Militia[1]

Trenton Jany 20th
1777
To Colonel Thomas Collins[2]

148

Addressee unknown[3]

Trenton Jany 22d 1777.

Sir:

I have sent you this morning a Company of Coll. Cook's Regiment Commanded by Captain Brady, and three Companies of Pennsylvania Militia Commanded by Coll. Stroud—I am Informed that there are a Considerable Number of Troops on the Road between Philada. and this and Expect them or most of them here this Evening. If they come they shall be Immediately forwarded to You—I am Sir your most obedt. Humble Servt.

CAESAR RODNEY, B. G.

149

To George Read

Trenton Jany the 23d 1777—

If I may Judge of you by my Self I dare venture to say You are antious to know What is going on in this part of the American World, And as it gives

1 When Rodney was ordered by Lord Stirling to take the post at Trenton, the Delaware troops were sent forward under the command of Colonel Collins. When they arrived at Princeton, General Putnam sent them on to Washington at Morristown. Like all militiamen they proved unreliable, and soon were clamoring to be sent home. Washington sent them back to Putnam at Princeton, thinking that Rodney had arrived there from Trenton and that they could be placed under his direct command and kept in check As will be seen in following letters, Putnam's order to Rodney to come to Princeton was countermanded without Washington's knowledge. Consequently, when the Delaware Militia reached Princeton from Morristown on February 4, Putnam permitted them to go on to Trenton the next day, and on February 6 they left Rodney at Trenton for Philadelphia and home.

2 Thomas Collins later in life became President (governor) of Delaware, serving from 1786 to 1789. He was, therefore, the Executive of the State when Delaware ratified the Federal Constitution on December 7, 1787.

3 In all probability the letter was sent to Major-General Israel Putnam at Princeton.

me pleasure to Satisfie the anxious Mind Would have wrote to you long ere this, but accounts of Every thing that happens are so various and perplexing That a man Who would wish to Support any degree of Credit dare Relate hardly any thing he hears. The first Engagement Between us and the Enemy after our Retreat from the North River was at Trenton, Where I am now not only playing the General but Commander in Chief. It happened the day after Christmas and you well know the circumstances attending it—On the Sunday following, Which was the twenty ninth of the Same month, General Washington passed the Delaware to Trenton again, and on Thursday the second of January had an advanced Post of three or four Field Peices, Covered with Six hundred musquetry, attacked (on the hills next toward Princetown) by (as the Inhabitants of the town think) a Body of about five thousand English and Hessians. In this Attack there was verry little done but discharging Field-Peices at each other, Washington Continueing to Retreat in and through the town, The Others, Commanded by General Cornwallis, Endeavouring to Flank them, till Washington Got over the Bridge in the town, and on the Side Where the Main Body of his army lay, and Where by his Order they had during the time of his Retreat been fixing a Number of Cannon. As Soon as these Cannon [were] discharged the Enemy Retreated Quite back to the first mentioned Hill, where they Remained till nine oclock the next Morning Expecting to be Reinforced and then to fight it out. Washington with his army Lay in the field and woods between the town creek and the River till about two Oclock in the morning and after having Caused the Fires to be well made up Marched his Army Round the head of the Creek into the Princetown Road so to Princetown Where a little on this side the town they mett the party Comeing to Reinforce those at Trenton. Here A Warm Engagement Came on, first with General Mercer's Brigade Who were far advanced and being overpowered with Numbers were oblidged to Retreat after having pushed Bayonets. This Gave the Remainder of Washingtons Army time to form and after Giving the Enemy two Rounds oblidged them to Retreat and Imediately after to Run. By this Means they Lost all their Baggage and only Saved themselves by our people's being so fatigued as not to be able to keep pace with them—Washington after following them a little beyond Kingstown filed off to the Left and made for Morristown—Mr Tucker of this town tells me he never see men so filled with astonishment as the English officers on finding that Washingtons army was gone; wondered how he Could have got over the River without being discovered &c He says that between Eight and Nine oClock that Morning two of the British officers Came to his House, ask'd for Breakfast, and Just as they had pourd out a dish of Coffee, heard the Cannon, and Imediately left it, thinking (as they heard the Cannon so verry plain) That Washington had Engaged their Body. However, verry soon Marched off. In this last mentioned Engagement we took about two hundred and thirty prisoners and at Trenton, the day before, Thirty—Since this, General Maxwell has taken Elizabeth town, one hundred and twenty prisoners and all their Baggage to a Considerable Amount. Soon after he took Spank-town about four miles from Elizabeth town toward Amboy on the Sound Where he took a few prisoners and a thousand bushells of Salt and some Baggage of Value—Col! Gurney, who was Sent by General Putnam with five hundred Men into Monmouth, has taken a verry large Quantity of Stores that were lodged there and Guarded by Skinner's Jersey Volunteers. Forty Waggon Load of them have arrived at Princetown, a Great Quantity of Cloths and other English Goods—There was a skirmish on Munday last between one of our outposts and a Superior Number of the Enemy Who Were forrageing. Our people drove them and took thirty one Waggons and Sixty five horses and have brought them Safe in—It is Said by those who Come from the Camp Every day That our Army increases Verry fast—I believe it does Increase some, tho great numbers are leaving it—Sure I am that if none would leave it for three weeks to Come—there would be Enough to Eat the Enemy up—Our Delaware Militia, in number two hundred and Thirty Eight, I sent to Princetown the day before Yesterday,[1] And Yesterday were ordered from there by General Putnam to Head Quarters[2]—I Shall leave this tomorrow and have the pleasure to inform you that I have not been in the least unwell since I left Home, not even with the Astma—In short I Every now and then Conceit I grow fatt—You May Readily Suppose there is nothing verry pleasing in a Cold Winter Campaign and Yet, if I Could but see those Parlimentary Robbers drove off and My old friend Livingston Restored to his Government, I Should Happy—Good God, What Havock they Have made. He that hath not Seen it can have no idea of it—The Dead Bodies of Col! Haslet and Major Morris are here on their way to Philadelphia for interment. Thus Ends a History Which perhaps will afford You much more trouble than Real Satisfaction. However, be that as it may, You must take it as the poor man took his Wife—

150
Addressee unknown[3]

Trent Town Jany. 21st 1777.

I have sent you this Morning the Delaware Batalion of Militia Commanded

---

1 Tuesday, January 21, 1777.

2 To Washington's headquarters at Morristown.

3 Original draft is in the handwriting of Thomas Rodney. The addressee was no doubt Major General Putnam at Princeton.

by Col. Thomas Collins. The Strength of the Batalion (by this morning Return) is Two Hundred & thirty eight including Officers. There are but about Eighty or ninety men now left here which I immagine will not be more than Suffitient for the Safety of this Place as there are Cannon & Stores. As fast as other Troops arrive and can be provided for they shall be Sent forward—a part of those now here are a part of Col. Cook's Regiment, they arrived last night—

P. S. I should be glad to know how many troops you think it will be necessary to keep here.

151

To William Killen[1]

Trenton Jany 27th 1777—

At a Time when Every Sensible Mind is filled with the greatest Anxiety for the Fate of America, When the Sons of Freedom have drawn their Swords and Nobly Stepped forth, in this inclement season, To defend Their most Invaluable Rights and priviledges—At a time of deep distress and danger. Thou Whose first and greatest Temporary wish is for the Freedom of The States art (no Doubt) Desirous to know The State of things in this Land of Tryal— This Scene of Action—This Frosty Warfare—Be it so—I'll Endeavour To Amuse if not Inform the Eager Ear—You have heard (Sad Intelegence) of Your Mercer and Haslet. Slaine. They fell, but nobly fell tho Butchered, And so Long as the Inhabitants of this American World Shall Continue to be a free people, So long (at least) will the name of Mercer and Haslet be held in Honorable Remembrance—Mercer's Charector is Excellent, but in Haslet We know we Lost a Brave, open, Honest, Sensible Man, One Who loved his Country's more than his private Interest—But While Washington Survives the great American Cause Cannot Die, his Abilities Seem to be fully Equal to the public Spirit That Called him forth—History does not furnish you with a greater Peice of Generalship Than he Exhibited on The day poor Haslet fell —He fought, he Conquered—And if we Continue to Improve the Advantages then gained, We Shall Soon put an End to the Dreadfull Controversy that Agitates and Distracts Us—And in Return have *Peace, Liberty* and *Safety* Heaven! What a Glorious Figure in the Eyes of Men and Angels will This Vast American World Exhibit, in its *Free Independent* State. Nothing will Then be wanting but better Men and Wiser Measures to make us a happy people—There has been no Capital Stroke Since our main army Left Princetown Tho' There Seldom a Day passes but Some Advantages are Gained

---

1 Elected first Chief Justice of Delaware under the State Constitution of 1776 in the year 1777.

Which Tend to distress, and in a Little time Must Ruin our Enemy—for the Particulars of these little Engagements Must beg leave to Refer you to my Brother and others That you will See from these parts, They Are too Numerous and Attended with too many Circumstances for my Time and Pen—I have been perfectly well in Health Ever Since I left Home, and do Assure you That I begin to play the General most Surprisingly. I would not have you Suppose I mean the fighting General. That is a part of duty I have not Yet been Called upon to discharge—But When Called I Trust I Shall not disgrace the American Cause Tis Glorious Even to die in a Good Cause. By Lord Sterling, Who I found in Philadelphia, I Was directed to Take the Command at this Place—to forward the Troops To the Army as fast as they Should Arrive Always keeping Sufficient for this Post—Since My arrival I have Sent forward Near two Thousand, Among others the Delawares Who first Went to Princetown and Then were sent by General Putnam to the Main Army to Convoy forty or fifty Waggons—Yesterday (by permission) I Set out myself for Camp—But on my way Received Orders to return to my Old Post Where I now am—General Mifflin is Gone to Philadelphia to forward the Troops there. In Short Every Step is taken, by fixing the Most Suitable persons in these places, to Strengthen our Army as Soon as possible—It is, I do Assure you, Increasing verry fast—The Cloud is fast Gathering all Arround, and I Trust will soon burst on the Tyrants Heads—As soon as the Chief of the Southern Troops pass this place I shall have leave to go and Join My Brigade.

152

To Lord Stirling[1]

Trenton Feby the 2d 1777—

When at Trenton, I mentioned to you my Desire of being Removed to Headquarters to Join My Brigade—and Wished to hear from you on that Head—However if upon advising with ye General, it is thought I can be more usefull at this Post, I Shall remain Here with the Greatest Chearfulness—Not more than four hundred Troops, Except the Light Horse, have arived Here— Since you passed through, and having Recd a Letter from General Putnam Requesting I would Imediately Send him four or five hundred to Replace that

1 William Alexander of New Jersey, whose claim to the title of Earl of Stirling was disallowed by Parliament. The title of Lord Stirling by courtesy was always accorded him by his American friends, by Congress, and by his fellow officers. The Delaware troops were in his brigade at the Battle of Long Island where he was captured. He was exchanged in September 1776. On February 19, 1777, he was promoted to the grade of Major-General, Continental Army. He died January 15, 1783.

many of Militia Whose time had Expired, have let him have upward of two Hundred with a promise to make up the Number he desired, as soon as so many Militia Shall Arrive—All the Continental Troops and the Remainder of the Militia Shall Imediately after their Arival be Sent to headquarters—The bearer of this takes with him a Letter to his Excellency General Washington, from a Hessian Captain, One of the prisoners at this place—He Informs Me the Contents is to Obtain his Excellency's permission to go to New-York for his Cloths and other Baggage—or be permitted to send an open Letter by a Flagg addressed to some friend of his there to send them to him—I doubted his Succeeding in his first Request—Tho he probably might in the Second— You will be pleased to let me know, by the first opportunity, whether it is thought best I should Stay here, or Whether I may with Equal Service to the Cause be permitted to Join the Brigade—

153
To Philemon Dickinson[1]

Trenton, Feb. 5ᵗʰ 1777.

General Putnam Told me the other day at Princetown That you hinted to him, my being Sent to the Post Where you now Command—I Suppose with a View of your being Released for here. I well know that it would be a Verry Great Advantage to you to be here, near Your Estate Which has and is now Suffering Much—I know also That the present Scituation of Your Wife and Children Must give you Such Concern That Nothing less than The Good of Your Country, Could detain you a Moment from them—These things wou'd Move me, Most Chearfully to Accept the appointment if made—But Sir, it would be with great Diffidence, Well knowing That my Experience in Military Matters must fall Vastly Short of Even those who are Inferior to you in that point—However as I have not much Doubt but That I Should Acquit myself with Some degree of Credit, Especially with a Small Matter of Instruction from you (Who I would Wish not to leave the post before I came) I Shall willingly Come provided You Can Obtain an Order for that purpose[2] —I have applied for leave to go to head Quarters & Join My Brigade there,[3] and

Did the General know that most of the Troops now go from Philadelphia

---

1 Brigadier-General, New Jersey Militia, and brother of John Dickinson.

2 An order from General Washington or General Putnam.

3 Refers to his letter of February 2 to Lord Stirling wherein he requests that general to suggest to Washington that he be permitted to join his troops at Morristown, whence (he now thinks) he might lead them to General Dickinson's post on the Raritan River.

by way of Curryell's Ferry He wou'd think my Stay here less Necessary, and of Course Give me leave—I have not Yet got an Answer, and if I don't Get one Soon, am affraid I Shall have no Brigade to Join[1]—Ten to one but they have, are now, begun to be Homesick—I have been Stationed Here, near Three Weeks—it was Much against my will, and Yet I think it has been of Considerable advantage, having time to improve by Practice without Hurry —As I have Turned out in this Frosty Season, and have Enjoyed a perfect good State of Health, Could wish to be Employed Longer (if with propriety) Than, I think the Troops of our State will Stay—Be pleased to let [me] Hear from the first Oppertunity

154

To Israel Putnam

[No date][2]

I Recollect when I had the pleasure of waiting on You at Princetown that You mentioned General Dickinsons haveing proposed my being ordered to his Post, and he ordered here—I Did not then attend so much to what you said on that head as I ought—But as I Supposed his being posted here, where he would be near to his (lately) much Injured Estate, wou'd be verry desirable —Shall have no other Objection to the Exchange if ordered—Than that I may want his Experience to discharge the Military duty, as I could Wish—If you Should approve and will let me know I Shall Set out for that place, where General Dickinson Stay till I arrive—I think there Can be no disadvantage attending this Post being without a General officer for a Little time Especially as most of the Troops now go from Philadelphia by way of Curryells Ferry—

155

To Lord Stirling

Trenton, Feb. 8th 1777

Your Letter of the 6th Instant I Recd Yesterday evening.[3] Am much

1 Rodney's fears were well-founded, for on the day previous (February 4), Washington had sent the Delaware troops back to Putnam at Princeton, due to their unwillingness to stay in camp, and, upon their arrival in Princeton, Putnam had sent them on to Rodney at Trenton on the very day this letter was written The next day, February 6, they left Rodney for home

2 Written probably on February 5, 1777 Rodney had tried to join his troops at Morristown once before when, by permission from General Putnam, he had left Trenton on January 26 with a view to reaching Washington's headquarters via Princeton However, he received a countermanding order from Putnam while on the road between Trenton and Princeton and returned to Trenton

3 In reply to Rodney's letter of February 2 requesting that Lord Stirling see Washington about

Oblidged to you for the Trouble you have taken in applying to the General—
But to my Great Surprise, and their everlasting Shame, the last of the Delaware Militia that I, with much pains, brought out to Serve the Cause, passed
through this Town, the day before Yesterday, on their way Home—So that
I have now no Brigade to Join, as Recommended by the General—They Spent
near or Quite Three weeks in marching up to Head Quarters, stayed There
about one week without Rendering a Single Copperworth of Service to the
Public—And then, Tho Solicited by the General to Stay only two weeks more,
Shamefully Set off, and, from any thing I can learn, without a discharge—I
have been in the Command at this place Ever since your Lordship appointed
me to it—and Shall, as matters are now Circumstanced, Continue Here, Untill
ordered to some other Post, or discharged—If I have given Satisfaction, and
can be longer usefull Here or Elsewhere, I shall, with the greatest Chearfullness Stay on the Service—If not, Shall Expect a discharge—Yesterday, I sent
to Head Quarters, by way of Princetown, Col! McCoy's Regiment of Continental Troops, the day before Col! Reeds Battalion of Jersey Militia went—In
the whole about Twelve hundred—More Troops are Just now arrived here
and shall be forwarded—

156
To Thomas Rodney

Trenton, Feby. 12th 1777.

I now set down to write you by Coll. Collins who was left Sick at Morristown and is not yet recovered. He came here the night before last & was detained yesterday by snow which fell the most of [the] day. As the first and
most material piece of intelligence, I inform you that I am in good Health and
have not been a moment otherwise since I left home. The day after you left
me, in consequence of permision had of General Putnam for that purpose, I
got a waggon, packed up All my Baggage and set out for Princetown Got
about four miles on my way and met orders from him to return to this Post,
letting me know that upon second consideration, he thought it as material a
post for any less than a General Officer. I returned and soon after I came back
Lord Sterling came to town, dined with me and promised that as soon as he
got to Headquarters where he was then going he wou'd prevail upon General
Washington to call me to Headquarters. However General Washington sup-

Rodney's joining his troops at Morristown. In his letter to Thomas Rodney, February 12, Caesar
Rodney refers to his having received orders on February 6 from Washington to join his troops at
Princeton under Putnam. Lord Stirling, in his letter of February 6, evidently refers to Washing-
ton's agreeing to his suggestion that Rodney be permitted to join the Delaware troops.

poseing I was by that time with Putnam, did not think proper to do it. Our people, or the most of them, by the time they had been a week at Camp got so uneasy to return that General Washington ordered them away to join General Putnam. They set out, came to Putnam's post on Tuesday, yesterday week,[1] and next day (as they informed me) by leave of General Putnam set out again and Came here and the next day set out for Philada. on their way home. Upon the Whole I think the General Hardly Expected they would go any farther than General Putnam's Post, Because on Thursday evening last[2] which was the day they left here, I rec'd orders from General Washington to take them into my Brigade with Putnam, supposing I had a Brigade under Putnam. All this appeared to be such a mistery that I could not tell what to think of it till Coll. Collins came and told me that the General finding that he could do nothing with them, said he would march them to Putnam where I was that I might try to deal with them, not knowing that I had been ordered back by Putnam.[3] However to do the men Justice who came from our County Coll. Collins says he is convinced every man of them would have staid provided those from Newcastle and Sussex would, but that they were determined against it.

Captain Manny had his men all turned out to stay Every man upon being addressed. For you must know the General Requested them to stay only two weeks and that he would then discharge them. I most sincerely wish they had, for their uneasiness drew from the General a very Severe Letter to them which Coll. Collins has.

I have Just Rec'd Intelligence of an Engagement between our Troops and those of the English at Quibble Town, the particulars of which are not yet fully known here, but are related as follow—That Coll. Scott of the Virginians with about four hundred men were attacked by a Forraging party Consisting of two thousand who beat him Back. Coll. Scott continued to fight and Retreat till he was Reinforced (which was in a verry little time from different quarters) to near as many if no more in number than the Enemy, and then beat the Enemy back to their Lines at Brunswick with the loss of all the Cattel Horses &c., they had been pillaging and three hundred or thereabout of their men Killed—Our people lost either two or three men.

When I shall be discharged the Service in order to set out home cannot yet say, but suppose it wont be Long—However am determined not to leave it while I am thought Necessary or Usefull, and have reason to believe the Generals have hitherto thought me both.

I have now a Set of acquantance here, both Gentlemen and Ladies, that do

1 Tuesday, February 4, 1777.   2 February 6, 1777.
3 When on his way to Princeton on January 26.

everything in their power to make my time agreable, and will I am Convinced, part with me, when Obliged to do it, with great Reluctance. You may think strange how this should come to pass. However I am certainly a man of Consequence here, tho of ever so little in my own State, and they have got it in their heads, tho ever so strangely, that I am a gentleman as well as a Whig.

157

From Israel Putnam[1]

Princeton 13th Feby. 1777

Coll. Taylor arrived here last night with a Company We continue to be very quiet in this Quarter.

158

From Thomas Rodney

Dover Feby 16th 1777—

I have not wrote to you nor recd: a letter from you Since I Came Home—The Night after I left Trenton I logd at Mr Coxes, the next at Philada the next at New Castle & the Next at home, where I found my famaly & all friends well—Since which there has nothing of note transpired to the Southward except the rising of the Tories to the amount of 2000 in Summersets who upon the arrival of Col: Hooper with about 500 men, all dispersed & fled, but he Took about 40 of the Principle ones and sent them To Anopolis

—By a letter from Mr Read to Mr Killen we are informed that McKinley[2] is appointed President or Gov. of this State by 19 voices out of 23—I think they have been very exact in their Choice as he is the only man that could so fully represent The Whig & Tory Complexion of this State—I make no doubt all their appointments will be of a peice with this and that the State will Continue in the same shackling condition it has been in some time past—without affoarding the least aid to the Union except the private influence of a few individuals—

Feby 26—

I have been from home & have not therefore had an opertunity of Sendg the above. I recd: a letter last night you sent by Collins The Great Assembly of the Dalaware State rose at last; have past a Treason Act, a Militia Act, and an act to Support the Credit of the Continental money with five or six other laws

1 Major-General from Connecticut Headquarters at Princeton from January to May, 1777.

2 Dr. John McKinly of Wilmington, the first President (governor) of Delaware under its first constitution.

I have not heard the Titles of—I have inclosed you a Copy of their appointment in the Executive Department—You will see that they have gone Great
lenths to Strip you but were Too Timerous to do all they wished—they have
left me out which no doubt they think a master Stroke, but it is what I
should have thanked them for if I had been obliged to serve if appointed—but
as that was not the Case & was determined not to Serve with such a motly
Crew the act is indifferent—But I am well Pleased that I Now Can Say I am
Truly a Free Man being neither the Servant of the King nor People—

> When Vice Prevails & Wicked men bare Sway
> The Post of Honour is a Private Station
>   Adison

Some of the members hearing reflexions Cast on the House for their Con-
trivance answed that you were to Chuse wither you would hold your offices
or be one of the Judges—but the faith of such men is but of little worth—they
have already degraded the Government to the Lowest degree; not regarding
either Merit, abilities or Publick faith in their appointments—But the Storm
I think will fall on their own heads in the long Run—one of their fast friends
in Mispillion "says they have made a law to hang their best friends" And what
will be their Complaints when they Come to Experience the administration
of Justice by the Ignoramuses now appointed to dispose of their property—
   Mrs Hazlett is dead of an inflamation in the throat & lungs, & the Estate is
in Such a Situation that Mr Killen presses my Taking the Probit of the Will,
says it will be Good if you avow the act, and as there is no doubt about the
Validity of it I have Consented to do it for the Estate is Suffering very much
—We have very little Business at Orphans Court—There is a Proclamation to
Continue all officers Till the new Comms. Come out—
Every [Nece]ssary of life is Gitting here to an extravagant Price and I am prepairing to move to the Landing in April to Contract expence & Trade a little
—Since I Came Home I have purchased about 1200 Acres of Land at a very
low rate Chiefly in Marshy hope, which I can Contrive to pay for very readily
I believe, as I have Great part of the money by me & can Collect the rest in
time—My inclination is Strong to go Some length in this Scheme as I was
offered any sum of Continen[tal] money at Philada without Interest, but dont
like to proceed beyond my own Stock before I have you opinion tho my own
is that the advantage will be very Great as Land will Certainly rise Shortly to
a great prices every thing it produces being Extravigant already—I have given
9/—13/6 & 14/ [per] acre for all but one Tract Viz. the Great Island at Vin-
cents Causway for which I gave 27/ [?] and Could now git I believe on
Trust £3. [per] acre—

We are very glad to hear you are well and in high Spiri[ts] I shall not neglect to attend your business—T. R.—we are all well at present

The officers of the Dalaware Batalion on the field are not appoint[ed] & Bedford it seems has refused—many of the Companies recru[it] but Slow the officers being determined to resign if the appoin[t]ment Talked of by the Assembly were made—The Batalion has been used in such a maner about the appointment or rather not appointmᵗ that I fear it will not be raised Unless the General who it seems now is to have the appointment should make Such a one as will please them—Your advise to him will have the Greatest wait Caldwell Certainly Stands first in merit & deserves the Command, but I fear his want of knowledg in business might make it To dificult for him—There is one appointment I believe would Please them, and the Honour & Safety of my Country almost induces me To mention it tho I feel unusually happy in the thought at present of being relieved from Publick business, & left at Liberty to pursue a private life to the benefit of my Children which seems at present to be my duty—But I have Tryed the Terror of the Field and feel no repulse from the apprehension of danger—If you have an opertunity you may determine as you please—be who will first—Caldwell deserves the 2 & Pope the 3 Comm.

159
From George Washington[1]

Headquarters Morris Town 18 Feby. 1777

Ld. Stirling did me the favᵗ of sending to me your letter of the 8th Inst. to him, mentioning your chearfullness to continue in Service, tho your Brigade had returned home, & waiting my determination on that head—

The readiness with which you took the field at the Period most critical to our affairs, the industry you used in bringing out the Militia of the Delaware State, & the alertness observed by you in forwarding on the Troops from Trenton, reflect the highest Honour on your Character & place your attachmᵗ to the Cause in a most distinguished point of view—They claim my Sincerest Thanks, & I am happy in this opportunity of giving them to you—Circumstanced as you are, I see no necessity in detaining you longer from yr. family & affairs, which no doubt demand yr. presence & attention—You have therefore my Leave to return.
P.S.

From the Enemy's maneuvres of late, especially their reinforcg. Brunswic,

1 Draft is in the handwriting of George Johnston.

I fear yr. Militia will be wanted again—You will therefore be pleased to keep them in readiness, till I call for them.

160
From William Livingston[1]

Haddonfield 24 Feby 1777

Among other Points that I have in Charge from the Congress to procure Affidavits of, concerning the Conduct of the Enemy upon their Irruption into this State, is their ravishing of Women. This however here is more difficult to prove than any of the rest, as the Person abused, as well as the Relations are generally reluctant against bringing matters of this kind into public Notice. But I am told that the Tavern keeper at Penny Town can prove a Rape against them, committed upon a Woman in his Neighborhood, or is able to direct to those who can. As this man is near your Quarters, & it would save the Expence of bringing him hither, I wish you would send for him, & have his Deposition taken there, & transmitted to me with all convenient Speed.

If you should still be stationed at Trenton when our Assembly rises (which I suppose will be in less than a Fortnight) I promise my self great Pleasure in seeing you in your military Character; & if there be any Wine in your Encampment (as there is no such thing here) to take a Glass with you—

161
Caesar Rodney's Commission as Brigadier-General

By His EXCELLENCY

JOHN McKINLY, ESQUIRE,

President, Captain General and Commander in Chief of the Delaware State. To Caesar Rodney Esquire

Reposing especial Trust and Confidence as well in your Care, Diligence and Circumspection, as in your Patriotism, Valour, Conduct and Fidelity, I have constituted and appointed, and I do by Virtue of the Powers and Authorities unto me given by the DELAWARE STATE, hereby Constitute and Appoint you to be Brigadier General of the Two Battalions of Militia in Kent County & of the Western Battalion of Militia in Sussex County in this State.
You are therefore carefully and diligently to discharge the Duty of Brigadier General by doing and performing all Manner of Things thereunto belonging:

1 Governor of New Jersey.

And all Officers and Soldiers under your Command are hereby strictly
charged and required to be obedient to your Orders as Brigad: General So are
you likewise to observe and follow such Orders and Directions, from Time to
Time, as you shall receive from the Commander in Chief of the said State,
for the Time being, or from any other of your Superior Officers, according to
the Rules and Discipline of War, in pursuance of the Trust reposed in you.
And for your so doing this shall be your Commission.

    Given under my Hand and Great-Seal of the State the Tenth Day of March
       in the Year of our Lord One Thousand Seven Hundred and Seventy-
       Seven.

By His Excellency's Command.

J. A. Booth, Sec^y

162

From John McKinly

Wilmington April 7, 1777.

Since you went abroad[1] I was forced to write to the several commanding
officers of the respective battaltions, in your brigades, & sent a parcel of copies
of the act, for Establishing a Militia in this state, to be properly distributed &
desired that they would severally take the most speedy & Effectual measures
to supply all the vacancies among the officers by Elections to be held, as in
that act is set forth, & that afterwards they would transmit to me the name of
the persons so chosen, the times when, & the particular officers to which they
should be severally Elected. Also Exact lists of the names, & Ranks, of the
several commissioned officers in their respective battalions, specifying the dates
of their several commissions, that accordingly Commissions may issue to them
respectively—I also desired that they w'd exert themselves, to know & perform
their several duties, & to hold themselves & those under their respective command, in constant readiness to oppose their Enemies, on Every Emergency.
These orders I hope you will take care to be speedily complied with throughout your brigade, especially as by a copy of a letter from Genl Washington,
dated the 31st, ultimo, Enclosed to me by Congress notice is given that 3000
British & Hessian Troops had Embarked about ten days before from New
York & Staton Island on board of Transports laying at the latter, & being uncertain where they were destined, advising therefore that we should be prepared to defend ourselves, in case of a descent or attack. The president of Congress having likewise transmitted a resolution of that Honourable Body recommending to the government of this State, to plan such a guard at Lewes

---

1 Refers to Rodney's being stationed at Trenton in January and February as post commander.

Town at the continental expense, as may be tho't sufficient, to protect the persons employed as Pilots, & such property of the good subjects of the United States, as shall be thrown on that or the adjacent Coasts & the same being laid before the Privy Council it is ordered as the best method of complying with that resolution, that a guard be furnished of the Militia of this State, for the purpose afforesaid, to consist of a Captain, 1 Ensign, 2 Leuts, 4 Sergeants, 4 Corporals, a drum man & a fifer, & 70 Privates, which we imagine ought to be stationed in two divisions, the one at the Light House, & the other at the false cape & relieve in rotation once a fortnight. I am to write to Congress to know in what manner they are to be furnished, paid, & Subsisted—You will be pleased to give orders to the commanding officers of the several Battalions of Militia in your brigade, that they may cause those under their respective commands, to get themselves in perfect readiness to perform this service, as speedily as possible & to be ready, to march completely Equipped to defend themselves, against their Enemies on the most sudden Emergency

163
To John McKinly

Dover April the 21st 1777—

Your Letter of the 16th Instant with General Orders inclosed, I Received on the 18th and Imediately Issued and dispatched orders to the Several Colonels and Commanding officers in My Brigade for the Imediate observance of those Inclosed—The Strict observance of the Militia Law, and makeing the Returns in due time, Recommended in your Letter, Orders were Issued for before my Return from York-Town—But from the best Information I Can get Great Numbers of the people are likely to decline Associating, Thinking it much Cheaper to pay the penalty than Equip themselves, attend Musters and lay themselves liable to be called into actual Service—I Think the penalty ought to have been so high as to have Compelled them to Associate—

164
From John McKinly

Wilmington 25th April 1777

I have recd. a Letter from the President of Congress enclosing some Resolutions of that Honble Body of the 19th Instant, founded on a Representation made by the Delegates of Maryland, of the imminent Danger of an Insurrection in the Counties of Somerset & Worcester in that State, & that the Insurgents may be joined by dissafected Persons in the County of Sussex in this State; & recommending Measures to the Government of said States to prevent such Insurrection, & to detect & defeat all Conspiracies that may be formed in those Counties against the Liberties of America—As this is the only Information I have had of any Danger of an Insurrection in the County of Sussex, & as it comes in such a manner, renders it highly necessary that a proper Enquiry shou'd be speedily made, as to the Conduct of the Inhabitants of that County, which may have occasioned the above Representation—& as the Western Battalion of that County belongs to your Brigade, & as I can place much Confidence in what you represent, I do earnestly request that you wou'd make a speedy & full Enquiry concerning this Affair, & write me your Sentiments thereupon that I may thereby be enabled, as early in the Sessions as possible, to give such Information as may be needfull to the General Assembly, who are to meet at New Castle next Thursday & that such Measures may be pursued as may appear most likely to conduce to the public Welfare—pray fail not— you may write by one of the Members of the General Assembly—

Pray how goes on the Militia—I have not yet recd. the necessary Returns required from your Brigade

165

From Robert Morris, Richard Henry Lee, and William Whipple[1]

Philadelphia April 25, 1777

By a letter lately received from Mr. Purdy at Lewis Town we learn that he has been pretty Successfull in collecting the goods that were Saved from the Ship Success lately blown up at the Capes; and that he was waiting for the Waggons which you were so obliging as to promise to Send down for the purpose of bringing up those goods—We doubt not these waggons are gone forward and must beg leave to trouble you further with this business—We request you will inform yourself of the Situation of the Enemys Ships of War in the Bay, and should you find that those goods can be safely transported by water from your Place or from Rheedy Island; that you will have them put on board some craft at either of the places, and sent up here as expeditiously as possible—Should this mode be dangerous, you will please to order the waggons to proceed up to this city.

We know your Zeal for the publick Interest will excuse the liberty we take in giving you this trouble, and if at any time we can render you services in return you may command us freely

1 Members of Congress from Pennsylvania, Virginia, and New Hampshire, respectively.

166

From John McKinly

Wilmington the 29th of April 1777.

Congress have made a requisition of 1500 of the Militia of this State who are to be well armed & accoutred & to rendezvous in Brandy-wine hundred in this Co. By the 15th. day of next month where a camp is to be formed & where tents & Camp equipage will be ready to be delivered to them—A Comm'ee of 3 members of Congress with Genl. Mifflin were appointed to confer with the President & Council of this State to enforce necessity of complying with the above requisition—who met here yesterday, accordingly when they showed the necessity fully, as from several circumstances Genl Howe will by that time make an attempt upon Philada. both by land & water, unless by our having a superior force ready to oppose him, he be deterred therefrom altogether—which makes the aid of the Militia absolutely necessary for about 6 weeks in which time it is expected that Genl. Washington (who is now very deficient but whose army is daily increasing fast) will have a sufficient number of continental Troops under his command—so that it is tho't the salvation of our country & every thing that ought to be dear to us depends under Providence on a hearty & speedy compliance—Another camp is to be formed at the same time of a suitable number of the Militia of Penn. near Philada. The following is concluded to be the most equal way of raising the quota of this State—to wit, New Castle Co. 550 in 8 companies of each 54 privates, serjeants, corpls drumr & fifer 10 commissioned offrs 4, in all 68—8 comps 544. Field & staff Officers 6–550. Kent Co. the same. Sussex, 6 Compies of the same number of privates & officers makes 408. Field & Staff 6, makes 414. Total 1554. I suppose you will speedily convene three officers you think proper in your County & Set about & complete this necessary business as speedily as possible, so as to raise the quota thereof in time. We were thinking that the Western Battalion of Sussex Co. under your command being more remote from the approaches of the enemy's ships & also much stronger than any of the others in that Co. should furnish one half of the Quota of that Co. However, you can settle that affair with Gen. Dagworthy to whom please to forward by Express as speedily as possible the letter herewith sent for him to your care as I have only got the bearer, who is an Ensign in the Delaware Battalion to go as far as Dover & I shall repay you the expense when you let me know it. The first division of the Militia, composed of the foregoing members, it is proposed shall stay 3 weeks & then be relieved by a equal number raised in the same manner & proportion in each of the 3 Counties who are to stay another 3 weeks which will complete the time it is tho't they may be wanted—You know the pay is fixed. Pray exert yourself & animate those under your command to a speedy compliance, as it is hoped this may be the last time the Militia may be wanted, but I have no doubt but that you will—the credit of our state & the liberties of America require it—Transmit me the names of the officers that may be appointed to the 1st Divisn (w'h may like the men, be taken from the several Comps. as Detachments) that I may issue Commissions—Write me frequently how you proceed as it is necessary I shou'd inform Congress—I am exceedingly hurried to get the Messenger off, so you will excuse any inaccuracy, as I have scarce time to read this long letter over again after writing. I sincerely wish you success & would fondly hope you will meet with it to the credit of the State & the good of our great-glorious & common cause—it behooves to settle the Quota with Genl. Dagworthy speedily—no time is to be lost

167

From Robert Purdy

Received from Robert Purdy the under mentioned Articles which I promise to Deliver Safe to General Rodney as I recd. them. Lewis 2 May 1777.

Elijah Berry Capt.

225 Baynets	12 Bales a 1. 12 Marked . . . W
167 Guns wanting Locks	3 Bales Stockings md. P. S. 300. 300 156
154 do with Locks	3 1/2 ps. canvass.
1 Barre[l] Pins marked 111	1 Small Trunk md. Geo. Ross
1 box pins. . . . %	1 Trunk belonging to Capt. Anderson
1 chest. . . . A B	7 Wagons in all
1 Barrell Gun Lock. . . . 11	

Sir above is all the cargo Saved of the ship Success. I hope to have the pleasure of Seeing you Monday Evening.

168

From Robert Morris

Philada. May 2d. 1777

Not meeting with an opportunity to send down the annexd letter[1] soon as intended We have now employed Capt. John Hun to go down & git the Goods shipped up—he will deliver you this letter & you'l please to direct that

1 Refers to letter dated April 25 and signed by Morris, Lee, and Whipple.

all the Goods be committed to his arangement and give him such advice or assistance as may be found necessary

169
From John McKinly

Wilmington 3d. May 1777

I mentioned in my Letter of the 29th Ulto. that the Companies shou'd be completed by Detachments from the several Companies but as you require a farther Explanation, I have drawn out the method agreed upon for this County which is so plain as to be easily understood & may with litle trouble be accomodated to your County according to Circumstances—The Officers who have met & been consulted are of Opinion that the Quota of this County may be raised according to the Requisition of Congress & I wou'd fondly hope that yours may likewise be raised—I have no doubt but the General Assembly will do every thing in their Power to encourage the same—If the People are aggrieved they shou'd apply to the Assembly to be redressed—otherwise complaining creates discontent & divisions which every real Friend to the Cause of their Country shou'd avoid & promote unanimity—pray exert Yourself as the Camp shou'd be formed by the 15th of this Month—a fine healthy pleasant & convenient piece of Ground is fixed upon near Naamans Creek—I have just now recd. a Letter from a Member of Congress urging a speedy complyance—

[P.S.] I expect you will direct the Levies from the Western Battalion of Sussex County—You will be pleased to communicate the Mode of raising & Arranging the Militia as inclosed to General Dagworthy when you have an opportunity to fix the Quotas of the two Battalions with him.

170
To John McKinly

Dover May the 6th 1777—

Yesterday the Militia Officers of this County met in Dover, persuant to my order, with the Enrollment of their several Companies as Well the Old as those under the new Militia Act—from whence we formed an Estimate of the Number Each Company Should furnish, having regard to the Strength and Scituation of the Company, and gave the proper orders for Enforcing a Speedy Compliance—We have appointed the Company Officers that Are to Serve in the first division, Who, as well as the men are to Parade, Those from the

Lower Battalion in Dover & Those of the Upper at the Cross Roads, on Tuesday Next, prepared to march Imediately from Thence to the Camp. In the mean time, be Assured, Everything that Can, Will be done to Inspire them with a Just and lively sense of their Duty on this Great & Most Important Occasion—As I am not fond of Trouble my self, it is disagreable to me, to lye under the Necessaty of being Troublesome to Other people, more Especially to one who is so much Engaged in business as I am Convinced you must be, But Sir, as I would Wish That in Matters of this kind, The Supreme Executive Authority of the State Should be the Rule of my Conduct, hope I Shall Stand Excused with you Tho the Enquiry s[h]ould be made—from a want of Understanding—as you Seem to hint in your last Letter—I have Inclosed you a List of the Officers appointed, That the Commissions may be filled Up, but think it might be better to send down Blank Commissions for the Field-Officers Who are not Yet appointed—I wrote to General Dagworthy Who left here Yesterday Morning, and Inclosed him the Copy as you Requested, and Sent Orders, by Express, to Coll. Polk to furnish the Troops Allotted the Western Battalion as agreed between General Dagworthy & me, Which is one half of the Quota of Sussex County—Be pleased to Let me know how the Troops are to be provided for between this and the Camp, whether they are to be Billitted at the Taverns, and out of what fund it is presently to be paid,—If it were possible they could draw Rations on their way, the Saving would be verry Considerable—Should be Glad to know whether it is Expected That a General Officer Should attend the Troops from this State—I am in great hopes the Militia of this County will Turn out Tolerable well But Shall be Able to Let you know more of that Matter some few days Hence.—

171

From John McKinly

Wilmington, the 6th of May, 1777.

I have heard a report that some officers from the enemies' ships of War were lately seen on shore near Muspilion [Mispillion] Creek & seemingly made welcome by some persons there. This, I hope, you will make a proper enquiry concerning & if found true that you will have such enemies to their country properly dealt with, the safety & credit of the State requires it. A report likewise prevails, that some parties of men from the said ships have landed near Jones' Creek in your Co. & have Killed several cattle & done other damage to the inhabitants. If this likewise be true, I think you should order a sufficient number of the Militia under your command to keep guard where it may be probable that they will land again, to give them a proper reception as I am persuaded a few spirited & successful attacks made upon them would have a happy effect & secure the inhabitants from their future depredations. I should be glad to be informed by you of the truth of these reports, as speedily as may be also should any thing of that sort happen in future in your country, also what success in embodying the militia to form the encamp! recommended by Congress, what numbers will march—how they are provided with arms & accoutrements & when they may be expected here—that provision may be made accordingly.

172

From Samuel Patterson

Xteen[1] May the 11th 1777.

I am now next Thursday to turn out as Col for the Camp at Naman Creek. At which time I cannot say who is to command us. Should be glad of your appearance there as Commander, as Brig. Gen!. I cannot say what orders you have rec^d but I must say I wish your presence. I shall be in the field by next Thursday, & hope to see you there.—
Have enclosed some advertisements as loan officer of this State, which begs you will distribute in your district. I have put in the public papers but this I thought necessary. I am to acquaint you that I have rec^d many sums, for such in this county.—none elsewhere. I would send some blanks to you, if I thought it would answer.

A line from you to the above would be acceptable

173

From John McKinly

Wilmington the 12th of May, 1777.

Yours of the 8th inst. I rec'd—As the battalion from this Co. will, I imagine be complete & as I flatter myself that from your county will be nearly so, I think a Gen. officer necessary to have the command, even should it happen that none should come from Sussex—I hope therefore, It will not be inconvenient for you to take that command to which I now appoint you[2]—As I understood from Col. Collins you had appointed Tuesday next to parade &

1 Christiana Bridge in New Castle County, Delaware

2 This appointment makes clear why Rodney was in command of the State Militia at the Noxentown Camp when the British invaded Delaware in August and September of the same year.

march the Quota from your Co. I have ordered those of this Co. accordingly so that I expect the whole will be at the place of encampm't near Naaman's Creek next Thursday eveg. which is very convenient & pleasantly situated & where I have ordered the Quarter-Master & Commissary here to leave the tents Camp Equipage &c which Gen. Mifflin promised should be furnished in readiness to accommodate the whole nor shall any thing in my power be wanting to make the service as agreeable as possible. The officers can receive their commissions when they come here—I rec'd the list you enclosed to me of the same & rank of those you have appointed for the 1st Division, but as the Subalterns are from different Companies, I should know the names of their respective Captains as also the dates of their former Commissions, or times when elected, as they are to be commissioned as officers of the Militia & not for this particular service only. I think it would be impracticable for the men to draw Rations on their march, as they have not Kettles &c to cook with. I fully approve of the method, I am told was recommended to the officers of your Co. for each man to carry provisions of his own for 3 days, but if nevertheless any should be unprovided that way you must do the best you can. The Gen. Assembly at this session have passed an act fixing the Tavern rates for Soldiers at 15 cents a meal & nothing for lodgins &c. You had better advance the pay for what is necessary & allowable on their march here & you shall be reimbursed. I hope the officers will set a good example & encourage their men to behave soberly & discreetly & to submit with becoming fortitude & manliness to those inconveniences that must be expected—a supplement has passed to the Militia law making all the fines for not enrolling or not attending on Muster days &c. just double to what they were, also that those who do not enroll are to pay an equivalent for every time the Militia are called forth into service. I hope to see you & those under your command in Health, Spirits & good Order, at the time appointed & that their appearance & behavior will do honor to themselves & this state—

174

To Samuel Patterson

Dover May the 13th 1777—

I Shall do My Self the Honr. of Taking the Command of the Delaware Militia Destined for the Camp Near Neaman's Creek, Expect to be there on Saturday or Sunday Next and Shall be Happy as I always was, in Your Company—I have Given Some Orders to the Quarter Master of the Kent Battalion Which he will Shew you and beg You Will Assist him.

175

From Charles Pope[1]

Camp Middlebrook 15th May 1777.

My not receiving any answer to my past letters, gives me reason to suspect they must been Troublesom to you, I do assure you they were not intended as such, as I have ever had the highest esteem for your person & character, I should been the most ungreatful Retch to Disturb that person I have so much Regard—notwithstanding I shall make free to Honour myself with directing this to you, & hope it may find you & Family in good health—as to news we have but little in this Quarter except the several alterations & movements, of the Army; the 3d Virginia Regemts, that composed it, are added to the two other Briggades of that lines, the Delawr. Regmt. is Ordered to join the 2d Maryland Briggade, (this is not a disaggreeable order to them,) which will be complied with as soon as we take the field, the Jersey Briggade & the 3d & 9th Pensylvania Regemts, are Ordered to the Westward, who are to march by Regemts. to Wyomen; one of the Jersey Regemts Marched through Bonbrook yesterday we have certain inteligence that four british regemts, (report say. 4,000 Troops) have sailed from New York & bound to the southward, its Conjectured their aim is Charles Town.

Our Officers, in Camp are very hearty some of them talk of petitioning the assembly, whilst others say they scorn to beg & say the Members cannot be strangers to the extravagence of the times as well as the Depresiation of the Currency—they are undoubtedly alarming circumstances and early Distressing to the Officers of the Army, as five days pay of a subaltern will now only purchase a Dinner—& other necessaries of life are equally as extravagant, it is therefore impractible for those distitute of fortune to Continue as Officers any longer in the service unless supported by their County, I have for your information inclosed a return of our Regemt. which is far short of the Establishmt., his Excellency says he expects something is doing for the Compleating it, wether his expectations will be favoured with success or not must leave you to Determine, much has been said rispecting our absent officers not complying with his Excly proclimation, the Brigadr & officers comd Briggades are desired to report all such. the comt. of our brigade has complied with that part —Capt Larmonth neglect of orders. still continue me in a very Idle Situation, having nothing to do but ride about & Visit the Army & view the County the

---

1 Formerly Captain in Haslet's regiment, now Lieutenant-Colonel of the Delaware Regiment of the Continental Line, which was authorized by a resolution of Congress in September 1776, and which had recently come up from Delaware under the command of Colonel Hall and joined Washington's army.

former gives some amusement whilst the latter affords a delightful prospect which at this season is very beautiful. As my return to the Delawr. Depends on the movemt. of our field Officers & the arrival of Capt. Larmonth, its therefore uncertain when I shall have the pleasure of Seeing you,

176
Addressee unknown

Dover June the 4th 1777

Several of the Waggons are Still behind, and Expected here today. This, as I am in advance to them, will make it necessary for me to Stay and Settle with them.—Should be glad therefore that you would take an Account of the Goods put in the Schooner till Loaded, and have the Remainder put in Mr. White's Store to be sent up as soon as possible in his Shallop—That no Goods be put on Dock but fill the Hole as full as possible. Take care that a safe hand has the management of the Veshel and that he has Sufficient strength of hands with him—Do endeavour to Learn of Mr. White whether the Veshel he was to send is gone and when, and Whether the Commander of the armed boats attended her, for I Could wish this Veshel to go with a Convoy—know of Mr. White what Goods went in his shallop and bring me an accot. of them as well as of those now going that I may transmit them by Mr. Purdy who will wait for that purpose—Desire Mr. White to send me, by You, an accot. of his Charge for Storage, Mending Guns, Boxes &c.—The freight I expect will be paid in Philad^a. If you should want to send to the Commander of the armed boats, in my name, to attend the Shallop, Mr. Skillington will find a Messenger—I have given you a great many matters in charge, however imagine you may get through them all in a Little time and Return home—

177
From John McKinly

Wilmington, the 16th of June. 1777.

I have enclosed to you a resolution of Congress to embody 1500 of our Militia & likewise the copies of some letters rec'd very early yesterday morn.g whereby you may perceive the necessity of marching the said Militia with all speed to a field near Naaman's Creek in this County where we propose the encampment. Tents, Camp equipage &c. are in readiness at Mr. Robinson's who lives near to the place.

With the approbation of the privy Council I have ordered 600 of the said

Militia to be raised in New Castle County & the same number in Kent Co. & the remaining 300 in Sussex Co. I have enclosed you the manner in which we propose to raise & officer the Quota of this County adapted to the particular circumstances thereof & shall leave the manner to you for your Co. whether the present or as you did before. The remaining 300 to be raised in Sussex Co. & divided into 4 Comp.ys under the command of a Major. We still think the Western Battalion as least exposed, should supply one half to be raised under your direction & to find the Major—the other 3 Battalions of that Co. to furnish the remaining 150 Officers still included. The whole to be under your command as Brigad.r Gen.l. The sooner you march them forward, the better. We expect by Friday next at farthest. They are to stay from the time of encampment 3 weeks & then they are to be relieved—to bring all the Arms that can be obtained & what may afterward be wanting, we must endeavor to procure. I sent 28 Bar.ls of Bread & 200 lbs. of Musket Bullets to you by 2 wagons yesterday. Please to forward the letter herewith sent to Col. Dagworthy by Express as speedily as possible. You must supply them on their march as well & as cheap as you can & you shall be reimbursed the expense. Pray exert yourself, but I know you will to raise & march the Quota of your Co. & that of Sussex Western Battalion as fast as possible. The credit of the state & our safety requires at this critical time every exertion. I hope therefore, The officers & men will be hearty & unanimous now when every thing that ought to be dear to us is at stake.

P. S. Excuse any incorrectness for I am greatly hurried to get the messenger off who is to return from your place. The 4 Comp.ies from Sussex must each consist of 1 Capt. 2 Lieut.nts 1 Ensign. 4 Sergeants 4 Corp.s 1 Drum.r 1 Fifer & 60 Privates, Major [?] to have the immediate command under you of those Companies—who is to hurry them forward.

178
From Thomas Collins

July 1777

The inclosed is a return of the first Battalion of Militia of this County also a roll of the Officers of sd Battalion with the dates of their Commissions & appointments. I have not been able to obtain a return from Capt. Bellach & Capt. Smith as to their arms & accoutrements as you see by the return—with respect to the Guard you Ordered to be fixed at Cross Roads, I immediately issued an order to Capt. Rees for that purpose, but he let me know after all his best endeavours he is not able to procure a man. I went through the Company myself and acquainted them of your order. They answered some of them. There was a lot of that Company refused doing any duty in the Company, and therefore say they, we will do no more until they take their turns of duty, and they further say that ye wages will not be half sufficient. I offered them 5/ per day finding themselves, but some of them say they will not undertake that business under 20/ per day. It really Seems to me that the devil or something else is got into the people for many of them is endeavoring who can make the most confusion. And the officers have no more authority over their companies than the privates have over their officers. What will be the consiquence I will not pretend to say, but I think at present that the Militia will not be worth a groat in a little time—

However I should be glad you would let me know the highest price that may be given for the Guard at Cross Roads, as well the officers as the privates. They all seem to be on the same key. Money is their principal object.

179
From John McKinly

Wilmington. the 10th of July, 1777.

Yesterday, I rec'd your favor of the 11th inst. & am exceedingly glad of your success in getting some of those vile traders secured which may be a means to deter others from such base practices. This care, vigilance & success of yours, I have taken proper notice of in a letter written this day to the President of Congress—Col. Cantwell was with me lately, with a deposition he had taken relative to the enemy's depredations on the night they went up Duck Creek— He then very much suspected Edingfield but could prove nothing against him. I wrote to him this day to use his utmost endeavors to apprehend & secure Conner. I have enclosed to you Commissions for the Judges of the Supreme Court & Court of Oyer & Terminer—& as I hope the chief Justice will qualify immediately on his knowing the great necessity there is at present for his so doing. He can give you the needful orders with respect to the prisoners as I look upon them to be in his Dept. I hope ere this you have got properly secured the red full-faced old fellow of the two-masted Boat from Murder Kill & his tall son with the rough, scurfy, sun-tanned face—&c. I have the greatest dependence that you will continue your care & vigilance. I have enclosed a general order to you for placing guards which I think will answer the best purposes. You must advance them cash as you shall see needful. I have likewise enclosed a commission for the Judge of the Admiralty. Your commission for the Brigr Gen. together with the commissions for the Field Officers of the two battallions in your county. I had enclosed in a paper for some time past directed for you but had no opportunity of sending until the other day by Leut. Col. Pope who promised to deliver the same to Col. Collins to whom I mentioned on the cover that he might open it so that he might see & take out his own commission & take care & forward the others to you, so as to save time & you some trouble as I had then no time to write to you or him. I have enclosed to you a copy of a resolution of Congress obtained on the representation of a few individuals from Sussex Co. sent by them & resolved upon by Congress, without giving me the least intimation altho' Maj. Null who carried the address delivered me a letter from Col. Hall on his way to Philad? with whom I conversed a considerable time & of whom I asked many questions relative to the affairs of that Co. but neither Maj. Null nor Col. Hall tho't fit to acquaint me with their application. However, the force may be necessary enough & I have no objections that Congress should thus have undertaken the expense. I have money of theirs in my hand wherewith I shall pay the Militia ordered by them on this service. I have requested from the President some éclaircissement as to the power with which Col. Richardson seems vested, seeing the detachement of Militia ordered by Congress to join him is only properly a Major's command. I should be heartily glad to have the whole under your immediate management which I hope will be the case. You hint at some exertion of Govt being necessary. Pray, be more explicit & write your opinion freely. I apprehend the Cos. of New.Castle & Kent must furnish the full number of Militia required who are to be regularly relieved & I imagine Kent Co. should furnish those who are to do duty first be pleased therefore to give directions to hold themselves in readiness to march when required. I expect to be informed by Congress when Col. Richardson may be there as I have likewise written to the President for that purpose.

P. S. July the 17th When I wrote the foregoing I intended sending the same early next morn. by Express but was disappointed in getting the commissions until this even. I have enclosed them seperate.

180

To John McKinly

Dover July the 11th 1777—

On Sunday last was apprehended and brought to Dover Goal, on Suspicion of trading with the English Men of War, One John Willson, a Residenter of New Jersey, On Tuesday I took his Examination in writeing wherein he Charged Jonas Edingfield of Bombay Hook in Newcastle County, John Ashworth of the Same Place and one John Conner who is said to live in Thorough-

fare Neck, of having Supplied the Men of War with Stock &c. In Consequence
of this I Got Mr Banning, a Member of the Legislative Council, the Only Civil
Majestrate in this Town, To Issue a Warrant for them in order that they
might be taken and Dealt with as directed by an Act of the General Assembly
of This State. Upon this Warrant Jonas Edingfield and John Ashworth were
Taken and brought here. When upon Examination after some little Time
They Confessed the fact with which they were Charged and now Stand Com-
mitted to the Sheriff and in Close Custody. I have Inclosed you a Copy of the
Examination and Should be Glad to know from you at the Request of Mr.
Banning, whether it will be most proper they Should Remain in Goal Here;
Admitted to go at Liberty on Giving Security, or Sent to Newcastle for Tryal
when the Supreme Court Shall be filled, or Whether, as the Tradeing was
had in the Delaware Bay, it falls within the Jurisdiction of The Admiralty
Court—John Conner it seems has not only been Tradeing with the Enemy
but was the Person who Pilotted the Man of War's Barges up Duck Creek to
the Cross-Roads Landing and is not Yet Taken—I have also, since I saw you,
taken the Depositions of three persons living at the Lower End of this County
Relative to the people in the Upper End of Sussex County and now send you a
Copy of them—This Evil is growing so verry fast That if not verry Shortly
put a Stop to by Some Exertion of Government We Shall be Overwhelmed,
we are most Certainly, Even now, in Eminent danger—Lt. Coll. Barrett the
Sheriff was with me Yesterday, and says That, a few days ago, in Consequence
of orders Received from me, He went to Mispillion Neck in this County, in
Order to Establish a Guard at that Post, being one of the three I Gave you a
Memorandum to have Established, and upon Applying to Mr. Nathaniel Luff,
who is Captain of the Militia in that Neck, for that purpose, was let to know
that he was Convinced it Could not be Done, for that the people in that
Quarter had so generally got into the Tradeing Scheme with the men of War,
That it would be dangerous for any Man Who's property lay among them, to
say a Word, or do any Act in opposition to it, and that if he Could procure
men Enough thereabout for a Guard He Should be doubtful of them. Mr.
Barrett Tells me That he is well Informed, they have got to so daring a pitch
in Sussex as to put forth a Proclamation in opposition to yours, and as he believes, offering a Greater Reward than is in Yours, for the Apprehending all
those who Shall attempt to oppose them in their present proceedings—I most
Sincerely wish that Some Method could be fallen upon by Which the State,
within itself and by its Own Authority, Might bring about that Subordination
and Good Order, by a due Execution of the Laws, So Necessary to good Government, The Safety of the people, and the Support of our Wholesom Constitution. And thereby prevent or at least render unnecessary, the Interposition

of our neigbouring States, Which by Some Information I have got since I saw You, is likely to be the Case—Pray Send me the order for Establishing the Guards in this County Which I spoke to you About, Our Temporary Safety depends much on their being Soon fixed—I must beg leave to tell you That John Willson Who Made the Information against the Others Expects the Benefit of Your proclamation.

181

From John McKinly

Wilmington—the 15th of July. 1777.

As I have rec'd information that there is a criminal intercourse kept up by some base, sorded, disaffected persons who reside within the district of your brigade with the Crews of the enemy's vessels of war, whom they supply with intelligence & provisions—as likewise that there is great reason to apprehend parties of men may attempt to land from the said vessels with intention to commit depredations upon the inhabitants who may be well affected to this state residing within the said district. You are therefore hereby, required to fix guards of the Militia under your command at such places & in such numbers as you may think needful to prevent such intercourse & depredations which guards you are to relieve regularly, by others of the same Militia for such time as the situation of the enemy's vessels of war in your opinion & according to your own direction may seem to render the same necessary. Be pleased also to give immediate orders to all the Militia under your command to hold themselves in constant readiness to march at a moment's warning completely fitted to oppose the enemy with effect, when & where they may be thereunto required.

182

To John McKinly

Dover July 19th 1777—

Yesterday (by Express) I Recd Your Letter of the 15th & 17th Instant with the Commissions and Orders, as also a Copy of the Resolutions of Congress Inclosed. The Commission of Oyer & Terminer and the Supreme Commission which belonged to him, I gave to the Chief Justice who let me know he would Qualify and Immediately take Order in the Several Matters cognizable in that Court—Mr. Cook's shall be delivered—The orders, and the several Matters Recommended to me Shall meet with all that attention & Vigilence I would wish to see paid to every wise Resolution of State by those in Authority under it—With Respect the Hint in my last. That Some Exertion of Government was necessary, Nothing more was ment than that the Evil and the Danger to the State, had got to Such Hight and Still growing, That, in my opinion some force had become necessary in Order to Reduce the people to a due subordination to Government, and tho the number of Disaffected was great, yet I had little Doubt but the well affected within the Government were sufficient for this purpose, If so, and the application had been first made to the Supreme Authority of this State Instead of its being made Elsewhere Surely it would have been more to the credit of the State to have taken it up, in, or nearly in the matter Congress have—I had when I wrote last heard that Congress had taken Some Order in this matter but did not till I Received Your Letter know what their Resolutions on that head were. I think they are wholesome and tend to give that Security to this State, so much to be wished by us, and so necessary to the Safety and Well-being of the United States. But, I am nevertheless of opinion This, tho' necessary, Step, Carries with it a Supposed disaffection in a majority of the Inhabitants, or a want of Energy in the Rulers of the State; I mention these things thus freely to you, because I allways have, and still am convinced that you would (not only) wish, but at all times Do, everything in your Power which you had reason to believe would tend to support the Constitution of this government and maintain the Independence of the United States as declared by Congress, and I verily believe you'd not meet with Censure, provided opinion in these matters was properly supported by all those who hold authority under the State; But there is Certainly that kind of Careless, Indifference in too many who are appointed to the Civil line of Duty, which Created the like Indifference and Even Neglect in the Military. That must tend to render Ineffectual your Orders as the Commander in Chief. I hope they will mend, Sure I am, it is in their Power to give order, Ease and Safety to the two hundred Militia Requested of you by Congress and which you mention proper to be furnished from the Militia of this County to join and Co-operate with Colonel Richardson's Regiment, Shall by my orders be, Immediately Draughted or otherwise procured from said Militia, and then Shall have Orders to hold themselves in readiness untill I shall Receive further directions from you, which, when you give them, you'l be pleased to make full as to time of Service, Relief &c—I think your observations with respect to the Command and powers with which Colonel Richardson seems to be vested by Congress, are Extremely just. It certainly would be a Reflection on this State, to Suppose there was no person Inhabitant thereof, of Virtue, Patriotism, prudence and knowledge enough to have the Superintendency of that business and the Command,—tis well known that my other public, as well as my private affairs must suffer by my absence at any time—But Sir when Ever I shall be thought usefull in the Service of my County, Either by Congress or you, I shall with the Greatest Chearfullness step forth, by whom are the offenders to be Tryed, but by the authority and the Laws of this State, if so, who is to report the proceedings held but the commanding officer? where is he to be found unless he be Resident within the jurisdiction of that authority? Tho' the General cause ought to be Supported at all Events, Yet many Inconveniences and Even Real Injuries to this State might be prevented by an alteration in the mode proceedure—hope therefore that Congress will weigh the matter well, when they do they seldom err. Mr. Killen is of opinion that the persons now in this goal ought to have their tryal in Newcastle County where the offence was committed—has therefore advised the sheriff to take order for their Removal, and says he will Immediately Issue Venires.

183
To Thomas Collins

Orders to Colonel Thomas Collins, or the Commanding Officer of the First Battalion of Kent Militia Present

Sir: Delaware State, Dover July the 23d 1777

In Virtue of a Requisition of Congress and an order of the Commander in Chief of this State you are hereby ordered Immediately to furnish from Your Battalion, properly Equipped, Ninety Nine of the Militia including Six Commission officers, to Join and Do Duty in this State with Colonel Richardson's Regiment of Continental Troops for the Term of one Month after their arrival in the County of Sussex, if in the opinion of the Commander in Chief of this State, they shall be thought so long necessary. When you have provided the above mentioned troops you are to cause them to hold themselves in Constant Readiness to March when they shall have orders for that purpose.

CAESAR RODNEY.
B. General.

N.B. a similar one to Colonel Rhodes of the Second Battalion

184
From John McKinly

Wilmington 26th July 1777

Your's of Yesterday's Date by Mr. Freeman I have just now received & am well pleased with the justness of your Remarks & the Spirit of Patriotism,

Love of Order & good Government therein expressed by You—& the great Attention which you pay to every Order sent you manifests your Sincerity—I am also much pleased to be informed by you of that readiness with which Mr. Chief Justice Killen is going to enter into the Execution of his Office—It would afford me the greatest pleasure did all others discover the same readiness to discharge the Duties of the several civil & military Offices to which they have been respectively appointed in this State—I have as yet recd. no Answer from Congress concerning what I mentioned to you in my last—when I do, shall let you know, & agreeable to your desire shall be full in my Orders, & in the meantime I hope that you will get the Militia required in readiness for that Service—I have inclosed to you a Newspaper with the Accot of the late unhappy Affair at Ticonderoga. No later Accot was recd. from thence at Philada. last Saturday's Evening, & this is very confused & imperfect—I have not the Evening Post of Yesterday but saw it to Day, there is a Letter of General Washington's published therein by order of Congress giving an Accot of a Party of about Forty Men under the command of Lt. Collo. Barton having gone from Providence to Rhode Island in two Whale Boats about Ten Miles by Water & then landed & marched a Mile to the Lodgings of Major General Prescot whom they seized together with the Major his Aid de Camp & Guard & carried them Prisoners to Providence, the whole performed with the greatest Courage & Conduct as they had the Enemy's Sentries & Shipping to pass very near. The Vessells at last discovered them & fired but too late—

185

From John McKinly

Wilmington 27th July 1777.

I recd. this Evening your Favour of the 26th Inst. by Capt. Manlove which afforded me the greatest Satisfaction to find that so many of those base & sordid wretches who hold an Intercourse with our Enemies, & of their Adherents who were so daringly wicked as to presume to rescue them in the way they proposed, have been apprehended & secured, in such a manner as discovers so much zeal & courage & such prudent conduct, as to reflect the highest honour on the Gentlemen concerned, & that those shou'd be of your County & under your command, enhances the pleasure.[1] A little after the above men-

1 McKinly refers to a capture, by a detachment of the Kent County Militia and some recruiting officers of the Delaware Battalion, of between twenty and thirty persons, who were selling sheep, poultry, fruit, etc, in the upper end of Sussex County to the crews of enemy shipping lying in the Delaware River, also to a capture of some ten of thirty other disaffected, who were assembling to proceed to Dover to rescue the prisoners.

tioned I recd. yours of the 23d. & Collo. Collins of the 24th, instant by William White together with a few Lines from Collo. Patterson concerning the Arms wanted but unluckily Collo. Patterson has neglected to particularize how many Arms he has belonging to your County, or in what Order they are—I am forced therefore to write him & waite for that Information before I know what Arms to send you—for as I am informed you have no Person with you who can repair Arms, it is in vain to send any but what are in good order; I shall therefore keep those that want repair & have them put in order as fast as possible & altho' we have very few Publick Arms belonging to this County, & know not what Hour we shall stand in need of them, yet I look upon the Business you are engaged in of such importance to the Credit of the State that I shall write as soon as possible to Congress for a Supply of some, altho' I was lately refused by the Board of War to whom I apply'd to purchase 500 Stand for this State, and it will be with much pleasure that I shall mention to that Honble. Body these Proceedings of yours & the Militia under your command, as I had ventured to write to them lately some opinions of mine concerning both which are now proved to be right—I have great hopes that this diligence & success of yours will be productive of the best Effects—as likewise the Attention given to this Business by the Chief Justice—You may both firmly rely on my hearty support as I have no doubt but you will perseveringly go on as you have begun firmly & vigorously yet with prudence & discretion—I shou'd be heartily glad for many Reasons you cou'd reduce those internal Enemies to a due Obedience to the Laws & Constitution, with the force of the Militia of your own County—but shou'd you perceive any necessity for the Assistance of the Militia of this County, let me know & I shall order as many of them as may be needful even before the Relief which you mention is necessary—I am well assured they will readily & cheerfully go at any time when ordered—The Commissary informs me that the Salted Beef & Pork he has will not do, being somewhat spoiled with keeping, so that you must purchase fresh Meat as you want, which I am persuaded you will take care to do on the best terms—You may be plentifully supplied with Bread when you require it—I much approve of your keeping up the Guard in your Place whilst any appearance of an Insurrection seems to require it—

186

To John Hancock, President of Congress

Dover July 30th 1777—5 OClock

Just now by Express from Lewis I am Informed that two hundred and Twenty Eight of the Enemy's ships have appeared in the offing—I have Sent

a fresh man and Horse that this Inteligence may be the Sooner with you[1]—
I believe our Militia (if necessary) will Turn out Imediately pretty Generally
—but must Let you know we are in great Want of Arms, Amunition & Camp
Utensils—if you Can, and think us Necessary, pray provide us with those
things as far as in the power of Congress—Consistant with their other Calls—

187

To William Rhodes

In Virtue of an Order Just Received from the Commander in Chief of the
Delaware State—

You are hereby Ordered, without further delay; To Make Regular Returns
to me of the Strength of Each and Every Company in Your Battalion. The
Number, Order and Condition of the Arms & Camp Utensils, as also the dates
of the Commissions or appointments of the Company and Staff-Officers.

You are also Ordered Immediately to Secure, or Cause to be Secured, all
Boats and Water-Craft whosoever within your Limits, in such Manner, as to
prevent any Inteligence being given to, or Intercourse with, the Enemy's Vessels—and further, for that End, to Place a Constant Guard of Six Men, including a Subaltern Officer, at the Cross-Roads near Craiges Mill on that side
next Dover—for the purpose, more Especially of Examining all travellers.

CAESAR RODNEY
B. GENERAL

To Coll. William Rhodes Esqr.
of the 2d. Battn. Kent Militia
or in his absence, the commanding Officer.

188

From Richard Peters[2]

War Office Aug. 1, 1777

I am directed by the Board of War to express the Approbation they think
you entitled to for your Activity & Zeal for the Service & to request you will

1 General Howe had sailed from New York harbor on July 23 with about 18,000 troops, together with horses and artillery. The British warship, *Roebuck,* which had been stationed in the
Delaware River and Bay over a year, signalled off Lewes that it would be too hazardous to sail
up the river. Consequently the British fleet, accompanied by the *Roebuck,* sailed down the coast
to Cape Charles and, entering Chesapeake Bay, the British army was landed near the Head of
Elk on August 26.

2 Secretary, Continental Board of War in Philadelphia.

continue your Exertions by calling forth as many of the Militia as you can *by any Means* arm. The Continental Stock here will afford but a small supply but the Board apprehend Measures may be fall'n upon to discover Arms throughout the Country. There must be Arms among the People as so many have been issued out of the Continental Stores & they cannot be annihilated. Your State has no Doubt its Proportion. You delivered up a Number last Fall, so did other States among whom Arms are daily discovered. There are such Numbers turning out to oppose the Enemy, that tho' we have many Arms, yet they will not be sufficient & we must give every one their Proportion. I have written to the President thro' whom any orders relative to your Brigade should regularly come, but the Board thought it best to request your Endeavours at getting Arms for Men as well as Men for Arms. We expect a speedy supply of a Number already on Terra firma. Let us but exert ourselves at this Time of Trial & we shall gain the Objects of our Wishes—Peace & Freedom to America

[P.S.] We have Ammunition & Camp Utensils in Plenty
Tents are very scarce.

189

From David Hall and Henry Fisher

8 O'Clock A.M.
Lewestown, August 2d, 1777.

Your Letter by Express arrived last Night by which I find you are anxious to know the movements of the Fleet—On Wednesday we first discovered them & in a little time we could make 23 Sail from the Light-House; they had every Appearance of coming into our Bay one of the small Vessels was placed in the Tail of the Hen & Chickens with a large flag as a Beacon for them & a Ship anchored in the Channel; thus they continued endeavoring to get in 'till the Evening when a large Ship which we took to be the Admiral fired a gun & immediately the whole Fleet tacked & stood off; except the Admiral with three or four others which lay close in the Cape 'till thursday Morning & about ten o'clock she fired a signal Gun and stood off for the Fleet which were to the eastward; immediately the whole Fleet changed their Course to about E.S.E. as near as we could judge the Wind being at S. and about four O'clock P.M.; they were out of sight; whether they were bound to New York or Virginia is not in my power to tell—Our disaffected were greatly disappointed by the Fleet not going up, as they expected the Matter would be shortly settled to their Satisfaction; several went on board of them from Indian River &

Nehemiah Field & Samuel Edwards (two Pilots) from off our Beach—The northern & Western Battalions still adhere to their former Principles as not above four made their Appearance under Arms at the Alarm

I am Sir Your humb. Servt
DAVID HALL.[1]

Sir/ After Colnel wrote this letter Mr. John Adams which I have as a proper Person to Attend at the Faulse Cape Came to town and says that there is no Ships nor Vessels Except one ship which lies at Anchor of Indian River, should any thing farther turn up I shall send my Express to you to forward to Philadelphia, I am sir Your Most Humble

Servant—&—
Aug. 2   HENRY FISHER[2]
Saturday 12 o'clock at noon—

190
From Tench Tilghman[3]

Head Quarters Philada. 2d. Aug.t 1777

Yours of Yesterday to Genl. Mifflin was delivired to his Excellency the Commander in Chief, who thanks you for the intelligence, altho' it was communicated to him before thro' another Channel. You will please to keep the Militia under marching orders till we hear whether the Enemy are really gone from our Coast, or whether the[y] mean another Feint.

191
From John McKinly

Wilmington 3d. Aug. 1777

I recd. your Favour of the 1st. Instant with the News of the disappearance of the Enemy's Fleet which I immediately communicated to Congress & find the same has been since confirmed by Letters from Lewes sent by Express & dated the 2d. Instant—had they approached I shou'd have put you to the Trouble of sending Expresses daily with Intelligence of their Motions & Proceedings,

1 Commanding Officer of the Delaware Continental Regiment; commissioned April 5, 1777.

2 Stationed at Lewes by the Pennsylvania revolutionary authorities to watch for hostile craft. Fisher's note appears on the second page of Hall's letter.

3 A volunteer military secretary to Washington from Maryland. Later was commissioned Lieutenant-Colonel and aide to Washington.

that Measures might be taken accordingly; however shou'd any thing yet happen, worthy of notice, I wou'd request that you wou'd communicate the same, as soon as possible[1]—I have again written to Congress pressing an Answer to my Demand, concerning the Power intended to be vested in Coll? Richardson, by the Resolution; & I expect the same every Hour, & therefore hope the Militia will hold themselves in perfect readiness to join him when required—Notwithstanding the disappearance of the Enemy's Fleet I have enclosed to You some general Orders which I issued the same Day after those sent You by Noarth, which You may perceive are merely discretionary & therefore to be put in partice [practice] only as necessity requires—The within Letter was enclosed to me by the Board of War, they complain of the Scarcity of Arms occasioned by the amazing Number annually distributed & never returned & alledge that our State must have it's proportion, yet still promise to supply our Deficiences as far as they can—they say Tents are scarce but Camp Kettles & other Necessaries may be supplied—they want to know the Number that want Arms & wou'd turn out were they found them—pray therefore hasten the Returns that I ordered to be made last March for that purpose—please to forward the Letter for General Dagworthy—

192

From John McKinly

Wilmington Aug 12. 1777.

I rec[d] a few days ago, the letter whereof the Enclosed is a copy, since which time I applied to the board of War, for as many arms, accoutrements, tents, camp Equipage, & ammunition, as would be necessary to supply the wants I had described, of the Militia of this State, as not Knowing how soon they might be called forth on duty, but I particularly urged that at least the detachment now ordered, on service into Sussex C? should be supplied. However all that could be obtained was a promise of 35 tents, & as many Camp Kittles, together with a sufficiency of Ammunition made up in Cartridges w[h] I expect here daily, & shall immediately forward to you by waggons; & in the mean time, hope the detachment will, in every other respect be in perfect readiness to march directly & join Col. Richardson's battalion & that you will as speedily as possible take the command of the whole, for which your Knowledge of the affairs of that distracted County, & of the character of Every individual of note, whose party disputes, private views, & personal animosities

---

1 Howe's fleet appearing off Cape Henlopen on July 30, with a view to coming up the Delaware, changed its course and sailed for Chesapeake Bay during the early morning hours of the thirty-first.

have in a great measure been the unhappy occasion, to bring matters there to the alarming situation they are in at present, has fitted you in a peculiar manner. This Knowledge incited by your zeal for the credit of the state, & for the Publick welfare, & directed by your prudence, will I hope be a happy means of restoring peace & good order there, by bringing those especially who seem desirous of distinguishing themselves as leaders to a due submission to the law & the present constitution & establishment to wh I am very sorry to observe so few have paid any regard—let me Know how Col Richardson's regiment is subsisted, whether the same commissary Can supply the Militia, or whether I am to apply to the commissary here for that purpose—or should anything besides be wanting that I can supply, you will, let me know—I shall answer your draughts for payment of the Militia, for such sums as you shall choose to draw for. I need not tell you that the payrolls should be proved on the oaths of the respective captains; let me know when they enter Sussex, that I may order the relief accordingly.

The Enclosed resolutions of the 31st ultimo, were lately transmitted to me, & in pursuance of them, I have, with the advice of a privy council, appointed such persons in this county, as we were of opinion would best answer the intention—but as neither myself nor the council were sufficiently acquainted in your county to take upon us to make proper appointments therein; We therefore made free to impose that task upon yourself & Coll Collins, to appoint such & so many as you may think most suitable to promote the main design, which from the readiness you have both heretofore shown on many occasions to serve the public cause, gives me reason to hope you will undertake & perform as speedily as possible & that as soon after as you can conveniently, you will let me know their names, & places of abode that I may transmit the same together with the names of others, that are or may be appointed in this State to Genl Washington, agreeable to his requisition, in his letter to me on that subject—please to advance what money may be immediately needful to go on with that service wh I shall reimburse you on demand, & likewise answer any draughts you may think proper to draw upon me for that service in future, as occasion requires. The place of rendevous has hitherto been at Wilmington, wh we have seen no reason to change—Altho' it is not in our power to augment the bounty, yet we cannot doubt but the General Assembly will consider & make satisfaction for any extraordinary charges that may incidentally happen on that service. Please to forward the letter herewith sent to Brigr Dagworthy, or Col Hall as soon as possible—should be glad of a few lines from you by return of the bearer.

[P.S.] Any of the recruiting officers of the Delaware battalion with you, will furnish [you] with forms, directions, &c. for Enlistments &c.

193
To John McKinly[1]

Dover August the 14th 1777—

Yours of the 12th Instant by Crampton, Came to hand yesterday, 6 o'clock P.M—The field officers will be with me this day, when I shall give orders for the Meeting and marching the Militia ordered to Sussex County. And hope the Tents &c. will be sent forward as fast as possible—I confess I want the Abilities necessary to qualify me for the task assigned, but be assured that Everything, in my power, that tends to give Peace, Safety and Good Order to the State shall be done—If I should be able to Remove Impressions & Practices, too predomenant, in that County & lower End of this, & Introduce good Order and a better opinion of the glorious cause for which we are contending, Even at the Expense of Blood Be sure, I shall be happy, not only in having Rendered great Service to my Country, which is and always has been my Chief, but of meeting Your Approbation;—I have sent you herewith, a Packet including the returns of Col. Collins Battalion and a copy of his letter to me on that head as also respecting the guards ordered for the purpose of Examining Travellors &c—It is difficult I confess but you may depend I will procure the returns of the second Battalion as soon as possible—Mr. Killen says he wrote to you respecting their sending the two Robinsons through this place who expected would have been brought before him for examination—for be it known that whatever might have been the case heretofore the Supreme Court, in my opinion, is presently filled with persons not only competent, but ready & willing to discharge their duty—The Chief Justice tells Me he intends to Issue a Venire for holding a Court of Oyer & Terminer in Sussex within the Time I shall probably be there, which I think will Answer a good purpose, as offenders will not therefore be detained long for tryal, and also Tend to introduce a practice some time out of fashion of holding Courts and putting in execution the Laws of the States—I submit it to you Sir whether our Company of Light Horse wont be very serviceable on this expedition to Sussex—I am apprehensive from the nature of the business they might be particularly so— but if found to be otherwise may be the sooner discharged, Be pleased to let me have your opinion and Order on this head—I believe they will Chearfully attend if called uppon—We shall immediately take order as to appointing persons for the recruiting service and advise me, and my wants make it necessary and advisable—write to you—

1 The original draft of this letter, from which this copy was taken, and the signature are in the handwriting of Thomas Rodney.

194

From John McKinly

Wilmington Aug 15. 1777.

Your favor of Yesterday I rec'd last Eveng with its enclosures, & you may depend that as soon as the Tents &c come to Hand, I shall forward them immediately. I am sorry to find such a backwardness in the Militia, as Col Collins Expresses in his letter which has no date—As to the orders for placing guards, they were issued on a presumption of the Enemy's fleet, proceeding up our bay & river, & were only discretionary to be fixed when & where you should see needful—they were placed here for some days, but were discontinued as soon as it was known, that the enemy had gone off from the Capes. I have written to Mr. Killen concerning the carrying the Robinson's Prisoners to Congress. it is no more than I expected, from those who I imagined would be Col. Richardson's advisers, who have never seemed to pay the least regard to any authority save that of Congress. I am of opinion that the light horse would be exceedingly useful & w'd advise to taking them. Could forage be readily had for them. It is undoubtedly at your own option, whether the 200 Militia be altogether foot, or in part horse. You comply with the resolution of August, & my orders Either way, So use your own discretion.

195

From John McKinly

Wilmington Aug 17, 1777.

I have just now recd by the bearer hereof a letter from the board of war, Enclosing copies of the resolution & extract, from which the enclosed are copied; by one of those resolutions you will perceive, that 20 Light horse are now ordered in the room of the 200 militia formerly required—I hope therefore, you will consequently get them raised & equiped immediately, & as quickly as may be, go with them into Sussex, & join Col Richardson & take the command of the whole & cause Cockayn, Walton, & Lightfoot to be apprehended & confined, agreeable to the other resolution. I am sorry I must give you this trouble, altho' I am persuaded you will cheerfully undergo the same, as it seems indispensably necessary for the credit & Safety of the state, Coll Richardson being a stranger to the laws constitution & establishment thereof in general, & to the affairs of that county in particular. I have informed him in a letter herewith sent, of your appointment to this command, & required him to pay obedience to your orders. I have no doubt but you will exert yourself in causing to be apprehended & secured, all persons offending against the laws, & deliver them over to the civil authority to be properly dealt with, to whom you are to afford Every necessary assistance, as well as to secure all those whose going at large in your opinion may Endanger the publick Safety. I have the greatest confidence that you will do every thing in your power, to promote peace & good order among that distracted people & convince them of the necessity of paying a due obedience, to the laws & authority of the state, as at present established—Let me Know your proceedings from time to time, & any wants I can supply.

196

To the Commander of the First Battalion, Kent Militia

Orders: Delaware State [Dover, Aug. 18 1777]
  Sir:

You are Immediately to Countermand the Orders You May have Issued in Consequence of My Orders of the Sixteenth Instant for Assembling the foot Militia of this County to March to the County of Sussex. As also the Orders Issued this day for Assembling the number of twelve of the Light Horse to go to the same place.

Ordered that you Cause, at least, twenty Men and Horse; to be furnished from the Light-Horse Company, belonging to your Battalion, to assemble in Dover on Thursday next by six OClock in the afternoon, fully Equipped, and in Compleat order to March with me into the County of Sussex. As this measure is Recommended by the Honble. Continental Congress and Expressly ordered by the president of this State. I hope it will be punctually obeyed.

CAESAR RODNEY,
B. GENERAL

To the Commandg. Officer
of the 1st Batta. of
Kent Militia.

197

To the High Sheriff of Sussex County, Delaware[1]

[August 1777]

Sir   A Party of Coll. Richardson's Men will deliver you the Bodies of Thomas Lightfoot and Thomas Cochayne, who in Virtue of A Resolution of Congress

---

1 On August 9, 1777, Colonel W. Richardson, commanding a regiment of the Continental Line in Sussex County, informed the Board of War at Philadelphia that he had taken from Thomas

and the Express order of the President of this State, I have taken into Custody, and now order you in the Most Possitive terms to keep them safe confin'd untill you shall receive Orders to the Contrary from the President

Caesar Rodney
B. General

Sussex County
Delaware State

To the High Sheriff of Sussex County
or to his Goaler—

On the 25th of the Month called August 1777 two of the Above named Richardson's Officers came to our House Just before Night and forced us the Subscribers to go with them to their Camp at the House of John Clowes, where we Arrived about the Middle of A dark Night, and gave us no reason why we were thus treated further than that they were Order'd to take us even at the Risque of their lives; and on the 27th of the same Month we were sent under

Cockayne, of Sussex County, 199 counterfeit thirty-dollar bills which Thomas Lightfoot had received from Walter Franklin of New York and delivered to Cockayne From papers found on the person of Cockayne, it appeared that he intended to circulate the money Lightfoot and Cockayne, having been brought before a local magistrate, were examined, but discharged, and Colonel Richardson, being uncertain how culpable the two men would appear to Congress, desired instructions. On August 15, 1777, Congress passed a resolution calling upon President McKinly of Delaware to order their arrest and confinement, and Caesar Rodney's order to the High Sheriff of Sussex County to receive the prisoners was issued, as he states, in accordance with instructions from McKinly. (See No 195, McKinly to Rodney, August 17, 1777.) In the same letter Colonel Richardson informed the Board of War that he had arrested Peter and Burton Robinson and sent them under guard to Congress "as there [was] no great probability that Tory Judges will punish Tory Offenders however Atrocious their Offence."

The order from Caesar Rodney here presented is taken from a copy evidently made by or for Lightfoot and Cockayne, to which is subjoined a defensive statement signed by them.

The letter from Colonel Richardson to the Board of War follows:

[*Papers of the Continental Congress,*
No. 78, XIX, folio 143]

Sussex County 9th August 1777

May it Please your Honours

Soon after my arrival here I waited upon the Gentlemen our Friends in Lewes Town to Consult them on the Business for which I was order'd Down, & laid before them the Resolution of Congress on that head. It was determined upon as the most effectual mode, that all the Water Craft in Cedar Creek & else where from which the Enemy are likely to receive Supplies, shou'd be collected into Lewes Town Creek, & put under the Care of the Armed Boat Stationed there Accordingly I issued Orders to Capt[n] Murphey who Commands the s[d] Boat to proceed to Cedar Creek and Seize all the Craft there; and to enable him to effect this without danger from the Inhabitants, I ordered down two Parties of Foot, one on each side the Creek, to Aid and Assist him However Capt[n] Murphy on his Passage up to Cedar Creek, on the 6th Instant, fell in with and took a Sloop from New York (of which you will be fully informed by Col° Hall and Major Fisher), which prevented him from executing my orders respecting the Craft I then sent Orders to my Officers to burn all a Guard of twelve Armed men and an Officer to Lewes Town Goal, with a Commitment from Caesar Rodney of which the Above is a true Copy, where we remain close Confin'd, and a Guard of Armed Men sit about the Goal by one Capt. Perry, who have frequently prevented our Friends from coming in to Visit us, and we have never yet been Able to know either our Accuser or Accusation—

Lewes Town Goal
12th of 10th Mo 1777

Tho Lightfoot
Thos. Cockayne

198

From John McKinly

Wilmington, 23d Aug. 1777.

I have rec'd certain advice that the Enemy's Fleet consisting of between 2 & 300 Sail which lately went into Chesapeake Bay were seen Yesterday's Afternoon off the Mouths of Elk & Sassafras Rivers & by their Movements seemed

the Craft in that Creek, and to disarm the Inhabitants, which I expect they will effect before they return to Camp.

In the Sloop taken by Captⁿ Murphey were found Several Letters and Papers, which I herewith transmit to you to be laid before Congress. As there is reason to believe that the Persons to whom these Letters are Addressed have Carried on a Correspondence with the Enemy prejudicial to the United States, I thought it my duty to apprehend & Secure them; And as there is no great probability that Tory Judges will punish Tory Offenders however Atrocious their Offence, I have sent Messʳˢ Peter & Burton Robinson under Guard to Congress (where they will be properly dealt with), rather than to the Civil Power of this County or the State. I also took Mʳ George Waltom into Custody, but have since set him at liberty on his giving good Security to be forthcoming when I shall receive Orders from Congress respecting him.

I have in my Possession One hundred and Ninety Nine Counterfeit thirty Dollar Bills, which I took from Thomas Cockayne of this County, Agent to a Walter Franklin of New York, & I transmit to you a Letter from Franklin to Cockayne which Accompanied the Bills from York. Upon examination it appears that a Thomas Lightfoot (who is Concerned with Franklin in an Iron Works) received the Letter and Bills from Simon Kollick, & delivered them to Cockayne. Lightfoot & Cockayne were carried before a Magistrate, and after being examined by him, they were discharged. By Propositions from Cockayne to Adams (a Copy of which I transmit) it is evident they had a design to Circulate the Bills, but how far Congress may think them Culpable I am not to Judge. I shall however be ready to execute any Order which that Honorable Body may Judge expedient to give me respecting this or any Other Matter.

From the best information I have been able to Collect, & from my Own Observations it appears that a large Majority of the Inhabitants of this County are disaffected; and would I believe afford the Enemy every Aid in their Power, except Personal Service in the Field, which the greater part of them want Spirit to do. They are a set of Poor Ignorant Illeterate People, yet they are Artful and Cunning as Foxes, tis hardly possible to detect the most Open Offenders, yet they are almost every Day Offending. I have had several of the most open and daring before me, but upon examination nothing has been proved against them that would Justify my keeping them Prisoners. I have read the Oath of Allegiance proposed in the Assembly of this State to them, and they declare they are willing to take it—I should therefore be glad to be impowered to Administer that

as if they intended for the latter where it is supposed they intend to make a
Descent in order to possess themselves of the Peninsula between Chesapeake
& Delaware Bays which we ought to endeavour to prevent by all the means in
our power as we are very deeply interested & therefore shou'd give every
Assistance we can to our Bretheren in Maryland & that as speedily as possible
to enable them to make a proper Opposition until the Continental Forces can
arrive—You are therefore to array the Militia under your command as speedily
as possible & have them well provided with Arms Accouterments & Ammunition & as much Provisions as they can. You know You have a Right by Law to
impress Waggons & Horses. I shall order You Bread & as much other Provisions as needful as soon as possible but should any be wanting You must procure & I shall pay for it.—You are to march immediately with the Militia ar-
rayed & provided as above & to such Places as may be most necessary to annoy

or such a one as Congress may Judge proper to be taken by these Rascals; for to apprehend, & turn
them loose again, with only a Reprimand, serves rather to harden than Convince or Convert them.

Have inclosed a General Return of my Regiment to the first of August—the Unsettled State we
have been in for some time past, has prevented me from making regular Monthly Returns for
which I hope to be pardoned. I shall take care to make them regularly in future. Our People have
been, & still are very Sickly, some have been taken off We are without Medicine—the Director
General promised to prepare a Chest and send it down to me, but I am afraid it has slip'd his
Memory· the inclosed Letter to him is on the Subject

We have not been Joined by any of the Militia of the Delaware State ordered by Congress—Nor
are they Necessary—Our Own Regiment Small & Sickly as it is, being sufficient to Oppose and
supress any inimical attempts of the Inhabitants. Ten or twenty Light Horse would render more
service than a Regiment of Foot in apprehending Suspected Persons—they are as wild as Deer &
run almost as fast. I have had a party after that Atrocious Villain Dorman Lofland these two
Days, but he has eluded their Strictest Search, and made his Escape into a large thick Swamp.
Yesterday evening I received a Letter from Gen¹ Dagworthey informing that he had Just received
a Letter from Col° Purnal by Express acquainting him that the British Fleet to the Amount of
two hundred and upwards appeared off the Bar of Sinapuxen, and were bearing to the Southward
with the wind about South East.

Have sent an Account of the Cloathing &cⁿ receiv'd from Major Harriso[n &] Col° Foreman's
Regimᵗ in Consequence of your Order.

I have the Honour to be with the greatest Respect

Your most obedᵗ Humble Servᵗ
W. Richardson

Endorsed: Colonel Richardson's
                Letter.
           Sussex County, 9 Aug. 1777.
           Letter from Colonel Richardson,
           enclosing sundry Papers, & Letters
           taken on board a prize from New York.

Addressed The Honorable
           The Commissioners of the
           Board of War
           Philadelphia.

the Enemy & prevent them from effecting their purpose of plundering the Inhabitants & possessing themselves of any part of the afores'd Peninsula but in a particular manner take care that they do not cut off your communication with the upper part of this State and by a timeous Removal prevent them from obtaining any Cattle or Provision of any kind neither Horses Carts or Waggons.—You are also to take especial Care that no Arms or Ammunition may fall into their Hands.—I shall from time to time endeavour to furnish You with such advice Orders & other things as may seem necessary pray exert Yourself & incite the Men under your command to shew themselves deserving of Freedom & Liberty, now is the time for every Exertion becoming Freemen —the Credit of the State—our own Safety—& the Happiness of the present & future Ages loudly demand it.

Burgoyne has met with a fortunate Check—2000 Militia of Connecticut under a General Stark—has totally defeated one of his Parties of 1500 whereof they killed about 200 & took about 700 Prisoners amongst whom their commanding officer a Lt.-Colonel Bern, Four brass Field Pieces, all their Baggage &c. the above certified by General Schuyler & published by Congress—so that if we do our duty here I believe their is no danger from that Quarter, the Militia there behaving nobly.

199
From John Dagworthy[1]

Indian River Aug^st. 24th. 1777

I Rec^d the letter you forwarded by the two Gent^n. of the light Horse ab^t 7 OClock this Evening,—we have nothing new in this quarter,—I am in hopes as you are so near you will give yourself the trouble to come & see us which will be a great pleasure to Sir Your most obedient Servt

200
From John McKinly

Wilmington 25th Augt 1777

The Enemy have landed this Morning at Cecil Court House & are proceeding towards the Head of Elk where there still remains a considerable quantity of Continental Stores, which his Excellency General Washington who is here,

---

1 Brigadier-General of Sussex County Militia.

is desirous that the Militia of this County shou'd cover the removal of & the first & second Battalion have proceeded toward that place accordingly—The third to follow—pray hurry the Militia under your command towards that place as fast as possible—Where you will receive further orders—pray make what haste you possibly can, the Continental Army is within a few miles of the place—

[P.S.] Just as I had finished the Letter on the other side I was favoured with Yours of the 24 Inst. by Mr Barret, pray come as fast as possible & take the command of the Militia of the State, the 1st & 2d Battalions of this county have turned out I believe to a Man almost, in high Spirits. General Washingtons Army near the place is said to be about 11,000 besides Light Horse & Artillery, I hope we shall give our Enemy's what they deserve a hearty drubbing pray bring as many from Kent as possible & as quick as possible—however you need not wait for them all—Excuse haste. I have had a busy Day

201

To the Commander of the First Battalion, Kent Militia

Dover, Aug 28th 1777

Such of the Company of Light Horse as attended me to Sussex under the Command of Lieutt. Carson Have behaved with such Cheerfullness and punctuallity in Executing, from time to time, my orders, as Demands my Thanks—Which they have most sincerely—You are to Give orders for the attendance of the whole Company Here tomorrow, properly Equipped, To march with me to Newcastle County, in order to Join the other Militia of this State.—

202

Addressee unknown

Wilmington Aug.t 31st 1777.

It is General Washingtons Express Orders that you Immediately Return from your present post by the same Road you came Untill you git to Cantwells Bridge,[1] and from thence as soon as you hear of the arrival of the New Castle Troops, to proceed to Middle Town. You may expect me to Join you—before you arrive—I am providing Commissaries &c.

1 Now Odessa, Delaware.

203

Addressee unknown

Wilmington, Augt. 31, 1777.

It is General Washingtons Express orders . . . that you immediately March from your present post to Middletown in This County or the nearest and strongest post to it, with the whole of the Newcastle County Militia Arm Rgts. Where I shall join and give you further Orders.—You are to give notice to General Maxwell[1] of this Movement and leave with him of the said Militia a Number of between Twenty & Thirty Men that are best acquainted with that part of the country you are now in as Guides to his other Troops—When you Arrive at or in the neighbourhood of Middletown you are to secure your Troops in the best Manner you can from any Surprize of the Enemy.

204

From Mordecai Gist[2]

Camp at Sarsafras[3] 2d. Sepr. 1777

I arrivd here to day at 4 oClk P.M. since which your Letter to General Cadwallader was put in my hands and in Answer thereto—have to Inform you that the Situation of the few Militia Embodied at this place will not admit of an order for their Joining you at present being in want of many Necessarys to equip and make them as formidable as cou'd be wished, a small space of time I hope will supply that deficiency when you may depend on my marchg. forward. I should be happy to keep up a line of communication with you & hope that any Movement of the Enemy that shall come to your knowledge will be forwarded.

205

To Captain Carty

Sept. 2nd 1777

You are, with the Light-Horse Militia under your Immediate Command forthwith to Set out Reconniter fully all the Grounds between Noxentown and

1 General Maxwell was in command of the American troops at the Battle of Cooch's Bridge, September 3, 1777.

2 Colonel of the 3d Maryland regiment.

3 Sassafras River on the eastern shore of Maryland.

the Head of Elk—You are also to take all you can of the Enemy Prisoners,
and bring them to me at Noxentown—You are to Return and make Report
to me by Seven o'clock this afternoon—

206

To George Washington[1]

[Noxonton[2] Sepr 3^d 1777]

Yesterday morning I took Post at this place between two and three miles
from Middleton. I have kept my Light-Horse, about seventeen or eighteen in
number, out beating up the Enemy's Quarters ever since and gaining what
intelligence I could of the Enemy's movements.[3] Last night a little after dark
they were close in with the Enemy at Carson's Tavern[4] where they encamped
exchanged some shott and allarmed their whole camp.

From the best information I can get, they are moving up toward Christiana
Creek. A person was with me this day who went to the Manor-Church and
below it, on purpose to make discoveries, and say, they have all left that place.
I have one prisoner and two deserters brought this day. They also confirm this
Acct. I should have sent them to head Quarters, . . .[5] I have now three hundred and seventy of the Militia all from Kent and with them am determined
to maintain the Post as long as I can and continue to give the enemy all the
trouble in my power in hopes still of being reinforced [from] some Quarter. I
am just now informed the Enemy's ships have all fell down, as if returning, except two ships of War that lay near the Ferry.

207

To George Washington

Noxonton Sepr 4th 1777—

I took Post in this place on Tuesday about 10 OClock being the most Secure
Considering my force—not being Joined as yet by more than forty or fifty of
the Newcastle Militia—I have Some more than four hundred, all but those few
before mentioned from Kent—I have kept out Scouting parties Rather more
than Equal to the force I now have—and my Light-Horse are Every day

1 Washington's headquarters were at Wilmington, Delaware, from August 25 to September 6
inclusive.
2 Near Middletown in New Castle County, Delaware.
3 General Knyphausen's division.
4 Same as Buck's Tavern, near what is now Summit, Delaware.
5 Last line of page 1 is missing.

within View of the Enemy—The night before Last they Exchanged Shot with and allarmed their Camp at Carson's Tavern[1] and last night did the Same at Aitkins's Tavern[2]—I have now two Scouting parties of foot out, one of twenty, and one other of fifty, the Light-Horse Just going out again—I Intend, in order to be more Convenient for this business, to move to Middletown to Morrow, and am in Great hopes Shall be Joined in a few days by the Militia from Maryland and this State—having advised Col! Gist of your Instructions and my Scituation, for that purpose—I am affraid the Newcastle Militia are so Intercepted as not to have it in their power to get to me—Four Deserters and one prisoner has been in to me. These Considering the difficulty in Sending to Wilmington I have [Sent] to Kent, and Given order for safe Keeping, indeed I have two of them at work Repairing our Arms in that County—from these Deserters, from the View my parties have had of the Enemy and from Some Land holders of this Neibourhood who been Seized taken into their Camp and Last night Released, They seem determined to push Immediately for Philadelphia—Some of those Last mentioned say the officers upon being told you had Thirty Thousand men under Your Command and Could have as many militia more, as you wou'd be pleased to ask—Said they wished most Sincerely You had an hundred Thousand—I wish, hope and Verily believe you have Enough to frustrate the Villinous Attempts of those Enemies to mankind and Pest to Good Society—

P.S. One of my Scouting parties Came in this minute & the Officers Reports the Enemy were Striking their Tents at Aitkins's Tavern and preparing to march toward Christina Bridge 7 OClock this morning

208
From Thomas Collins

Sept. 4 1777

I received you favour by Mr. Rees, with respect to the Arms belonging to Mr. McGarmant. I was yesterday about setting out to purchase them, but re-

1 The division under General Knyphausen was approaching from Cecil Court House and Carson's or Buck Tavern served as that officer's headquarters for a short time. This division joined the rest of the army under General Howe at Aiken's Tavern on Wednesday, September 3.

2 Now Glasgow, Delaware. General Howe with the division under Lord Cornwallis reached this point early on Wednesday morning, September 3. With his headquarters here, General Howe sent forward Hessians and British troops on the road leading to Cooch's Bridge. Sharp skirmishing between these and American Light Infantry under General Maxwell occurred along the road, culminating in a severe fight at the bridge referred to. After Knyphausen joined the British at Aiken's Tavern on the same day, the British army remained entrenched from that point to Iron Hill and beyond for five days, when on Monday, September 8, it filed off to the left through Newark, Delaware, toward Kennett Square, Pennsylvania.

ceiving certain Inteligence that McGarmant is not at home, he is some where
upwards with his Drove of Cattell, therefore thought it Needless my Going
unless I could purchase the Arms, however I have wrote to Mr. Banning, to
inquire the certainty of the Arms being there, how many there are and what
kind they are of, and likewise to send all the publick Arms at Dover to Cross
Roads in Order that they may be Repaired by the two Deserters you sent here
yesterday, they are giting in Order at Rees Shop to do this kind of business,
and seem very thankful they can be of use in this way and Promise to be very
assiduous in their business. I shall take care to collect all the publick and
private Arms and send to them for immediate reparation, which shall be sent
to you as soon as done—Cambell the other Deserter I have with me—I also
Received yesterday from two Negroes, [be]longing to Moses Coughran a
small cart, to horses, and some other Articles taken by them—I was . . . to set
out this day to your Quarters before I received . . . ter, but shall Decline
Coming until I have the Necessary business of Repairing the Arms done or in
a fair way of being done, more Especially as our Battalion with you is week
and seems to be well officered with field officers as Col. Battell & Major Raymond is there. However when you think my presence is necessary with you
youl please to Order it—as I am ready on the shortest Notice to give my Attendance I cincerely wish you Success in your Progress

209

From George Washington

Head Quarters Wilmington 5th Sept. 1777

Your's of yesterday reached me last night. I hope as the Enemy have moved
further towards the Head of Elk that the New Castle Militia will find an
Opportunity of joining you with safety. I last night sent an Express to Colo.
Richardson of the 5th Maryland Battalion to march up from Lewis Town &
join you, but as there is a possibility that the Letter may have miscarried, I
enclose you a Duplicate, which I beg you will be kind enough to forward to
him. For the present you can do no more than keep Scouts and Patroles
towards the Enemy to watch their motions, but as soon as you are joined by
more force from this State, by the Militia of the Eastern Shore of Maryland
and by Richardson's Battalion, I would have you move as near the Enemy as
you can with safety, that you may, if they move on towards Philadelphia, get
between them & their Shipping and cut off their Communication with them
or at least render it difficult. You will endeavour to check any parties that the
Enemy may send out to collect Horses, Cattle or Forage; and give me intelligence of any Occurrences that may come to your Knowledge—

P.S. The light Horseman who brought your letter informs me that the Enemy's Shipping all fell down from Cecil Court House last Tuesday and were out of Sight, be pleased to inform me whether this be true, and if it is, endeavour to find out how low they have fallen down. If you advance toward the Enemy always keep your Baggage well in your Rear that you may not be encumbered by it.

210
To George Washington

Middletown Septr 6th 1777

Immediately on the Rect of Your Letter of Yesterday I dispatched one of my Light-Horse with yours to Col! Richardson who he fortunately found at the Head of Sarsafrass—by the Same hand I wrote to Col! Gist to obtain and Give me the best Information of the movements of the Enemy's Fleet, and have Inclosed You his Letter to me on that head—He mention's the riseing & Embodying of Some Tories, and Refers to another Letter sent here with. As to those mentioned to be in Kent on Delaware. I am apprehensive it must be without foundation, because I have Verry Good Inteligence from that Quarter Everry day and have heard nothing of it—When I arrived here yesterday was informed by a number of people that four hundred of Enemy had Landed that morning at Town Point, the farthest point of Land between the Rivers Elk & Bohama.[1] I Immediately sent a party off that way. The officer has Returned and Reports that he was down on the point and all through that neck, and that there were none of the Enemy to be seen—I have a party of foot Just Setting out to take a View of the Enemy about Aitkins's Tavern, where I am Informed they still Lye—I had forgot to tell you that the Officer of the Horse informed me he took a View of the Elk River and that he saw but three or four Veshels, small Veshels of War—Before I left Wilmington I Drew five Boxes of Cartridges, Could not then obtain a Waggon to bring them. The President[2] promised to have them sent Immediately. However by Some means or other they are not Come—for want of them I am much distressed, not having more than four Rounds—I think the Newcastle Militia now may, and hope they will, Join me—
P.S. A person Just Come from Kent on Delaware Says, there is a Report there that a Number of Tories on the Borders of that County and Maryland have Embodied, that Some of them are taken, and that it is believed they were encouraged to it by the Methodists, Many of whose preachers are in that Quarter.[3]

1 Bohemia River in Maryland   2 President McKinly of Delaware State
3 This postscript does not appear in the original draft.

211

From Tench Tilghman

Head Quarters Newport[1] 7th Sept. 1777

His Excellency, being called out to the lines this morning, commands me to acknowledge the Rect. of your favr. of Yesterday. We have undoubted information that the Enemy have sent all their Baggage and Tents on Board, and have drawn their whole force on this side the Town of Elk, having destroyed all the Grain which they found in Store there. This being the Case, the General desires that you would keep Strong parties nearer the Enemy than you are at present, in order to keep them from making excursions to collect Horses of which I fancy they are in great want, to move their Artillery with expedition. If you find, upon a Consultation with the other officers, that you can, consistant with the Safety and Conveniency of your men, move your whole Force nearer the Enemy than you are at present, it will answer two Valuable purposes. You will effectually check all but large Parties from coming out, and you will be ready to fall upon their Rear should they move towards us. In this the General wishes you to consult and cooperate with Coll. Gist, Coll. Richardson and Gen. Cadwalader, who, altho' he bears no rank in Maryland, has been very active in collecting the militia, and is a Gentleman upon whose Judgment you may rely. I hope if any Spirit of disaffection Should appear below that it will soon be checked by making a severe example of the Ringleaders.

212

To George Washington[2]

Noxonton Sept!. the 9th 1777—

I am here in a disagreeable Scituation unable to Render you and the States those Services I both wished & Expected—A few days ago I moved from hence to Middletown in order to induce the Newcastle Militia in this Quarter, Who had Shown great backwardness, to turn out—Especially as by that Move, Most of their farms & property Were Covered. However all this has answered no purpose, for tho' I believe most of their Officers have been Vigelant, but verry few have Come in at all, and those few who made their appearance in the

---

1 A few miles west of Wilmington, Delaware

2 Howe's army having on September 8 marched through Newark with the evident intention of flanking Washington's right wing near what is now Marshallton, Delaware, the American commander had led his army in the early morning hours of the ninth in the direction of the Brandywine River, crossing it at Chad's Ford and at fords below on the tenth.

Morning took the Liberty of Returning, Contrary to[1] Orders, in the Evening. There [Their] increasing the duty of, and Setting so bad an Example to the Troops from Kent, about four hundred in number, and the only Troops I had with me—brought about so General discontent and Uneasiness, Especially as they were more Immediately defending the property of those people, as Caused them in great Numbers. to leave me, Tho I Must Say the Officers did all they Could to prevent it—

Finding this the Case paid Col!. Gist a Visit myself to know his Scituation and when it might be possible for him to Move forward with Col!. Richardsons Battalion and the Militia of the Maryland Eastern Shore, Who let me know he was doing all he Could to Collect them and would move forward as soon as he Should have it his power—the two Upper Battalions of Newcastle County have never Even Assignd me a Reason Why they have not Joined me —Under these Circumstances I Removed to Noxontown Where the Camp duty, on the few I have with me is less Severe, Untill the other Troops Mentioned Shall be Ready to Move forward, and have Wrote this day to Col! Gist on that Head—Yesterday Evening I Sent a party of my Light Horse to take a View of the Enemy and Gain In[telli]gence. The Officer with his Men Returned this Morning and Reports, That he was in Aitkin['s] Tavvern-House, passed Some Miles through the late Encampment of the Enemy Round about that place, Saw, and was among the fires they had left burning. That the Extreem part of their Right Wing Was at Cooch's Mill, Their left toward Newark—This Inte[lli]gence Makes me the More Anxious to Collect and Move forward Such a Body as would be able to Render you Signal Service by falling upon and Harrassing their Right Wing or Rear—Be assured all I Can do Shall be done—But he that Can deal with Militia may allmost Venture to deal with the—. As Soon as I Can Set forward Shall advise you—God Send you a compleat Victory[2]—

213

From John McKinly

Wilmington Septr 9 1777.

Yesterday morning, the British Army made a general movement from the place of their Encampment on the Iron hill, proceeding northward thro' Mill creek Hundred. Our Army at that time expecting they would take their rout

1 In the letter sent to Washington, the word "their" was inserted between the words "to" and "orders."

2 Rodney wrote this letter two days before Washington was defeated at the Battle of the Brandywine.

thro' this place, over Brandywine Bridge entrenched themselves very well on the Eastern bank of Red Clay creek, about a mile westward from Newport, where they had moved the day before & waited their approach in the highest spirits imaginable; but the enemy has for the present given them the slip, having moved farther north to pass Brandywine, at a Place called Chad's Ford, about 9 or 10 miles above this place, but were pursued, or rather attempted to be outmarched, head[ed] & interrupted, in their rout by the whole Continental Troops under Genl Washington who set off for that purpose from their lines at four o'clock this morng accompanied by his excellency, the commander in chief, & the other general officers, & hope they will accomplish their intention, & that victory will be ours. The Enemy I suppose by way of decoy, & to amuse our Troops from pursuits, have left a body of their's on a high hill,[1] about 3 miles west of Newport, who shew themselves very freely both last Eveng & this day on the skirt of a piece of Woods. Various opinions are Entertained concerning their numbers, some alledging them to be only 150 others vastly more—Nothing would please me more, than that they would be made prisoners by the militia of this state, & I have no doubt had the numbers, which first marched to the Head of Elk of the first & 2nd Battalions of this County, been now under arms, they could Easily have accomplished that desirable service by to morrow morng; but they are dispersed, taking care of their Effects which lay directly in the Rout which it was supposed the Enemy w'd take, so that I have no hopes from them at present, unless you could bring immediately, what Troops you mentioned in your last, to have under your command at your present station, to join with such as Could be readily convened here of the 1st & 2nd Battalions, & then I think there would be no danger of succeeding. There are two Brigades of Militia from the state of Pennsylvania, under the command of Brigadiers Potter & Irvine now lying here—But they must wait the command of Genl Washington, who it is possible may order them forward—As the fleet of the enemy is sailed & no danger from them or their army at present in the neighbourhood where you are; & Genl Washington has now left this state, perhaps it w'd be very agreeable to your officers & men, to perform this piece of service which would redound so much to their own Honor, & the credit of the state—I have the Cartridges you wrote for, but the waggons are so much engaged with the movements of our Army, that I could not procure any to forward them to you—No news from the Northward —My best respects to all friends, particularly your privateer, Mr. Dickenson[2]— [P.S.] Should you think proper to come, the sooner the better

1 Near Mill Town

2 John Dickinson, the well-known statesman, was at this time a private in the Kent County Militia.

214

From George Washington

Head Quarters near Chads Ford 10th Sept. 1777

I am favd. with yours of Yesterday, and am sorry to find that so irregular a Spirit and temper prevail among your Militia. The New Castle County people have no excuse for not joining you now, as the Enemy has in a manner left good part of the Country. I have recd. Advice that their advanced Guards are within five miles of this place. I wrote to you Yesterday to follow upon their Rear with all the Force you could collect, and I now press it upon you in the most urgent Manner, because if we Should be lucky enough to give them a Stroke at this distance from their Ships, you will be ready to intercept them. You will also be in the way of intercepting Convoys going to and coming from their Shipping. I desire you will be very particular in keeping the Returns of what militia are in Service and the time of Service, because when the Rolls are brought in for pay, I shall expect them to be certified by you. For want of a little Care in this respect the public has suffered monstrous impositions.

215

From John McKinly

Wilmington Septr 10. 1777

I wrote you yesterday by Express, informing of the movements of the Enemy & that a party remained behind which I was desirous should be made Prisoners by the Militia of this state under your command, since which I have had authentic intelligence, that the sd party have moved on after the main body. Our Army is on the East side of Chad's Ford, in a strong post, & so have baulked Genl How who tho't to have stolen a march & passed that ford, before Genl Washington could have reached it. Genl. How's army Encamped about 5 miles west of the aforesaid Ford last night—No news this morng but what the bearer can inform you. It is generally tho't that How must alter his rout, & perhaps endeavor to get into the great road from Lancaster to Philada. But I hope our army will still keep ahead of them. Our Army are in the Highest spirits & seem most Eager for an attack, & I am well persuaded that if How does not make one, Genl Washington will.[1] One Jacob Hollingsworth, a credible person saw the whole English Fleet evening before last off Spesuti

---

1 The Battle of the Brandywine was fought on September 11, the day after this letter was written. McKinly was captured by the British when a detachment from Howe's army occupied Wilmington two days after the battle, September 13

Island, before the mouth of Susquehanah river—I have not seen the commissary of purchases since I recd yours, but I have no doubt of getting Mr. Haughey's appointment confirmed by him—there is no possibility of procurring a team, to send you the cartridges at present—but hope soon to get one—As I expect His Excellency Genl Washington has sent you orders by this conveyance, I shall not interfere—My respects to Mr. Dickenson &c—

216

To the Officers of the New Castle County Militia

As The Enemy have now Chiefly Left this State, and the property of the Inhabitants Thereby Rendered more Secure—His Excellency General Washington fully Expects The Militia of Newcastle County will Immediatley Join the Troops now Marching Under my Command.—

You are Therefore, without delay, to make the Associators Acquainted with the necessaty of the Utmost Exertion at this time, and Use your Utmost Endeavours to Assemble and March them out to me, by Companies or otherwise, as Quick as Possible—And as a Number of Felling-Axes will probably be Extreemly Usefull, You are to Cause about an hundred of them to be Collected, if possible, Immediately and Sent forward to me.—

Noxonton Sept. 10th 1777—

Caesar Rodney—

B. General

To the Field and Company Officers of the Newcastle County Militia, not now on their March—

217

Caesar Rodney's Orderly Book
(June—September, 1777)

On the following pages, 225 to 233 inclusive, appear the contents of Caesar Rodney's Orderly Book, all in the handwriting of Thomas Rodney, who evidently was serving his brother as an aide or secretary. The dates of the entries are from June 10 to September 11, 1777, and cover the period when Caesar Rodney issued orders for sending a detachment of the Kent County Militia to Naaman's Creek in June, when he commanded an expedition in August into Sussex County, and when he commanded the State Militia in the same month and in September, following the landing of the British at the Head of the Elk and their invasion of Delaware.

B Gen:l Rodneys
Orderly Book—1777

Be it Remembered that I Do hereby appoint Thomas Rodney Esqr., Brigade Majar to me and My Brigade This   Day of   1777—

In Congress June 10. 1777—

Resolved—That it be earnestly recommended to the President and Council of the State of Delaware To Give Orders to the Militia of that State to hold themselves in readiness to March at a Moments warning & to Take Measures to Call forth into actual Service 1500 of the Militia as Soon as possible & that They Order the Said Militia to rendezvous at or near Wilmington or Chester—

Coppy
Wilmington 16th June 1777—[1]

*   *   *   *   *   *   *

Wilmington 16th June 1777—

Dear General/

I herein enclose to you a Resolution of Congress to embody 1500 of Our Militia & Likewise the Copies of Some Letters recd. very early yesterday morning—Whereby You May perceive the necessity of marching the said Militia with all Speed to a field near Naamans Creek in this County where we propose the Encampment—Tents, Camp Equipage &c are in readiness at Mr. Robinsons who lives near to the place—With the Approbation of the Privy Council I have ordered 600 of the said Militia to be raised in New Castle County—and the same number in Kent County—& the remaining 300 in Sussex County—I have inclosed you the manner in which we propose to raise and officer the Quota of this County adapted to the particular Circumstances thereof—& I shall leave the manner to you for your County whether the present or as you did before—The remaining 300 to be raised in Sussex County & Divided into four Companies Under the Command of a Major—We Still think the Western Battalion, as least exposed, should Supply one half to be raised under your Direction & to find the Major—the Other three Battalions of that County to furnish the remaining 150, Officers Still included—The Whole to be under Your Command as Brigad. General—The Sooner you March Them forward the better—We expect by fryday next at farthest—They are to Stay from the Time of Encampment three weeks and then to be relieved—To bring all the Arms can be Obtained, and what May afterwards be

1 Enclosure with President McKinly's letter of same date, a copy of which follows

wanting we must endeavour to procure—I sent twenty eight Barrels of Bread
& 200P of Musket Bullets to you by two Wagons Yesterday—Please to forward
the Letter herewith Sent to General Dagworthy by Express as Speedily as
possible—You must supply them on their March as well and as Cheap as you
Can—& you shall be reimbursed the expense. Pray Exert your Self, but I know
you will, to raise and march the Quota of your County and that of Sussex—
Western Battalion as fast as possible—the Credit of the State and our Safety
requires at this critical Time every exertion—I hope therefore the officers &
men will be hearty and Unanimus now when every thing that ought to be
dear to us is at Stake. I am with much Esteem & Regard

Dr. Sir
Yr. very Hum Servt.
Jno. McKinly

*　*　*　*　*　*　*

Orders for the uper Battalion Kent Malitia
In pursuance of express Orders from the Hon. the President of this State for
the immediately imbodying and Marching fifteen hundred of the Malitia—
You are hereby Ordered forth with to form four Companies from your Bat-
talion To Consist each of one Captain, two Lieutenants, one Ensign, four
Sergants, four Corporals, one fifer one Drummer and fifty Privates—You are
Also hereby Directed to nominate the Captains & Subaltern officers to Said
Companies for My Approbation—You are to raise these Companies from the
Several Companies of Malitia belonging to your Battalion By Draughting
them in Such proportions as you Considering their Situation Strength and Circumstances shall think most proper and Convenient, and Parade them at
Dover, Ready Equiped to march in as few days as possible—You are to Use
the utmost deligence and Activity to Comply with these Orders and Make Report thereof to me

C. R.　B. G.

June 17th 1777
To Col: Thomas Collins Esqre.

*　*　*　*　*　*　*

Orders for the Lower Battalion Kent Malitia
In pursuance of Express Orders from the Hon. The President of this State for
the immediately Imbodying and Marching fifteen hundred of the Malitia—
You are hereby Ordered forthwith to form five Companies from your Bat-
talion to Consist each of one Captain, Two Lieutenants, one Ensign, four
Sergants, four Corporals, one fifer, one Drummer and fifty Privates—You are

Also hereby Directed to Nominate the Captains and Subaltern Officers to Said Companies for My Approbation—You are to Raise these Companies from the Several Companies of Malitia belonging to your Battalion by Draughting them in such proportions as you Considering their Situation Strength and Circumstances Shall think most proper and Convenient and parade them at Dover ready Equiped to March in as few days as possible—You are to use the Utmost deligence and Activity to Comply with these Orders and Make Report thereof to Me—

June 17th 1777—
To Col: William Rhodes Esqr.

* * * * * * *

General Orders—

As a number of persons supposed to be disaffected to the present Constitution and Government &c. have been lately apprehended brought to, and Confined in, Dover Goal, as it has been with the Utmost Difficulty that I have been able to procure from the Malitia a Suffitient Guard from Time to Time to prevent those persons being rescued, and as Col: Richardsons Regiment of Continental Troops and as Suffitient number of the Malitia of this County are actually Ordered and in a short time will be ready for the purpose of bringing the disaffected in this State to a Sense of their duty and a strict obedience to the Laws thereof by bringing the offenders to Justice &c.—And as I have been informed that a party of the Malitia is now marching up for the purpose of, as They say, Taking Tories, Whereby for want of prudence & good Order Many Mischiefs may arise to the good & well disposed Inhabitants of this State &c. These are therefore Ordering and Commanding all Officers & others within My Brigade to desist from any such purpose or expedition without first making the design known to Me and receiving My special orders and Instructions for that purpose.

CAESAR RODNEY
B. General

July 29, 1777—

* * * * * * *

Ordered that all the officers of the Malitia of Kent County Use their Utmost diligence to furnish from the Several Companies the number of men ordered to Join and co-opperate with Colonel Richardsons Batalion so that they be ready to March immediately on receiving orders for that purpose—

C. R.
B. General

July 29: 1777

* * * * * * *

Dover

In pursuance of a Recommendation of the Honourable the Continental Congress—It is the express Orders of his Excellency the President of this State To Me to Cause all the Malitia of this County (lately ordered to hold themselves in readiness to go to the County of Sussex and there join and co-operate with Col. Richardsons Regiment of Continental Troops) to March to that place as soon as possible, and when joined to take the whole under My Command.

You are therefore hereby Ordered to cause the officers and privates belonging to your Regiment and assigned to this service to assemble in the Town of Dover on Thursday next by Ten of the Clock in the forenoon, Where they will receive necessary supplies and marching Orders—They are to bring with them all the private Arms, Cartrige Boxes, Canteens, Blankets &c., they Can procure fit for service.

As the Troops now Ordered from this County will shortly be relieved by the like number from Newcastle County I hope and expect they will enter their services Chearfully—

                                                                C. R.

Aug 16. 1777   B. General

To Thomas Collins Esqr. Col. of the first Battn. Kent Malitia or in his absence to the Commanding Officer—

*   *   *   *   *   *   *

Dover

In pursuance of a recommendation of The Honourable Continental Congress—It is the express orders of the President of this State, To me, to Cause all the Malitia of this County (lately ordered to hold themselves in readiness to go to the County of Sussex and there Join and co-opperate with Coll: Richardsons Regiment of Continental Troops) To March to that place as soon as possible and when joined to take the whole under My Command.

You are therefore hereby Ordered to Cause the officers and privates belonging to your Regiment and assigned to this Service, to assemble at the House of John Bell in Mispillion Hundred (or where else you may Think more Convenient) on Thursday next by Ten of the Clock in the fore noon, Where they will receive necessary supplies and further orders—They are to bring with them all the private arms Catrige-Boxes, Canteens, Blankets &c., they can procure fit for Service—As the Troops now ordered from this County will Shortly be relieved by The like number from New Castle County I hope and expect they will enter the Service Chearfully

                                                                C. R.

Aug. 16. 1777   B. General

To William Rhodes Esqr. Col of the 2d Regiment of Kent Malitia or in his absence to the Commandg officer—

P.S. Perhaps it will be more proper that those persons belonging to your Battalion that are to go under the Command of Captn. Lockwood should assemble at Dover.

* * * * * * *

In Congress 15th August 1777—

Resolved that it be Recommended to the President of the Delaware State to Order Twenty Light Horse to Join Col: Richardson in the County of Sussex & give him All Assistance in their power to Execute the Directions of the said State, in the Room of the Militia ordered there.

Copy from the Journals

William Z. Houston D. Secry.[1]

* * * * * * *

In Congress 15th August 1777
Resolved

That a Copy of that part of Coll. Richardsons Letter which relates to Thomas Cockrane & George Walton and Thomas Lightfoot of Sussex County in the State of Delaware be transmitted to President McKinley & That he be desired forthwith to take orders for the Apprehension And Confinement of the said Cockrayne, Walton and Lightfoot & That Coll. Richardson be Ordered to afford every assistance in his power to President McKinley & the officers whom he shall employ in this necessary Service.

Copy from the Journals

William Z. Houston D. Secry[2]

* * * * * * *

Extract of a Letter from President McKinly

Wilmington 17th Aug. 1777

I have just now received by the bearer hereof—a Letter from the Board of War enclosing Copies of the Resolutions & Extract from which the enclosed are Copied—by one of those Resolutions you Will perceive That twenty Light Horse are now ordered in the Room of the 200 Militia formerly required—I

---

1 Enclosure with McKinly's letter of August 17.
2 *Ibid.*

hope therefore that you Will consequently get them raised & equiped immediately & as Speedily as May be—go with them into Sussex & Join Col: Richardson and Take the Command of the Whole & Cause Cockrayne, Walton & Lightfoot to be Apprehended and Confined agreeable to the other Resolution—

I have informed him (Col: Richardson) in a Letter herewith Sent of your Appointment to this Command & required him to pay Obediance to your Orders—I have no doubt but you will exert your self in Causing to be Apprehended & receive all persons offendg. against the Laws & deliver them Over to the Civil Authority to be properly dealt with, to whom you are to afford every necessary Assistance: as well as to secure all those whose going at Large in your Opinion May endanger the Publick safety—

*   *   *   *   *   *   *

Dover Augt. 18th 1777—

You are immediately to Countermand the Orders you May have Issued in consiquence of My orders to you of the Sixteenth Instant for Assembling and Marching into the County of Sussex Two Hundred of the Militia of this County—As by a recommendation and an Order from the President of this State the whole Company of Light Horse are to go with Me instead of the foot Malitia afsd.

To the Commandg. Officer ⎰
of the Second Battalion   ⎱

*   *   *   *   *   *   *

Dover Augt. 18th 1777—

You are immediately to Countermand the orders you may have Issued in Consiquence of My Orders of the sixteenth Instant for assembling the foot Malitia of Kent County to March to the County of Sussex as also the Orders Issued this day for Assembling twelve of the Light Horse to go to the same place—
Ordered

That you Cause at least twenty men and Horse to be furnished from the Light Horse Company belonging to your Battalion to Assemble in Dover on Thirsday next by six OClock in the afternoon equiped and in Complete Order to march with Me into the County of Sussex—As this Measure is recommended by the Honourable the Continental Congress and expressly Ordered by the president of this State I hope it will be punctualy Obeyed—

To the Commanding Officer ⎱
of the 1st Battalion Kent Malitia ⎰

* * * * * * *

Sir

Such of the Light Horse as Attended me to Sussex Under the Command of Lieutt. Carson Have behaved With such Chearfullness and punctuallity in Executing, from time to Time, My Orders as Demands My Thanks—Which they now have Most Sincerely—You are to Give Orders for the Attendance of the Whole Company Here Tomorrow properly equiped to March with Me to New Castle County in order to Join the other Malitia of this State—Dover Augt. 28: 1777—

To the Commanding Officer ⎱
the first Battalion Kent Malitia ⎰

* * * * * * *

Ordered that all the Malitia Troops now in Noxentown Draw one days Rations, and March This morning by Eight OClock to Middletown—

Noxen Town Sept 11th 1777—

* * * * * * *

As the Enemy have now Chiefly left this State and the property of the inhabitants thereby rendered more secure—His Excellency General Washington fully expects the Malitia of New Castle County will immediately join the Troops now Marching under My Command—You are therefore without Delay to make the Associaters Acquainted with the necessaty of the utmost exertion at this Time—and use your utmost endeavours to assemble and March them to me by Companies or otherwise as Quick as possible—And as a number of felling Axes will probably be Extremely useful, You are to cause about an hundred of them to be Collected if possible immediately and sent forward to Me.

Noxtown Sept. 10th 1777—

To the field and Company Officers ⎤
of the New Castle County Malitia ⎬
not now on their March.   ⎦

* * * * * * *

Sir

You are to March the Malitia of this County assembled at the Cross Roads tomorrow Morning by nine oClock by the nearest and most Safe way to Join the Malitia of New Castle County Unless you receive other Orders from Me in the Meantime

Dover Aug. 29th 1777—

C. R.

To the Commanding Officer of the ⎫
Kent Malitia in the Delaware State at ⎬
Cross Roads ⎭

*   *   *   *   *   *   *

Sir

You are with the Light Horse Malitia under your Command forthwith to Set Out—Reconniter fully all the Ground between Noxen Town and the Head of Elk—You are also to Take all you Can of the Enemy Prisoners and bring them To Me by Seven OClock this afternoon

C. Rodney
B. G.

Sept: 2d: 1777—
To Captn: Carty

*   *   *   *   *   *   *

Countersign—Washington
Ordered that Col: Collins establish a Guard at Duck Creek to Examine all Travellers who have no papers and especially to Stop all the Malitia now on duty who have not passes from the General.

Noxen Town Sept. 3d. 1777—

*   *   *   *   *   *   *

Ordered that Captn. Carty of the Light Horse and Two of his men immediately to apprehend John Cain, Othaniel Cain and Benjamin Parker (who deserted from Captn. Berrys Company of Malitia now at Camp at This place) and bring them back to Camp—

NoxenTown Sept. 3. 1777—

*   *   *   *   *   *   *

Head Quarters

Camp at Noxen Town Septr: 3. 1777—

The Enemy being within a few Miles of this Camp it appears necessary and is therefore Ordered that Every person not in the Service be brought before some Field Officer and examined as to his business and Cause of Coming

Hence—This Order is not intended to prevent well disposed persons Visiting the Camp—

Ordered That no Soldiers be permitted to pass the out Guards and Centinels without a pass from his Captain or One of the Field Officers—

Countersign—Hancock

* * * * * * *

As there is no Commissary of purchases provided in the Regular Channels to Supply this Camp and as a Supply of Provisions is immediately necessary for the Troops here, You are hereby directed and Ordered to discharge that duty Until a regular appointment by the proper Authority can be made—

                                                        C. R.
Head Quarters Middle Town   B. G.
Septr. 8th 1777
To Mr. Robert Haughey

218
From Mordecai Gist

Christeen Bridge 15 Sep. 1777

having receivd orders last night per Express to remove from this quarter, [I] propose marching Immediately to the left, which will leave this place open to the ravages of the Enemy, and as I have certain Intelligence of their Intention of Crossing in Small Foraging parties on the New Castle side, have thought it necessary to advise you of it per Express that you may as far as in your power comply with his Excellencys Instructions in removing the Stock, for which purpose hope the Soldiers of your Brigade will readily turn out. I am likewise Informd by good authority that the Comdg. Officer at Wilmington orderd a mustring of the Inhabitants last Saturday to quallify them to the quantity and quallity of the Stock removd, and to oblige them to attend their parties to the place to deliver the same, for which they are promisd a genteel payment.

I attempted this morning about day break to secure and bring off their Picket, but the party being misled by the Guide faild in the Execution. We got one man wounded, drove them in and retd.

Colo. Pattersons Regt. meets to day. I can get no arms from him.
I am advisd of an Intended route of Colo. McDonnalds to day to drive with a friend of his, a small party is now waiting for the event which I hope will prove Successful as soon as they return I march.

N.B. the party are returned and have only but Mr. Malcomb prisoner, who was Just setting of to go over to the Enemy, who are now Entrenching round the accadamy in Wilmington.

4 oClock

The Inclosd is this Moment come to hand. I therefore transmit it to you.

my orders last night was from Congress to repair Immediately with all the force I had to Join the main army. Since which the Inclosed came to hand.

219

From Samuel Patterson

Christiana bridge Sept. 19, 1777

Yours of the 17th came to hand by Express, note the contents, for answer have done all in my power to assemble the militia but to very little purpose. I have disposed of them, viz. one company made out of three, along the neck & down along the Delaware to Hamburgh, one company at Xteen under a subaltern about 15 men, to take it in rotation, & one in the Welsh Tract, to keep people from plundering one another. The Cattle is mostly all drove off from the riverside. This I shall attend to. As to Col McDonough's Battalion, I think they will not move from their own district, without you should come up to this place. We are all open to be plundered down to the bottom of the State. All our rich have deserted us; What can be done when such is the case?

I am in hopes Genl Washington will assist us; Such I have ordered to be applied for. My officers never come near me nor men scarcely. The few I have will, if not assisted, will break off, as in fact they will be sacrificed if their numbers are known. I have the floor to lay on & that's almost all, as all this part has fled.

As to the news from Genl Howe, I hear it was true in part but was going to New York by land, & was interrupted & to what you say. We have no news here as our passage is blocked up. Genl Washington advancing to attack them. Last accts, they are yet near Shad's ford. 6 ships was of Xteen Creek, 1 brig with 12 Guns, run into Xteen Creek, lies a mile above the town. Some Cannon fired this morng—the cause have not heard.

220

To George Washington[1]

September the 21st 1777—

There has Just fell into my hands, found in the Tract of Enemy by Some

1 At the time Washington's army was in the vicinity of Potts Grove, Pennsylvania

of my people some Eight or ten days ago, One of the Enemy's Orderly Books. It Commences in April last, and Ends Since they landed at Elk. I have perused it, and being of opinion that it might be Verry Usefull provided you are not previously informed, as to the matters it Contains have sent it you by a private of my Light-Horse who I believe to be Verry Trustworthy—Last fryday week in the Afternoon I Arrived at Christina Bridge and That Evening Wrote you by one of my Horse who in a Little time after Unfortunately fell into the Enemy's hands with the Letter, as they were Comeing to take possession of Wilmington.[1] He was a private but a well behaved Trusty Young fellow, possessed property which is in Trade and therefore Must Suffer Verry Much; If under these Circumstances an Exchange without Interuption to the Important business before [you?] Could be soon made for him, it Would give me great pleasure, his name is William Berry—The Next Morning after the Enemy had taken possession of Wilmington We got Inteligence of it, and by the Evening had no More of the Delaware Militia than Sufficient to Conduct their Baggage Home, and these, their Officers let me know, were determined to go that Night. Therefore thought it best to give them that Charge and let them go—The Next day I left Coll. Gist with the Continental Troops, and the Militia from the Eastern Shore of Maryland at the Bridge—And have Eversince, but am sorry to Say, to no purpose, been Trying to rouse and Get them to the field again. Except a few small parties near Christina Creek Removing Stock &c out of the Enemy's way—The people Complain the Militia Law by the Insufficiency of the fines Compells none to turn out, That the people of property, Who are Disaffected Avail themselves of it And Therefore the Burthen too Great on them—In Short it does not Seem Ever to have intended by the Law They Should be brought forth—I am much hurt by not having it in my power to go forward with Coll. Gist to Join General Smallwood with propriety, Especially as the Cause, at this time, So Loudly Calls Assistance. If there are any Services I Can Render be pleased to Command;

P.S. Should be glad to hear from You—

221

From Samuel Patterson

Trap Tavern[2] Sept. 22d. 1777

I[n] consequence of your letter, I came to this place on Saturday night. Yesterday was appointed for a meeting of Collo. McDonaghs Battl. I waited,

---

1 Friday, September 12.   2 Near St. Georges in New Castle County.

but am Sorry to say, it answered no purpose. Not a field officer here. Mr. Vandyke Just Cald at the house. After this a 2d Division of the Enemys fleet Appeared. Then to move them, if in a Body, I thought rong.

Ordered them one half at a time to Guard their Shore as long as the Enemy
lay there; when movd. up, to Join me at Xteen, but no hopes at any rate. And
I dont much blame them, as all our big men have left us. I wish Sincearly
you could come, if only your horse, to give some heart. If no help, the few I
have will disperse.

I expect Mr. McKean at Xteen to act as presidint of this State to day.

Our Presidint is prisoner on board the Roebuck; went on board Saturday.

Per Last accompt, I find wee have Surrouned Mr. How at the Great Vally[1]

222

From George Washington

Camp, Four Miles From Potts' Grove, September 24, 1777.

—I last night read your favor of the 21st, and am much obliged to you for
the book. This, and the one taken in the action at Chadsford, complete general
Howe's orders from April to the 10th inst.[2] I am sorry for the captivity of Mr.
Berry, whom you mention to be a young man of merit, but no proposition for
his exchange can be made at this time, nor can he be exchanged but in due
course, which is the only rule by which equal justice can take place. The conduct of the militia is much to be regretted. In many instances, they are not to
be roused, and in others they come into the field with all possible indifference,
and, to all appearance, entirely unimpressed with the importance of the cause
in which we are engaged. Hence proceeds a total inattention to order and to
discipline, and too often a disgraceful departure from the army at the instant
their aid is most wanted. I am inclined to think, the complaints and objections
offered to the militia laws are but too well founded. The interest of the community has not been well consulted in their formation, and, generally speaking, those I have seen are unequal.

I wish I could inform you that our affairs were in a happier train than they
now are. After various manoeuvres and extending his army high up the
Schuylkill, as if he meant to turn our right flank, general Howe made a sudden countermarch on Monday night, and in the course of it and yesterday
morning, crossed the river, which is fordable in almost every part several miles

1 On the day this letter was written General Howe succeeded in crossing the Schuylkill River
at Swede's Ford (now Norristown).

2 The Battle of Chad's Ford or the Brandywine was fought September 11.

below us; he will possess himself of Philadelphia in all probability[1]—but I think, he will not be able to hold it. No exertions shall be wanting on my part to dispossess him.[2]

223

From Thomas McKean[3]

Newark[4] Septem half past five P.M. the 25th 1777

I have only time to send you the inclosed, and to beg your utmost assistance at this time—Every nerve must be strained—Be not discouraged—Let us acquit ourselves like men determined to be free.—

Take care that the Election be held—Send the Dover Light-Horse, or at least six of them, to the assistance of Colo: Patterson. You shall hear from me very particularly in a few days. I took the command on Monday,[5] with no other view but to do all I can, in the worst of times, to save my Country. Adieu.

224

Caesar Rodney's Commission as Major-General of the State Militia

COMMISSION
Major General of the
Delaware State, Sept. 26th, 1777
    to
C. Rodney.

THE DELAWARE STATE TO CAESAR RODNEY, ESQUIRE, GREETING. KNOW you, that the PRESIDENT, with the approbation of two of the Privy Council of the said State, reposing especial trust & confidence in your patriotism, valour, conduct & fidelity, doth by these presents constitute & appoint you to be Major General of the Militia of the said State, for the protection of the same State against all hostile enterprizes, and for the defence of the liberties & inde-

1 Howe occupied Philadelphia September 26.

2 Washington here is referring to his plans which culminated in the Battle of Germantown, October 4.

3 In the capacity of Speaker of the Delaware House of Assembly, McKean was at this time Acting President of the State on account of the capture by the British of President McKinly in Wilmington, September 13, and the absence from the state of the Vice-President, George Read.

4 On account of the British ships being on the Delaware River off New Castle, McKean made Newark, Delaware, the temporary capital of the state.

5 September 22.

pendence thereof, and of the UNITED STATES OF AMERICA. You are therefore
carefully & diligently to discharge the duty of Major General as aforesaid by
doing & performing all manner of things thereunto belonging. AND we do
strictly charge and require all officers and soldiers under your command to be
obedient to your orders as their Major General: AND you are to observe and
follow such orders & directions from time to time as you shall receive from the
Commander in Chief of this State according to law, and pursuant to the trust
reposed in you. This commission to continue in force during the present war
with Great Britain. WITNESS the Honorable THOMAS MCKEAN, ESQUIRE,
Speaker of the Assembly, President, Captain-General and Commander in
Chief of the said State, &c. and given under his seal at arms at Newark, the
twenty-sixth day of September in the year of our Lord one thousand seven
hundred and seventy seven.

Thos. McKean.

225

From William Peery[1]

Lewes October 3rd 1777

I suppose before this reaches your Town you will have various representations of what happened here on the late Election day, in which I make no
doubt my Charecter among others must suffer much, I have therefore undertaken to give you a true state of the whole matter in order to enable you to
judge impartially thereon.—For sometime before the Election various stories
were circulated through the County to inflame the minds of the disaffected
multitude here, one of which was, that if the Whigs got into the Assembly
the Militia would be draughted and obliged to go to the Camp, in consequence
of which the disaffected came out almost to a man; as soon as they had collected in Town they began in thier usual strain of drinking prosperity to King
George, Damning the Whigs, and swearing there was not Rebels enough in
Town to take them up &c. I order'd some of them under Guard and had one
of them Bound to appear at the next Court of Oyer and Terminer.—

This behaviour of the Tories determin'd a few Whigs to send for the Sheriff
and propose to him that no man should be suffer'd to Vote who refus'd to take
the following Oath. "I —— do swear that I renounce and refuse all allegiance
and obedience to George the third King of Great Britain &c., and that I will
discover, and make known, to the President, or some Judge, or Justice of the
Peace, of the Delaware State all Treasons, or Traitorous conspiracies, that I

---

1 A captain commanding a company of militia at Lewes.

now, or hereafter may know, to be form'd against the same" and requested the Sheriff to propose it to the People which he at first agree'd to, but in some short time after told us he was threatened to be thrown Neck and Heels out of the Court-House if he tender'd any such Oath.—Col. Conwell, Major Fisher, and myself, then went into the Court-House and proposed it to the Inspectors who (in our opinion) would have adopted the measure had not Jacob Moore, and John Wiltbank, come in and oppos'd it which drew on a pritty warm debate between Moore and myself, in the course of which Moore said he had opposed any such Oath in the House of Assembly and always would, that he would take no such Oath, and if any Inspector refus'd his Vote he would bring an Action against him, and he would find one hundred and fifty more should do the same, whereupon our proposal was rejected and the Election opened: we then retired into a Room and sent the Sheriff a Note to the purport following.

Sir
A number of Whigs have met and are determined no man shall Vote at the Election this day unless he take the oath prescribed in the paper put into your Hands.

To John Woodgate Sheriff
Wm. Peery

This note was deliver'd by Major Fisher who return'd with an answer in the Sheriffs name tho in Moores Writing.—That he Could only conduct the Election according to Law, and if I impeded the freedom there of by an Armed force he would adjourn it and I must expect to be answerable for any consequences arising. On recieving this I sent the following answer.

Sir
I Expect to be answerable for any Consequences arising from my Conduct respecting the present Election, be that as it may, Either adjourn the Election, or Administer the Oath prescribed, or I will make Lewes Town too Hot for every Tory in it.

To John Woodgate Sheriff
William Peery

This was also deliver'd by Major Fisher who was waiting an answer when he was Seiz'd by Isaac Bradley and others who Beat him with thier Fists, Clubs, and Stamped him, untill the Militia now on duty and the Soldiers was call'd to his relief, who instantly rushed in and rescued him or he must have been Murdered in a few minutes more.—The people Enraged to see the Major thus basely treated, Beat without distinction every one of the party that came in thier way, one of them fir'd a Gun at Bradly in the Street which made the Tories fly to thier Houses with all possible speed some Jumping out of the Court-House Windows and getting off as fast as they Could the Soldiers pursuing and firing several Guns after them and it was with difficulty they could be restrain'd by the Officers who Exerted themselves on the Occasion—The Sheriff and Inspectors also quited the Court-House and the Election broke up in confusion—This Sir is a true state of the whole matter so far as I am able to Collect—My Conduct may be censurable but when the State of this County comes to be fully consider'd I hope I shall stand Justified in the judgement of every friend to the American Cause—

226
From William Peery

Lewes Oct.ʳ 5ᵗʰ 1777

This morning 36 Sail of the Enemies Ships went past this Town up the Bay, and this Evening 47 more were seen from the light House Standing in for the Cape, and while Writing being Nine oClock, find by the lights in the Bay and firing Signal Guns, they have Anchor'd in our Road, I hope they also will pass by without Vissiting us.

On the appearence of the Fleet last evening all the Boats along Lewes Creek were brought up to the Fort and a Centinel placed over them to prevent any person going off to the Ships, but notwithstanding this precaution, Abraham Wiltbank, his Son Jacob, and Luke Shields Jun.ʳ, went on Board the Fleet, they had taken a small Boat a Cross the Creek some time Yesterday and left her where she could not be discover'd, and in the Evening went over in a Cannoe, and then haul'd thier Boat a Cross the Cape to the Serf, and we suppose went to Ships who were then anchor'd in the Road.

I have been advis'd to place Guards at thier Houses and have thier Goods Inventory'd, but have declin'd the measure untill I shall receive orders from you respecting the matter, should therefore take it as a favour if you would be so kind as to send me your opinion on this Head—

227
To George Washington[1]

Dover Oct.ʳ yᵉ 7th 1777

Captain Peery who commands a Company at Lewis-Town writes me as

1 Washington's army was at Pennypacker's Mills on the Perkiomen River.

follows—"Lewis Octr ye 5th 1777. This morning 36 sails of the Enemy's Ships went past this Town up the Bay, and this Evening 47 more were seen from the Light House Standing in for the Cape, and While writing being nine OClock find by the Lights in the Bay and firing Signal Gun they have Anchored in our Road."—Captain Peery Says Several of the inhabitants run off to them that night. Tho he tryed to prevent it—

The Enemy that possess Wilmington By permitting the Inhabitants of this State to pass in and out the Town freely and—bring their Effects to Market, by furnishing them with articles much Cheaper than they were used to get them &c have already So Corrupted them—That to talk of Giving the enemy any opposition, or to prevent this free, dangerous Communication, is more than any, now, dare Venture—In Short we are now in a most alarming Scituation—

228
From Thomas McKean

October 15th 1777.

I am sorry I was not at home when your favor of the 29th ulto. by express was left at my House, being then with the Congress at Yorktown in Pennsylvania,[1] soliciting the affairs of the Delaware State. Every friend of mine, nay every man of common sense or common honesty must know that nothing under Heaven, but the love of my country & of the virtuous part of the Delaware State, could have induced me to have undertaken the command in chief when it was the duty of the Speaker of the Council[2] in the first place, or at least to have requested it of me; but from whom I have never yet heard, tho I wrote to him on the 26th of last month and delivered my letter to his cousin Major Evans one of the Privy-council: I say no man could suppose it to be eligible in one who had quit the State and accepted the office of Chief-Justice in another, where he could have remained in peace & honor and taken care of his own property & domestic affairs without censure from any one, to neglect them all and step forth to save a "poor & distressed State" without a head, without a shilling, public records & papers in possession of the enemy, together with their capital & principal trading town; the militia dispirited & dispersed, many of them fled out of the State for safety, and a majority of the rest supposed to be disaffected to the glorious cause we are engaged in, and to undergo

1 When the British were approaching Philadelphia, Congress adjourned on September 18 to Lancaster and from there proceeded to York, Pennsylvania.

2 McKean is referring to George Read, who did not go with Congress to Lancaster and York, but remained in Philadelphia until September 26 (the day the British occupied the city), escaping across the river to New Jersey and returning to New Castle via Salem, N.J. Read then took up the duties of acting president or governor of Delaware.

all the difficulties and discouragements, he was sure to meet with, and which has since been realized. No Secretary, no Great Seal &c., &c., to be heard of. The command to continue but a few weeks, and another person to succeed, who might either disconcert every plan he should propose or adopt, or reap the honor of it. Tho' sensible of all this, yet I have done it, and by the favor of God will go thro' with the business.

You have new orders enclosed: Please to advise with General Dickinson & whom else you please about the method of carrying them into execution with the utmost speed. There is something more in view than what is mentioned, but I am under an obligation to the General to keep it secret. This hint must not be mentioned. I must beg you will give orders to the Dover Light horse to hold themselves in readiness to march on a day's notice. I purpose to be at Dover next week.

Your commission as Major General is inclosed. Please to forward the packet for Brigadier Dickinson,[1] who is appointed next to General Dagworthy; Colo' Patterson is appointed third.[2]

Our affairs are again in a most prosperous way. General Burgoyne's army of about seven thousand surrounded in a swamp by Twenty thousand Americans, his retreat and all supplies cut off,—General Howe's army, consisting on the day after the battle at Shad's Ford on the 11th of September of 8304 including the sick, and since reduced by the battle of the 4th instant inclusive of the sick to about 6,000. soon to be attacked again by General Washington & an army of more than double the numbers; and the row-gallies, Batteries &c., playing their part most nobly indeed. In short a month more will in my opinion give us peace, liberty & safety. I know your utmost exertions will not be wanting. Let us quit ourselves like men, like freemen, and convince the world we deserve liberty.

You have the copy of a state of the British forces at & after the 11th September among the papers, it was found in the pocket of a British Major, now a prisoner taken in the last action.[3] General Agnew was killed, a Hessian general supposed Lieut. Gen. Kniphausin mortally wounded[4] and another Hessian General severely wounded, besides a great many Colonels &c., and upwards of a thousand soldiers killed, and above an hundred waggon load of wounded were brought into the city on the 4th. A Quaker from their yearly

---

1 John Dickinson was appointed brigadier-general for Kent County to succeed Caesar Rodney. He did not accept the commission, however.

2 Samuel Patterson was appointed brigadier-general for New Castle County to fill the vacancy caused by Dr. John McKinly's election to the presidency and his subsequent capture by the British

3 The Battle of Germantown on October 4.

4 A false rumor.

meeting told me this, and that he saw the two Hessian Generals in the condition I mention. General Washington in his letter of the 10th to me says, "If the uncommon fogginess of the morning & the smoke had not hindered us from seeing our advantage, I am convinced it would have ended in a complete victory: But we must not repine, on the Contrary should rejoice that we have given a severe blow to our enemies, and that our ranks are as full or rather fuller than they were before. . . ."

229
From George Read

Dover[1] November 1st 1777

I inclose you a Copy of certain Resolutions entered into by the Legislative Council of this State with the Approbation of thirteen of the members of the Assembly signified by their subscribing the same as they could not nor did not form a House to do Legislative acts—The critical Situation of the State having the Enemy on its borders without any Armed force to repel their Attacks induced the Council to adopt the Measures contained in the Resolution afsd therefore I must request you forthwith to proceed in the Nomination of the Officers, and raising of the Quota of militia assigned for Kent County agreeable to the Scheme and General Orders of Mr President McKean of the 14th of October last transmitted to you, and that you do appoint a Commissary to supply them with Rations of 1lb Meat, 1lb Bread or Flour, and ½ a Gill of Brandy or Whiskey per man per day 3 Pecks of Potatoes for 6 men per Week, or other Vegetables in Proportion, 1 Gill of Salt per man per week and 5lb Candles for 50 men per week for Guards &c—These militia when raised are to be employed under your Direction and order in protecting and defending the Inhabitants of the State and their Property from the Attacks and Depredations of the Enemy—In preventing and putting a stop to all Traffick or Intercourse with the Enemy and generally in opposing and distressing the Enemy by every way and mean and also to aid the Civil magistrate when called upon, in the due Execution of the Laws—I have not appointed any Person as Paymaster for your Quota of Troops but leave this to be done by you in such way as you judge best for the Publick Interest.—

By the 2d Resolution of the Legislative Council I am directed to draw the sum of £5000 out of your Hands as Trustee of the Loan Office for Kent County, this I must do by partial Draughts from time to time—I now inclose

1 Dover became the capital of Delaware in the fall of 1777, the General Assembly having decided at its meeting in New Castle the previous summer to hold its sessions in that more centrally located place.

a Draught for £500 in Favour of Brigadier General Dagworthy which you are to pay to his order when called upon—another of £1500 in favour of George Latimer Esq! for the Pay and Subsistence of the Quota of militia to be raised in New Castle County—I am well convinced of your Zeal for and attention to the Welfare of the State and therefore desire that you will as Commanding Officer of the whole militia give such Directions from Time to Time as you may judge necessary for the Rendering the Service of the 600 militia afs! or any other part of the militia in this State, you may order forth to support them, as useful and effectual for the Protection and Defence of the State as may be—I wish you Success in this business.

P.S. You are to consider the march and
Rendezvous of the Kent Quota at
Middletown in New Castle County
as directed by M! President Mc Kean
to be revoked.—

230

To Major James Raymond

Dover, Nov. the 3d, 1777.

The General Assembly has directed that Six hundred of the militia be raised, paid and subsisted for two months unless sooner discharged. The President has ordered me to take upon me the Chief Direction of the whole as occasion may require, and to appoint the Officers for those to be raised in this County as its proportion of the whole. This County's quota is two hundred, formed into four Companies, and to be now immediately commanded by a Major. I have appointed the several Captains, Lieutenants and Ensigns, and have sent them their orders, and now appoint you to be the Major. I expect you will therefore immediately, or as soon as your business will possibly permit, call upon me in Dover that I may furnish you with instructions for this purpose. Convinced of your zeal for the Cause. Do not doubt your activity on this occasion.

231

To Captain Mark McCall

Dover Nov!. the 8th 1777

Having Certain Information that a Number of people in the Lower part of

Duck Creek hundred are avowedly Aiding & Comforting the Enemy by Supplying their men of war with provisions &c and that a party, on the last evening, attacked the dwelling House of Col! Collins &c. all in open Violation of the Laws of this State

You are therefore, with the party under your Command, Immediately to proceed to that part of Duck Creek hundred afs^d. by way of the Bridge Called Martin's Bridge, and Cause all the Shallops, Boats, or other Small Craft to be so Secured as to prevent their Trading with the Enemy in future but to do no Injury to the Said Shallops, Boats, or Other Craft, other than is necessary for the purpose afs^d—You are also to apprehend secure and bring to Justice all such persons as are Concerned in Such Trade, as also such person or persons as have had any hand in attacking, or have been aiding in attacking Col^l Collins's House—When You shall have Joined Col^l Collins, Major Raymond or other your Commanding Officer, You are to take their order for Executing these or other orders they may Give you, first Showing them these, as they are to be observed by them. When you shall have Joined other Troops and find no Superior officer, you are in that Case to Cause these Orders to be Executed a[nd] make Report to me—Unless you sh[ould] in the mean time Receive other O[r]ders from me or other your Super[ior] officers—

232

From Thomas Collins

Nov: 15th 1777

There was taken and sent to me by Capt Snow and his party Sundrey Articals the property of Danl Morris taken out of a Batua coming from his Shalloop, this hapened before he (Morris) gave himself up, Viz. about 6 or 8 gallons of Rum, 100 ^{wt} of Brown Sugar, 1 Loaf of Sugar, 6 ^{lb} of tea, 1^{lb} of Pinns.—Now S.^r I wait your Order what is to be Done with those Articals, as Daniel Morris has been here about them I could give him no Answer Other than I should make a Report to you of them and take your Order in the Matter and then he might be informed.—

N.B. I had information last Evening of some of our raschals returning in the Lower part of Dutch Neck where they were carousing and some of them fuddeled, I sent orders Express to Capt Snow to rais his Company or such part as was Necessary and indevour to take them, but it seems the Orders was not obeyed as it said the men would not turn out.

233
Instructions to Delaware's Delegates to Congress[1]

In Council, Wednesday P.M. Dec. 17, 1777

Whereas Caesar Rodney, Nicholas Vandyke and Thomas McKean Esquires have been chosen, by joint Ballot of the two Houses of Assembly, to represent the Delaware State in the Continental Congress:

Resolved,

That they, or any one or more of them are hereby fully authorized and impowered for and in behalf of this State, to concert, agree to and execute any Measure, which they or he, together with a Majority of the Continental Congress, shall judge necessary for the Defense, Security, Interest and Welfare of this State in particular, and America in general, with Power to adjourn to such times and Places as shall appear most conducive to the Publick Safety and Advantage.—

Extract from the Minutes of ye Council

Sent for Concurrence

Ben: Vining Clk of the Council—

In the House of Assembly, Eodem Die
Read and concurred in.   Sam. West Speaker

234
From John Dickinson

December 21st 1777

The Bearer is well known to me—He is a very honest, inoffensive, worthy man—tho very poor—He has a Wife and three small children, one of them blind—Mrs. Dickinson says, she knew his Distresses were very great before she left Philadelphia—

He came from Philadelphia in a Row boat & has brought down John Palmer taken some time ago by the Enemy—His companions are John Rollison and John Prefontaine, persons in his own situation, and Wm. Douglass a young man who came to help them—The three first have bought a small Beef, a few

---

1 The previous year, 1776, the conservative element in Delaware's legislature had declined to return Caesar Rodney and Thomas McKean to Congress. George Read was re-elected at that time but John Dickinson and John Evans were elected to succeed the more radical members of Delaware's first delegation to Congress In 1777, after Delaware's soil had been invaded by the British, the radical element was in control of the legislature again, and Thomas McKean and Caesar Rodney were restored to the delegation while George Read was left off Rodney did not, however, attend the Congress after this election, at first on account of his military duties, and later, because he was elected President of the State in March 1778.

Hogs and three Barrels of Flour for the use of their several Families, all articles of Provision being exorbitantly dear in the City—

The Bearer assures me, and I entirely believe him, that the Enemy never takes any kind of provisions from poor persons who procure it by going out of the City—

Under these Circumstances I earnestly entreat you to give a Passport for the Bearer & his Companions to return to their Home, with their little vesel & Cargo,

[P.S.]

I desire you will be so kind as to dispatch the Bearer as soon as possible for as the Boat is small they will be in Danger of suffering great Harships, if a sharp spell of Weather should set in He tells me it is the general opinion of the Inhabitants of Philadelphia, that the number of the Enemy's Forces in Town does not exceed 12000—tho they say they are 20000 strong. He also says, the Fleet appears to be but poorly man'd—

[Rodney's Endorsement]

Decr. 21st 1777. As I cannot be Supposed to have so general a View of matters as to Justifie the Granting a pasport in this Case, must Decline it—Therefore would recommend an application to be made to his Excellency General Washington, who's advice and Direction I shall stricly observe—

Caesar Rodney
M. General

235
From George Read

Dover 21st. December 1777.

I have this moment received Information by Letter from His Excellency General Washington, that he has Reason to believe that the Enemy mean to establish a Post at Wilmington for the Purpose of countenancing the Disaffected in the Delaware State, drawing Supplies from our country, and securing a Post upon the Delaware River during the Winter; that he has detached General Smallwood with a respectable Continental Force to take a Post at Wilmington, but this he apprehended may not be adequated to the Business, therefore he expects that I will call out as many Militia of this State as I possibly can to rendezvous without Loss of Time at Wilmington, and put themselves under the Command of General Smallwood—In Consequence of this Application I must desire that you will forthwith issue your Orders to the Officers of the Militia, particularly of your County, to examine into the State of the Arms & Accoutrements of the Men, that the same be put into the best Order that your Circumstances will admit and be prepared to march upon the first Notice—. The General Assembly have ordered that the Six Hundred Militia, directed to be raised by the Resolution of Council of the 29th October last, should be continued for other two Months in the Service of the State, therefore I desire that you would issue your Orders for compleating the Companies, particularly those of Kent County, as I expect that you will, upon the first Notice of the Enemy's Attempt to seize the Post at Wilmington order the march of that Corps of Men as well as such of the Militia of Kent as may be got together.—I rely on your paying a particular Attention to the State of the whole Militia and issuing such Orders as you may deem necessary for complying with the Requisition of General Washington; and in Case of ordering forth the whole Militia I would recommend the Mode prescribed in the Act for establishing a Militia in this State for making a Signal of Alarm, to be adopted, that we may have it in our Power to punish Delinquents—I have wrote to Brigadier Dagworthy mentioning the Purport of General Washington's Letter with Directions to examine into the State of the Militia, their Arms &c. and have them ready to march on the first Notice, and to proceed in the raising and compleating of the two Companies of the afsd. Six Hundred, that had been alloted as Sussex County's Quota.—I shall write to General Patterson to the same Purpose.

236

From William Smallwood[1]

Wilmington Decem. 22d 1777

His Excellency General Washington having it in View as much as maybe to cover the Country, & prevent the Depredations of the Enemy, has detatched a Body of Troops under my Command to take Post at this Place, with Instructions to fortify it strongly, & to sollicit your Aid in drawing together a Body of light Horse & Militia to co operate with the Continental Troops for its defence; & the construction of Works; this in either Instance cannot perhaps wholly be effected by the small Number of harrassed Cont.l Troops; & the Necessity of speedy & vigorous Exertions to frustrate the Enemys Designs must be obvious, therefore make no doubt but you will be induced to give every countenance & Aid in your Power, to promote & facilitate an Object of such Importance.

1 Brigadier-General William Smallwood was ordered from New Jersey by General Washington (writing from Gulf Mill, Pennsylvania, December 19, 1777) to proceed to Wilmington, Delaware, and take measures for the defense of that town. He commanded troops of Maryland and Delaware of the Continental Line.

237
To Thomas Collins

In virtue of the most Earnest Requisition of his Excellency General Washington, That the Militia of this State, if necessary, Should Join and Co-operate with the Continental Troops now within the State under the command of Brigadier General Smallwood—and in Virtue of orders from the Honorable George Read Vice President and Commander in Chief of said State directed to me for this purpose. You are Immediately to see that all the officers and Companies belonging to your Battalion, be forthwith equipped in the best manner that, in our present Circumstances, They possibley can, with Arms & accoutrements. And hold themselves in Readiness to March under Your Command and Rendezvous at such place, within the State, as shall be here-after thought most proper to Cooperate with the Continental Troops sent here for the defence of the State under the Command of General Smallwood, for which purpose you Shall Have orders from me, in Case it should be found necessary.

CAESAR RODNEY
MAJOR GENERAL.

Head Quarters. Dover
decr. the 22d 1777.
    To Coll. Thomas Collins Eqr.
    of the 1st Batta. Militia.
    [of Kent County]

238
To William Smallwood

Dover decr. the 25th 1777—

Your letter of the 22d Instant, by Doct. Spencer Came to hand, and I am happy to find you have taken Post at Wilmington, a movement which, in its event, must tend to Secure the persons and propery of the well affected in this State, Against the depredations and Insults of a cruel Enemy and their cruel abetters—Mr. Read the Vice President, left this town on Sunday last, a few hours before he set out, he received a Letter from his Excellency General Washington advising him of the design to take Post at Wilmington, and Requesting the aid of the Militia &c. He Immediately directed me to order the Militia of this County to hold themselves in Readiness to march at a moments warning in Case it should be found necessary—These orders have been issued, and am sorry to say that I believe they will be verry little Regarded, A want of Zeal in some and disaffection in others is so prevalent that little good is to be Expected of them in this way, it is a misfortune that our Militia Law is not calculated to bring them to the Field—I have issued orders to my Light-Horse to go Immediately to your Assistance and shall do everything in my power to get them there—I make no doubt but the Militia of Newcastle County, who are near at hand, will generally turn out—I have, in this Town & near it, about one hundred men what are engaged and under pay for two months, but they are constantly employed in keeping in awe and preventing the disaffected carrying on a Trade with and Supplying the Enemy with Provisions, I have many of those Traitors now in goal and should be glad of a place of greater safety for them than this is. Should therefore be pleased to know of you whether you'd approve of their being sent to your Camp. I shall be glad to hear from you by the bearer, and be assured I shall do every thing in my power to assist you.

239
To Captain Caldwell

Dover dec:. 28th 1777—

I Received your letter of this day's date—If the Commissary promised to Attend you he has done verry wrong, and upon presumsition that he had Neglected his duty Sent for him, and he dinies your Ever Giving him Any Notice to Attend, But says he will attend to morrow morning—However be that as it may, You have by a Neglect of Your Orders, and Your possitive Engagement, occasioned Such a disappointment That in all probability there will not be a Single person left to do duty in the Town and that at a time when the prison is full of Offenders, and what may be the Consequence I Shall leave You to Judge—The people know their pay and Rations were sure to be had at any time therefore that Could not Justify their not attending as you Engaged—As to their pay if you had asked me for more money when in Town You Might have had it, and may have it when Ever You are pleased to Call for it—I dont Recollect What the pay is, and have not a list of it by me, or would send you one—Captain Delancy says that upon Your promise his Men have Stayed verry Patiently till now, but that they will now go home—If this is to be the Case the public money is bestowed to verry little purpose, and Patriotism at a Verry low Ebb with those I Expected to find it, which Give no Small Concern, as I always have and would Still wish to Encourage Such. I hope You will Exert your Self and Endeavour to be more punctual, for the future in Military Matters nothing is More Necessary.

240

From Samuel Patterson[1]

Wilmington January 10th 1778

Your favour came to hand of the 8th and observe the Contents. For answer am sorry that it did not suit you to have come sooner than Sunday. As you say times are much altered in the Spirit of the Delaware State, but hopes times will Mend.

Never was America in so fair a way to compleat the grand Struggle in our favour from every quarter and Accompts—nothing here very Material acc.ts from Head Quarters every day alls quiet diserters and prisoners comeing in there every day.

There is an affair of much consequence to our State and directly wants attention paid. I have wrote our Vice president on the Occassion—A Schooner drove a shore in the Ice the other day at Reedy point near white head Jones. . Not a person on board and encloses you a list of part of her Cargo, worth £100,000. She in my oppinion is a prise to our poor state. If so you can command, if Mr. Read is not here. As you know, I am here commanded, and no troops as Usual. Ordered Col.o McDonogh to send a Comp. down to secure Effects &c. One Continental also went from here to bring all thats fit for the army. Agreed, but how is it to be ascertaind and Valued.

241

From William Hooper[2]

Cape Fear, North Carolina, January 22 1778

My dear Caesar,

Or if you rather choose the more sounding military epithets with which your Country has honoured you.

Most respected Major General

I cannot omit this favourable opportunity to assure you that there is still in the land of the living a man who sincerely esteems you & numbers amongst the happiest moments of his life those that composed the short hours which he and you laughed away in Philadelphia together—May he hope that that

1 Brigadier-General of the New Castle Militia.

2 A delegate to Continental Congress from North Carolina, who, although not present when Richard Henry Lee's resolution for Independence was passed on July 2, nor when the Declaration of Independence was adopted on the fourth, nevertheless signed the Declaration on or after August 2, 1776, when it was presented on parchment to the members of Congress for their signatures.

friendship is mutual & flatter himself that this scrawl which is all that he has an Opportunity to say at present may tempt you in return to say upon paper that you exist, for to know even this alone would add much to the happiness of My dear Sir

Your Friend & Obed. Sev.

W^m. Hooper

242

From Samuel Patterson

Wilmington Jan. 28. 1778.

I wrote you the other day to which I refer you of the accompt of our prize. She is not unloaded all yet. turns out better & better. as we come lower down. Some fine old Maderia.

As to the militia in my brigade, am sorry to say by the reports my officers, a total defection appears, & no hopes of turning out at present, not above 20 men & they will not stay.

I have wrote to Mr. Ried[1] the President to come here if possible to know what part we are to act, or give up the State to its ruin. Which from the general behaviour of our people, they are pushing on fast, for if the Continental troops are let loose on us, for our conduct, I dread the consequences, but from some appearances believe it will be done.

As to news have none only two ships burnt by our people, near Gloster, every day taking some prisoners.

243

To William Smallwood

Dover Februy 21st 1778—

This letter will be delivered you by a Miss. Langdell, some five or Six Weeks ago from Philadelphia, Where her Mother now Resides. This Young Lady, who came here on a Visit to her Sister who married in this Town, now Wants to return, And has applied to me for a Pass to Carry her to the City. My not having so General a View of the propriety or Impropriety of these matters as Those who are Immediately Engaged in the Military Line, Induced me to refuse giving One, But Referred her to You Who I know to be Competant, and Who, I am Convinced, will decide in this Case without Love, fear, favour or

1 George Read.

Affection—Miss Langdell Tells me She is to be accompanied by Mr John Casson of this Town he, I believe to be an honest man, but as he belongs to the Light-Horse here, and has been Verry Active I think him Greatly to Blame in Attempting it, However have not Seen him.—

Your favour of the 18th was delivered me by Captain Lee, and be assured Every Assistance in my power Shall be Given him. I hope and believe they will act with prudence—The Militia to be Sent from this County are ordered and the day fixed for their March. I wish They may more than answer My Expectation; but Liberty, Freedom &c are but dull Sounds in their Ears, and am Affraid will not so Sound as to be heard throughout the Assembly; He that hath Ears to hear let him hear, let him hear or Abide the Sentence. However I flater my Self there are a Majority now Who are disposed to Emerge from the former Torpid State of the House—There seems to be many late manoeuvres of our Army Which I don't Seem able fully to account for, Nor would I wish to know at the Risque of divulging that to the World which ought to be a Secret. It is Sufficient for me That I believe and Trust Every thing is done for Best—

244

To Thomas McKean

Dover March the 9th 1778

This letter will be delivered you by William Frazier Lieutenant of the Militia Light Dragoons—He is sent by Mr Read for a further Supply of Cash to be applied in recruiting the Delaware Regiment, and I have the pleasure to inform you that the Officers appointed to this Duty have Succeeded far beyond my most Sanguine hope, haveing got, in a verry few days near Seventy Recruits—The Vice-President, who is now here, came Near Three weeks ago to meet the General Assembly, I believe, with a full determination to have something done to effect. For this purpose, when they first met, they passed a Law to give a Representation to the County of Sussex, who then had no members in the Assembly and wanted two Councilors—In Consequence of this Act the Election was held at Lewis on Munday last, when the following Persons were Elected—To wit, for the Council John Clowes & William Conwell Esquires—for the Assembly Captain William Peery, Doct.^r Joseph Hall, John Collins, Nathaniel Waples, George Adams, Major Simon Kollock and Levin Derixon,—These men Joined with the Representation from Newcastle County, you'l be apt to think with me, will produce not only wholsom Laws & Regulations but Energy in the Execution of them, and thereby rouse this little Branch of the Union from its heretofore Torpid State, which God of his

Infinite Mercy Grant—I need not tell you How disagreable the Scituation of those in this Peninsula, who Openly profess friendship to the American Cause, a narrow neck of Land liable to the incursions of the Enemy, by water, in small Parties and therefore their property Exposed. The militia not to be brought forth to the protection of the State, tho: frequently Called upon in the most pressing Terms for that purpose—I Do not Doubt, my dear Sir, Your desire to See me in Congress or at least that I might be Ready to take my Seat when you shall be necessarily called off to the discharge of your duty, in another Public department. I wish to be with you, but think it highly necessary I Should wait the Close of this Sessions of Assembly. You know I may be of Service. One thing, among others, absolutely necessary to be done, is an allowance to the Delegates, which many of the members have promised me shall be ample—Let this Sessions, in which much is Expected, be done away, and I Come Immediately—I am not a little astonished that the appointment of the Delegates was not published in the papers, as Individuals who may have applications to make to Congress, will not know who to apply through—Mr Read lets me know that he applied to you to Solicit the Excha[n]ge of our late President, which if accomplished might be as well for the Honor as the Interest of the State. I cannot help thinking he ment well tho he might have been deceived by many in whom he placed Confidence. However the Question is, How his Release can be brought about, for my part I cannot Figure to my self the means by which it may probably be done, if I Could I would Recommend the Execution of the plan to you and do not doubt you would undertake, tho he might never have discharged the Duty of that Station with that Energy that You and I Could have wished—By your Letter to Mr Read you are informed that the President Lodges with his old friends Robinson & Manlove and that He seems perfectly satisfied.[1] It may be that those traitors[2] to their Country have Visited him, tho it be merely to Insult him in his unfortunate Scituation. But, Sir, I am well informed that Robinson has Lodged at Joshua Fishers ever since he first went to the City and that Manloves place of Abode is at one Snowdens over the Drawbridge—Sir, as I have declared to you my Intention of Comeing to Congress in a Short time,[3] and as I apprehend Lodgings in York-Town not only verry Expensive but Extreemly Scarce and difficult to be Got must beg leave to Solicit your Endeavours to procure such for

---

1 Rodney is referring to a letter from McKean to Read, dated February 12, wherein McKean in alluding to McKinly's captivity in Philadelphia wrote. "I was told the other day that he lodged at widow Jenkin's, along with his *old friends* Robinson and Manlove, and seemed very *happy* "

2 Thomas Robinson and Boaz Manlove were two Delaware Tories, who had escaped to the British.

3 Rodney did not go to York, Pennsylvania, where Congress was then sitting, on account of his election as President (Governor) of Delaware by the General Assembly the same month.

me as you, who know me well, may think Suitable, and that you would write me fully on all these matters

P.S. While writing am Informed of a number more Recruits. Therefore don't delay the mesenger with the Money, or I shall be run aground—

245
From David Hall

Wilmington, March 15th 1778—

Your favor I received & am exceeding glad to hear our recruiting goes on so successfully, am in hopes it will continue & the regiment be once more on a respectable Footing. I have applied for the Cloth but the General[1] objects to sending it to the Cross Roads[2] but hath given me Leave to send it to Newark[3] where I have ordered the Taylors from Cross Roads; the General desires me (as he is exceeding busy) to acquaint you that he has detained the waggon in expectation of Ammunition from Head-Quarters but it not arriving he has sent the waggon with the Cloth to Newark & from thence it is to proceed down—as soon as we get a Supply of Ammunition the General says he will send what you want, but at present we have but 12000 spare cartidges on hand —we have received information that the Flat Bottomed Boats are on their way down, thinks it would be insecure to send the Cloth down he advises that Coll. Pope immediately remove the Taylors and Shoe-makers with their Cloth & Leather to Newark—We have nothing new—

246
From George Read

Dover half past 4—Monday afternoon.[4]

Capts. West & Clark just from the Cross Roads bring intelligence that a considerable body of the Enemy supposed to be 700 landed this morning about Listen's Highlands and were on their March up the Thoroughfare Neck—it is highly expedient that Col. Pope repair immediately to the Cross Roads in order to secure the Cloathing &c there belonging to his Battalion—and that you forthwith give orders for the assembling of the Militia—Col. Collins is

---

1 General William Smallwood, who was ordered by Washington in December to Wilmington with Maryland and Delaware troops while the main army lay at Valley Forge.

2 Now Smyrna, Delaware   3 Newark, Delaware.

4 In all probability the date was March 16, 1778

doing a part of the business here and will set out for the Cross Roads in a few minutes

247
From Charles Pope[1]

Cross Roads Duck Creek March 17th. 1778

Capt. Skillington just this moment Returned from the River Shore near to Listons high woods—he informs that yesterday about 30—or 40 mereens landed & took of some cattle &c. & Returned like wise that at eight oclock this morning the fleet consisting of about 35 Sail weighed & Stood Down the bay wind & at N.W. 3/4 flood—a Sloop & the unfortunate Schooner Virtue Orphan Tacked & stood up the River I sent up to Listons woods this morning Mr. Lt. Quenault with three of Cap Cartey's light horse to observe the motion of the Vessels—with Orders to continue there with Causion until tomorrow morning, shall send the Tradesmen & Cloaths leather &c of tomorrow morning—Capt Skillington with the flag Did not get on board the friggate—

248
Minutes of the General Assembly Recording the Election of Caesar Rodney as President of Delaware

IN THE GENERAL ASSEMBLY OF THE DELAWARE STATE
Tuesday, March 31st, 1778 A.M.

The Council proceeded to the Assembly-Room, and there met the House of Assembly, when several Persons were put in Nomination for the Office of President, and their Names taken down for the Consideration of the Members of both Houses:

Resolved,

That the General Assembly meet in the Assembly-Room to ballot for a President of this State at 3 o'clock this Afternoon.

Eodem Die. P.M.

The Council met the House of Assembly in the Assembly-Room, and there in General Assembly preceeded to the Election of a President for the State, and the Members of both Houses, to wit, Eight of the Council and Sixteen of the House of Assembly then present, having prepared Tickets with the Name of the President to be appointed, and put the same into the Ballot-Box. The

1 Lieutenant-Colonel of the Delaware Regiment of the Continental Line under General Smallwood.

Speakers of the two Houses in the presence of the other Members examined the Ballot-Box, and it appeared that 20 Votes out of 24 put into the said Box, were in favour of the Honourable Caesar Rodney, Esq. Whereupon the said Caesar Rodney, Esquire was declared duly elected President of this State for the term of three Years next ensuing and until the sitting of the next General Assembly, thereafter, and no longer, agreeable to the present Constitution or System of Government.

On motion resolved,

That the Speaker of the Council nominate five Members of the General Assembly to wait on Caesar Rodney Esquire, and inform him of his Election and Appointment to the Office of President of this State, and know whether he will accept the Office of President, and make Report thereof to the General Assembly and thereupon,

Messrs. VanDyke, Clowes, Ridgely, Patterson and Bryan, are appointed for this Purpose.

Extract from the Minutes—

Benj. Vining, Clk of the Council.

249

Message of Caesar Rodney to Legislative Council (Upper House)

April 3rd 1778.

Gentlemen of the Legislative Council.—

Complaint is just now made to me as Commander-in-chief of this state, by Thos White Esq. who says a continental officer, in virtue of an order or resolution of Congress, has taken him into custody, & as he believes with design to carry him out of the state. He says further that he is ready & willing to answer any charges alleged against him; but thinks he ought to be charged within the state &c. As the General Assembly is now sitting, I have thought it proper to lay this complaint before the Honorable, the Council, for their direction. I have also made the House of Assembly acquainted with it.

250

To William Smallwood

Dover April the 5th 1778

I received a letter from you by Col! Hall of the Delawares requesting me to afford him such assistance in the military line as he might Stand in need of for the apprehending Messrs Gordon & White. I afford'd the aid required and the men were Taken and brought to Dover.—This done, I received a message from the Council requesting me, as President, to Issue an order for the detention of the prisoners untill the general Assembly Should Consider the propriety of seizing the persons of those men other than under the authority of the State. I Issued the order and Col! Hall accordingly detained them for the purpose above mentioned—I believe the House has come to no resolution as Yet at least I have heard nothing from them since—However I have now to inform you that the Prisoners have applied for and obtained from the Chief Justice a Habeas Corpus. The Chief Justice now desires to know what the Offence is with which they are charged, and the Cause of their Imprisonment, by the Military and applied to me to write you concerning it, which I now do by express, and shall be glad of an answer by him;—Among the Prisoners I sent to your Camp was the Captain of the Schooner Reed. The veshell is Libeled in the Court of Admir[alty] and the Judge requests his being sent down here. I shall be therefore Oblidged to you to give him a furlow and orders for that purpose. You'l be best able to Judge whether it will be safe [to] send him alone,—it seems the Veshell can't be [con]demned without him, the State will pay t[he] Expence of his comeing—

251

From William Smallwood

Wilmington April 6th 1778

I have just received your favor of the 5 Inst. and in Answer there to, have inclosed a copy of the Act of Congress, which gave rise to the Orders issued by me to Col.o Hall for apprehending & forwarding to this Post, Thomas White, and Charles Gordon which Act I still hold myself bound in honor & Duty to execute, and shall direct the Orders issued thereon, immediately to be put in Execution in the most pointed manner—conceiving myself neither at large, or bound to give in a charge against those Persons to the chief Justice, or to wave the Execution of such an express Order derived from the supreme Authority of the United States of America—to which your Legislature must apply for Redress, if they conceive the Act to be an Infringement of their Internal Police —for as a Military Officer and in point of Propriety, I can neither mitigate or suspend the Execution of the Order. Impelled by these Motives, I hope the Legislature will excuse my directing the Orders to be enforced,—at the same time allow me to assure you & them, that Nothing but the strong sense I have of the Ties of Duty and Honor, wou'd prompt me to do an Act that might give Umbrage, or in the least Interfere with your Police.—
P.S. The Cap.t you mention has some Days past been sent to Lancaster. Hav-

ing been much engaged in the Examination of Tories & Refugees your Boy has been detained this Evening. have also inclosed you Copies of the Presidents Lt. & mine to Col.º Hall directing the Order to be inforced that he may incur no Censure on the occasion.

252
From Samuel J. Atlee[1]

April 6th 1778

Untill the 27th of Aug.t 1776 the Bearer Mr. Alex.r Stewart then Lieut. in the Delaware Reg.t was unknown to me; his Behaviour on that day under my own Eye has convinced me he greatly merrits the Notice and Reward of the Executive Councill of the State.

He chooses to continue in the Millitary Line (notwithstanding the wish of his Parents, whose desire is that he shou'd enter into the Hospital) provided that Justice is done to this Merrit, which he thinks himself intitled to—and his promotion according to the former Rank he held in the Reg.t is secured to him.

I think his demand very reasonable, and no more than what in Justice is his due.—

I must beg leave in the Strongest manner to recommend him to the Notice of the Executive Councill &

253
From Charles Pope

Grog or Whiskey Town Apl. 14th 1778

It is with a Certainty I can inform you that the report of the Tories having a fort built is a truth for this Day myself with a party of about forty was within gun shot of their works—on our appearance upwards of one hundred sallied out, several shot was Exchanged[2]—After taking a full view of their works & finding it proff against our small Number Forced the party to Retreat, We kill'd one of their party. Mr. Derough of Cross Roads was shot through the thigh.

as there is no provisions in the place have Ordered twenty four men to Do the Duty of the Night & the Rest to look out for Quarters with orders to at-

---

1 Late Colonel of Pennsylvania "Musqt B "

2 The Tories were under the leadership of one Cheney or China Clow, a Tory officer. Born in England, he was brought while still a child to Queen Anne County, Maryland, by his parents. After his marriage he lived on a farm which was on the Delaware-Maryland line, his house being some two hundred yards to the eastward of the line in Kent County. This Tory uprising in Kent County hastened the passage of the Test Act by the General Assembly in May 1778.

tend tomorrow morning—pray Send us what Cartridges you can spare—like-wise—Whiskey & provisions—without which I cannot Carry the fort, I have Wrote Genl. Smallwood on the Subject & Request his sending a light field piece.

254
From Charles Pope

Grog Town Aprl. 16th. 78—

In my last I informed you that for want of provisions I was to Order the Militia here Except twenty that was for Duty to Return to their Several homes or where Else was convenient for getting provisions & Returning to Day—at the same time Expected a full Supply from you this morning, but am much Distressed to find only fifty wt. of meet & one bbl. of bread—for upperds of one hundred men.—if you mean to have the Militia kept to gether pray Send us a Supply amediately otherways it will be out of my power to keep them longer than this night, by the next opportunity shall furnish you with the Ri-turns of our several Companies—& I hope a good acct of Colonl. Clowes & his party—I have ordered the Militia from Head of Chester to Join me at Marches Quarter within one mile & half of their fortress, at which place we shall be this Evening—if you have any arms to spare shall be glad you would furnish us with them as they are much wanted here—it will likewise be necessary that what ammunition you have can be prepared should be forward here.—pray corect the above as I am D—blly Bothered—now on a line of march

255
From John Dagworthy[1]

Dagsberry[2] April 18th 1778

A Commander of a Schooner with his Mate and eight Sailors having been made prisoners and their Vessel taken by a Number of the inhabitants of In-dian River I send to recieve your orders in relation to them.—

256
To Thomas McKean

April 18th 1778—

I Recd yours of the 8th instant by Mr. Robinson the Post. Am much pleased

1 Brigadier-General of Delaware Militia for Sussex County.
2 Dagsboro in Sussex County.

that the General Assembly have your approbation in their appointment of me to the Supreme Command in this State, and do not doubt your willingness to tender me your best Services.[1] I shall often stand in need of your advise—and shall thankfully Receive it whenever given—The General Assembly is still Setting. Much business in hand and but little finished as yet—In the House of Assembly we have a majority of men disposed to do whatever they think tends most to support the American Cause, but Sir, They Labor under some disadvantages, they are most of them new members, They want a Pen. They want you, business goes on Slow and the Slower too as they want Patience, added to all these inconveniences we are frequently alarmed. Our Situation is at best unsafe, and the General Assembly no small Object—I am in great hopes However that in a few days we shall have a Militia Law Through both Houses, Calculated to bring forth the Militia on any Requisition of Congress nothing shall be wanting on my part whenever they are Regulated under the Law which will take some time—There is a Matter I would wish to mention to you as one of our Delegates, which, if Congress should approve and adopt, I think and am convinced would tend more to the Security of this little State than any other Plan in that way we can fall upon, and be of infinite advantage to the neighbouring States and indeed to the cause in general—You know Sir we have a verry considerable water frontier, bordering on which are our best grass & farm Lands well stocked, and a number of Salt works, not only necessary but convenient for the support of our army, which I hope will be large; this property so situated must be protected where they are, as there are no other grounds within the State that can subsist Stock, and the Salt works cannot be removed—Now I would wish and do think it highly Expedient, that Congress would Order an Independent Company of an hundred men on the plan of the one fixed at the Cape under Captain Perry—To be stationed in Kent at Such place or places as I shall from time to time direct, the company to be raised for one year at least—It may be said that it will better suit the Militia to defend this part of the Country, but sir I have got to be Tolerably acquainted with Militia in general and particularly with ours, and do know that so near to their homes they cannot be kept to duty, that subordination which know to be necessary cannot be maintained unless they are Joined and acting with Continentals—Therefore could wish that this plan might be adopted, and that any number of the Militia which may be thought necessary to assist the Continental Army, and defend this river side, may all be sent to the army, for sure I am that one hundred men under Subordination will be of more service here, than all the Militia in the State—The night before last a part of the Militia of this County which I ordered out under Lt. Coll. Pope of

1 Refers to his election as President and Commander-in-Chief by the General Assembly.

Delaware, against Genl. China Clow, and his army of Refugees, came up with
them on the Western Borders of this County, and verry soon routed Mr. Clow
& his army, and burnt the fort—This Villian clow had about one hundred
and fifty men, they left in the fort about a thousand weight of Bacon and two
barrels of flower which they Stole—I Pray dont neglect the affair of the Company, I would wish Congress to Establish.

257
To Henry Laurens[1]

Dover April the 24th 1778

I recd. you letter of the 15th instant relative to the Order of Congress for securing persons of Thomas White, Charles Gordon & others residenters of this
State, and beg leave to give Congress by you, a Short State of the facts and
what has been construed to have given disgust to this Government concerning
them;

These men were taken by order of General Smallwood in virtue of the Resolution of Congress, The Officer, sent on this business, was directed to apply to
me for aid which was immediately afforded. The men taken and brought to
Dover—In the mean time I was appointed President of the State, and Mr.
White, protesting against the Legality of his being taken and carried out of
the State without knowing the Offence with which he was charged and applying for relief, I laid the matter before the General Assembly, then Setting, for
their direction, who desired me to detain Mr. White untill they Considered
of the matter. I issued an Order for this purpose and immediately advised
General Smallwood thereof, as also that said White with Mr. Gordon had
obtained of the Chief Justice an Habeas Corpus—General Smallwood thinking himself bound to Execute the Order of Congress Caused Mr. White to be
brought to him—This procedure the General Assembly Countermanded because they had full confidence in Congress, and that, as they had a more general view of matters might see a danger unobserved by the Assembly. But Sir
whatever may have been the Case with respect to the Assembly of this State
in the opinion of Congress, I can venture to say that the present General Assembly, at least, a great majority of the Members are, and would wish to be
thought as warm friends to the American Cause as any within the United
States. And therefore cannot help thinking that Congress, for whom they have,
and are determined to pay the highest respect, might have committed that important business to their Supreme Majistrate and that if aid was thought necessary, That Continental Troops might have been ordered to that purpose, for

1 President of Congress.

that, in their opinion, The consequences of the governing Powers of a State is so lessoned, in the Eyes of the people, by such procedure, as to prevent their being able to render these Essential Services, to the United States, they could wish, when called upon by Congress—

I am sorry to say, The suspicions Congress entertains of the disaffection of the people is too well founded, but as the people at large are generally directed by those at the Helm, Hope, they will soon mend—I trust nothing will be wanting, on my part, to Effect it, and that I shall, to the utmost of my power, as well comply with the Requisitions of Congress from time to time as to maintain the Honour and independence of this State.

258
To Henry Laurens

Dover April the 24th 1778

There is a Matter I intended, but Neglected to mention in my other Letter of this day—On Tuesday the fourteenth Instant I Got information that About one hundred and fifty Insurgents under the Command of one China Clow were Armed and Assembled on the Western side of this County near the borders of Maryland. I, as soon as possible Collected and Sent About one hundred and forty of the Militia of this County, under the Command of Lt. Col'l Pope of the Delawares, against them.—The Insurgents had built a Fort which the Militia Surrounded on the Thursday night following, but Mr. Clow and his Gang, hearing of their approach, fled—The Militia burnt the Fort and secured all the Stolen Effects in and about it and Returned—I then fitted out a number of Horse-men, Since when many of them have been taken and others Surrendered to the number, in all, of about fifty, about twenty of whom being single men, are sent off with a recruiting party of the Delaware Regiment to enlist or do Worse—so that with what the Maryland Militia have done, this infernal set are, I believe, broke up, and I hope to hear in a few days that the Villain Clow is taken.[1]—

1 Although Clow was not captured at this time, he was arrested in 1782 for treason, having failed to take the oath of allegiance under the act of 1778. The arrest was only effected after a member of the sheriff's posse, named Joseph Moore, had been killed in an exchange of shots at Clow's home in Little Creek Hundred, Kent County. Clow was brought to trial for treason and acquitted after showing the jury his commission as a captain in the British army and asserting that he was not guilty of treason and could not be tried in a civil court. He was not released from jail, however, his enemies now being determined to have him indicted for the alleged murder of Moore. In 1783 he was brought to trial on this charge, and although there was only flimsy evidence to show that Clow had shot Moore in the darkness of night, he was nevertheless convicted of murder, and condemned to death by hanging. After five years of delay, during which time he was kept in jail, he was finally executed late in the year 1788.

P.S. They increased verry fast and I believe, if they had not been opposed very suddenly and with Spirit they would have become formidable in a Little time.

259
From Thomas McKean

York Town, April 28th 1778.

Your favor of the 18th instant came safe to hand. If the General Assembly continue to sit a few weeks and I can be informed of that intention, and that it would be agreeable to them, I shall do myself the honor to wait upon them upon notice, being anxious to render any and every service in my power to that virtuous Body. The affair of the hundred men I have not yet had opportunity to move, but am told three hundred are ordered to be raised on the Eastern shore for the purpose you mention, which it is thought will be sufficient. I congratulate you on the success of Lieutt. Colo. Pope, and should be glad to know whether any prisoners were taken and what has been done with them. The Congress sometime ago passed an Act for the apprehending Charles Gordon and Thomas White Esquires and such others as were notoriously disaffected and active agt. their country in the Delaware State. This took its rise from a motion of the Delegates of Maryland, founded on an Information given to, and an intercepted letter of Thomas White's laid before the Governor and Council of Maryland, and some kind of claim they had to the persons named, they being lately subjects of that State, living upon their borders and carrying on an iniquitous conspiracy within that State. The intention was to have them imprisoned in Maryland, and to prevent any revenge on the part of these men or their adherents agt the Executive Power of the Delaware State, and also to prevent their being rescued out of our Goals by the Enemy or the Tories, or their being liberated by habeas corpus, as the General Assembly had not suspended the habeas corpus Act. I have heard that they have since been taken, and discharged by ha. cor. and that Gordon has again joined the Enemy. Tho' it was perfectly right to enlarge them on this committment, yet the charge made agt them by Congress would have been sufficient ground for my brother Chief Justice to have bound them to the[ir] Good Behaviour.

I should have mentioned this affair to you or Mr. Read before, but that it was ordered to be kept secret, lest the execution of it should be frustrated. I was called upon to name some of the most dangerous men in the State to be added to the others, but I refused, alledging the people there were now becoming good Whigs, and I hoped there would be no occasion.

Now for most important intelligence. You will receive ten papers herewith, published by Congress, which will give you part of it, and which I must beg you will distribute among the Members of the General Assembly. The Bills have been passed into laws, and Lord Amherst, Admiral Keppel and General Murray are the Commissioners. This whole affair will (I know) surprize you, but it has been owing to preliminaries for a treaty with Congress from France being intercepted, tho' the duplicates have not yet been received here. I have not a fear of an Acknowledgm't of our Independance, and an honorable peace, if British Honors, Offices and Gold do not tempt and corrupt your Members of Congress and the Generals and principal Officers of the Army. Do Sir, as I have not time to write to any body else, press the General Assembly to send two more Delegates here, and inform them that you know with certainty I am determined never to give up the Independance of the United States, after so much expence of blood and treasure, whilst I have a breath to draw; that I shall neither be allured nor intimidated into it; and that, if this resolution should not meet with their fullest approbation, they would be pleased to remove me immediately.

God grant us virtue and fortitude in this hour of trial. I have worked double tides (as the Sailors say) all the last week, being every day in Court, and also in Congress, which latter sat on the Fast Day and also yesterday. Our Officers will be allowed half pay for life, under sundry limitations and restrictions; the thing not finished but near it. The Bell tolls for Congress. Adieu.

260

From Charles Pope

Wilmington May 3rd 1778—

Your favour of the 28th Inst. pr. Lieutenant Queenault is at hand I Expect to Receive the Cloth from Mr. Lattimore to Morrow. Have Ordered the Officers late in the Recruiting Service to Extrefis [?] their Respective accounts against the Delaware State and Shall Transmit them to you by the first Opportunity. I have been All-most Troublesom to the General Respecting the Cartridges as their is none to Spare in this Garrison, have Pressed the General to give me an Order for 13,000 that was taken in the Brig Simetre, but must Send to Nottingham for them. I shall procure a waggon at the Expense of your State to take them Down to your Place. The troops belonging to this Division is very Healthy. I fear our Regt. Will suffer for Linen unless it can be procured for them Shortly. as to other Clothes they do not want for. Lieut. Rhodes Informs me that you have been a tory Kitching. I am sorry to hear my Relation Stokely was so lost to Virture as to be one of that number but you cannot Expect anything Else whilst the Executive Power of your State is so Relax, and nothing but Publick Examples will put a stop to that Evil Practice of Trade. Popes Jack was Hanged on Wednesday last a debt due one third of your People but as it is not the Only instance in which the State may be be cald bad Paymaster have Reason to Judge, that shee would Prove a Bankrupt was shee to attempt to pay of their Creditors their Just Demands— or D——d Demmit Should you want hangmen send a line to me and you may have the Regiment as it is not likely we shall have much Else to do but to Subdue our Internal Enemies and we who have bled in this Contest I think it no disgrace to serve our Contry in any Public Capasity. I have the pleasure to Transmit you a Copy of part of an Express which arived here yesterday from his Excellency Genl Washington to Genl. Smallwood. Glorious newes and not the least to be doubted. Pray send Lieut. Willson to Camp he being much Complained off and should he not Come in a short time matters may grow worse with him then he may Expect.

261

To John Dagworthy

Dover May the 7th 1778.—

I am informed by the Judge of ye Admiralty, That the Court ordered the Cargo of the schooner Fortune to be Sold in order to prevent waste and the Expence of Guards &c—That Col! John Jones was appointed Marshel Who had Given Bond for the discharge of his Duty as to the Selling the Cargo and returning the monies to the Judge for distribution among Such as Should be Consider and Adjudged, by him, to have a Just Claim—That Mr Jones in Virtue of this appointment had Advertised the Cargo to be Sold by him on Munday Next—The Judge now informs Me that a Set of Men under the name of a Committee have in Open Violation of the Civil Authority undertaken not only to pull down the Advertisements of the Marshal but to Set up Others, under their Authority, for the Sale of the Cargo aforesaid, as of tomorrow.

As I find by the depositions taken in the Court of Admiralty, That Captain of the Schooner Surrendered the Vessel and Cargo to You as Commanding Officer, I am not a little Surprised that these people, Whoever they be, Should have the possession of this Cargo Unless by Your Authority—However, be that as it may, As Commanding Officer of the Militia You are by Every Means in your power Immediately to put a Stop to this Riottous proceeding,—and you are Also by your authority to Afford Every Necessary protection to the Marshal, And for that purpose, in case you Should be too Unwell to Act in

Person, You Are Immediately to Issue Orders to Your Inferior Officers,—And report to me How you and Your Officers Shall have Conducted Yourselves in the premisses.

262

To Thomas McKean

Dover May the 8th 1778

I received your favour of the 28th—I am Apprehensive the Assembly will not Continue to Sit more than a day or two. I know not the Cause But really think they might as well never have Met for all they are likely to do—I certainly know This that I have been furnished with but one Bill Yet to put the Seal to, Tho they have been Setting near Three Months. Shall be able to let you know More of this Matter by the Next Post—I wish to God you had been here to have lent them Your Assistance four Weeks ago—

Mr Thomas White is verry Anxious to have a hearing with respect to the Charge against him. When You think it can be done with propriety I don't Doubt You'l Move it.—

We are Constantly Alarmed in this Place by the Enemy and Refugees. and Seldom a day passes but Some man in this and the Neighbouring Counties is taken off by these Villians. so that many, near the Bay, Who I know to be hearty in the Cause, dare neither Act or Speak least they Should be taken away and their Houses plundered—These fears will certainly increase till Some protection is afforded them; Therefore I must again Solicit your Moveing Congress in the Most Earnest manner for the Company I mentioned in a former Letter—if it is obtained our persons and property may be tolerably Safe, if not I fear I must Decampt.—I thing [think] Congress ought not to hisitate Especially when you Consider that the number of Guards heretofore Necessary to the defence of a people Situate as we are, has Exosted our funds. The practice of landing in Small parties and taking men out of their Beds is so Villainous, and is so Generally adopted by the Enemy as may be Sufficient to Call the Attention of Congress for Retaliation. Some punishment for this Offence Might be adopted by this State More properly were they in proper Force for that purpose—The Three hundred men Ordered for the Eastern Shore upon the plan you have Mentioned, I have not heard of. However, Sure I am, if they are not Stationed on the Delaware, they will be of little or no Service to Us—

Lord North's Speech is certainly the production of a King and Ministry hard pushed and wicked even to the last, for tho their Salvation depended on their acknowledging the Independence of America, and Entering into a Commercial Treaty with them—By their plan they are trying to divide us—However Virtue and firmness will, with the Blessing of God, as well frustrate them in this as in all their other damnable projects to cajole and Enslave—Since I wrote You last a Sloop drove a Shore at the Cape Richly Laden With Wine, Spirits, Porter, Cheese and a Great Quantity of Dry-Goods. The Cargo is all Saved and Supposed will Sell for Sixty Thousand pounds. There were a great Number of letters from New-York to Philadelphia. I have Sent you, in a packet, all Such of them as, in the least, Speak of Politicks. There Seems to be verry little of Consequence even in them—We are Still Continueing the Recruiting Service and of course Shall Stand in Need of the other ten of the forty Thousand Dollars this State applied to Congress for, for that purpose, and Granted by Congress and Thirty Thousand Sent—let me knew when we Can have it and it Shall be Sent for—I Just now Got certain Inteligence from Port-Pen That Ten people residenters in That Neck Were taken off and Carried on board the Enemy's Veshells Last Night—

263

To Thomas McKean

Dover, May the 22d, 1778.

Mr. Read has put into my hands an order of the General Assembly, in your favour, for Ninety Pounds and eleven pence halfpenny, which I will pay you or your order when directed as to the time and place most convenient to you and me. I have rec'd no letter from you since I wrote you last which is now two weeks ago. This I cannot account for unless you have forgot that I mentioned to you the conveniency of writing by our Post who rides every week from this to Lancaster and is instructed to enquire there at the Post and Printing Offices for letters to me. Our Assembly have broke off without haveing compleated their business, but expect they will meet on Monday next with a greater stock of patience. I wish I could induce you to believe your business would justify your spending even one week with them; if you cannot come pray let me hear from you fully as to the business I have heretofore wrote you.

264

Writ to the Sheriff of New Castle County for Summoning the Members of the General Assembly for the County

The Delaware State To the Sheriff of New Castle County, Greeting; Whereas His Excellency Caesar Rodney, Esquire, President and Commander

in Chief of the State, by and with the Advice of the Privy-Council, Doth declare it necessary, that the Geneeral Assembly of Delaware should be called together on the Seventeenth Day of June, Instant, to consult about and provide for the Weal and Safety of the State, Therefore it is commanded you that you summon as well each and every of the Members of The Council, as each and every of the Members of the House of Assembly, Chosen for and representing your county the present year in the General Assembly of Delaware, to Caesar Rodney meet on Wednesday the Seventeenth Day of June, Instant, at the Town of Dover in Kent County, in General Assembly, and that you then and there make known to the President, or Commander in Chief, in what manner you shall execute this Precept, and of this fail not. Witness His Excellency Caesar Rodney Esquire, President, at Dover, the eighth Day of June in the year of our Lord One Thousand Seven Hundred and Seventy-eight.
Attest.

Jas Booth Secy

265

The Answer of the Sheriff of New Castle County to the Above Writ

I do hereby Certify to the Hon. Caesar Rodney Esquire President and Commander in Chief of the Delaware State that agreeable to the Command of the within Writ, the Legislative Council to Wit. George Read Nichlas Vandyke Peter Hayett, and the members of Assembly of my County for the Present year to wit, George Craighead, Robert Armstrong, Samul Patterson, Isaac Lewis, William Clark, James Black & Robert Bryan, were summoned to appear at the town of Dover in Kent County within the Said State on Wednesday the Seventeenth Instant to meet in General Assembly for the purpose within Mentioned—So answers

Jno Clark Shff N. Castle
County

266

To Thomas Rodney

Newark[1] June the 9th 1778

We have no news of Consequence to be depended upon, Except that the Fleet in Delaware Consisting of upward a hundred & fifty Sail, Continue in the Same place they were four or five days ago—And that the Commissioners arrived on Saturday last, in the Trident of 64 Guns, off New-Castle, and Im-

---

1 Newark, Delaware.

mediately proceeded to Philadelphia in one of the Eagle's Tenders—The Commissioners are—The Earl Carlisle, Lord Amher[s]t, Lord V Howe, M.r Jackson & M.r W.m Eden, brother to the late Governor of Maryland—I suppose we Shall soon hear more of them—[1]

P.S. a Sloop has run into Christina with salt, tea and limes, which will be Libelled—

267

To Thomas McKean

Newark June the 9th 1778

Your favour, I Recd by the Post on my way to this place where I have Summoned the Privy-Council[2] for the purpose, more Especially, of Calling the General Assembly, who verry imprudently dispersed and thereby are disolved unless called by me, after which they may set on their adjournments as before —The Summoning them is the more necessary as they have left us without even one Supreme Judge in the State, having before they Seperated, for the purpose of getting rid of John Cook, Got both Killen and him to resign, the first of whom they intended to re-appoint together with David Finny of New-castle County and John Jones of Sussex—I am much Obliged to you for your Care in procuring the money. Shall Send an Express for it before I leave this together with the order in favour of you which you will be pleased to deduct, unless General Patterson Should fail in procuring one which he has promised —I shall write you by the Express—The Commissioners arrived off Newcastle the day before yesterday in the Trident of 64 Guns & Immediately went on bord the Eagle's Tender and proceeded to Philadelphia—They are Earl Car-lisle, Lord Amherst, Lord V. Howe, M.r Jackson & M.r W.m Eden—

---

1 British Commissioners were on their way from England to Philadelphia for the purpose of negotiating with the Continental Congress, sitting at York, Pennsylvania, for a settlement Since the Commissioners would not recognize the independence of the United States, nothing came of the negotiations and the Commissioners left Philadelphia when that city was evacuated by the British army, June 18.

2 The colonial government of the Three Lower Counties on Delaware had been fairly simple with a unicameral legislature of eighteen members, six from each county, and with a Penn pro-prietor as governor or (if the Proprietor lived in England) someone designated by him as deputy-governor. The government set up for the State by the first constitution of 1776 was more cumber-some, the executive's powers being restricted by the fact that he was elected by a bicameral legisla-ture, not by the people, and that all of the President's acts must be concurred in by a small council of four, called the Privy Council, two elected by the Legislative Council (upper house) and two by the House of Assembly (lower branch). The Privy Council was abolished by the second State constitution of 1792, and after that year the governor was elected by the people.

To Thomas McKean

Newark June the 11th 1778

I wrote from this place last Tuesday in a great Hurry as the Post was waiting, wherein I Acknowledged the Rect of your favour of the 31st of May. I mentioned to you the Sudden departure of the Assembly-men from the necessary business they had in hand &c, but now mean to answer by Mr Lattimer your Letter more fully—I have inclosed you the order of the Assembly in your favour, you will be pleased therefore to deduct the money, Enter a Rect on the back of the order, and deliver both the order and the ballance of the money to Mr George Lattimer who undertakes to give you a Rect and bring the money Safe to Dover.

You and I have both had our disagreable moments with respect to the Complection of the Delaware State. However those who dare persevere in Such days of Tryal cannot now be Doubted. He that Dare Acknowledge himself a Whig near the waters of the Delaware, where not only his property but his person is every hour in danger of being Carried off is more, in my opinion, to be depended upon than a dozn Whigs who are in Security—You have had your times of Tryal here, You know how precarious their Scituation, and you also know their firmness—They did not bear that proportion to the disaffected that I could have wished. Yet while they dared to Contend, I hoped Congress would not have Supposed the State Lost. I thank God Affairs now wear a different Complection, and Can I but have the Countenance and Support of Congress which I, no doubt, Shall, Civil Government, I am Convinced, will soon be in such force as to cause those who have offended to Tremble—I have received from the President of Congress, the Treaty of Amity & Commerce with the Resolution of Congress thereon before the rising of our General and laid them before the House Immediately with a Message. These together with all the other Acts Transmitted me by the President They have neglected to finish. Some indeed they have not as yet taken into Consideration—

The House of Assembly have a fee-Bill in which they made an allowance, to each of the Delagates in Congress, of Three pounds a day, and sent it to the Council for Concurrence. But owing, I believe, more to Ignorance than to any Evil intention or even inclination to offend, They have, in the manner of doing it, insulted the delegates, by makeing it necessary for them to have a Certificate from the Secretary of their Actual Attendance. The Council are for allowing them the Same Sum per day from the time they leave home until they return according to their own account rendered to the House, and it would have passed in that manner had not the Assembly gone off as mentioned before. I have Issued writs for calling them together again on Wednesday next, when, if possible for you to come, you might render great Service.—

With respect to the Confederation our General Assembly, I think, Stand Something Excusable in not furnishing you with Instructions on that head as Congress, so far as I have knowledge in the matter, have neither Specially recommended it to them or even furnished them with a Copy, which probably has been done as to the other States[1]—Perhaps it may have been neglected in Consequence of their thinking us Lost—However they had taken it up Just before they parted, and when they meet again they will, no doubt, furnish you with full Powers—I am Just now informed, from Camp, that Congress have finished the regulation of the Army, be Pleased therefore to Send me a Copy—Well knowing Your Scituation I have been urging the Sending more members to Congress, but they have as yet appointed no person in my place and you know that Mr Vandike is not only a little unwilling to leave home so far, but much Engaged of late in the General Assembly—If you think you cannot be Spared to Come down to Kent, pray do not neglect to give me Every information and advice Respecting Public matters—It is Certain that the Commissioners are Come for the purpose of Treating, but hope Congress, in whom I fully Confide, will not Treat without they first acknowledge *Independence*—I don't understand the withdrawing their Fleets and armies unless it is Intended they Shall actually go back to England—Our whole army have moved Three miles nearer Philada than before, and am Just informed that the British, Except the Grenadiers and light Infantry, are Incamped on the Jersey Shore—Their Fleet, Consisting of one hundred and Seventy sail at least lay between Readen point and Bombay Hook Except the Eagle, Trident, Phenix and two or three armed Veshels.

P.S. The Assembly during their Setting, passed a Test Bill, Militia Bill, one against desertion, a Bill to prevent the inhabitants Trading with the Enemy or refugees and one or two others.

269

From Thomas McKean

York Town, June 17th 1778.

Yesterday I was favored by your's of the 11th instant, inclosing a draught in my favor for £90.0.11½, for which I have given a recet to Geo. Latimer Esquire. He will deliver you the ten thousand dollars, deducting the above sum.

---

1 McKean had requested instructions to sign for Delaware the Articles of Confederation.

This day you inform me the General Assembly are to meet. I should with pleasure attend them, but am afraid, tho' I should thereby act to the great satisfaction of many, yet some would take it amiss and charge me with deserting my Post, especially at this most critical period.

I have lived to see the day when, instead of "Americans licking the dust from the feet of a British Minister," the tables are turned. The Commissioners are, Frederick Earl of Carlisle, Rich.d Viscount Howe, Sir Henry Clinton, W.m Eden Esquire (one of the Lords for trade & plantations & brother to the late Governor of Maryland) and Captain George Johnstone, commonly called Governor Johnstone. The last Gen.n sent me a Letter from an old Correspondent in London, warmly recommending him as a Commissioner of peace, and begging that I would receive him among my friends, as he most ardently desired it &c—Several Members of Congress have received such Letters; but no Answers will be given by Individuals, it being treason to correspond with Enemies by the laws of Pennsylvania. The Commissioners have sent us again the three Acts of Parliament, their Commissions from their Sovereign, and their Propositions; w.ch in brief are, to suspend hostilities by Sea and Land immediately, to join in supporting our Paper money, to agree that we shall govern ourselves in all cases, excepting matters of trade, and for the equal adjustment of that, the British Nation shall have Agents in Congress to have a voice there, and Congress or the several States to appoint Agents in Parliament, who are to have a voice there; and in fine seem willing to any thing but a total seperation; they desire we should have the same King, the same wars and the same peace. In my opinion their propositions cannot be fully supported by the Acts of Parliament: Be that as it may Congress will again repeat; acknowledge our Independence or withdraw your fleets and armies, and we will enter into treaty with you. This answer will be sent off today, and as soon as it is received you may expect to hear the Enemy have evacuated Philad.la, if that should not be done sooner.[1]

Be upon your guard with regard to Letters from the Enemy; they intend to seduce, corrupt & bribe by every method possible. Keep the whole militia under marching orders, if you have the power—Warn the people to double their vigilance, and not be lulled with these pleasing prospects, lest they meet with some terrible stroke, when they do not expect it.

Present my best compliments to your good Brother Thomas, and tell him I am much instructed and obliged by his strictures on financeering and our paper money, but have not time to write to him. Also let Doctor M.cCall know,

1 The answer was agreed to unanimously by the thirty-one delegates present in Congress at York, Pennsylvania. The British army evacuated Philadelphia the day after this letter was written, June 18.

that I have rece. his letter, & wrote to the Commissionary General of Prisoners &c. &c. and that Mr Adams and myself will take every step in our power
for the exchange of his son the Captain, and also Mr Pope.

Remember me with particular attention to Messrs Read, Killen, and the
Gentlemen of the Assembly. Confederation is put off till Friday, tho' it has
been the Order of the day for two weeks. New Jersey is in my situation with
regard to Powers but they expect them daily.

P.S. Blessed is he that endureth unto the end, for he shall be saved.

270

To John Dagworthy

Dover July the 4th 1778

Mr. Read, one of the Council for the State, in the Claim against the
Schooner Fortune, Says it will be Absolutely Necessary you Should attend
the Court of Admiralty in order to declare your knowledge concerning said
Vessel, Cargo &.^c, and that a Summons has Issued for that purpose. This being
the Case make no Doubt you will Chearfully attend, if able, Tho the ride may
otherwise be ever so disagreable—I am Extreemly sorry to put you to this
Trouble as I well know you are generally in a bad State of Health, But as
your not comeing will occasion a delay in the determination, to the great disadvantage of those to whom the prize may be hereafter adjudged, hope I Shall
Stand Excused in Earnestly requesting Your Attendance,

P.S. I have inclosed you an Evening Post, in which is a Letter from Genl
Washington giving an acount of a Genl Engagement.[1] You'l see we have
gained the Field. I had it also by Express. It seems we have killed and taken
upward of a Thousand of the Enemy, our Loss inconsiderable. Besides this,
best accounts are, about three Thousand of the enemy deserted—Great News—

271

From Charles Pope

Cross Road D[uck] Creek[2] July 8th 1778.

The bearer Mr Clark, who I had imployed to make hatts, for our regmt.
Called on me this Morning for Money—which he says [he] stands in much
need of, to pay his workmen &c—I have recd about 100 hatts from him in aprl.

1 Refers to the Battle of Monmouth, June 28.
2 Now Smyrna, Delaware.

last. he now informs me that he had 200 more ready—they are an article that the Regemt. stands in much need of at present but I cannot with propriety Call on Mr. Clark for any more until he is payed for those allready Recd as I am Convinced from his losses occasined by his moving out of the Way of the Enimy, that he must stand in need of money more especially as he put of all other business in Order to Serve the Regemt. and as I have no publick money in my hand—have made free to recommend him to you for yr. Direction in the matter and hope for the above reason you will give him all the redress in yr. power should have waited on you myself but am not so hearty as I could wish—

272

From David Hall

Lewestown, July 9th 1778.

Captain Nicholson who came Passenger with the honourable S. Dean[1] in the Admiral Ship Languidor commanded by his Excellency the Count Destaing;[2] will present you this—he is on his way to Congress[3] with Express from the Admiral.[4] I shall refer you to him for particulars about the Fleet as he is more capable of giving you Satisfaction in that Matter than I am—

273

To William Patterson

Dover, July 11th, 1778.

As the enemy have now entirely left the Delaware, and a large French fleet on our Coast, there does not appear to be that danger to this State which was justly apprehended by the General Assembly when they passed the Act for establishing the independent company you were commissioned to command in the County of New Castle. Therefore, in virtue of the power and authority to me given by the said Act, the said independent company for the County of New Castle is hereby disbanded, and you are immediately to discharge the

1 Silas Deane, first American diplomatic agent, after signing, together with Franklin and Arthur Lee, the treaty of alliance with France on February 6, 1778, sailed in April with Comte d'Estaing's fleet in company with Gérard, the recently appointed minister to the United States.

2 Comte d'Estaing, who commanded the first French fleet sent to aid the Americans after the treaty of alliance.

3 Congress had returned to Philadelphia from York, Pennsylvania, July 2, following the evacuation of the former city by the British army.

4 The admiral's first objective was to bottle up the British shipping in the Delaware River, but he arrived on the American coast too late.

officers and privates thereof from further duty. You are, as soon as convenient, to return me the number of those who served in said company and the time they did serve. You are also to cause the commissary to make a regular account of their supplies which you are to certifie.

274
From Jonathan B. Smith

Philadelphia July 15ᵗʰ 1778

I am informed that a party of the militia of your State has destroyed all my buildings on Bombayhook; & it is said to have been done by your orders on an idea of its being necessary for the public service. In this case I would not presume to suppose you judged wrong, & my uniform opinion has been that private interests must give way to the public necessities. But as I have also been informed that it was a voluntary sacrifice on the mere inconsideration of the persons who made it, & some suggestions have been intimated that personal & interested motives had some influence with the party, I beg the favor of your Excellency to indulge me with information of the orders under which the militia acted, if they had any. The loss of the buildings, of the current rents, & of considerable arrearages which must take place is considerable, & not merited by a person who has sacrificed already so much of his interest, & his whole time for several years to the service of his country.

I beg your Excellencys pardon for giving you this trouble, and shall only add that if you, or the government of your state have directed the measure, I shall have the fullest confidence in its having been proper & necessary.

275
From Samuel Patterson

Christiania bridge July 20 1778

I am Just return'd from the City and am to inform you with all my Industry I have procur'd four chests of public papers, many of the books, half-usᵈ and torn. I found them in near a hundred places, barbers, Taylors Shops &c. should have got many more if our old president had let them alone, but he gathered them to better Security as he thought. and Mr. T. Robison laid hold of a number that he may make his peace I sepose—they are both at New York. I pᵈ. cash to all the Persons I got of—Should be Glad to know who I am to deliver them to as they are wanted to be arranged. Shall wait your commands for that purpose. am afraid if monseur plays a good Game we may bid adeiu to the rest, as they will burn, I sepose before they will give up 600 Sail Vessels which by best acc.ts lay at New York. As to news nothing from N. York particular on Sunday morning. Every person, open mouth, at the Coffe house for the Event of the fleet. you may expect it every hour. I would have sent you the papers of saturday but sepose before this you have them; wee have had a smart Skirmish with the Indians up Susquehannah. kild 13 and took 4 of them, wee lost 10 men kild. wee have sent force sofitient up now. Congress recd a letter from the commiss: from N. York, say they had no right to Make an alliance &c. and now will appeal to the People and treat there, at large. Congress will not answer such Stuff. G. Washington has had an Aid D. Conj. [aide de camp] on board the french Admiral, so they understand Each other. a packet Taken by Mon.s of N. York and many Prises taken by both sides will be up to the City. Goods are now put to Show and Falling, and whigs are going to drive the tories to the D''l. whats our sloop about taking prises.

276

To Captain Carson

Dover July the 22d 1778.—

As the English armed Vessels have all now left the Delaware, and as a powerfull French Fleet is lying off our Coast, The Inhabitants of this State Do not in my opinion appear to be in that danger from an invasion of the Enemy, so Justly apprehended by the General Assembly, When they Entered into the resolution for Establishing the Independent Company you Command in this County—I do therefore, in Virtue of the powers Given me by the General Assembly, hereby Disband the above mentioned Independent Company, You are therefore Immediately to discharge the officers and Privates Thereof from further Service—You are also, so soon as it may be Convenient, to make me a regular return of those who may have been Engaged, and done Duty in said Company.

N.B. The Newcastle and Sussex Companies were ordered to be disbanded on the 11th Instant.—

277

From John Gibson[1]

Treasury office. July the 24th 1778.

The board of Treasury by a resolution of theirs of this day have directed me to salute your Exᶜʸ & request in their name that you would give orders to the

1 Auditor-General.

Treasurer of your State to make monthly returns to their board of the sums of money paid into his hands for the purpose of supplying the continental Treasury conformable to a resolution of Congress of the 22nd of Nov. last & to answer the draughts of the President of Congress for such sums.

278

To Henry Laurens

Dover July the 31st 1778

I verry lately Received your favour, of the tenth Instant, Concerning the Confederation, which is the first application of Congress, on this head, to the General Assembly of this State and is the reason assigned me, by several of the members, why it was not taken into Consideration heretofore—The General Assembly of this State will, by adjournment, meet in this place the tenth day of August next, when I shall Lay your letter before them as Requested. I Shall urge them to as Speedy a determination as its Importance will admit of, and will cause their Resolutions thereon to be Transmitted to the Delegates of this State to be laid before Congress.[1]

279

To Edward Cole

Dover, Aug 8th 1778.

You are to take the prisoners belonging to the Mairmaid Frigate, to wit: John Addams, John Holes, William Cozens and John Martin, from hence to Philadelphia and there deliver them to the Commissary of Prisoners and take his rect. You are also to take with you a Chest and Box said to contain medicines taken from on board said ship and deliver them to the proper officer to take charge of them. There are some bundles of cloathes, supposed to belong to the prisoners, which you are to take in your waggon.

280

To Jonathan B. Smith

Dover August the 11th 1778—

I Recd, Yesterday Evening, a Letter from you dated the 15th of July last, Concerning the distruction of your Farm Houses, and other buildings on

---

1 At this time only three States had not instructed their delegates in Congress to sign the Articles of Confederation, namely, New Jersey, Delaware, and Maryland.

Bombay-Hook—The loss to you is, no doubt, verry Considerable, and your Submitting to such a Sacrifice for the public Good is a further proof of that Patritism you have hitherto Shown—It appears that Inhabitants of that Island were a wicked Set, and carried on, for a considerable time, a most Villainous and distructive trade with the Enemy—and were so Scituate between the other Inhabitants of this State and the Enemy That they could not be easily prevented, Which, I make, no doubt, was the cause of this Severe Step—But Sir it was not done by any order of mine or any resolution of this State—We were not, at that time, in force to have done it, and defend our other Posts from the Incursions of the Enemy and their abettors, the Refugees—who were on our Coast from one End of the State to the other—I am informed, and beleive the fact is, That it was done by a party of Continental Troops from Wilmington Under The Command of L:t. Col:l. Pope, Who I presume had his orders from General Smallwood. I make no doubt that Some Individuals of the Militia, who lived near the place and had Suffered by them, went over to the Island with, and assisted the Co[n]tinental Troops—I am Much Concerned Whenever the opperations of War are Such as Make it Necessary to Sacrifice the property of Whigs. When rascally Tories are accumulating Wealth for Which They are Claiming, and indeed obtaining The protection of that Government they Never Sought to Establish—

281

From Samuel Patterson

Xteen Bridge. Aug. 17th 1778.

Your favor is rec:d of the 31st ult. Observe the contents. I shall deliver the records agreeable to your orders. Young Rich:d McWilliam I am told has reassumed the recorder's office. Those I shall make free with your indulgence to retain a while & see if the judges of the pleas will remove him. His conduct about them when first removed is scandelous. Judge Finney called on me, he tells me there was a general goal delivery. I expected such. I wish that you could leave them & come up this way. There is but a few in your county to stand by you. They will now grow insulting. I wish you would send, for the officers of the Independent Co. was here, to peremptorily to attend you at Dover a certain day in order to settle the whole acc:t The poor unfortunate Commissary lost his life about 3 weeks ago by a fall out of his chair—broke his leg & mortified. It would be in my opinion best to order the Capt. to bring his acc:ts to the Commissary:s or all he has, as also an acc:t of left provision on hand, if any—he is to sell them & give the Commissary credit for them.

My reason for pointing this business to your Ex:cy I am afraid bad acc:ts of the £300. I gave the Capt. an order on Stockton—for £150 of said cash to pay his men &c. off. He rec^d it. I am also sorry to hear that our Assembly did not meet. Such conduct in representatives does not bear the test. I have now been nearly about 3 weeks confined to my room & bed—a bilious complaint mending very slow. I intend to decline being member of Assembly at our next Election—as confinement would absolutely Kill me. I can not say whether they would vote me or not but I shall act my part. I will push Mr. McKean. I think we can carry him & he will not refuse. I plainly see that the old leaven is at work below & I am afraid some of it is got up here. Your moderate people —a proper term in this contest for a villain in disguise.

The officers of the militia here have no notion of mustering this. Can not hear one a stirring. I wrote to one Dep^y of the County to exert himself in ordering them to observe the law, as my confinement prevents my aiding. It is a good law & if it neglected in the first instance it is totally gone. What the enemies of our state wish—I shall watch them as well as I can to complete it.

Col. Ramsay called here on Saturday last & left the enclosed acc^t He says the sloop should be sent out with a load of tobacco. If such could be got. I also approve of it. No news but what is in the papers, which I make no doubt you have read.

282

To Henry Laurens

Dover Augt the 22d 1778

In my last I informed you that the General Assembly of this State were to meet, by adjournment, on the tenth of this Instant, when I would lay before them, for Consideration, the Confederation and Your Letter on that head— The Assembly did not meet according to adjournment and Therefore, by the Constitution cannot Assemble unless Called by the President—However I Shall meet the Privy-Council at Newcastle on Monday the 31st of this Instant. Therefore if Congress think it necessary and will advise me of it, I will then Isue writs for calling the Assembly for that purpose previous to the anual Election to be held on the first day of October. The Assembly then Chosen will Set on the twentieth of the Same month—

283

To Henry Laurens

Dover August the 24th 1778.

Mr. McKinly the late President of this State Informs me that General Clin-

ton has Enlarged him, on Parole, for one month, from the fifth of this In-
stant, in order to Effect an Exchange for Mr. Franklin late Governor of the
State of New Jersey—That the proposed Exchange has been laid before Congress, by Mr. McKinly, for their approbation—That the matter was taken up,
Debated upon and, for some Reasons, postponed on Thursday last—Mr. Mc-
Kinly also says that, one objection was that, no application had been made in
his favour by the authority of this State—With respect to the application to
Congress in his favour. The President and Privy Council were not advised of
the Measure and therefore could not apply—The other reasons why Congress
have not acceded to the proposed Exchange I cannot Judge of, as they have
not been Communicated to me—Certainly Congress, who have the most Extensive View of these Matters, can best Judge of the propriety of Exchangeing
Mr. Franklin—However so far as Mr. McKinly's conduct and services from
the beginning of this great Contest to the Declaration of Independence, In
adopting and Enforcing the Resolutions of Congress from time to time, both
as a Member of Assembly and Member of Committee, His Activity as an
officer in the Militia, his obtaining Subscriptions and collecting Money for the
Poor of Boston, Will recommend him to the favour of Congress and the good
opinion of all other friends to our glorious Cause. I am persuaded he is deserving—Soon after the Declaration of Independence and the adopting the
present Constitution of this State, Mr. McKinly was appointed President.
From that appointment until he was taken Prisoner, all his Letters and orders
to me as commanding officer of the Militia breathed the same Spirit of Patriotism—I cannot pretend to Judge of Mr. McKinly's Secret Intention or
wish, But his public Services, in this great Contest, induces me to wish him
restored to his Liberty—Colo. Bedford and Colo. Latimer fully concur with
me in this. The other two members of the Privy-Council are absent, one in the
State of Maryland, the other with a Sick family.—

284
To Thomas McKean and Nicholas Van Dyke[1]

Dover August the 24th 1778

On application of Mr. Mckinly, and taking into Consideration his distressed
Scituation and the Services he has heretofore Rendered in our Great contest,
Tho I do not alltogether approve his Conduct, I have wrote the President of
Congres Soliciting his Exchange, would therefore refer you to the Letter and,
so far, as you think you can with propriety, would Wish you to lend your aid

[1] Delaware delegates in Congress.

in bringing it about He is an old man and can Illy support himself under his present misfortune[1]—While I am Speaking of an Exchange Give me leave to mention to you a worthy active man in the American Cause now a prisoner on Long Island and as I am Informed, much distressed, I mean Silas Snow a Captain in the militia, he was taken in the dead of Night out his warm bed by the refugees and Carried on board of Ship without Clothes or money &c.— There are now prisoners of this State and on Parole in Philadelphia a Captain Nowls, a Captain Burrows and Mr. Young, a merchant, why might not one of these be Exchanged for him? In short he was so Servisable That rather than not have him I would give them all—Major Hodgson was also taken off. Should be glad he could be Exchanged.

285

From Thomas Bradford

Phila Sept. the 17th 1778.

About 3 weeks ago I wrote you respecting some prisoners of war I was informed was in Dover, since which I have not been honored with your answer, from which concluding my letter has miscarried. I am not [?] to request you would order to my care in this city all the Prisoners-of-War of all degrees as also all the paroles of Prisoners that may be lodged with you, that we may be enabled to exchange & release from a cruel captivity a like number of our Countrymen many of whom have families among us. I am the more urgent on this matter as an exchange of Sea-men is now going on & we shall fall short of the quota necessary to release all ours in New-York. Your answer will much oblige.

286

To Henry Laurens

Dover Octr 18th 1778.

Your favour of the 16th Instant inclosed with an Act of Congress of the same date, I Received at 6 OClock this Evening by Express. And Congress

---

1 When President McKinly was captured by the British in Wilmington on the night of September 12, 1777, following the Battle of the Brandywine, he was kept aboard the British warship, *Solbay,* in the Delaware River, until the British military forces succeeded in capturing the forts below Philadelphia When the last fort at Red Bank, N J, was captured in November and the British shipping could pass up to Philadelphia, McKinly was brought to the city and kept a prisoner there until General Clinton evacuated the place, July 18, 1778. McKinly was then brought by sea with other prisoners to Flatbush, Long Island, where he remained until paroled with a view to securing his exchange.

may be Assured that every necessary Step, in my power, Shall be immediately taken to enforce the Act above Mentioned. Your favours of the 7th and 13th of this month, mentioned in the 16th. are not come to hand.

287
Message to the General Assembly

Gentlemen of the Assembly—

At the request of the Honorable the Continental Congress I now lay before your Honors a Letter received from the President dated the Tenth day of July 1778 urging your takeing into Consideration the Confederation of the United States &c—With the President's Letter of the Seventh Instant, I received and now send you, by the Secretary, two Acts of Congress, One passed the Second day of October 1778, for Continueing the present Embargo on provisions until the last day of January 1779, and for other purposes therein mentioned, The other, an Act passed the fifth of October 1778, for exchanging with Continental Currency Such Local Bills of Credit as have been received in the Loan-office of Each State respectively—In a Letter of the Thirteenth Instant from His Excellency the President of Congress, I received an Act of that Honorable Body passed the twelf[t]h, for Encouraging True religion and Good Morals and for the Suppression of such Entertainments and diversions as have a Contrary Tendency—As I have been favoured with no more than one Copy of each Act, Hope Your Honors will, as early as possible this Sessions, lay them before the Legislative Council for their perusal also—

Caesar Rodney

Dover, Octr the 23d 1778

288
To Henry Laurens

Dover Octr the 27th 1778.

Since my Letter of the 18th Instant, I have received your favours of the 7th and 13th with the Acts of Congress inclosed. I have laid them before the General Assembly now setting. And whenever they come to any determination thereon Shall take the Earliest opportunity to inform Congress.

We have not, as yet, been honored with any Flags from the High & Mighty British Commissioners, Tho prepared to give them a proper reception and such Quarters as Congress would Wish and they justly Merit.

289

Message to General Assembly

Gentlemen of the Assembly

I beg leave to inform you, that In Virtue of a Resolution of the General Assembly passed the twenty sixth day of June last, Impowering the President to Appoint a proper person to go to the City of Philadelphia, Make Enquery for, demand, receive, Secure &c the public papers belonging to this State that had been taken away by the English, I Appointed Samuel Patterson, Esq. who in pursuance of Said Appointment proceeded to Philadelphia and by the papers returned me procured many of the Records above Mentioned, and lodged them in the Office of Newcastle County to which they belong. He has also lodged with me an Accnt of his Expences, which with the other papers reported to me Accompanies this Message, for your perusal and Approbation.[1]

Caesar Rodney.

Dover Oct. the 29th 1778.

290

From Henry Laurens

Philadelphia 1st Novem. 1778

I am just now honored with your favor of the 27th Inst. which shall be presented to Congress at their meeting to morrow.

A budget of Manifestoes said to be from the British Commissioners was lately thrown up by the Sea on the Jersey Shore, it contained one Package marked Delaware supposed to have been intended for that State, another marked Pennsylvania, the whole number were brought to my House & by me laid before Congress. Congress would take no Cognizance of the Waif; the Vice President of this State declined touching the bundle marked Pennsylvania—if your Excellency believes that which was possibly intended for Delaware worth carriage, it shall be immediately transmitted. I make no doubt Sir of your having heard that a Flag Vessel on board of which was a Lieut.t Midshipman & thirteen people of the Preston British Man of War, [who] had been wrecked some days ago on the Coast of New Jersey, two of the people were drowned. Those who reached the Shore alive having no Credentials by flag

1 New Castle County records and probably some colonial records of the "Government of the Three Lower Counties of New Castle, Kent and Sussex on Delaware" were captured by the British when they occupied Wilmington on September 13, 1777, following the Battle of the Brandywine. (See Samuel Patterson's letter to Rodney, dated July 20, 1778.)

or otherwise were conducted as prisoners of War to the New Jail in this City where they remain.

I am directed by Congress to recommend to the State of Delaware to supply immediately a proper number of Representatives in Congress; for some considerable time past the State has been almost wholly unrepresented. The Honorable Mr. Vandyke having retired on account of the bad state of his health & the Honorable Mr. Chief Justice, McKean detained by unavoidable attendance on his duties of his Office. Also to request the State to give Instructions to their Delegates to Ratify the Articles of Confederation; New Jersey will accede in a few days, as Congress is informed by her Delegates & we hope Maryland will no longer delay—the accession of these three States will perfect the foundation on which the happiness of our general Union [depends?].

Inclosed with this will be found Sea Manifestoes by Congress, will Your Excellency be pleased to distribute by proper means to public view in your State—
Copies are sent to all the posts of the Enemy

291
To Henry Laurens

Dover Nov. the 4th 1778—

I Recd your favour of the 1st Instant, by Express, this day—

I Suppose there is little doubt that the package Marked Delaware, is filled with Manifestoes from the British Commissioners, if so, I would not be at the Trouble of opening it for the Contents, and as I received no British favours when on better terms than we now are am determined against taking this

In My Letter of the 27th of October I informed you That I had laid before the General Assembly, Then Setting, The Several Acts of Congress inclosed with Yours of the 7th and 13th, together with the Confederation and That I Should take the Earliest oppertunity to Make Congress Acquainted With their determination—I am Now to inform Congress, and it is with Concern I do it, That by Some means or other in the course of Yesterday and to day the Members of the House of Assembly have dispersed and thereby the House dissolved without having Compleated any one peice of business laid before them —This precedure of theirs laid me Under the Necessaty of Immediately Calling the privy-Council to lay an Embargo for Thirty days, to take place at the Expiration of the present Act of Assembly—This is all we can do Touching that business—At the Meeting of the Council I purpose Issuing Writs to Call the General [Assembly] to Meet on the fourth day of January Next, if Congress think their Meeting at a Shorter day Absolutely Necessary Should be Glad They would let me know it by the Nint[h] of this month That I may then propos[e] it to the Council—

The Hon⁰ M⁰ Vandike let me know he intended to Congress in a few days. No New appointment of Representati[ves] in Congress for this State has been Made—

The Manifestoes of Congr[ess] Shall be made public.

292

From Henry Laurens

Phila. Nov. 7, 1778.

I had yesterday the honor of presenting to Congress Your Excellencys favor of the 4th Inst. and received an Order from the House to request that Your Excellency will call the General Assembly together as early as possible, this will more fully appear by an Act of Congress herein transmitted.

It is the earnest desire of Congress that the Assembly may attend to the Articles immediately after their Meeting and be decided in their Instructions to their Delegates.

293

To Henry Laurens

Dover Nov⁰ the 8th 1778—

I Received this morning about 11 OClock, Your Excellency's favour of Yesterday with the Act of Congress inclosed—

I Expect the Privy-Council, Agreeable to Summons, will meet here tomorrow, and do not doubt they will Concur with me in calling the General Assembly together as Early as possible in order to Compleat the business so Earnestly recommended by Congress. I Shall let Congress [know] the time fixed for the Assembly's Meeting.

294

To Henry Laurens

Dover Nov⁰ the 13th 1778

I now beg leave to inform Congress that, with the Concurrance of the Privy-Council, I have, by writ, Called the General Assembly to meet at Dover on Monday the Twenty Third of this Instant. Therefore, if Congress have any matters they would wish to have laid before the General Assembly other than Those already recommended, hope They will furnish me with them—

295

From Henry Laurens

Philadelphia 16th November 1778

Within the present inclosure will be found two Copies of the undermentioned Acts of Congress viz.

An Act of the 26th August 1776 for establishing a Provision for Soldiers and Seamen Maimed or disabled in the Service of the United States.—to which is subjoined a supplementary Act of the 25th September 1778 for the benefit of maimed and disabled Volunteers in the service of the States antecedent to the date of the first above mentioned Act.

An Act of the 26th September for organizing the public Treasury, and for providing an House for the several officers of Treasury.

17th You will likewise receive an Act of Congress for holding a general Thanks giving throughout these States on Wednesday the 30th December next—and three Copies of the Treaty of Amity and Commerce and of Alliance eventual and defensive between his Most Christian Majesty and these United States for the information and use of the State of Delaware. *18th* Your Excellency's favor of the 15th [November 13] this Morning presented to Congress afforded the House much satisfaction.[1]

You Sir, and the privy Council have done your part. Congress confide on the General Assembly to Co-operate with you for the benefit of the Union, particularly by acceding to the Articles of Confederation. The State of Jersey have Resolved to Ratify, we trust that Maryland and Delaware will not much longer be delinquents.

296

To Henry Laurens

Dover Novr. the 22d 1778—

This morning, half after 10 OClock, I Recd Your Excellency's favour of the

1 In Rodney's letter of November 13 he stated that with the concurrence of the Privy Council he had called the General Assembly to meet on November 23 Rodney had explained in a letter to Congress of November 4 that the General Assembly which had been called together principally for the purpose of taking action upon the Articles of Confederation had, by the dispersion of the members, become dissolved. Congress had thereupon requested him to call the General Assembly together again "as soon as possible " (See the *Journals,* November 6, and Laurens' letter to Rodney, November 7.)

16th, 17th and 18th Instant, with the Several Acts of Congress and the Treaty of Amity and Commerce—Such of them as Require the Consideration of the General Assembly Shall be laid before them Immediately on their making a House—

297
From James Booth

New Castle 23ᵈ November 1778.

Agreeable to your orders I reminded the Members of the Privy Council both before and at the Court of writing to you respecting the appointment of an Attorney-General. I have since understood from Col? Bedford, that, altho' they have not wrote, it is their Request that you should nominate whom you pleased; I therefore mentioned to him my Apprehension that this would not be altogether Satisfactory to you, which if it should be Case, I suppose the[y] will write speedily.

Col! Evans informed me that according to your Directions, with which I immediately acquainted him upon my Return from Dover, he had Sent one of the Proclamations to be inserted in the Papers, but as I have not seen it published I suspect that the Person by whom he sent it has been guilty of Neglect.

I herewith transmit the blank Marriage Licences by a special Messenger, who also carries down the Papers belonging to the Assembly, and I hope that both your Excellency and the House when you advert to the present Situation of the public Business of this County, will excuse my Non-Attendance at this Time, or for a few Days.

298
Message to the General Assembly

Gentlemen of the General Assembly

The calling you together at so Short a day from your last Setting gives me no small concern. I am not Ignorant of the great sacrafice you make to the public by leaving your Families and private Affairs so frequently. But am nevertheless persuaded that the importance of the business which you are now called to decide upon will, in your opinions, justify the Act of convening you.

I must beg leave to recommend to your Honors the compleating the several matters laid before you, by Message, at your last Setting, particularly, the Articles of Confederation. Congress are verry pressing to have the General Assembly decide upon that Matter and to Instruct their representatives in Congress accordingly.

Since your last Setting I have received and send you herewith Several Acts of Congress to wit. An Act of the twenty Sixth day of August 1776, for Establishing a provision for Soldiers and Seamen Maimed or disabled in the service of the United States—to which is Subjoined a Supplimentary Act of the twenty fifth of September 1778, for the benefit of Maimed and disabled Volunteers in the Service of the States, antecedent to the date of the first Mentioned Act—An Act of the twenty Sixth of September 1778 for Organizing the public Treasury and for providing an House for the several offices of Treasury—and An Act for holding a general Thanksgiving, throughout the United States, on Wednesday the thirtieth of December next.

Give me leave to put your Honors in mind of the Delaware Regiment now in the Continental Service. Their Situation and circumstance at this season of the Year will no doubt call your Immediate attention, and Urge you to make, so far as may be in your power, every necessary provision for them—I have sent herewith a petition & remonstrance of the Officers of that Regiment Addressed to the General Assembly, and two Letters One from Lt. Coll. Pope, the other from Captn. Patten addressed to me.

Gentlemen. I have been informed by the deputy residing here in the Quarter-master's department that, in consequence of Orders he has received, He is building Stables for Sixty of the Light-Horse, and no doubt, Similar Orders are given to other deputies within this State. If this should be the case, the troopers are probably intended to be Quartered upon the Inhabitants. And as there has been no Application to the Civil Authority, it is reasonable to Suppose they intend Quartering them by their Own, and in Such Manner as they may think proper. Now to avoid that uneasiness in the Minds of the Inhabitants, Which is often occasioned by immaginary, and too Often by real impositions, I would wish the General Assembly to take this Matter Under their consideration and make such regulations as they may think best calculated to afford a comfortable Support to the troops and at the same time preserve Peace and good Order.

Gentlemen. I am requested to inform you that this State has been verry Seldom represented in Congress for twelve months past, and that Congress are verry desirous the General Assembly Should take Order therein.

CAESAR RODNEY

Dover November
  the 27th 1778

[Endorsement]
(A message to the General Assembly
  Nov. 26—1777—Read 1st time
In council
  Read the first Time.)

299
Message to the General Assembly

Gentlemen of the General Assembly

Since my Message to you of the twenty Seventh Instant, I have received and send you herewith An Act of Congress, dated the tenth day of this month, appointing Mr. Scudder, Mr. Morris and Mr. Whipple a Committee to Superintend and regulate the departments of the Commissary and Quarter Masters General.—I send you Also three letters, of the eleventh of this Month, from the above mentioned committee addressed to me, requesting I would recommend to your Honors, the Enacting Laws for the prosecution and punishment of persons in office under the Continent[al Congress], for offences committed within this State,—To prohibit the distilling Spirits from Grain and to prevent Engrossing.

I have received from the President of Congress and now present your Honors a Copy of the Articles of Confederation and perpetual union of the States.

CAESAR RODNEY

Dover, November
the 28th 1778

[Endorsement]
(Message to the General Assembly
Nov. 28, 1778.
Read 1st Time)

300
Thanksgiving Proclamation

[December, 1778]

By His Excellency
Caesar Rodney Esquire
President, Captain-General and Commander in Chief of the Delaware State

a

Proclamation

Whereas the Honorable the Continental Congress did, on the Seventeenth day of November last, Resolve towit. That &c. (here insert the resolution of Congress at large) And Whereas the General-Assembly, on the fifth day of december Instant, did take into Consideration the resolution aforesaid, and having approved the same, Did request me to Issue my Proclamation Accordingly—I Do Therefore appoint Wednesday the Thirtieth day of this Instant december to be observed as a day of Thanksgiving and praise Throughout this State— And I do most earnestly recommend it to the Inhabitants thereof To Omit on that day all recreations, Unsuitable to the purpose of Such Solemn[i]ty, To attend places of public Worship and there with a decency and devotion becomeing good Christians, acknowledge their obligations to Almighty God for the Benefits they have received.

301

From Gunning Bedford, Junior

Philada Jany 16th—1779

I wrote to you when I was down at the last NCastle court, which letter, Bedford[i] informs me, from a late message of yours to him, he believes you did not receive. Had I known it sooner, you would have had the trouble of reading another letter from me before this, but as I did not, & if it had not been on business, I dare say you would readily excuse me.

In that letter Sir, I expressed my wishes to accept of the office of attorney General for the State. Bedford had informed me you were so obliging as to incline to favour my application in preference to some others that had been made, if I had any intention of coming into the state to live. In answer to this, I expressed my gratitude to your Excelly for your favourable disposition toward me, I further told you, from the favourable prospect of business & the introduction that the appointment might give me, I was much inclined to settle in the State. I still continue of the same opinion, & if I am so happy as to have your approbation, & nothing unexpected happens, I think I shall have the honor of being your neighbor the next summer. I shall at any rate ,(unless I hear from you,) be at the next Dover Court, when I hope to have the pleasure of taking you by hand.

Mr Rush I am told, is a powerful antagonist, & has large recommendations. Perhaps I have presumed too much on your Excellys personal knowledge of me? If I have, it is my misfortune. At the time I applied indeed, there was no other application that I had heard of, otherwise I should have been more particular.

Mrs Bedford begs her compliments to you. She is favourably inclined to Dover, & I do assure you her high esteem for Genl Rodney does not contribute a little to it.

---

1 Gunning Bedford, the elder, at this time was a member of the Privy Council.

302

From Gouverneur Morris and William Whipple

In Committee of Congress   ⎱   Philadelphia 19ᵗʰ Jan. 1779.
on the Commyˀ & Qᵗ Mᵗ Dept. ⎰

    We did ourselves the honour to write to your excellency the 11ᵗʰ of Nov. last, on the subject of Engrossing. Permit us to call your attention once more to that subject. The evils feared when that letter was written now rapidly approach and the letter from the Commisʸ Genl. of which [we] enclose [you] a copy gives us the most alarming apprehensions. The wisdom of the state you preside over and your own exertion will not we are confident be wanting to prevent the mischiefs arising from that insatiable thirst of gain which knows neither principle or bounds. We will not insult your good sense by dwelling upon this fruitful topick. Your knowledge of the cause & prudential foresight of the effects, will doubtless stimulate you to every measure which you shall deem necessary for the public service.

303

Message to the General Assembly

Gentlemen of the General Assembly—

    Saturday afternoon I received by Express a Letter from his Excellency General Washington requesting That I would give the Deputy Quarter master Authority to Canton Pulaski's Legion within this State, And as I would wish the General Assembly to take order in this matter, have directed the Secretary to lay the Letter before you—I have also directed him to lay before your Honors a letter of the 19th Instant from the Committee of Congress on the Subject of Engrossing,[1] with the Copy of a letter from the Commissary-General of purchases to them on That Head.

Caesar Rodney

Dover January the
25th 1779

304

To George Washington

Dover Janʸ the 27th 1779—

    Your favour of the 19th instant came to hand, by Express, the 23d in the afternoon, I immediately laid it before the General Assembly who are now

---

1 Monopolizing or cornering the supply of food or other important articles by war profiteers.

taking order in the Matter, be assured nothing in my power to aid the Quarter Master Shall be wanting—

I am apprehensive Your Excellency Must have been misinformed with respect to the County of Sussex being able to Maintain a part of the Horse. They have no forage but what is taken from the Indian Corn and Salt Marshes— The Indian Corn has produced verry little this Year owing to a Storm before the time of Gathering—The Counties of Newcastle & Kent will be able to Maintain a considerable Number, and believe the Quarter Masters have got Stables, already Erected, Sufficient for Polaskis Legion—Mr Quarter Master Wade has not Yet Called upon me.

305

To Nathaniel Scudder, Gouverneur Morris, and William Whipple[1]

Dover Jany the 27th 1779

Your favour of the 11th of November last, refered to in that of the 19th of January Instant, was recd and Immediately laid before the General Assembly then Setting, and Whenever they Shall have taken Order in the Matter recommended I Shall communicate it to you with out loss of time

306

Delaware Ratifies the Articles of Confederation[2]

His excellency Caesar Rodney, Esq. president, captain general and commander in chief of the Delaware State, to all to whom these presents shall come, greeting:

Know ye, that among the records remaining in the rolls office in the Delaware State, there is a certain instrument of writing, purporting to be an act of the general assembly of the said State, which said act is contained in the words and tenor here following, to wit,

Anno millesimo septingentesimo septuagesimo nono.

An act to authorize and empower the delegates of the Delaware state to subscribe and ratify the articles of confederation and perpetual union between the several states.

1 Continental Congress Committee to superintend and regulate the departments of the Commissary and Quartermaster-General.

2 Thomas McKean laid before Congress the proclamation on Tuesday, February 16, 1779. He signed the Articles "On the part & behalf of the State of Delaware," February 22, 1779. John Dickinson and Nicholas Van Dyke likewise signed them on May 5, 1779.

Whereas Articles of Confederation and perpetual union between the states of New Hampshire, Massachusetts Bay, Rhode Island and Providence Plantations, Connecticut, New York, New Jersey, Pennsylvania, Delaware, Maryland, Virginia, North Carolina, South Carolina and Georgia, signed in the general Congress of the said states by the honorable Henry Laurens, Esq. their then president, have been laid before the legislature of this State, to be ratified by the same if approved: and, whereas, notwithstanding the terms of the articles of confederation and perpetual union are considered as in divers respects unequal and disadvantageous to this State, and the objections stated on the part of this State are viewed as just and reasonable, and of great moment to the welfare and happiness of the good people thereof, yet, under the full conviction of the present necessity of acceding to the confederacy proposed, and that the interest of particular states ought to be postponed to the general good of the union; and moreover, in firm reliance that the candor and justice of the several states will, in due time, remove, as far as possible, the objectionable parts thereof:

Be it enacted by the general assembly of Delaware, and it is hereby enacted by the authority of the same, that the hon. John Dickinson, Nicholas Vandyke, and Thomas M'Kean, Esqrs. delegates appointed to represent this State in Congress, or any one or more of them, be and they hereby are authorized, empowered, and directed, on behalf of this State, to subscribe and ratify the said articles of confederation and perpetual union between the several states aforesaid.

And be it further enacted by the authority aforesaid, that the said articles of confederation and perpetual union, so as aforesaid subscribed and ratified, shall thenceforth become obligatory on this State.

Signed by order of the house of assembly,

NICHOLAS VANDYKE, Speaker.

Signed by order of the council,

THOMAS COLLINS, Speaker.

Passed at Dover, February 1, 1779.

All which, by the tenor of these presents, I have caused to be exemplified. In testimony whereof, the great seal of the Delaware State is hereunto affixed, at Dover, the sixth day of February, in the year of our Lord, one thousand seven hundred and seventy-nine, and in the third year of the independency of the United States of America.

CAESAR RODNEY.

By his excellency's command,

JAMES BOOTH, Secretary.

307

Message to the General Assembly

Gentlemen of the General Assembly,

I have just received, by Express, from His Excellency the President of Congress, a Letter of the 22ᵈ Ultᵒ inclosed with divers Acts of that Honorable Body on the Subject of Finance, which I have ordered the Secretary to lay before your Honors for your Perusal.

Caesar Rodney

Dover, February 1, 1779.

308

To John Jay[1]

Dover Febʸ the 4th 1779

I have the pleasure to inform your Excellency that I this day fixed the great Seal to an Act of the General Assembly impowering the delegates to Ratify the Confederation on the part of this State and the Delegates Shall be furnished with a Certified Copy of the Act as soon as possible for that purpose.

309

From Samuel Patterson

Xteen Feby 14. 1779.

Yours of the 11ᵗʰ came to hand last Evnᵍ note the contents as to the cash sent for the office by Mr. Rodney to you. I wish it was at hand, that I might get clear of it. I cant devise any way but to send it up by some safe hand. It was his business so to have done. You mention news if any to advise. Have sent you a paper by this opportunity, Mr. Mitchell who promises to deliver it to you. And have news every day but cannot give it under my hand, as it frequently tells otherwise by next day.

Gold is fell much, also Rum 20 p [?] per gallon in one day. Spain in our favor offers a loan to Congress, of hard 15,000 dollars.

310

To the Governor of Massachusetts

Delaware State March 1ˢᵗ 1779

A few days since a Letter signed by you in behalf of the General Court

1 President of Congress.

dated the 14th of January last and addressed to the Honᵉ George Read Esquire
was put in to my hands as President of this State—By this Letter I am Informed That you are verry apprehensive of Suffering for want of Grain in
your State, and that you have prayed Congress to recommend to the Southern States a Suspension of the Embargo as far as relates to the Exportation of
Grain to the Eastern States.— . . . Act passed in this State prohi . . . of Grain,
Except disposition of the Inhabitants of this, toward those of the Eastern
States leads me to make no doubt that the Council will readily Concur with
me in Granting permits Unless Congress who have as yet taken no steps with
us as to your Prayer, Should advise the Contrary, To such persons as Shall
come into this State for the purpose of purchasing and Transporting Grain to
Any of the Eastern States for the Concumption of the Inhabitants, Provided
they bring with them proper Credentials—But Sir I have to inform you, and
it is with much concern . . .

[The rest is missing.]

311

From Gunning Bedford, Junior

Philadelph.ᵃ March 8th 1779

I was much pleased the other day, when your neighbour Mr. Robison called
on me & proposed an exchange of houses. I unfortunately had engaged mine
the day before he came to me, but urged him to call on the gentlemen who
had taken mine, & get the refusal of his, which he did. Mr. Robison now tels
me, he believes his house is engaged when he leaves it, (which is some time in
june) to Mr McCombs, but that I may go into it when he leaves it til his time
is out. More certain terms, you know, would be much more agreeable to me.
Tilton too passed through town, & I had not an opportunity of seeing him. I
must beg the favour of you Sir, to interpose your good offices with those who
may have an interest in the house, that I may if possible get into it.

I am informed a Mr. McCall is come up from Dover to town to live; I dont
know what house he lives in, but Mr. Robison tels me he thinks I might be
accomodated in that house with a part of the house that fronts the street, which
he thinks might be procured.

As I have determined to go down, I should be glad to get fixed by some
means or other, by the middle of April. Mrs. B is very anious about it, & thinks
she should be much happier if she can get next door to his Excelly I dont
know how it comes General, but you still hold your place as a great favourite,

& I dont know but I had better counteract her in her wishes as to that point—However, I will run the risk for the sake of the house.

We have nothing material in politicks—We are determined to have no convention—our last one made such a damned bad constitution, we are afraid to trust another—Sic et citeris [ceteris]

I shall esteem myself happy, in being favoured with a line from you—If left at the Coffe house, I shall get it safe—

312
From Samuel Patterson

Xteen Bridge. March 12th 1779.

I am to acquaint you that I have paid to the continental treasurer, Francis Hopkinson Esqr. 60,000 dollars as his receipt of the 9th inst being our full state tax of '78. I send it under a small guard of light dragoons continental & Capt. Dunn. We are the first state have paid such in full & but one before—any part.

As to news, we have none but what you must have heard before this, sooner to hand, it is all good. The sun in the American Horizan shines bright for our independence. I was for the honor of our state to put in of my own cash to make out about £1100 to be early & clear of charge of cash.

313
From James Booth

New Castle 23d March 1779.

I received yours by the Express, with Directions to attend at Dover on Friday next, which I am sorry to inform your Excellency will not be in my Power, having been extremely ill for some Time past. Could I even bear to ride down it would answer no good Purpose as I have almost totally lost the Use of my Hands and Arms which renders me unable to write, nor have I been one step from my Bed since the 10th of the Month, owing to the same Debility in my legs; tho' I think the Strength of Both are returning, slowly, and I hope, once more, God knows when, to be very well.

[P.S.] I should be sorry any Business your Excellency may have would be delayed by my absence. And respecting the Conversation I had with your Excellency when last at Dover relative to the SecyShip I would wish you to do therein that which is most agreeable to you, which would also be most Satisfactory to me.—

Excuse this Letter I write in great pain

314
From Gunning Bedford, Junior

New Castle April 6th 1779.

I wrote to you some time ago from Philadᵃ & expected to have had the honor of hearing from you before this time—I must again beg leave to trouble you with a few lines—I am a[n]xious to know either there will be a possibility of getting a house in or near your town; the spring will soon be over, & I shall miss every opportunity of making any little improvements in the garden way —Mᵣ Basset has promised to look out for me & seems pleased that I talk of coming down, wether he is sincere or not I dont know—I am afraid I shall be obliged to attend your court of oyer & Terminer, before I go down to Lewis; I could wish to save the time if possible—

We were flattered with having the pleasure of seeing you here while the court were sitting; we have made out to convict one of your traitors, what more is to be done with him will be left to you—

315
To John Dickinson

Dover April the 17th 1779

Some Seventeen or Eighteen months ago, General Smallwood, in Virtue of an order of Congress, Seized and imprisoned Thomas White Esquire of this State on Suspicion, as is said, that he held Correspondence with the Enemy— Mr. White is still under Parole to General Smallwood, and therefore wishes, if they have any thing to alledge against him, to have a hearing, or to be discharged—as his request seems to be reasonable, you will be pleased to move Congress for that purpose—Mr. White's papers are in the hands of the Honb. Nicholas VanDike Esqr.

I wish you would Endeavour to know how Captain Silas Snow and Mr. Robert Hodgson, late residenters of the State and now prisoners on Long-Island, are provided for, and what probability there is of their being Exchanged—There was Captain Knowls and Mr. Young, prisoners of this State and whose Paroles I now have, Sent to Philadelphia. I think they ought to have been Exchanged for Snow & Hodgson and wrote to our Delegates to that Effect, but have not heard from them concerning it—Captain James Moore and Lieutenant Hyatt of the Delaware Regiment are also prisoners with the enemy and on Long-Island.

I must beg leave to mention to you a Matter which gives me and, I think, must give every real friend to American Independence Great Concern—I mean the management in the Quarter-Masters and Commissaries departments—The prices now given and likely to be given for every kind of forage, and provisions together with the Expences of Transporting are so Enormous that I much fear they will in the end, if a remedy cannot be fallen upon, tend verry much, if not Effectually to ruin one of the most glorious Causes a people ever engaged in—It is difficult to know how these people manage their business, but it appears strange to me that they should necessarily be obliged to give such Extravagant Prices, When there is no other Market for those articles—but be this as it may, I must beg leave to submit it to you Whether every purchaser in the Quarter-Master's and Commissaries departments to, being obliged to submit his accounts to, and obtaining the Certificates of their having passed the Inspection of the Supreme Executive Authority comprehending the district to which they belong, or such other as they or the Congress might constitute for that purpose—would not in Some Measure be a remedy—for tho' people in General are not willing to become informers, they are generally free to say the Truth when called upon, Especially where they are known and can have an Easy access. However it appears Clearly to me that there is an evil, and would wish to submit the contriving a remedy to the wisdon of Congress —I am persuaded that you have seen & heard enough of this matter to be convinced that the public are much Injured, and your own good sence will better direct you how to remove the Injury than I possibly can—I rest assured that you will, from time to time, let me know, so far as this State ought to know, how matters go on in Congress, and that you will freely give me your friendly advice in Conducting the business of my department. Your advice, especially as you are now situate, may Cause my acts, the better to correspond with my wishes for the public wellfare.

316
From Gouverneur Morris

Phila: 21st April 1779

Having given Orders that the Commissaries of your State desist from farther Purchases of Flour permit me to intreat that your Excellencies known Attachment to the Interests of America will urge the rigid Obedience of this Order. If at the same time Flour can be had at £15 per Ct. I am content that it be taken by such Person as you shall appoint for that Purpose notifying me as soon as possible of the Quantity purchased and the Place where it shall be lodged. It should be put in store and kept at my orders (ie.) the Store Keeper should deliver it as I may direct. Every Measure becomes necessary to prevent that Ruin which menaces us from Commissaries and Quarter Masters.

317

From John Dickinson[1]

Philadelphia, May 10th 1779.

This Morning Congress receiv'd Intelligence from the Commander in Chief, of a very considerable Embarkation of Troops from New York. The Destination of this armament cannot be ascertained, but from its consisting in part of Horse, and from other Circumstances, it is believ'd to be designed against some of the Middle or Southern States. I therefore think it my Duty to give You the earliest Notice of this Advice, that in Case the Enemy bend their Course to our Bay or to Chesapeak, the Delaware State may be in preparation for defending itself or cooperating in the Common Cause.

I would be more particular on this subject but that Congress has this Moment resolv'd to send Copies of the Dispatches to the Southward, and M[r]. Jay assures Me You shall receive one—

Your Letter came to my Hands, but I have not been able to obtain any satisfactory Information, concerning the prisoners you mention—Humanity & your Recommendation will powerfully induce Me to pay Attention to their Case, and I shall transmit to you the Result of my Enquiries & Applications.

I mention'd M[r]. White's affair to M[r]. Vandike, who tells me, the papers are in M[r]. M[c]Kean's Hands—He is now on the Circuit. When he returns, I will endeavour to have that Business finish'd according to your Desire.

The very important Business of the Quarter master & Commissaries departments demands the most speedy & vigorous Measures—You know, how much my sentiments correspond with your own on that Head, and I have the pleasure to inform you, that there appears in Congress a hearty Inclination to probe the Disease to the Bottom—For my part, I must say, that as I do not know a more effectual Way of rendering essential services to my Country, than by contributing any Assistance whatever it may be, to the Relief of these Evils, so I shall industriously labour to perform my part of this great Duty.

I think You mentioned to me, before I left Kent, that You had some thoughts of coming to Philadelphia this Month. I most earnestly wish You would, and if possible, before the Meeting of our Assembly, which I understand, is to be on the 17th—If you cannot, I wish to receive the sense of yourself and as many of the legislative Council & Assembly, as can be conveniently collected, as soon as possible, on a general Question, which may be of eminent Use to my Colleagues & myself in regulating our future Conduct. We have most momentory Business to transact. It may happen in managing the Affairs

1 John Dickinson was elected a delegate in the Continental Congress from Delaware by the General Assembly on January 18, 1779.

of so extensive a Confederacy, that particular States may be more interested in certain points than other States or than the Confederacy in general—

My opinion is clear, that the Interest of each State being Objects comprehended within the Confederation, are to be regarded as the Interests of the whole, & as such to be contended for and defended—[On] Interests of this kind, Difficulties, I apprehend, will not arise—but on Interests beyond these Limits they may. On these, my opinion is also clear, that as a Delegate I am bound to prefer the general Interests of the Confederacy to the partial Interests of Constituent Members, how many soever they be, & however respectable and meritorious; and further, that if ever such a Competition should arise it is my Duty to prefer the particular Interests of the State that honours Me with her Confidence & invests me with a share of her power, to the particular Interests of any other State on this Continent—

I cannot be more particular on these very important Considerations, not being at Liberty to disclose the Subjects of Debate to which they may refer— But obviously just as my Determination seems to Myself on the most mature Deliberation to be, yet so strangely hooked do the plain Lines of sound policy appear by passing thro some Mediums, that I should receive great satisfaction in finding Myself fortified in the Resolutions that will actuate my Conduct, by knowing that the Sentiments leading Me to those Resolutions are approv'd by my Country.

[P.S.] Captain McClean's Company[1] is by a Resolution of Congress annexed to the Delaware Battalion.

318
From John Jay

Philadelphia 19th May 1779

I have the Honor of Transmitting to your Excellency herewith enclosed a copy of an Act of Congress of the 18th Inst, for affording Releif to the distressed Inhabitants of Bermuda—

319
From John Jay

Philadelphia 22nd May—1779

You will receive, herewith enclosed a Copy of an Act of Congress of the 21st Inst, calling on the States for forty five millions of Dollars.

The late rapid depreciation of the Currency demanded a speedy & effectual

---

1 Allen McLane's Partisan Company.

Remedy While the great purposes for which the money was originally issued are Remembered, there can be no doubt that every Measure calculated to support its credit, & prepare the public faith, will be readily adopted—

320
Message to the General Assembly

Gentlemen of the General Assembly,

Since your last Sitting, I recd a letter from the Honorable the President of Congress, with an act of that Honorable body, dated the ninth day of March last, recommending it to the several states to make up & complete their respective battalions, to their full compliments by draft, or in any other manner they shall think proper, & to have their quotas of Deficiences ready to take the field & march to such place, as the commander in chief shall direct without delay &c. As there is not a power vested in any but the General Assembly to comply with the act on the part of this state; & as this is the first opportunity I have had, I must beg leave, tho late in the year, to lay the letter & act with a return of the regiment, before your Honors for consideration.

The Secretary will lay before your honors with the President's Letter, two acts of Congress—one of the 23rd of March last, for regulating the clothing department—the other of the 5th of April providing for the pay of the officers Employed in it. He will also lay before you a letter from Mr. Pomeroy:—the commissioner appointed to settle & pay all accounts of arrearages for clothing, due to the Troops of these States, for the Year Seventeen Hundred & Seventy Seven, requesting a return of the Expenditures of this state; & also an act of congress the Second of March to that effect.

By the Secretary I have sent you a letter from his excellency the President of the State of New Hampshire, enclosing an act of the General Court of that State. To prevent returning into the state, certain persons therein named, & of others who have left or shall leave that state, or Either of the United States of America, & have joined or shall join the Enemies thereof.

Permit me to inform your Honors, that in virtue of a recommendation of Congress, I have with the advice of the Privy-Council, suspended by Proclamation under the great seal, a part of the act, "to prohibit the Exportation of provision from this state beyond the seas, for a limited time," so far as the same relates to Massachtts Bay. And now I send you with a copy of the Proclamation above mentioned, a recommendation of Congress, for affording relief to the distressed inhabitants of Bermuda.

I have just recd & beg leave to lay before you, a letter from the Hon John

Dickinson Esqr one of the Delegates in Congress on the part of this state, by which you will find Congress have called upon the United States, in addition to the sum required, by a resolution of the Second of January last, for their respective quotas of 45 millions of dollars, to be paid in to the Continental Treasury before the first day of Jany next; that the Quotas are to be in the same proportion with those of the fifteen millions, & that the quota of this state will be four Hundred & Fifty Thousand Dolls.

You will receive herewith a remonstrance, signed by a number of the officers of the Delaware regiment, addressed to the House, & put into my hands to be laid before you.

Caesar Rodney

Dover, May 24th, 1779.

321

From Samuel McLane

Philada May 27th 1779

I have agreeable to your request made every necessary Enquirey Respecting the Sale of the Charriott & find there is Severall to be disposed of in this City, Coachmakers & others Say they can give no Opinion of it unless they see it whether it woud be likely to Sell. I have Described it & Shall use every method to get a Purchaser but I fear there is not much demand for Such at Present—A Spirit of regulating the prices of goods & rising the Value of the Money have taken place here it alarms the Monopoliser. The Committee apointed at a Town Meeting are Active. many bad Characters are Confined & its expected some will be sent into the enemys Lines. God knows its time something is done to help the Credit of the Curency—Its hoped it will have a good effect—

Reports from the Southward still Bad—please Sir accept these from your Very humble

322

Message to the General Assembly

Gentlemen of the General Assembly,

Since my message of the 24th Instant I have received and now beg leave to lay before you, a Letter from the President of Congress with an Act of that Honorable Body, calling on the States for Forty five Millions of Dollars.

The Secretary will lay before your Honors for Consideration the Application of Captain William Murray of the Island of Bermuda, for Leave to exchange Salt for Corn; and I am to inform you that M$\underline{r}$ Murray wishes to be called before the House and examined touching his Application.

Caesar Rodney

Dover, May 28$\underline{th}$ 1779.

323

From Francis Wade[1]

Wilmington 31$\underline{st}$ May 1779

Just as the Express return'd the Inclos'd Came to hand, Gen$\underline{l}$ Guist pass'd here this morn$\underline{g}$ on his way from Camp to take the Command of the Millit$\underline{a}$ in Maryland, a number of officers is gone to the southward, Coln$\underline{l}$ Lawrence the late president of Congress's. son, has been wound$\underline{d}$ in an Engagement there, supposed to be the same mentioned in the inclosed pape[r] that Count Polaskie was ɪn, the Pensyl[vania] troops was to move near the Enemy a[t] New York this day, which is the pri[ncɪpal] [ne]ws I could Collect from the Gen[eral]

324

From John Dickɪnson

I have the pleasure to inform you, that the news of our success in South Carolina, is so far confirm'd, tho we have not yet receiv'd any Express, as to put the Truth of it beyond all Doubt—The Enemy attack'd our Lines at Charlestown, and were bravely repulsed—They attacked a second time, & while the action was well maɪntained on both sides, a Column of Lincoln's army appear'd in the rear of the Enemy, & immedɪately falling upon them, put them to a total rout, with a very great loss of kɪll'd & taken on the Spot—and then pursued them as they were scattered in small parties to make their Escape, which perhaps is the Reason, that we have not yet had any Express from him

It is said, the Enemy's numbers were 4000 British, & 3000 Tories, the latter of which made little or no Resistance In short, tho the partɪculars cannot be authentically ascertained, Congress is convɪnced, that the affaɪr is another Bourgoɪgnade,—and every successive Blow of that kind, must be more severely felt than the precedɪng, because it is striking upon a place already sorely weakened.

Let us all at this important Crisis intensely recollect our Duties to Heaven & our Country—cooperate in our several stations with the Efforts of our gal-

---

1 Deputy Quartermaster-General of the Contɪnental Army.

lant Brethren in the field, and after vanquishing & win[ning] in fair fight, not suffer ourselves to be ruined in our internal & domestic affairs by the most contemptible vermin that ever crept upon the Earth

I saw a letter yesterday from the Quarter Master General—He mentions the Enemy's having gone up in Force to West point on North River, an important post of ours well situated, fortified, and garrisoned—after viewing it some time, part of them return'd down the River, & from circumstances it is believed, an Irruption into New Jersey is intended—My Brother came to town last night, from General Cadwaladers, & tells me he came up in Consequence of an Express, to collect the Jersey Militia with all possible Expedition—It is supposed, but without any Evidence that can be depended on, that Genl Clinton may take the Field with 8 or 10000 Men—Such a force will not be able to accomplish any great matters

If we baffle the attempt of our Invaders this Campaign, & convince them, that our Finances are not in an utterly irrecoverable Disorder, I hope this year will crown our Labours with peace Liberty & safety—

[P.S.] I sent down by Jo, 19 copies or setts of the Journals & Minutes of Congress, for the Counsil of Assembly, but have never heard, whether they were receiv'd—I now send down 19 setts more—from the 17th of April to the 22d Trust Thomas Smith will deliver them

325
To John Dickinson

Dover June 13th 1779

That you may, in some measure, be acquainted with the proceedings of our General Assembly at their late setting, I have inclosed you Sundry resolutions for filling up the Delaware Regiment, and Supplying the officers,—and also the Titles of all the Acts they passed—[Towit, "An Act for the recovery of public monies from the late Trustees of the Loan-office of Sussex County, and others therein named.—An Act for the better securing Elections within this State.—An Act for the Speedy recovery of Public Debts. A Supplement to an Act, intituled, "An Act of Free Pardon and oblivion, and for other]¹

And am Sorry to inform you that when these and some other things of less moment were done, two of the members of Assembly, according to Custom, went off, and thereby dissolved the House, Tho much business of importance nearly finished.

1 Evidently a draft, as the words within the brackets are crossed out.

I don't like to make use of harsh Expressions relative to these gentlemen's Conduct—But wish most heartily they had a deeper sense of their Duty.—

It gives me much pleasure to find your name at the head of a Committee appointed to remedy, if possible, Some of the public abuses.—

I Just now received your letter of the tenth instant and am happy in our Success at Charles-Town—if That be Confirmed we have nothing to fear from the Enemy, and Congress may turn their attention to our internal affairs—

P.S. Mr Collins told me he had received the minutes of Congress sent

326

From David Hall

Middle Brook June 24th 1779

Your Favor of the 9th Inst I received by Captain Patten with the Resolutions therein mentioned inclosed therewith. In consequence of the Resolution for filling up the Regiment after consulting his Excellency I have sent down Lts Mc Kinnan Quenouault & Hosman who together with Lts Rhodes & Skillington who are already in the State are to proceed on the recruiting Service. Captain Patten is sent down with them to superintend that Business—There is nothing new stirring, both armies are lying still, ours at Smiths Cove, the Enemy at Kings Ferry where they are fortifying

327

From John Jay

Philadelphia 29th June 1779

Your Excellency will receive, herewith enclosed, a copy of an Extract of a Letter from General Washington to Congress of the 11th Inst; and of an Act of Congress, which it gave rise to, of the 28th—By the latter you will perceive that Congress have again thought it requisite to call on the several States to fill up their Battalions by the most speedy and vigorous efforts—

The necessity of this measure is too evident, to need any Arguments to press your Excellency's Attention to an object of such movement to the freedom and Independence of America.

Your Excellency will perceive the Expediency of keeping the General's Letter as secret as the nature of the case will admit—

328

From James Booth

New Castle 3d July 1779.

On my way up from Dover I called upon General Collins in order to have the Draught for the 36,000 Dollars, signed, but not finding him at Home I left it, requesting that he would transmit it by the first opportunity to either Mr Vandyke or myself. Since which I have not heard from General Collins, and have therefore drawn another and delivered it to Lieut Queenault who promises to call upon the General in order to have it completed.—With the latter Draught, after Mr Vandyke had signed it, I waited upon Genl Patterson, who declined entering his Acceptance upon it because it was incomplete, but said he knew such a Sum had been directed to be drawn for by the Speakers of both Houses, and with or without a Draught from them would answer every Order of Yours to that Amount while he had a Shilling of the Public Money in his Hands.—He also informed me that at present he had little or no money, but that Dr Ridgely, as Treasurer of Kent, had a Considerable Sum in his Hands due to the State Treasury, which he had directed him to pay to your order, and that he had acquainted you therewith before he left Dover.

Lieut Queenault who waits upon your Excellency with this Letter, will deliver you £309"14"4 the amount of the Order drawn in Favor of Capt Mc-Lane and by him assigned to you, which I received from the State Treasurer.

329

From George Craghead[1]

Xteen. Hundd July 6th 1779—

In my last (by Captn McCall) was Inclosed the Invoice of the Cloth Received of Coll: Pope, having measured the White Naps—Captn Patten, Put into my hands, last Saturday, a Copy of the Resolve of the General Assembly, for Giveing the officers of the Delaware Regiment a Quantity of Rum, Tea &c, and make no Doubt but the Clerk of the Assembly hath Furnished Your Excellency with a Certify'd Copey of the same;

And as Your Excellencey is therein Impowred, & Requested to Draw upon the State Treasurer for One Thousand pounds to Inable the Clother General to Put said Resolve into Execution; I shall be obliged to Governour Rodney for to send His order for that Purpose, by Captn Patten, Lieut McKannon (or

1 Clothier-General of Delaware.

any other safe hand) as the expence of my going to Dover for it, must be charged to the state; which I wish to avoid, I have ben at Philada and Purchased Cloth for Coats for the officers of s.d Regiment, (at a high Price) which with that I had Purchased before for Jackets & Breches, is makeing for those who hath had their Measure taken; and as soon as the Trimmings is compleat, Will send the Bill of Costs, that Your Excellency, may see how farr the 12000 Dollers, Granted hath gone towards the same; which will be found not sufficeant for the above and Two Shirts a Peice; (as I had to Pay for makeing the last sett of overalls, out of it;)

What is be done for Cash to Purchase the Remainder of their Cloathing; Particularly Shoes, Stockings & shirts, I cannot say, but must submit it to Your Excellencey; But will beg leave say, that if Governour Rodney, would Direct to Cash for to Compleat the Resolve I am Clear that the General Assembly will Chearfully Repay him; The Gentlemen, haveing Depended on that Resolve, is unprovided, and must be in Great Distress; I have Received several Letters, which all mention the Great want they are in of all the above Articles. no news hear.

330

From John Jay

Philadelphia 8th July 1779

Herewith enclosed is a copy of an act of Congress of the 29th Ult.º for borrowing twenty millions of Dollars on the terms therein specified.—

331

To Samuel Patterson[1]

Dover, July the 10th 1779.

By certain Resolutions of the General Assembly entered into on the fifth of June last, The Clothier General of this State is impowered to purchase sundry Articles for the [?] Supplying the Officers of the Delaware Regiment, while at camp—and by the said Resolutions the President is impowered to draw his Order, from time to time, on the Treasurer of this State, in favour of the said Clothier General, for monies for that purpose.—

You will therefore be pleased to pay Immediately into the hands of Lt Coll George Craghead Esqr the Clothier General of this State, for the purpose above Mentioned, The Sum of One Thousand pounds out of the public monies in Your hands, take his Rect., and Charge the Delaware State therewith.

1 State Treasurer of Delaware.

332
From Francis Wade

Wilmington 17th July 1779

Having Occassion to send an Express as far as Duck Creek, have taken the Oport.y by him to forward you the annexed piece of Inteligence Just rec'd by an Express from Charles Town south Carolina

Charles Town 22d June 1779

An attempt was made to dislodge the Enemy from thier Intrench'd post at Stone ferry Early in the morn.g of the 20th of this month. The attack was made at half past seven & the Action Continued with Considerable warmth for the space of 56 minutes dureing which time they were drove into thier works, but it being found that their works were so strongly Constructed, that our light field pieces Could make no Impression on them and that they had been Considerably reinforced from Johns Island dureing the Action, our troops were withdrawn from the lines, which was perform'd in good order, the light Infantry Covered the rear & maintain'd so good a Countenance, that the Enemy did not attempt to follow more than 400 yards and that at a respectful distance. The highlanders made a desperate sally early in the Action, but were drawn back leaveing 27 dead & several wounded on the field their loss is not ascertained, but as the above was only on one part of the field many more are thought to have fallen, besides what were killed without the lines, our loss is 32 killed and about 90 wounded many of them slightly, Coln.l Roberts of the Artillery & Capt.n Dyget of the Infantry are among the slain—our troops are now Convinced they are a full match for the best of the Enemies forces, who they find are as liable to be alarmed at abreast [?] Charge of Baynets as those they have affected to despise.—

N.B. the above was Copy'd from one the Express had, said to be wrote by Gen.l Lincolns Aid D. Camp & the Express adds that before he left Charles town that Gen.l Moultrie with Coln.l Laurence & a body of troops had got between the Enemy & their shiping, & Cut down a swinging bridge the Enemy had Erected, & had blocked up several of their gallies &c.

333
To James Booth

Dover July the 20th 1779.

The business of State makes it necessary I Should Convene the Privy-Council. You will Therefore let the members, residing in Newcastle County, know

That I expect their punctual attendance, in Council, at Dover on Tuesday Next, the 27th Instant—If there be any thing not heretofore furnished in the Minutes and proceedings of the Assembly Necessary for me to act upon, you will be pleased to bring Such business with you properly certified—

As Congress have, by an Act of the 9th Instant, Vested the Executive Powers of each State with further Authority respecting persons Employed in the Quarter master General, or purchasing or issuing Commissary's Departments —And, as George Evans and John Lee Esquires, have informed me of Sundry Complaints against Mr. Francis Wade D.Q.M.G., You will be pleased immediately to see Messrs Evans & Lee and let them know That Such persons as have any thing to alledge against him are requested to attend the President & Council at the time and place above Mentioned—And also that you Acquaint Mr. Wade with this Matter, That he may, if he thinks proper, attend on his part—

It is with reluctance I assign you so much Troublesome business previous to your comeing down to Council, And as punctuallity Seems to be Necessary hope you'l Execuse me—As I purpose having a Colle[c]ter appointed for the port of Lewis, it would be well to bring your Commission or Appointment with you—

334
From John Dickinson

Philadelphia, July 22nd 1779

I send you by Mr. Wm. Brown the Journals of Congress from the 1st of February to the End of March, & from the 21st of June to the 26th—20 setts of each which, with those I have already sent, form compleat Journals of Congress from 1774 to this Day, excepting the third volume not yet published, and the Journals from the 20th of last month also not published—When these come out, I will send you twenty setts of each, with which I will beg leave to trouble you for the use of the Legislative Council & Assembly.

335
To Thomas Rodney

Dover, July the 24th 1779.

Genl Wayn with 1200 Light Infantry marched up in the midst of a heavy fire & took sword in hand without firing a gun—the enemy's fort at Stony Point on the North River. The whole garrison consisting of 500 fell into his hands, 15 pieces of Cannon & all the stores. This is published by Congress in the Tuesday's paper which I have not now got. I have not rec'd a paper since. P.S. The above is one of the greatest strokes struck this war.

336
To John Jones

Dover July the 24th 1779.

I am informed by Congress that Captn. Young on the 18th instant Landed at Senepuxent 64 Prisoners taken on board the British Sloop of War Harlem by Captain Barry &c that when landed Colo Purnal, Col Handy or Handley & Mr. John Bailiff were applied to take them in charge, but that they had not —Congress have therefore requested of me that, in Case they shall not have been secured and sent to Annapolis, I would order a Sufficient Guard to take them into Custody and have them sent to Philadelphia at the most moderate expence possible and that the Expences shall be paid immediately on their arrival at Phila.—You are therefore, as Genl. Dagsworthy, I understand, is from home, first to know whether they are secured and sent to Annapolis, if not immediately to order a Guard of about 20 men from your Regt. direct their being sent to the lower end of this State, Where your Guard may take charge of and bring them to the lower end of this County or to Dover, and there deliver them to a Captain and guard with an account of Wages and Expences which account is to be delivered to me so that the money may be had of congress for their use.—This letter goes by an Express by whom you may forward a message to the Neighbourhood of Senepuxent in order to have the prisoners Conveyed to this State—You may also direct this Express to wait for and bring you an answer—You will be pleased to pay due attention to these Orders immediately on the Receipt of them, and inform me as soon as possible what you shall have done therein.
P.S. Gl. Waine with the L.I. has taken Sword in hand the Fort at Stoney Point on ye N. River with ye. whole Garrison consisting of 500 men 15 Pieces Cannon all ye Stores &c this is published by Congress and may be depended upon.

337
From James Booth

New Castle 7th Aug. 1779.—

About half an Hour ago I received from Wilmington the printed Copies relative to the Continental Loan, which M.ʳ Lyons to whom I delivered them promises to do himself the Honor of waiting upon your Excellency with, tho' from his Impatience to ride I could not write by him.—Inclosed is the Record of Judson's Conviction complete, which I had at Dover but forgot to deliver.

I congratulate your Excellency upon the Reduction of Grenada by the French Arms, and the Success of D'Estaing's Fleet, whose Superiority over the British in Naval Force will, I hope, by these and future operations be productive of immediate and permanent beneficial Effects to the United States—tho' I suppose before now you have had more particular accounts than we can inform you of.

338
From Francis Wade

Wilmington 9ᵗʰ Aug.ᵗ 1779

The inclos'd Came to hand by Express this morn.ᵍ I have taken the earliest opport.ʸ of forwarding it, Mr. Coakley in a late lett.ʳ to me has intimated that your Excellency is in future to have the diricting of the prices to be given by the purchascing Commiss.ʸˢ &c. of forage &c., which will give me infinate pleasure dureing my stay in the department, as it will be a means of stoping in some measure the reflections thrown out ag.ᵗ the departm.ᵗ for raising the prices, for sake of the Commiss.ˢ. We purchase every article wanted in this quarter, & Oats in great plenty at the regulated prices fixed by the Committee which makes the business Exceeding Easy & no murmuring among the people or attempts to break through them. I have herewith Inclos'd the last news paper.

339
To George Read

Dover August the 13th 1779

As the Case of Creed & Hutton has been represented to me in a favourable point of view by you, the attorny General & M.ʳ Vandike I have inclosed you a Pardon for them.

Sally who intends to Newcastle with me, is not a little concerned to find you are under the necessaty of being in Philadelphia at the time—However we Shall take up our Quarters with Miss.ʳˢ Read and leave you, tho crowded with the great ones of the Earth to envy our happiness—

340
From Francis Wade

Wilmington 14ᵗʰ Augᵗ 1779

we have accounts last even§ that Antagua was in possession of the French, that the grand fleet on the Coast of England cant keep the sea that the Spaniards have actually Joined France & 25000 men were Embarked for Ireland if all those accounts proves true, which I most sincerely pray may be the Case, we will soon be Clear of those Usurpers & every man can live in peace under his own roof which no man wishes more for then

341
To John Jay

Dover August the 20th 1779.

Your Excellency's favour of the 14th instant, I recd this day, and Congress may be Assured that, every thing in my power, to comply with their wishes By filling up the Battalion as soon as possible, and by calling forth the Militia if it shall be found Necessary Shall be done.

The Success of the party now recruiting for the Battalion, by report of the officers, exceeds my Expectation. The Officers are verry industrious, and had the Orders of Congress been made last winter, I am convinced the Battalion might then have been filled in two or three weeks time.

342
From Eleazar McComb[1]

Philadelphia 24ᵗʰ August 1779

Agreeable to your Excellency's desire I waited upon Mʳ. Dickinson on Saturday evening, and had some Conversation with him on the Subject you recommended. He inform'd me that the Committee appointed to frame some regulations for the Quarter-Master and Commissary departments, (of which he was a Member) had deliver'd in their Report.—That He expected Congress would take it up in a few days, and he hoped such Resolutions would be passed as fully to answer your Wishes. In the meantime He is of Opinion that

1 Member of the Privy Council.

the Act of Congress already passed gives full power to the Executive authority of the several States to ascertain the districts of the Purchasers so as that one may not encroach upon the purchasing Ground of another.

I should most certainly have waited upon your Excellency this day, if I had not hoped that the other Gentlemen of the Privy Council would attend, and render my presence unnecessary. If this should not be the Case, M^r· Magaw will come up here immediately, and I will drive down the Carriage he brings up with the least possible delay.

343
From George Washington[1]

West Point August the 26th 1779

In a letter which I had the Honor of addressing to Your Excellency on the 22^d of May I took the liberty to mention the inconveniences which had prevailed for want of System in the Cloathing department and the necessity there was for an early appointment of State or subCloathiers, agreeable to the Ordenance established by Congress, by their Act of the 23^d of March, with which I presumed Your Excellency had been made acquainted. I am now under the necessity of troubling you with a farther address, upon the subject of Cloathing itself. From the best information I have been able to obtain, both from Returns and particular inquiries, I fear, there is but too much reason to apprehend, that unless the 11 Respective States interpose with their exertions, our supplies of this essential Article will be very deficient, and that the Troops may again experience on this account, a part of those distresses, which were so severely and injuriously felt in past stages of the war, and which a regard to the interests of the States as well as the duties of humanity should prevent if it be practicable. I do not know exactly how matters will turn out with respect to Woollen Cloathing, I should hope tolerably well, but if the attention of the State should ever go to this, there will be little probability of our having an over supply: But the Articles to which I would take the liberty to solicit your Excellency's more particular attention are Blankets, Shirts, Shoes & Hats, (more especially the two first) as our prospect of these is by no means pleasing and such indeed as decides, that the supply from the Continental Cloathing and agents will fall far short, or at least stand upon too critical & precarious a footing. The importance and advantages of good supplies of cloath-

1 This communication was addressed to the States of "New Hampshire, Massachusetts, Rhode Island, Connecticut, New York, Jersey, Pensilvania, Delaware, Maryland, Virginia."

ing are evident and they have been most remarkably and happily demonstrated in the health of the Troops, since they have been pretty comfortably provided for in this instance,—a circumstance of all others the most interesting.

While I am on the subject of Cloathing, I would also beg leave to add that the condition of the Officers in this respect appears to me to require the attention of their states. It is nearly in many instances painfully distressing. The want of necessaries and of the means of procuring them at their present exorbitant prices have compelled a great many Officers, of good reputation and merit, to resign their commissions;—and if they are not relieved, it must be the case with many others, as they will have no alternative.

344
From George Washington[1]

August 26th 1779

I have the honor to enclose Your Excellency a list of sundry officers belonging to your State who have been in captivity and are reported by the Commissary of prisoners as violators of parole. A conduct of this kind so ignominious to the individuals themselves dishonorable to their country and to the service in which they have been engaged and so injurious to those Gentlemen who were associated with them in misfortune, but preferred their honor demands that every measure should be taken to deprive them of the benefit of their delinquency and to compel their return. We have pleged ourselves to the enemy to do every thing in our power for this purpose and in consequence I directed W. Beally Commissary of Prisoners to issue the Summons, which you will probably have seen in the public papers. But as it is likely to have a very partial operation, I find it necessary in aid of it to request the interposition of the executive powers of the different States to enforce a compliance. Most of these persons never having been and none of them now being in Continental Service, military authority will hardly be sufficient to oblige them to leave their places of residence and return to captivity against their inclination. Neither will it be difficult for them to elude a military search and keep themselves in concealment. I must therefore entreat that Your Excellency will be pleased to take such measures as shall appear to you proper and effectual to produce their immediate return. This will be rendering an essential service to our officers in general in captivity, will tend much to remove the difficulties

1 This letter was addressed to "Governor Clinton, Governor Livingston, President Reed, Governor Johnson, President Powel, Governor Rodney, Governor Trumbull."

which now lie in the way of exchanges, and to discourage the practice of violating paroles in future.

345
To John Jay

NewCastle; 26th Aug? 1779.

I have to inform Congress, that the Act prohibiting the Exportation of Flour, Grain &c. expires the first Day of September. By the Constitution of this State, the President, with the Advice of the Privy Council, is vested with Power to lay an Embargo for thirty Days. The Privy-Councillors are now with me in NewCastle, and will attend me here again on Tuesday next, therefore if Congress think it necessary that the Embargo should be continued, and will advise me of it by that Time, I have no Doubt the Measure will be adopted.

346
From Jesse Root[1]

Philadelphia September 3rd 1779

The Commissaries of Purchases have directions from the Committee to enter into Contracts for the purchase of as large quantities of Flour as they can, not exceeding two hundred thousand Barrels on the most reasonable terms they shall be able—that being the quantity necessary to Supply the Public Exigences the Current Year—This quantity must be drawn principally from the States of New York, New Jersey, Pennsylvania, Delaware, Maryland and Virginia— of which the quota of your State is calculated at twelve thousand Barrels—The present exhausted Condition of our Magazines having not more than a Supply of three weeks on hand as appears by the inclosed Extract from the Commissary Generals Letter, the impractibillity of drawing any immediate Supplies from the States of New York and Jersey calls for the most vigorous Exertions of the powers of your State to Co-operate with and facilitate Col. Ephraim Blaine Deputy Commissary General of Purchases for the Middle District in procuring the Supplies of Flour so immediately wanted.—

Your Excellencys well known ardour in the Common Cause will need no Incitements to induce you to lend Col. Blaine every assistance in your power

1 Member of the Continental Congress from Connecticut.

to promote a business so pressing and Important in such way and by such means as Your Excellency with him shall think most proper and necessary—

Signed for Order of the Com.ttee for Superintending the Commissary & Quarter Masters departments

347
From John Dickinson

Philadelphia, September 8th 1779.

Monsieur Gerard yesterday communicated to Congress a Letter to him dated the 29th of June last from the Count de Vergennes Minister of France for foreign affairs, informing, "that in Consequence of the decided part Spain has taken, the Forces of that Kingdom & of France are in Motion to effect a Junction, in order to direct their united Efforts against the Common Enemy —that Great Britain unwilling to renounce America, meditates the deluding her by sending over two Emissaries to offer a Truce & the drawing away the British Forces, on Condition that these states shall break their alliance with France & enter into a Treaty with her"—on which Point the Count makes such Observations as are commonly made among us on the supposition of such a project being really designed by Great Britain—

I think the Count does not speak positively of this Measure being adopted by the Enemy—His Expressions are unusually vague—& perhaps it is only a political Touch on an important string, to try the Tone of America, after the Accession of Spain to the War—If he doubts our Temper, his apprehensions will soon be satisfactorily removed

I mention this affair to you, because it has produced already in this Town an multitude of Falsehoods, which, I suppose, will be still gathering as it rolls as far as Dover

348
To George Craghead

Dover Sepr. the 11th 1779

I have Just Recd a letter from his Excellency General Washington, one from the Clothier General and a Copy of one from the Board of War to him, all on the Subject of Clothing the Army—I have inclosed you Copies of all these letters and beg You will Use your Utmost Endeavour by every Means in Your Power to Supply our Quota—I am convinced you labour under one difficulty—the want of Cash. Which is not easy to be remedied but by the General Assembly. How ever do all you can immediately—and do not delay to let the Clothier General know the State of Your business so far as relates to the Quota of this State.

349
From Francis Wade

Wilmington—the 14th of Sept. 1779.

Notwithstanding I may be singular & unsupported in my observations & complaints against some men committing practices, injurious to the Country yet I presume it will not be deemed forward in me to make known in part some matters that has come under my notice since my entering in the duties of my office in this state. As George Evans, Esq. who we should look up to for justice & uprightness, from the station he holds will be a principal, I shall begin with him, by enclosing you copies of his different accounts with some observations on them. (I shall pass over his being concerned in taking & selling the people's cattle & retaining to this day the money.) This gentleman, I took notice of early as looking upon him to be a good friend to the Country & employed him in his branch of business in consequence thereof, which I continued until the Commissaries had orders for the purchasing of the wheat when I called on him for his accounts which remains in an unsettled state to this day. However, on receipt of the accts rendered me as per. copies enclosed, I made some observations on them, necessary for a settlement & for me to account for the disposal of this property. Consequently, they created some jealousy in a man of his disposition not to have his bare word taken for the deficiency of his acct. being at loss to know what other part to act. He from that time to this has done every thing in his power to shew his own resentment & to raise the resentment of the people against me, in an underhand, unbecoming manner & catched at every turn & expression of mind & construed it to my prejudice. His first attack was joining in urging a summons to be issued gainst me at the sitting of the Court for expressions that I let drop as was said on the Thanks-giving day, derogatory to the dignity of the Magistrates which I cleared up long before to the satisfaction of 3 of that body. However, at the sitting of the next Court the matter was revived & I was summoned to attend, without any excuse being admitted altho' it was a time of danger & attend I did. & after being detained a considerable time & requesting to know the charges by one of the Justices (Doct. Clayton) I rec'd for answer that the court was too much engaged & could not attend to it & that he was of opinion it was a trifling matter so that I was at liberty to withdraw without fine or submission & there the matter rested. In the affair of Rumford, he used uncommon pains to bring me to condign punishment & had the whole town ransacked for evidences against me & on the examination encouraged a person who came in to throw out the most injurious insinuations against me & when I called on him to support one sentence of what he advanced, he could not do it, however, Mr. Evans to keep him in countenance declared him to be as good a Whig as any in the States, altho' it is well known that he nor none of his family ever took up a fire lock in defense of their Country but remained under the protection of the enemy (this by way of, I will support you now) if you will support me when tottering another time. So far Mr. Evans, thinks it necessary to keep in with those kind of people, well knowing that he is losing ground with the honest Whigs altho' he has made advances to please both parties, but knowing my turn & that I was not to be pleased by double dealing, which I always declared my abhorrence of he has carefully avoided me & begun to work another way as the moles do under the surface, but to keep up a show of attention to his country's welfare, altho' it may well be supposed it was more designed to support his own consequence with those that had the matter at heart. He joined in taking notice of Rumford's shipping the flour & gave out that he had been guilty of dirty tricks before, which he no sooner discovered to be disagreeable to the opposite party, than he began to contradict what he had said & joined Rumford who he had repeatedly abused before (that he might have full scope. Knowing he could have no other hold) to attack me. He met with a proper instrument to carry on his dirty purposes with turnings, twistings, twinings & evasions to the last minute & now Rumford wants to take me by the hand after he has gained his end that of soaking my pocket, as Capt. Lee has done, who now says that he was led to join in the letter to you by Mr. Evans & declared in the presence of a gentleman that he had no charge against me. I shall leave those gent? for the present & shall take no further notice of the person who the qualification now enclosed is against them mentioning him as one of the same cast as Mr. Evans & of the same clan who are eternally plotting & contriving to frustrate & break the spirits of every attentive observer & well-wisher to his Country's welfare, but I am not to be intimidated or deterred from doing my duty like some of their neighbors after so long persevering in the same line. The attempt made by another gent? to have me removed to make room of office for himself, namely, Doct. McMahon at Christ? Bridge being some what curious, I cannot omit mentioning it. He got his negroes to let down the fence about the public Hay, drove cattle &c. in & when in the worst condition he could put it in, took Gen! Scott who was then at his house to look at it, prevailed on the Gen! to represent it to Gen! Green by letter in the most shocking destructive light possible. To give the Gen! his due, he did not spare words to effect his design & recommended the Doct. in the strongest manner to supersede me, but unfortunately for the Doct. I happened to be in Phil? when he delivered the letter & had judicious impartial judges to judge of my conduct who immediately sent for me & I confuted every charge & bro't the above charges against the Doct. & mentioned my authority to support them, but the Doct. like a prudent man, let the matter rest & sneaked off like another curr with his tail between his legs. I then ordered my assistant to lay wait for him & his negroes & some time after he catched his negro in the dead of night with a load of Hay on his back who declared he was taking it as he had done before by his master's orders. (These are only a few of the number that I have in tow.) Exclusive of the most barefaced extortions, breaking of the most solemn contracts after receiving the public's money as an earnest for their performances &c; & those are the kind of men who have put their heads together to get me put out of their way, to make room of office for themselves or connexions, that they may connive at each other's actions. There can be no tolerable apology made for Mr. Evans conduct to me except that his natural disposition of jealousy of office has superseded every other consideration with him. Altho' it should seem strange that a man should complain of others without thinking of the cause given others to complain of him, but Providence often makes use of such instruments as him for the benefit of the injured party. How far I have claim to it, I must leave it to others to determine, but I must say that he has shown a want of integrity, want of sincerity, want of humanity, want of charity (as to honor, it is out of the question) with him when he dare not force a man to vindicate it. Insolence & imprudence is natural conclusions of selfish, dastardly minds & these qualifications he abounds with. If those matters are worthy of your Ex?y? notice, well; if not, I must beg your excuse for troubling you with them.

350

From John Dickinson

Philadelphia, September 15th, 1779.

By a late letter from the Board of War it appears, that they *despair* of being able to provide Cloathing for the Troops—The Several States will be depended on by Congress for the necessary requisite for their respective Lines—I therefore think it my Duty to give you this Intelligence, as I do not doubt but *immediate* and *effectual* Measures will be taken in our State, for comfortably cloathing our worthy & brave officers & soldiers

351
To George Craghead

Dover Septr the 19th 1779.

About seven or eight days ago I wrote you on the Subject of providing in time for the Delaware Regiment & then inclosed you Copies of Letters from the Board of War, Clothier General, [and his Excellency General Washington] on that head. I now beg leave to inclose you a Copy of a late resolution of Congress, I am Just now furnished with, to the same purpose, and must beg leave, tho perhaps unnecessary, to urge your immediate attention to this business, that you do not neglect as soon as possible to lay a full State of it before the board of War, & the Clothier General, and that you also furnish me with another, in order that I may be enabled to lay the Same before the General Assembly at their next Meeting and urge their making ample provision for carrying the requisition of Congress into Execution in future.

352
From George Craghead

New Castle County Sept. 20th 1779

Your Letter of yesteday & the Inclosed is Just Come to hand, and haveing Answered Your Excellincy's of the 11th of [?] as soon as Come to hand, (which I sent by [?] as also sent a Just State of the Buisness [?] my care; to the Clothier-General of the United States; I have nothing New to Inform Your Excellency off.

The Dificulty as to Purchasing Linnen, is not Yet Removed and as to Blankets, I have not yet had any Orders from the Board of War, Concerning them, but have mentioned it, to the Clothier General.

I shall take Pirticular care of Provideing a Pirticular Return of all in my hands and what I have don in the Department before the General Assembly meets; and hope to have the Pleasure then of seeing your Excellency

353
From John Dickinson

Philadelphia, September 25th 1779.

I have the pleasure to inform you, that the President of Congress this moment call'd upon me, to inform me, that he has receiv'd advice, that the Count D'Estaing with a formidable Fleet has arriv'd at Georgia, with a very considerable Body of Troops on Board—one of the principal officers landed in South Carolina, held a Council of War there, in which the plan of operations was settled, and then return'd to the Count—and, if no *Blunder* is committed, the Event will be what we wish it to be.

The Enemy is fortifying New York incessantly—They have done a great Deal, but still are not contented. Our Intelligence is well authenticated that they meditated an Embarkation of several thousand men—The Count's arrival in all probability will put a stop to it, unless they slip out to the West Indies, while he is approaching—which is not unlikely

General Sullivan has beat the collected force of the Enemy, of which too formal an Account is published—tho the Consequences are said by such as understand Indian Affairs, to be of importance to the peace of our Frontiers[1]—

Mr. Gerard has taken Leave of Congress, & is expected to sail every day in the Frigate, *Confederacy*—We have dismist him with as honorable Testimonials respecting his public & private Conduct as we could give.

I have been for some time exceedingly indisposed—I intend soon, if I get better, to make a Trip to Kent—& if the State has any particular Business requiring immediate Dispatch, I should be glad to have advise of it as early as possible.

I beg leave to recommend in the most earn[est] manner the providing every kind of Cloath[ing] for our Battalion of brave & worthy officers & men and also the having our militia in the most respectable Readiness for Action. I speak the sense of Congress on these subjects—

354
From Samuel Patterson

Xteen October 6. 1779.

I have just recd a letter in much confusion that a party risen in Philad[a] last Monday against the merchants &c were engaged to a large number both sides by which some were killed dead on the spot. & several badly wounded—some of which are dead, amongst them a Capt. Campbell, of the Invalids & a Colonel his name not yet to hand.

1 General John Sullivan with troops collected in the Wyoming Valley, Pennsylvania, and with men under General James Clinton from the Mohawk Valley, New York, fell upon a force of Tories and Indians strongly fortified at Chemung (now Elmira), New York, and dispersed it on August 29, 1779. Then the Americans, during the course of the succeeding three weeks, devastated the country of the Seneca Indians in the Genesee River region in New York, destroying upwards of forty Indian villages and many cornfields, orchards, and vegetable gardens. This widespread destruction was the patriot answer to the terrible Wyoming Valley massacre perpetrated by Colonel Butler's Indians in the night of July 4–5, 1778.

Mr. Sharp Delany badly wounded & Mr. John Berclay wounded & was thought next day would be more terrible. God help us—Terrible times, when all is in our favour.

Next shall write you more. The poor starving here & rise for redress.

[P.S.] Many flying the city for fear of Vengeance.

355

From Samuel Patterson

Xteen Octr 9, 1779

I wrote you a few days ago, & promised your Excellency a farther acc't of the disturbance in this city. I have rec^d such by letter from one that was in the city light horse, a gentleman who opposed the rioters. He writes me nearly this acct.

On Monday morn^g a Handbill appeared for the Militia to collect on the Commons, in order to fall on a plan, to drive from the city, all disaffected persons, & those who supported them, & made out a list of their names that he intended to seise & put on board the prison ship to be sent to New York. Among those names was Reck Sims & Thos Story. & Jno Drinker. Those they catched & had them prisoners at Paddy Burns, till they got the whole. The next they were after; was James Wilson, the lawyer, who had always plead; for such he applied to the Assembly for protection. On hearing he was amongst the number they referred him over to the Governor & Council, but in the mean time he found the militia even coming. Before civil aid was at hand, called in a number of his friends & armed, secured the doors. However a fireing began, when they were opposed. Some say that one began first, & the others contradict it. The firing continued on both sides some time, in the House fell Capt Cammel of Invalids, wounded Sam! Cadmorris thro' the arm; John Mifflin, a ball thro both hands, Sharp Delancy a slight wound; the others doing well. Four of the Mob & Negro boy were killed. in all 14 wounded. In the mean time the Governor had ordered out the Light Horse of the city, who just came in time to save the lives of all in the House, for they had forced the doors, & the cry was blood for blood. The Governor ordered them to charge with Swords,—they did—& after some cutting they broke them for that time. The Governor hearing that the Germans were coming down to reverse [?] the loss of their Countrymen, as 3 killed, were dutch, he went up with a Troop & pacified them, for the present. At present there is a parley. The president, magistrates, & clergy of all denominations, met the militia & with very great difficulty, prevailed on them to lay their grievances before the Assembly, & have chose a captain & 2 privates, out of each battalion, to lay a state before the assembly. But he thinks it is not over. They will have blood for blood, & dreads the consequences yet, & says they are very numerous.

356
To John Dickinson

[Dover, Oct.r 17, 1779]

You will Oblidge me in applying to Congress for Thirty Six Thousand dollars for the payment of the Bounties allowed by Congress for the recruiting Service. I have Actually advanced the greater part of that sum to the officers now on that duty And they inform me they Shall verry Shortly want a further supply—You will be pleased to desire the Committee, appointed to take order for the procuring Flour &c for the army, to let me know what the persons employed in That service are to be allowed, or whether they mean I Should procure it to be done upon the best Terms I can—You may Assure them I Shall do every[thing] in my power to forward the business, but expect the flower will come high, as those termed Speculators are as thick and as industrious as Bees, and as Active and wicked as the Devil himself—I doubt much Whether any of the Taxes mentioned by the Committee are, as yet, paid into the Treasury. However I have wrote to the Treasurer, Expect to hear from him in few days, and will immediately let them know—I Shall Expect to hear from the Committee immediately

357
To John Dickinson

Dover Oct.r the 27th 1779.

I Recd your letter of the 21st instant, and Immediately laid the inclosed printed paper before the General Assembly—

Since I wrote you last I have, in Virtue of the power Vested in me by the Congress and the Delegates of Delaware, Maryland and South Carolina, appointed a person to Superintend the purchasing the Quantity of Flour recommended by the Delegates. In order that he might set about the business I Gave him an order on the State Treasurer for Sixty Thousand dollars, and wrote to the Treasurer to give me an account of the monies in his hands and the probability of his being supplied. I have inclosed you his answer by which you will see it is not likely that I shall be enabled to Comply with the requisition of Congress from that Quarter.

358
Message to the General Assembly

Gentlemen of the General Assembly:—

I have just received by express an Act of Congress dated the twentieth instant, recommending to the several States, that Thursday, the ninth of December next, be appointed a day of public Thanksgiving, which I have ordered the Secretary to lay before your Honors.

Caesar Rodney.

Dover, Octobr. 27th, 1779.

359
From John Dickinson

Philadelphia, October 29th 1779.

I recd yours of the 27th this Day, and have this Moment communicated its Contents to Congress, who have referr'd an Extract to the Treasury

I have not yet been able to procure a Report from that Board, tho I have sollicited them every Day, on the recruiting Business which was referr'd to them some time ago, as I informed you

I have applied to the Delegates of Maryland &c for Information concerning the Terms on which the supply recommended by Congress should be obtained—but they can say nothing on the subject—It is expected each state will manage the Business with a laudable Conpetition for Frugality—

I write this letter in Congress—this Instant We receive advice, which seems to come in a very good private Way from the Fleet at New York that there has been a severe Engagment in Europe between the combined fleets of France & Spain[1] & that of Britain, in which the latter was defeated & oblig'd to retreat into harbour—that in the Battle, the ardent, admiral Gambier went to the Bottom with Colours flying—

360
To John Dickinson

Dover November the 5th 1779

I recd yours of the 29th Ulto a few days ago. Am much oblidged by your attention to the business recommended. I wish that part relative to the recruit-

---

1 Spain joined France in an offensive alliance in April 1779 and in August a combined French and Spanish fleet attempted an invasion of England.

ing Service to be Compleated as I have already given orders for the whole of the monies Granted by the State for that purpose—

If money is not Supplyed by Congress, the other measure proposed, relative to the Supply of Flour, must fall through.—

The General assembly of this State adjourned on Saturday last to the Twenty ninth of this month, Then to meet at Wilmington for the dispatch of business—All the public business Committed to my Charge was laid before them as soon as they made a House, but nothing done in it previous to their adjournment.

I am much obliged to you for the news you gave me. Such Strokes will force them not only to acknowledge us a free and Independent people but put it out of their power to Vex us hereafter at least for a long time.

361

From Samuel Patterson

Xteen Bridge. Nov. 5th 1779.

Last Eve? was presented to me by Capt. Patten your Ex^{cys} draft for $6000 dated the 29th ult. I am sorry to inform you that the bank is out on paying bills at Dover. However, I gave him an order on Col. Bryan, our county Treasurer who from conversation have some faint hopes. If not paid by him perhaps if in cash shall advance my own on so important business. Our clothier Gen! called at the same time to see if I had orders to pay him cash. I answered that I had none such to hand & bank stock out. I wish to have my bank better supplied to answer every draft. Nothing shall be wanting on my side.

As to news here, there is nothing new. All is in impatience for the arrival of the Count[1] but it is generally believed that the combined fleets of France & Spain have beat Admiral Hardy & blocked them up in 2 ports in England & taken the Ardent man of war &c. Small news plenty, of our success near New York, by Genl. Washington.

362

From George Craghead

Wilmingtown Nov? 12th 1779—

I am just Returned from Philadelphia, where I have ben applying for such

---

1 The French admiral, Comte d'Estaing, was expected to cooperate with General Lincoln in recapturing Savannah.

Cloathing for the Delaware Regiment a[s I] apprehended could not be provided in Time, in this State and have suczeded so well, notwithstanding the scarsety in the Continental Stores, that the Cloathing I Expect will set off the begining of next month, Expect Blankets, for which I Could get an order, for onely One Hundred; what will be don for the Rest, must be (I suppose) Determained by the General Assembly.

I am now so supply'd with Cloth & Linnens that I Expect not to Purchase any more then what is Ingaged at Present—That Cloth which Your Excellency was Pleased to Mention [sp]airing off, as I then apprehend we would be in Great want, may be sent by the serjant, which Lieut: Purvis, is to send up with Cloth & Linnen from Dover, if it can Conveniantly be spaired. *News,* The *Count* is gon to the West Indies and General *Lincoln* to Charles Town—[1]

363

Writer unknown[2]

Philad^a Novr 16th 1779

The very alarming Prospects which present themselves to publick View with Respect to supplying the Army with Provisions will I trust make any Apology unnecessary for troubling your Excell.y on this Occasion—Notwithstanding the Importunity of the trading Interest in which the Views of many of the Farmers coincide, the Sense of the Legislature of this State has steadily been to prohibit the Exportation of Provisions, & we have on all Occasions exerted ourselves to have this wholesome Regulation observed. I need not enumerate the other temporary Expedients which have been adopted for the Reduction of Prices in which the Goodness of Intentions were sufficiently demonstrated whatever Argum[ents] may be offered against them founded on commercial Wisdom or Propriety. These being removed or rather having ceased Prices have not only increased very rapidly but there is a general Indifference almost amounting to Disinclination to sell even those Commodities most necessary for the Army. The Commissaries seem to apprehend that no inconsiderable clandestine Trade is carried on in Provisions which mutual Vigilance in the three States on the Delaware & Chesapeak would do much to correct. We have therefore form'd new Regulations, added Penalties & are

1 The British having captured Savannah in December 1778, General Benjamin Lincoln in co-operation with the French admiral, Comte d'Estaing, had attempted to retake the town in October 1779, but was unsuccessful. The French fleet then proceeded to the West Indies and the American army under Lincoln marched to the defense of Charleston, S C

2 Probably a draft of a letter written by the President of the Supreme Executive Council of Pennsylvania.

resolved to stop the pernicious Practice while the publick Necessities continue, but unless [y]our State concurs with us, such is the powerful force of private Interest that we [?] ineffectual for the great Purpose in View. A Limitation of Price not having been deemed proper in Maryland their Example [was followed by this State], but the inordinate Desires of the Holders of Provisions soon raised them up to such a Height that we thought it best to suspend the Purchases of this State by the publick Commissaries, which seemed the more necessary as New Jersey & New York having limited the Price of Wheat to 20 Dollars per Bush.ˡ while our Commiss.ˢ were left to give curr.ᵗ Prices reach.ᵍ £15—We farther hoped that an indifference of Purchase would give an Alarm favorable to the Reduction of Price, of this we cannot yet judge, but I beg leave to assure your Excell.ʸ that every thing will be done in this State as well to accomplish this desirable Purpose as to produce effectual Supplies proportinate to the Ability of the State. Col. Blaine, whose Assiduity in Business is truly laudable, having requested these Observations from me as supposing they might be of some publick use I could not refuse him

364

From Ephraim Blaine[1]

Wilmington 19ᵗʰ Nov. 1779

The letter which will be delivered you by the Express I expected to have been the bearer myself, but as I am going to Annapolis and the want of flour for the Army—requires my utmost exertion, and hoping to have the Opportunity of seeing you and the Council in this Town upon my return, (Declin'd going by Dover), for god sake fix with McGarment or some other person to be Commisary and adopt such means as will enable them to procure the Quantity of Flour Demand from your State.

365

From John Rodney

Lewes Novᵣ 24th—at 10 p.m [1779?]

I have sent by Mᵣ Samuel Rowland the sum of Seven thousand & Forty eight pounds eighteen shillings & 6ᵈ—being the exact balance due to the State Treasurer on the Continental Tax laid by Act of Assembly for raising 198000 Dollars in the Delaware State, towit, for Sussex's Quota—I say it is the exact

---

1 Deputy Commissary-General of the Continental Army.

balance according to my Acc. which I sent last month to General Patterson Inclos'd in a Letter—And as he inform'd me that he Expected you to draw on him for a large Sum, & very soon, & as I presume you are going up to meet the Assembly[1] I have made bold to trouble you with the money once-more which will save me the Expence of an Express—The difficulty of getting one, & the Cost Attending it is no inconsiderable sum out of those small Commissions Allowed by the Act. If any exceptions should be made to any of the money sent, should be glad that the Name of the person our of whose bundle it may be taken might be marked upon such bills in order that I may return them, and that you will be so good as to pay M. Patterson for such deficient bills in order that I may get a proper receipt in full of that Tax, and you may depend upon my repaying you for the same with punctuallity and dispatch I hope General Patterson will excuse my not writing to him on the Occassion, as I but just now heard of Mr. Rowland's going up and had not time to write.

You were [?] me a Commission for t[he] office of Collector of port Lewes, but I should rather declin[e] to Qualify for several Reasons, which would time permit, I could render—I am obliged to you for your good will but had much rather some other person may be appointed.

366

From Thomas Rodney

Dover Dec. 9th 1779—

Your letter as well as M. Carty informs me that the purchase I expected is made by M. Morris—But M. Carty mentions a very good house and Lot in Town for Sale, which he says he mentioned to you—but he could not describe it to me so that I Could recollect it—However he says the House is Good, & room enough in it—That there is a good garden & Grass lot—and that the Situation is on the hill part of the Town & Commands the prospect of the River—That it's on the left hand of the streat going up—and near the House where the assembly sits—If any purchase of this sort may be made that you think may sute me in price as well as in a good House garden and lot, I should be glad to git it, and Spoke to Major Carty to mention this to you, but have this opertunity by M. Shee to write before he goes up—Not recollecting any house, but that of Crips's, which I formerly wanted near the College, I was afraid Major Carty at a Slight view, had been rather favourable in his relation; but upon view you Can readily Tell whether this place he mentions may Sute

1 Probably referring to the approaching session at Wilmington, which was held from November 29 to December 28, 1779.

me—However as the Times are yet unsettled I am not anxious to give what you may think an Extravagant price in the Town—But I would be willing to give from four to five thousand pounds hard money for Malkoms place, provided from two to five years Credit could be obtained; I only mention this in Case any thing of this Sort Should fall in your way—No news here but that all are well at your house and mine

367

From Silas Snow[1]

Flat Bush Decemr the 13th. 1779

I wrote you a Letter Some time ago informing you that those prisoners not taken in Actual Service,[2] Received no part of the Last Continental Supply, of which Maj Hodgson & myself are the only two from the Delaware, you can Redily conceive the Distress we must be in for want of cash, having Recd only twenty five pounds a pees Since we were prisoners. Congress have been Addressed upon the Subject, Major Beaty has been wrote too but as no answer has been Recd. from either, it Remains uncertain if we Shal Receive any farther Supply from that Quarter. If we Should Not I hope you will Lay our Case before Our Assembly or make use of what means you may think proper to procure us a Suficient Supply to Discharge Our board and provide us Necessaries &c

368

From George Washington[3]

Head Quarters Morris Town 16 Decr 1779.

The situation of the army with respect to supplies is beyond description alarming.* and We have not more than three days bread at a third allowance (on hand) nor any where within reach. When this is exhausted we must depend on the precarious gleanings of the neighboring country. Our magazines are absolutely empty every where and our commissaries intirely destitute of money or credit to replenish them. We have never experienced a like extremity at any period of the war. We have often felt temporary want from accidental

1 Captain in the state militia referred to in Caesar Rodney's letter to Thomas McKean and Nicholas Van Dyke, August 24, 1778.

2 Having been captured by the Tories while in bed and put on board a British ship in the Delaware River and carried to New York, Captain Snow had been discriminated against in the distribution of supplies sent to prisoners within the British lines.

3 This letter was addressed to "Governors Reed, Livingston, Lee, Clinton and Rodney."

delay, in forwarding supplies; but we always had something in our magazines and the means of procuring more. Neither one nor the other is at present the case. This representation is the result of minute examination of our
resources. Unless some extraordinary and immediate exertions are made by
the States from which we draw our supplies, there is every appearance that the
Army will infallibly disband in a fortnight. I think it my duty to lay this candid view of our situation before your Excellency and to entreat the vigorous
interposition of the State to rescue us from the danger of an event, which if it
did not prove the total ruin of our affairs, would at least give them a shock
from which they would not easily recover and plunge us into a train of new
and still more perplexing embarrassments than any we have hitherto felt.
* It has been five or six weeks past on half allowances.

369
To Thomas Rodney

Wilmington dec! the 17th 1779.

I sent you by M! Bassett the Tuesdays paper, and both Hall's and Bradford's of Wednesday—and now M! Bell promises to leave you Thursday's
and the postscript to it—I imagine the Assembly will hardly rise soon enough
for me to Eat my Christmas Dinner at Home[1]—Hope you have taken Care
of my Corn and other matters committed to you. I have been something uneasy about the corn as the weather has been verry Bad since I left Home—
Col! Washington[2] with his regiment of Horse is now here on his way to
Charles-Town South Carolina. The North Carolina Troops passed here above
a week ago for that place, and the Virginia line are at Philadelphia on their
way there—The main army are gone into Winter Quarter at Jockey-Hollow
near Morris-Town leaving the forts at West-point well Garrisoned—

370
From Samuel Huntington

Philadelphia Dec! 21st 1779

In pursuance of the enclosed resolution passed by Congress, I think it my
duty to inform you that the accounts received from our army call for the most

1 The General Assembly adjourned on December 28.
2 Colonel William Washington, with whose men the Delaware Battalion under Captain Robert
Kirkwood was closely associated in the Southern campaigns of 1780 and 1781.

immediate & strenuous exertion of your State to forward a Supply of provisions.

The enormous prices to which the necessary Supplies for the Army have been raised have drained the public treasury, and the sole dependance of Congress for the Support of an Army & defence of our liberties must rest on the exertion of the several States. The present exegence admits not of the least delay, it is therefore hoped that you will procure & forward with all possible expedition as much flour as can be obtained in your State which shall be passed to your Credit in part of its Quota lately called for and due care will be taken that Justice be done to the State.

371
From Francis Wade

Philad.ᵃ 29th, Decembʳ 1779.

Your orders by letter rec'd this evening should have been immediately Complied with had I not been prevented from going by M.ʳˢ Wades Illness, I however hope to be at liberty to go in a day or two, I dont mean to make any Enquiery about the house of Assembly takeing up the several matters in the staff departmᵗ no doubt they thought it right, & necessary so to do but I must say I have been a little hurt by Expressions, I hear has been thrown out by Individˢ of them, be that as it will, my attatchment to my Country, and the Army, with the respect I have for your Excellʸ are sufficient Inducements for me, to obey your summons, to resume my station, until a proper arangement takes place until which time, you may rest assured, that I shall use every exertion in my power for the speedy supply of the Army, whose wants I am no stranger to, but the want of Cash for that purpose, is such a stumbling block as I wish to have removed. I believe every thing is doing that Can be done, and we must hope for the best,

372
From Mordecai Gist[1]

Camp Near Morris Town 3ᵈ Janʸ 1780

I have directed Captain Learmonth Lieutenants Cox—Kid[d]—& Anderson, to proceed to the Delaware State on the recruiting Service, with orders to wait on your Excellency for Instructions respecting that duty, as also for or-

1 Colonel Gist had been promoted by Congress to brigadier-general the year before.

ders on the Treasury for such sums of Money as may be necessary to pay the State & Continental Bounties to such recruits as they may enlist.

I herewith enclose you the monthly Return of the Regiment for your Inspection, as also a Bond of Mr. Malcombs for £3,000: who I hope has not broke the Condition by a Forfeiture of his Allegiance to the State.

The Homeward Bound fleet from N. York Consisting of 102 sail put to sea about ten days ago, an embarkation said to be of 8. or 10.000 Troops saild the 26th Ultimo, Supposed to be destind for the Southward. this fleet Consisted of 101 sail 91 of which were square Rigg'd Vessels.[1]

Colo.s Morgan, Matthews, Ely, & Ramsay left N York the 25th on parole for 28 Days. They are now at Head Qrs with proposals for an exchange of prisoners from the Commanding Officer at N York, which I have reason to believe his Excellency with the approbation of Congress will accept of.

373
From John Patten[2]

Camp near Morris Town Jany 17th 1780

I should have sent you the arangement of the Del Regt by Col. Craighead had not some claims been laid in by the officers which I have been hithirto unaquaintd with, and which will require some little time to adjust and determine—but as soon as I can satisfy my self in this respect and be able to satisfy others with regard to them, your Excellancy may depend on receiving it—

I have Inclosed you a return of the Regt Taken from the one deliverd in for the last week, by which, compard with those you have receivd before, you will find recruiting has renderd us more respectable as to numbers, and which I have not a doubt but you will do every thing in your Power to continue, as officers are sent down for that purpose—

The Army has been reduced to the most Extreme want for provisions, having subsistd five days on half a pound of salf Beef and half a pint of Rice without any other kind of support whatever—you who are a friend to the Military will feel for, and applaud those brave men who suffer so much in the defence of their Country and bear it with such patience and Fortitude—Provisions are now comming in fast, and from the Exertions made by this State and what we are told is done in others, we have now the pleasing prospect of being amply supplied in a short time, unless some change of weather should take

1 Refers to Sir Henry Clinton's expedition against Charleston.

2 Being senior captain, John Patten was promoted to major in the Delaware Regiment December 14, 1779, to succeed Major Joseph Vaughan, who the same day succeeded Lieutenant-Colonel Charles Pope, who on December 13, had resigned his commission.

place on which in my opinion much depends—for as the snow is Exceedingly deep in this Country and the Roads well beat, it affords a happy means of conveying supplies on sledg⁸ which makes ample recompence for the stoppage of our Rivers—

A large Detachment of our army was day before yesterday on Staten Island under the command of *Lord Stirling* having passed the sound on the Ice— their Intention it is said was to *sweep* the Island Why the[y] did not do it I am not at present able to tell you—though perhaps may be well enough Infor⁴ to Instruct you in my next—We hear they drew up in the face of the Enemy and remain⁴ there for some Hours without firing [scarcely] a single shot. Then retir⁴ after stripping some small Vessels of their Rigging and burning them and bringing off some Blanketts and Military stores—. Rivingtons Royal Gazette will no doubt in a little time give us a Pompous description of this adventure of his Lordship—However I do not undertake to say but he acted on justifiable principles—

I have the pleasure to inform you that our Regt is rather better Clothed than any in the army, a little care and attention will make them the foremost in which sittuation I most ardently wish to see them—The stores we brought up with us as well as the Clothing was a happy relief to the officers as they stood much in need of them—This is a cold mountanous Country and little supplies of any kind to be had in the neighbourhood of the Camp, which makes our sittuation les agreable than that of Middle Brook last winter—To make all things easy we will wait and Expect—

374
From George Craghead

Jan: 24ᵗʰ 1780 Willmingtown—

Haveing just Returned from Camp, beg leave to Inform your Excellency, That I left the Delaware Regiment *Well* and Better Cloathed, than any Regiment in Camp. Yet not quite Compleat, as their was not the Articles, which they wanted in the Publick Stores: (which are 200 P⁺ Wollen Overalls & 70 Bla[n]kets,) nor know I how to get them, unless the officer Destraining for Militia Fines, would Levey on such Articles—Inclosed is a Return of Stores Purchased & Delivered to the Officers of our Troops; it was thought best to Deliver them as far as the would go, to the Officers Present & those going up Immediately—as the others may be Provided when down—

I had to Pay £24″10″0 for Rum, 47/6 for Sugar, 18£ for Tea, 11 Dollars for Coffee, 100 Dollars for Stockings, 92½ Dollars for Shoes and for Linnen

£21:15:0, which far Exceeded what I expected, I could not get to purchase white Broad Cloth for Weast Coats & Breches, Except a few yards at 600 Dollars, (which I Declined)—

As Lieut! Queanault is to Come up in a few Days, Your Excellency's Order, on the State Treasurer for the 1400 £ might by him come safe; If thought best to send it.—I must refer to Major Patten & Doctor Tilton's Letters for *News* my Ink & Penn haveing ben Frose, and I cannot better them—I have got hurt in my Ears & Feet, with the Frost, Yet hope soon to get over it.

375
From Thomas McKean

Philadelphia, January 27th 1780.

Your favour of the 20th instant was delivered me by Captain Learmonth, who has received thirty six thousand dollars for the recruiting service in our State, which is to be paid into your hands and charged to the State—When this is expended, on your application more will be obtained. I hope every exertion will be made to fill our Battalion, as peace will in a great measure depend upon the numbers of our army and the time they take the field—Every State in the Union is sensible of this, and I rest assured we shall have in consequence the largest army next campaign we ever yet had, and that this circumstance will determine our Enemy to peace or war, as our success or the contrary in this measure may prove—

Our army has been almost starved and our Treasury empty; but both are again in a good way—Our resources are great if properly and timely called forth.

We have no news of Importance.—

376
From Thomas Rodney

Wilmington Sunday Jany 30th 1780—

Yesterday and the day before was so Cold that we only arrived here Eleven oClock to day—Capt? Walker is arrived in New York one of the hands has come out—Loss—no account of the other Vessel—The Convention has broke up for want of representation from Several States—They have now arrived and the convention is to be called again, as it is said.[1] It is also said that Spain

1 On October 20, 1779, a convention of the New England States and New York met at Hartford, Connecticut, for the purpose of regulating prices. This convention proposed a similar con-

has offered America any number of Ships & Troops, and any Quanty of money they want, & that this offer in part or the whole is accepted and a vessel sent express to the Havanah for the purpose—

377
Addressee unknown

Dover February the 3rd 1780.

With the monies now put into your hands you are immediately to Enter upon the recruiting business and as a Peace and the Terms of it will much depend on our having a respectable army ready to take field with the parties under your direction early in the season, You are to use every Exertion to fill the Regiment of this State.

You are to enlist none but those who are able Bodied and fit for service and carefully to avoid any British or Foreign deserters;

You are to send your recruits to Wilmington, Dover or Lewes to be mustered immediately after enlisting them, and you are to advance as little of the Bounty to them as possible until they are mustered.

As it is your duty to treat the Inhabitants of this State with respect, and as your gaining their confidence and good opinion will tend to aid you in this most essential Service, I expect you will pay strict attention to the conduct of the parties under your direction and suffer them by no means to insult or ill-treat any. But on all occasions to aid the Civil authority when properly called upon for that purpose.

Whenever you stand in need of a further supply of money for the service, you are to apply to me for it, and frequently advise me of your success and the State of the business.

You are to apprehend secure and take the most effectual method of sending to Camp all such deserters from the Continental Army as may fall in your

---

vention of all the States as far south as Virginia, to meet on the first Wednesday in January (the fifth) in Philadelphia. The latter convention, being only attended by commissioners from New Hampshire, Rhode Island, Connecticut, New Jersey, Pennsylvania, Delaware, and Maryland, decided that it had no authority to proceed, especially since a resolution of Congress, which was passed after the calling of the convention, recommended the regulation of prices, and consequently, seemed to have disposed of the question. The convention, therefore, adjourned *sine die*. However, when in a few days a commissioner appeared from Massachusetts, the convention was organized again with all states present except New Jersey and Virginia. An adjournment was taken to Wednesday, February 2, to give the New Jersey commissioners time to return. It was then adjourned till April to give Virginia another opportunity to send commissioners. No more meetings were held.

way, and to proceed against all those who may be found to harbour such deserters in the manner directed by an Act of Assembly of this State constituting it an offence.

As you have hitherto given the most convincing proofs of your attachment to the Liberty and Independence of this Country, I am persuaded you will discharge this important duty with Honor to yourself and satisfaction to the State—

378
From Henry Lee[1]

Philadelphia, February 16th 1780

Congress have been pleased to order an addition to my Corps.

Cap.t M.cLane is put into your state for the purpose of recruiting.

Be pleased sir to give him proper authority & money. The soldiers enlisted are rated as part of the quota of the State of Delaware.

379
From George Craghead

Pleasant Hills New Castle County Feb.y 21.st 1780

In the last I had the Honour of Addressing Your Excellency in this way I mentioned some of the wants, to Compleat the Cloathing of the Delaware Regiment: and I am sorry to say it is yet out of my Power to have them supply'd I left full Power with L.t Roché to Draw when to be had; I apply'd at Philadelphia and having not Cash, I can do but Little and so the are yet not supply'd—

I mentioned that if the Justices would Order the Militia Fines (Where they must be Levied) to have Blankets Executed, that we might have sufficient I am more & more Convinced of the Propriety of it; as then if the[y] would not help one way the[y] must the other; and one Blanket would Pay several Fines and as the[y] would not Receive Back the Overpluss, if Lodged in the Justice's hands might save even to them another Execution; If your Excellency should approve of it, I Doubt not but it would be Caried into Execution—

I mentioned in a Letter to Coll: Hall and to have it Try'd, (if agreable) *their* I Expect it will be hear.—

1 Light Horse Harry Lee, the father of General Robert E. Lee.

In Closed is a Letter from Doctor Tilton, and as I know not what to Do, in his Case; Must Request Your Excellencys Advise in a Matter of so much Consequence to him; I shewed his application to the Board of War—who Informed me that the knew of no such Resolution; He Informed me that as to Cash he Expected his Bro: Coll: Tilton would advance it (if I could not get it) until the General Assembly would meet—

I have not Received yet the Remainder of the 15000 £ so am stopped in Purchasing the Officers Cloathing & stores—
P.S.

New Castle Feb. 23rd I find that the 10,000 £ Intended ⎫
by the House of Assembly for to Purchas Summer   ⎪
Cloathing for the Regiment, was not Compleated   ⎬
by Council, so that none can be had for them   ⎪
untill the General Assembly meets   ⎭

380

From the Board of War, by Richard Peters[1]

War Office March 7th 1780.

We are alarmed at the accounts we have just received from the Com. Genl. of Issues of the State of Magazines of Provisions at Camp—Unless the spediest relief is afforded it is by no means improbable that the army will be compelled by famine to disband; the vicinity of the Camp & indeed the whole State of New Jersey being exhausted by its exertions for the supply of the Troops this winter—We have therefore most earnestly to request the assistance of Your Excellency & the Honl. Council upon this distressing Exigency & to beg that you will cause as much Flour as possible to be forwarded from your State that the distress likely to fall on the Army & the dangerous Consequences which may probably attend it may be prevented.

381

From John Johnson, A.D.Q.M.G.

Head of Elk. March the 9th 1780.

Inclosed you will receive a letter from the Honorable Board of War of Phila which came inclosed in one to Col. Henry Hollingsworth acquainting him of the present distressed situation of the Army the Col. being absent in Kent Co. having dispatched the bearer, Tom Giles, Express to you.

---

1 Secretary of the Board of War.

382
From Samuel Huntington[1]

Philadelphia March 14 1780

Enclosed your Excellency will receive a Recommendation of Congress to the several States to set apart Wednesday the 26th of April next as a Day of fasting, Humiliation and Prayer.

383
From James Booth

Lewes, Monday 11 o'Clock A M. Apl 3—[1780]

There are now seven Members of the Assembly in Town and I expect they will be able to form a House this Evening, when I shall lay before them your Excellency's Message and the other Papers.[2] The members wish your Presence here which I hope a speedy Recovery and good weather will permit. The Air of Lewes at present seems very clear, and free from those damp vapours that I apprehended Sea-Air was generally impregnated with, and should it continue in the State it has been since I came here, it is thought your Excellency will be under no apprehension of an attack from the Asthma. The Accomodations and Table are very good, nay they very much surpass my Expectations and equal my wishes. Major Fisher has also provided a Quantity of good Claret and fruit, which with Rehoboth Oysters &c. &c. tend to make the Place more agreeable. The Gentleman from New Castle County have likewise desired me to acquaint you that they consider themselves here in a Place of tolerable Security. I am very happily lodged at Mr John Rodney's, with Colo Barratt. How it happened that my good Stars were so very propitious I know not, perhaps it may be imputed to your Excellency's name, tho' I can assure you I did not make use of it, but was informed by a messenger that my Lodgings were to be at this House, without any Application of mine and this [?] Friend, on the Occasion, was this word *Secret[ary]*

384
To the President of Congress

Dover April the 20th 1780

I lately Convened the General Assembly of this State and laid before them by Message the following Acts of Congress: two of the 13th & 14th of January

1 President of Congress.
2 The General Assembly met in Lewes for one session from March 28 to April 16, 1780.

last—One of the 25th of February, and two of the 18th & 20th of March. I have now to inform Congress that the Assembly have passed the following Acts to wit—An Act for regulating Prisoners of War brought into this State, An Act for Confering certain Priviledges and Immunities on the Subjects of his Most Christian Majesty the King of France, and an Act for raising the Quota of Supplies recommended by Congress to be raised by this State—They then adjourned to the end of the year, without taking into Consideration the other resolutions. I believe most of the members disapprove the plan, and are rather inclined to think the money will gain more credit by being left to itself than by any Act of the Assembly—They have also repealed the Embargo Bill. [Letter incomplete.]

385
From Baron de Kalb[1]

Philadelphia April 24th 1780

The Troops under my Command being on their Rout to the Southward and most of the officirs very much distressed how to bear the Expenses of so considerable a March. I applied to Congress and the Board of War for money to assist Such as would be unable to preceed without, but being answered that the Continental Treasury is quite exhausted, that in consequence of a Resolve to make good to the Army the depreciation of the Bills of Credit, it had been recommended to the States to make what advances they should think proper to the officers of their Respective Troops and that Congress will give credit for the Same. I therefore hope, Your Excellency will take it into consideration and be pleased to grant as ample a Supply to the officers of the Delaware Regiment as the Length of this march demands.

386
Addressee unknown

Dover May the 6th 1780

I received a letter of the 24th ulto from the Baron de Kalb a Major-General in our army requesting an immediate supply of Cash for the officers of the Delaware Regiment now moving to the Southward, to be advanced them by this State in consequence of a resolution of Congress to make good to the army the depreciation of the paper Currency—As it is highly probable the General will not Join the troops before their embarkation at the head of Elk, I must beg leave to give the officers, thro you, such answer as I should have

[1] Major-General Baron de Kalb was leading a force including the Delaware Regiment to the Carolinas. He was mortally wounded at the Battle of Camden, August 16, 1780.

given him. There is little doubt but the officers wishes and perhaps their expectations are equal to their wants, if so, their disappointment must be great. I am well acquainted both with their wants and their worth. it is therefore with great concern I tell you that no such resolution as above writed has been communicated to me by Congress and that there are no monies granted by the General assembly of this State, subject to my order, in favour of any person, save the State Clothier. Whenever I have it in my power, be assured I shall not want an inclination to serve the Delaware officers.

387
From George Craghead

New Castle County May 11th 1780,

I find that the General Assembly hath Impowered Your Excellency to Draw on the State Treasurer, for what money may be wanting to Cloath the Officers in the Delaware Regiment and for supplys of Stores, and as it is Expected that their will be money shortly in the Treasurry and I have ben under the necessaty of Running much in debt to Provide those Articles of Cloathing that were to be had as they past to the Sowthward, I am under the necessaty of Requesting your Excellency to Draw an Order in my Feavour for the Sum of Ten Thousand pounds to Inable me to Dischare said Debts; and as it will be necessary to Proced Immediately their Cloathing for the present year, that the may be Ready to send or give in Time, I shall be further obliged to Your Excellency for an other Order, in my Feavour for the sum of Fifteen Thousand pounds to Inable me to Proced Immediately in so Issential a Buisness—

Lt Roché, having Refussed to receive any more Stores and my orders being to send them to him, I beg your Excellency to give me your opinion or Order what is best to be don in Regard to them—

I should have don myself the Pleasure of waiting on you for the above Orders & Instructions but knowing that you do not Desire me to Run to Expence if it can be Avoidd and allso that Col! Bedford, is to be next week at Court, Do therefore Request the Feavour of their being sent by Him.

388
To Thomas McKean

Dover May the 12th 1780

The refugee Boats have taken many of our shallops, and also a great number of people belonging to this State all of whom as well passengers as others they have laid under parole to appear at New York within thirty days from the time of signing the parole—many of whom seem to show an inclination to go there. I should be glad to have the opinion of Congress, through you, how far this plan of their's ought to be complied with, or whether the executive authority of the State ought to interfere in it, least under pretence of being under parole a great number of the inhabitants may establish an intercourse with the enemy injurious to the State. Be pleased to let me hear from you as soon as possible.

P.S.—I am in want of a few blank Commissn's & Bonds for fitting out armed Vessels &c—be pleased to contrive me some

[Endorsement] "No. 41
   Letter from Gov.r. Rodney
      to Mr. McKean May 12, 1780 Read 15th
         Referred to board of War
            (postponed)"

389
Appointment of William Millan

Dover, May 24.th 1780.

By virtue of the Powers vested in me by an Act of the General Assembly, intituled, An Act for furnishing Supplies within this State, for the Army of the United States, for the ensuing Campaign, I have constituted you, William Millan, Receiver of Supplies for the said Army within the County of New Castle:

You are therefore to qualify yourself for the Execution of that office by giving the Security required by the said Act.

You are to provide Store-Houses and Hay-Yards for the Reception of the Supplies of your County in such Parts thereof, as that said Supplies may, with the most convenience, be transmitted from [or] to Wilmington, which will be the Repository of the whole Supplies to be furnished by the State:

You are therefore to provide at Wilmington a sufficient Number of such Stores and Yards for that Purpose.

You are to make exact Returns to me from Time to Time of the Quantity and Kind of Supplies which shall have been received by You: And for more particular Instructions herein I refer you to the Directions prescribed in the Act of General Assembly afs.d

Caesar Rodney

To M.r William Millan; Receiver of Supplies for the County of New Castle
   Attest.
      Ja.s Booth Sec.y

390

From Samuel Patterson

Xteen[1] May the 30th 1780

I wrote your Excellency a few days agone by Doctor Gilder. to which I refer you to—

Not hearing from you. have appointed the Review of my Brigade. viz. Coll?. Duffs the 5th June Monday. The 6th Coll? Bedfords the 7th Col? McDonoughs, as the season is getting warm. was the occasion, and Not hearing from you. I wish you could attend in my oppinion it would give life to the militia. Your Presence. as commander in chief. would in my oppinion animate us and revive the Spirits. which am sorry to say. is drooping by too much Security.

That is the only Time of danger in my oppinion. the Bearer hereof goes down to your place one Purpose to satisfie our officers. have paid him 20375 doll? which he takes down for that purpose, and orders on your County Treasurer for the Completion. of your Two orders if in his Power.—should be Glad of a line

N.B as to news refer you to the Bearer. much Vague

391

To George Washington

Dover June the 3d 1780.

Major John Patten of Delaware Regiment informs me that there are four vacancies of Ensigns in the Regiment, and that taking into consideration two of the officers being at this time Prisoners, it is necessary there should be some new appointments made, two least—As the Congress have advised the States to make no new appointments without first consulting your Excellency on the propriety of the Measure, and as the General Assembly are to meet next week, I would, as soon as possible, wish to have your advise in the matter.

392

To Samuel Huntington[2]

Dover June the 3d 1780.

Immediately on receiving your Letter of the 19th of may with the Resolu-

---

1 Christiana Bridge in New Castle County, Delaware.
2 President of Congress.

tions of Congress of that date, I issued writs calling the general Assembly, who stood adjourned to the end of the term for which they were Elected, to meet at Dover on Monday the fifth instant, when those Resolutions with one of the 24th of May shall be laid before them. I have wrote the Committee of Co-operation that their dispatches, just now received, shall also be laid before the General Assembly, and that on my part all possible dispatch shall be used in the execution of such Measures as they may recommend.

393
From Samuel Patterson

Xteen. June 3rd. 1780.

I think it my duty to acquaint your Ex:y that most of the officers reccom-mended for going out seem to decline, from their sundry private affairs. You must judge of the bad consequences of such refusal if commissioned as others will not accept after such a refusal. I wish your Ex:y could spend a day or two here for that purpose or any other mode you should think best to obviate such a refusal.

For further affairs, I refer you to my last, We have had a severe brush at West Point with Gen. Clinton. We beat him & he is returned to New-York says report. We lost not a man in the fort. The British had Killed near 400 men. The whole of the British has returned to New-York by the last accts. Count de Esteing has taken a 74 & 2 of 50 gun ships on the coast of France. No word of the French fleet. It is expected every hour.

P.S. The British drove in at Charles Town. The Gov: of Georgia was at Xteen last evening.

394
Message to the General Assembly

Gentlemen of the General Assembly

A circular Letter of the nineteenth of may last which I have received from the President of Congress with an Act of that Honorable Body of the same date calling upon the several States from New Hampshire to Virginia inclu-sive to furnish their Quotas of Ten Millions Dollars for immediate use, have, from the importance of the subject, determined me, with the advice of the Privy-Council, to convene you at so early a day after your last setting, both because the most Speedy complyance with the act, and the most vigorous exertions in carrying the same into Execution, appear to be equally obvious and essentially Necessary, I have therefore directed the Secretary to lay these papers before your Honors for immediate Consideration.

Since issuing the Writs for convening the General Assembly I have received a Letter from the Committee of Co-operation at Morris-Town of the twenty fifth Ult? with a Copy of a Letter from the Commander in Chief of our Army and other papers of the same date, which I have also directed the Secretary to lay before you, and am persuaded that the powerfull Naval and Land force expected here from his most Christian Majesty our good Ally to forward the operation of our arms, together with your Zeal and affection for the interest of your Country, will lead you to every exertion in your power, consistant with scituation and circumstance of the people you represent.

The Secretary will deliver you an Act of Congress of the Twenty second Ult? for laying an Imbargo within this State.

Gentlemen

I have this day received from the President of Congress, a Letter of the Twenty Ninth of May, with two Acts of that Honorable Body of the Twenty sixth and Twenty seventh of the same month, the one recommending to the States where any debts are due to their inhabitants from the Quartermasters and Commissary's department, by Notes or Certificates, to make provision for discharging the same—The other adopting measures to equip for Sea the Naval Force of the United States, promoting Harmony and forwarding the common Views of France and America.—One other Act of Congress of the first instant making farther provision respecting such supplies as any State may furnish, other than, or over and above their Quota of supplies required by the Act of the Twenty fifth of February last. These papers also The Secretary will lay before you for Your Consideration.

Caesar Rodney

Dover June 8th 1780.

395

Message to the General Assembly

Gentlemen of the General Assembly

Yesterday evening I received a Letter from the Committee of Co-operation at Morris-Town, dated the 12th instant, together with Copies of two Letters from his Excellency General Washington to the Committee, all which I have directed the Secretary to lay before your Honors immediately, and as the

General is verry pressing, I am persuaded you will do every thing in your power, without the least delay, to answer his expectations.

Caesar Rodney

Dover June the 17th 1780.
[Endorsement]
   Read the first time.
In the Council, Tuesday
Jun. 20th, 1780 A.M.
Read the 1st Time.

396
To Samuel Huntington

Dover June the 22d 1780.

Your Letter directed to me and the several Acts of Congress accompanying them from the 24th of April last have been laid before the General Assembly of this State, and at their request I have inclosed you a Copy of a resolution of that Honourable Body[1]—I have further to inform Congress that the General Assembly on a requisition made by his Excellency the Commander in Chief and the Committee of Co-operation, have passed an Act for embodying Three hundred and fifteen of the Militia of this State immediately to be formed into one Regiment and properly Officered, for the purpose of reinforcing the Army of the United States[2] and to continue in the Service until the first Day of November ensuing and an Act to prohibit the Exportation of Provisions from this State beyond the Sea until the twentieth day of October Next, and have Vested me with powers for carrying the above mentioned Acts and the one referred to in the inclosed resolution into Execution—They have also passed an Act for furnishing the Continental Treasury with One Hundred and Thirty two Thousand eight hundred Dollars by Loan on the credit of the State.

397
To the Committee of Co-operation

Dover June the 22d 1780

In consequence of the requisitions of Congress & the Commander in Chief and you the Committee of Co-operation, I convened the General Assembly.

---

   1 The General Assembly met at Dover from June 5 to June 21, 1780, at the call of President Rodney.

   2 Second Delaware Regiment of the Continental Line, officially known as Continental Regiment No. 38, mustered into service at Philadelphia, July 10, 1780, and discharged October 28 same year. Stationed in Kent County, Maryland.

They adjourned yesterday and as I Think it my duty to give you the earliest inteligence of their proceedings relative to the business recommended, beg leave to inform you that during their setting they passed the following Acts. An Act for furnishing the Continental Treasury with the Sum of One Hundred and Thirty two Thousand Eight Hundred Dollars by Loan on the Credit of the State—An Act for immediately Embodying Three Hundred and fifteen of the Militia of this State for the purpose of reinforcing The Army of the United States, to continue in service until the first day of November Next unless sooner discharged and An Act for procuring an immediate supply of Provision, Waggons, Horses &c within this State for the Army of the United States.—At the request of the General Assembly I have inclosed you a copy of a Resolution entered into by them—& Gentlemen you may be Assured of the greatest exertion on my part, to carry into Effect the Above Acts so far as I am vested with Authority for that purpose.

398
To George Washington

Dover, June 22ᵈ 1780

In Consequence of the Requisitions of Congress, the Committee of Cooperation, and your Excellency, transmitted to me and laid before the General Assembly of this State, I beg Leave to inform your Excellency, that they have passed the following Acts—An Act for furnishing the Continental Treasury with One Hundred and Thirty Two Thousand Eight Hundred Dollars by Loan on the Credit of the State—An Act for immediately embodying three hundred and fifteen of the Militia of this State for the Purpose of reinforcing the Army of the United States, to continue in Service until the first Day of November next, unless sooner discharged—An Act for procuring an immediate Supply of Provisions, Waggons, Horses &c. within this State for the Army of the United States. The above are the only Acts passed during their Sitting that I think necessary to make your Excellency acquainted with. At the Request of the General Assembly I have inclosed you a Copy of a Resolution entered in by them.
P.S. The General Assembly of this State adjourned Yesterday to the Twentieth of October next.

399
From Samuel Patterson

June 22ᵈ. 1780. P.M. 5

(Private) I never was so deceived in my Politics, as on yesterday. By plan it was agreed by a majority of both Houses, that you were to be invested with martial law during the recess. It was drawn up—I saw it, & approved of it, to be introduced, the last paper before breaking up. A full majority fixed to carry it through both houses. To my great surprize, when every moment I & others expected its appearance; the notice was, the Assembly was adjourned.

I must confess I was startled, & now reflect on their timidity. Nothing can be done without it, as sacrificing the State, by continual callings & sittings &c. &c. I am tired with such complacency, & am almost determined never more to appear in that public body who cannot see the necessity of spirited measures; & in their power—& no triming now. Have sent the last paper at hand,—much news but not digested yet, as to truth—when so you will hear from [me.]

400

To William Millan[1]

Dover, June 23rd 1780.

You are hereby directed to proceed in the Receipt and Collection of the Supplies of Flour and Indian-Corn, agreeable to my former Instruction: And you are hereby further directed, to purchase, on the Credit of the State, giving Receipts therefor, the monthly Supplies enumerated and required by the Act of General Assembly, intituled, "An Act for procuring an immediate Supply of Provisions within this State for the Army of the United States of America, and for other Purposes therein mentioned," passed the 21st Day of this Instant June; and in Case such Supplies cannot be so procured you are to seize the same for the Use of the Army, first making Application to me, and receiving my general Direction for that Purpose, as by the said Act you are directed.

You are also to procure by Purchase or Hire, on the Credit of the State, the Waggons and Horses required by the abovementioned Act, and if the same cannot be so obtained you are to impress such Waggons and Horses, conducting yourself therein agreeable to the Directions of the said Act.

You are to make monthly Returns to me of the Quantum and kind of Supplies received, and when Teams or Vessels may be necessary for the Transportation of those Supplies, you are to give Information thereof to me, and orders shall issue for obtaining the same.

As the Supplies of Provisions are immediately wanted for the Use of the Army I must beg leave to urge as speedy a Collection of them as possible, and that as soon as you shall have procured a Quantity sufficient for loading a ves-

1 Receiver of Supplies for New Castle County.

sel at any one Post, that you procure one for the transportation thereof, and make me acquainted with it, and so continue to do from Time to Time; You are, nevertheless, to make your monthly Returns with Punctuality.

When Aids of Money may be found requisite for the Discharge of the Trust, assigned you, with particular Dispatch, on your application I shall draw upon the Treasury for them: and for a more particular Rule of Conduct in the Execution of your office I refer you to the before recited Act of Assembly.

401

To William Millan

By His Excellency Caesar Rodney, Esquire, President, Captain-General and Commander-in-Chief of the Delaware State.

In virtue of the Powers vested in me by an Act of the General Assembly, intituled, "An Act for procuring an immediate Supply of Provisions within this State for the Army of the United States of America, and for other Purposes therein mentioned," I do hereby impower you, William Millan, Receiver of Supplies for the County of New Castle, to take to your Assistance any sufficient Number of Persons and seize upon, impress and take, for the use of the Army, all Horses, Mares or Geldings within your County that may be in Keeping for Racing, or at a Race-Ground for the purpose of Running, and report the same to me. Given under my Hand and Seal at Arms, at Dover, the twenty third Day of June in the Year of our Lord One Thousand Seven Hundred and Eighty.

402

From John Mathews and Nathaniel Peabody[1]

In Committee of Congress Morris Town June 23. 1780

Impressed with the necessity of giving you the earliest information of every important occurrence, We therefore inclose you Copy of a letter from the commander in Chief this moment Received.—

From the accumulated destresses of our Army which we are daily Spectators of, the jeopardy we have twice seen them in and the fatal consequences that must have resulted from a defeat (which would inevitably have been the Consequence had the enemy at first, and still will be, should they even now

1 Members of Congress, from South Carolina and New Hampshire, respectively. These gentlemen together with Philip Schuyler, a member of Congress from New York, were appointed a committee on April 13, 1780, to proceed to Washington's headquarters to bring about closer cooperation between the Army and Congress.

pursue their object) We are constrained again to call on you in the most pressing manner to forward your Quota of men and supplies agreable to our estimate of the 2ᵈ Inst. and prevent the Total sacrifice of the few brave & intrepid
Spirits that at present compose our Army, and avoid the indelible stain that
must consequently be fixed on these States, Should such an event take place.—

403

From David Hall and Henry Fisher

Lewes Town June 24 Day 1780.

We juged it our Duty to Send up to your Excellency Two Prisoners Huge
Elias & [?]. Brought here by Cap Goodwin which he Tuck in a Schooner Be-
longin to Sunnipuxion Commanded by Cap [?] Purnell which they had
Taken in a Barge that they came from New York in we ordered them to Be
Delivered to Coln Rhoads to Be guarded up to Dover
P.S. Two Ships with Flags from South Carolina came into the Bay yesterday and have Taken Pilots on Board for Philad. Genel Lincone and a number of his officers is one Board with a Number of outher Prisoners To the
amount 350.

404

To Samuel Huntington

Dover june 26 1780.

I wrote your Excellency the 22ᵈ Instant that I had called the Genᶫ Assembly
of this State, and laid before them the Requisitions of Congress, The Com-
mitee of Co-operation and of His Excellency the Commander in Chief—and
therein gave you the Titles of the Acts passed in Consequence of those requisitions—I have now to inform Congress that immediately after the House
adjourned I issued orders to the proper Officers throughout the State for collecting and forwarding the Supplies, and have urged in the most pressing
manner a speedy Execution of them—every thing in my power shall be done
to turn out and forward to the Army of the United States the 315 rank & File
properly Officered from the Militia. Congress may expect copies of the Acts
passed this Sessions when they come from the Press which will be in a few
days—I shall write to Congress & the Committee of Co-operation freequently,
relative to the supplies of men, provisions, &ᶜ. expected from this State—Sir
you may expect the returns requested by the Act of Congress of the 17th instant as soon as time will Permitt

405

From Samuel Patterson

Xteen. June 26. 1780.

This morning Capt James was with me on hearing his name was mentioned, as one of the Capts to your excellency, he says he can go at this time, but is willing to take his class tour. He is a good Whig, & always ready to turn out, & is yet; if in rotation. I wish we had gone in that line, only raised the fines. He desired me to write you as above.

As to News, I suppose you have it mostly, before my letters arrive at your place.

The British Army is moving; last accounts they were at Springfield in force to attack West Point; it is said 8000 men are there in the fort of ours.—The city of Ph^d militia, march^d yesterday.

General Lincoln arrived in a flag at Philad^a, a few days ago, lost Charlestown for want of provisions; & only 600 militia, with all the puffs south ward was there. General Clinton has arrived at New York, with 6000 men, & said to be in the field with the Troops. Since the reduction of Cha^sTown, we have lost 400 men, & forty wagons with stores, going to our Army, 100 miles this side of Cha^sTown. Part of Genl Scotts Brigade, who were cut to pieces by about 700 Cavalry; Our people fought them bravely; Killed near 300 of the British. 10,000 Virginians are under marching orders to Carolina; also the Militia of North Carolina. Genl Gates is gone to command to the southward.

The Holker has brot in a fine Jamacnia [?] man, last week.

406

From Samuel Patterson

Xteen June 27, 1780.

Yours of the 24th came to hand last night, with the resolutions of the Genl Assembly, as also your excellency's appointment as Brigadier General, recruiting Sergeant for the Delaware Battalion. There is no appointment you can give in that way, will hurt my honor for such superintendance. I said in the house I would do without for a reward, also your own observations on future Economy.

At present no such attempts of Enlisting can be entered into. Till the Quota of Militia is marched, as they are giving £1000 to £1500 for a man. If I am to be Sergeant Kite, I must be indulged in my plan. I am not afraid of success. To be furnished with a good sergeant drum, & fife, it will be attended

with no extra charge,—rations & a house can be had. Without those how can
it be expected I shall succeed? You can order them—If not I will do all I can.
But those are the main ingredients. Cash I shall draw, when expended only.
refer you to my 2 last letters for news.
Excuse Humer
N.B.

A certain Robt Wilcocks has applied to me to recommend him to you, as
surgeon to the militia going out. He was over Commander Hopkins fleet as
such.

407

To the Board of War

Dover July the 7th 1780.

By Sergeant Eshom I have sent a James Cooke and a John Bryan of the
Delaware Regiment. They have hitherto behaved so ill that the officers of the
Regiment when they Marched to the Southward left them here, and advised
their being put on board one of the Continental Frigates. If you approve of
this you will be pleased to Order the Necessary Steps to be taken for that purpose—if not, I would Submit it to the Board Whether it will not be best to
order them to Join some Regiment in the Pennsylvania Line until they may
have an opertunity to Join their own Regiment now in South-Carolina—It
may be necessary that the Sergeant, who is ordered to return here on the recruiting Service, Should have a rect for them—

408

To Samuel Huntington

Dover, 11th July 1780.

Agreeably to your Excellency's Letter of the 21st Ulto. accompanying an Act
of Congress of the 17th, I beg leave to inform Congress of the Transactions of
this State respecting the several Recommendations of your Honble Body, made
at different Periods, which are enumerated in the above mentioned Act. I
have therefore annexed a List of the several Resolutions, with their Dates, and
subjoined to each Resolution the Measures taken by the Legislature of this
State in consequence thereof.

Congress will observe by my former Letters and the Acts of General Assembly of the 21st of June last, that the Legislature have enacted Laws for
furnishing the Supplies of Provisions, Forage, Horses and Waggons, agree-

ably to the Requisition of the Committee of Congress at Head-Quarters, and also a Regiment of Militia to Join the Army under the Command of General Washington, in Conformity to another Requisition of the said Committee and the Commander in Chief, who also recommended an Augmentation of the Troops of this State to the number of 504 Rank and File, which the Legislature have no otherwise complied with, than by appointing Persons within the State to the Recruiting Services, owing to the Regiments' being to the Southward.

Congress will also perceive from the above recited Acts what Powers I am invested with, which they may be assured I shall vigorously and unremittingly exert for the Good of the Service.

I hope the Regiment of Militia will be ready to march at the Time directed by the General.

409

To Captain Peyton

Dover, 11th July 1780.

I just now received your Letter of the 8th Instant, referring to one sent me some Time ago which I so far complied with as to cause Advertisements to be wrote and set up, but do assure you I am so much employed in Business of more Importance, that I have not Leisure for apprehending, securing and forwarding Deserters. It is a Business I did not expect to be engaged in, and hope you will in future direct your orders to a proper Person for that Service —perhaps a Serjeant may be equal to the Task, and such a Person may expect my Countenance and Support.

410

From James Glasgow[1]

Christiana Bridge 12 July. 1780—

I had the honour this Day to receive from your Excellency by the hands of Generall Patterson a Commission in the Regt raised by this State which Commission I have returned to the Genl—I Beg that your Excellency would not impute my resignation Either to Cowardice, Disafection or any Cause Whatsoever, but the true state of my health I do assert to you on My honor that I am

1 A lieutenant in the Christiana Hundred Company of militia in 1779 and 1780 Commissioned by Caesar Rodney July 11 as lieutenant in Lieutenant-Colonel Neill's regiment of the Continental Line.

incapable for the Service on Acc^t of Bodily Infirmities. If there was Occassion to prove it the Doctor in this Town under whose hands I am would attest to the fact above mentioned

411

To George Washington

Dover, 13 July 1780

I heretofore informed you that the several matters recommended by your Excellency and the Committee of Co-operation as well as those recommended by Congress were laid before the General Assembly, and since they adjourned wrote your Excellency how far they had complied with the several requisitions, but find by your Letter of the 30th Ult., I have not been sufficiently explicit with respect to filling up the State Regiment to the number of 504 rank & file—I am sorry to inform you that the Legislature have no otherwise complied therewith than by appointing Persons within the State to the recruiting service, owing, as I am informed by some of the members, to the Regiment being to the Southwards.

I have appointed the officers and issued orders for Assembling the Regiment directed to be raised from the Militia of this State, and am in expectation that they will be at the place of Rendezvous by the time asigned in your Letter of the 30th Ult. However am of opinion that the great bounties given for men to fill this will effectually prevent our recruiting in future the State Regiment which I am persuaded is of much more importance—

You will find by the Act for furnishing Supplies of Provisions, Forage &c., The General Assembly have invested me with certain Powers for the more speedy obtaining the same, which powers your Excellency may be assured I shall vigorously and steadily exert for the good of the service.

412

From Samuel Patterson

Xteen July 13th 1780. 4. P.M.

I wrote your Excellency this morning by Coll. Battell. At the time I wrote, nothing but dunning for public dues hardly knows what I wrote.

Now alone for answer have enclosed your setts of commissions to each capt. this morning, & your letters, to congress's sent forward, since my prior letters. Mr. Mc Cracken was with me at the time he was recommended, he was Ensign. Since he has been elected a Lt. he will not go under such a commission. This was unknown at the time.

In the hurry of breaking up the Genl Assem^ly many names were mentioned. I think all good men. My former letter, had your Excellency thought proper to communicate your intentions, whom you would commission, should have waited on them in person, to have had their answer & willingness. This was a matter I could by no means arrogate, but wishes it had been done for the good of the service & the Honor of our State, as their refusal of the commissions must have a fatal tendency, to procure good men. No person of spirit will take the refusal, had not your Excellency ordered me to send the commissions to them directly, I should not have done it, this depend. I always will obey letters, and as no time was left for altercation; obey^d have sent the last paper to which I refer you.

413
From John Jones[1]

July 13th 1780

Our situation here is truly alarming the Enimy being almost Constantly in the River; we therefore should be greatly Obliged to your Excellency for an answer by the first safe Conveyance.—We have neither Lead, nor flints, Could you furnish us with afew of those Articles we should esteem it a particular favour

414
From Samuel Patterson

Xteen. July 14th 1780.

I wrote you last eve. by Col. Battell. Now enclosed, you have Capt. O'Flynn's Answer.

The commissons he sent back to me. I have them in my possession. I am sorry such are so bad sale. It will have a very bad consequence I am afraid as but few will now take their refusals. I wish you could come up or order some thing to be done. I expect you will hear from Capt. Moody in the same way, or a refusal with some excuse. No news but as Per sent you.

P. S. Capt. Joseph Israel of the New Castle Co. would have gone & wanted to. He is clever, will not vouch now his accepting. I will sound him.

1 Colonel, next to Brigadier-General Dagworthy in command of the Sussex County Militia.

415
To John Jones

Dover July the 15th 1780.

I received your letter of the Thirteenth instant with an instrument of Writing, signed by a great number of verry respectable people, setting forth your
scituation to be at this time verry alarming, and, if it was in my power you
and those Gentlemen may be Assured, I would with the greatest Chearfulness
relieve them from their distress, but am sorry to say there is, presently, too little
in my power—I have inclosed you a Copy of the Resolution entered into by the
General Assembly—By this Resolution you will find that I am to Commissionate Barges & Boats &c to cruize in the Bay & River, and to direct their proceedings from time to time, That the expences of Equipping the vessels and the
wages of the Crews [?] are to [be] discharged by the State &c—Now if any
Gentlemen in yo[ur] Quarter should think proper to Equip or cause to be
Equipped an[d] manned any such Vessel, They may be Assured of every Aid
and contenance, on my part, according to the powers with which I am invested
by the General Assembly—You all know that our Treasury is not presently in
Cash, and if it was, That there is but little subject to my Order except by special
direction of the House according to the several Bills & Resolutions for raising
it. However I can regulate and direct matters, You can under these circumstances Trust the State and I believe the State will repay you when able.

416
From Samuel Patterson [?]

Xteen. July 18th 1780.

Never was your presence more wanted in this county than at present. I wish
it suited you.

Yesterday our county Lt. ordered their Capts to bring their quota of men to
this place, All that had notice as report says appeared; & must say as I was
there, about 50 fine men appeared.

The[y] could not know what to do with them, not one officer, to receive
them, were sent home with full rations as he had no orders from you, & a
general murmur who was to be their officers, by what I find they wish the
militia officers of that line to command them.

Also, a continental vessel was ordered to attend at this place, to carry them
to Trentown by some report to Mr. McKean, that, they were to attend here
that day; where he got his report cannot say, for the above, a letter to me by

the Capt. came for that purpose. I told him to return, with his lading stores from this place. He is gone, as nothing could be done without orders from you.

As most of the officers were here of my Brigade, they were sounded. Some found that would be willing to go; their names I have but could not inshure any, nor did. A list I have by me. I advised Col. Evans to write you. I would forward it, he has not sent it to hand. Mr. Miller told me, you talked of coming up in ten days. I wish it in one. As to news I now can, but suppose you have as good authority or better; but depend on this, the French Fleet is arrived at Rhode Island, the 10th Inst in the evening. & a Capt. Rudulph of Major Lee's horse, was at my house today, & was [Incomplete]

417
To John Holker[1]

Dover July the 24th 1780

I Just received your letter of the 11th instant relative to your appointment of Turnbull & Co. purchasers of flour for the royal marine, and the permitting that Article to be carried from this State to Pensylvania, and have to inform you that the exportation of Flour from this State is, by law, prohibited until the requisitions of Congress are complied with—However, as we have all one point in view, if the Hon^e the Congress will signify to me thier desire that your Requisition should be Complied with, I shall immediately and most cheerfully order my receivers to permit flour to be sent there on the Terms you propose on Condition that the receivers take care to secure the quantity required by Congress which the Act has principally in view.

418
To Samuel Huntington

Dover July the 24th 1780.

Your letter of the 29th of June, with the resolution of Congress inclosed, I did not receive until Yesterday at 12 O Clock. How it has been thus delayed I cannot say. However I have wrote you several times since the adjournment of the General Assembly. Those letters may in some Measure Answer the One now received—I have now to inform Congress That the Troops, directed to be raised from the Militia of this State to form a Regiment, are under Marching Orders for Wilmington, Where I expect they will be verry soon Assembled in order to march from thence and Join the Army of the United States and

1 French consul.

as the Board of War has promised to have Arms and accoutrements ready for them on their arrival at Philadelphia I have advised them That the Troops are in Motion.

419
To the Board of War

July the 24th 1780

Your Letter of the 23 instant relative to the issuing provisions to soldiers wives came to hand yesterday—I know of no Issuing Commissaries within this State at present but such as are under my appointment and direction. They shall issue no provisions to soldiers wives absent from their husbands,—and they shall pay obedience to any other orders you may think proper to give for the good of the Service and Communicate to me—There is no Law of this State that Specially provides for the maintenance of soldiers wives. However the laws that provide for support of the Poor in general, I think, comprehend them. If there should be any complaint on this head I will lay the matter before the General Assembly at their next meeting—I have now to inform you Gentlemen that the Troops directed to be raised from the militia of this State to form a Regiment for the purpose of reinforcing the army of the United States are under marching orders for Wilmington, where, I expect, they will be assembled in a short time, so that you may be prepared to Equip them with arms and accoutrements on their arrival at Philadelphia agreable to promise— [Incomplete.]

420
To Samuel Patterson

Dover, July the 24th, 1780.

Your letter of the 23d accompanied with one of the 18th I had the honor of receiving yesterday. Within a few days past I have received several other letters from you of an older date all of them principally relating to the officers lately appointed to serve in the Regiment now raising from the Militia of this State to serve in the Army of the United States, refusing to accept of their commissions. By the act for raising the above Regiment I am invested with the power of appointing the officers without being confined to any County for obtaining such gentlemen I should think best calculated to serve and answer the expectations of the public. I nevertheless thought it a compliment due to each county to give them an opportunity to furnish an equal number of officers, therefore in order that this might be done prudentially I consulted the representatives who recommended to me a number of worthy characters, and they were commissioned accordingly. Now Sir, is it not strange that any of these gentlemen, who were all well known and distinguished for their patriotism, and pointed out to me by their representatives, should refuse to accept their appointments without the strongest reasons why they could not serve. Many of them no doubt are able to assign very good reasons for not serving, and such as were unknown at that time to those who recommended them, such ought to be excused. I have given commissions to a number of promising young gentlemen in this county upon their personal applications, and could ere this have filled up commissions for all the Companies in the Battalion in the same way had not the respect I have for the gentlemen of your County and the one below inclined me to proceed as I have in this business. However, I intend to fill no more commissions until the troops are all assembled at Wilmington where they are already ordered. I intend to be there and shall see what vacancies there then are and fill them as well as possible. There is no doubt with me that the Regiment will be well officered. It is probable that I shall not have the pleasure of seeing you before Saturday or Sunday next as I intend to have all the troops sent forward before I leave Dover. My purpose is to see you at Xteen Bridge on my way to Wilmington.

421

From Thomas McKean

Philadelphia, July 24th 1780

You will herewith receive the Votes & Laws of this State passed during the last Sitting of the General Assembly, which are transmitted thro' me by the President and Supreme Executive Council to you. It is wished that the Votes & Laws of each State could be sent thro' the like Channel to the other States; this would conduce to a uniformity of proceedings and to the ease & improvement of legislation throughout the United States.

The public duty I am obliged to perform is too much for me, and as our State affords me no relief in Congress I shall be obliged to decline the Delegation. The truth is, should my health & strength hold out, my finances will not; while I continue in the station I will support the Rank of a Deputy of the State, and this I find so expensive in these times that without some support from the Government I cannot endure it much longer. I have not received a farthing since the first of January 1779, and I am not a single day out of Congress unless when attending some court of Justice, so that I cannot attend in the least to my private affairs, nor to the wants of my family: however I will endeavor to persevere until the General Assembly meet again, especially as the difficulties & dangers we have had to encounter, owing to our change of system for the support of the war by taxes & loans, are not yet over. For God's sake exert yourself in enforcing the collection & payment of the public taxes, or we may yet be ruined; if we had but money we could finish the war in all probability the present campaign, notwithstanding the loss of South Carolina.

A fleet of eight sail of the Line, besides several frigates & armed transports, with 5,000 troops on board, are safely arrived at Rhode Island from France, sent for our assistance by our great and good Ally, whom God protect. This fleet is superior to that under Admirals Graves & Arbuthnot, notwithstanding what you may have seen or heard to the contrary. Be that as it may, believe me we shall be *vastly superior* to the Enemy on this Continent very soon. Keep this hint to your self, as you love your Country; *verbum sat sapienti.*—The Tories will propagate, and, I will suppose, do believe the contrary; I hope they will gain credit for a time.—Notwithstanding the *res arduae domi,* and appearances abroad, you see I have some consolation in being a member of Congress; and if I had not now and then these grateful animating cordials, yet I will not quit the Helm in the midst of a storm.

I cannot conclude without informing you, that Delaware at present stands high in the opinion of Congress, and that if they had revised and altered the tender law, and adopted the plan of discharging the national debt of the 18th of March last (for which omissions they are alone censured) they would have stood higher than any State in the Union.

422

To John Holker

Dover July the 26th 1780

I wrote you the 24th instant and therein neglected to inform you, That it will be necessary & Convenient you should appoint some person as purchaser within this State. Not only that I may be means thereof have it in my power to keep him within the line of his duty according to your Instructions, but because this State has a Port and Market which it is as much my duty to encourage as it is the duty of any other Executive Authority their Ports so that if Congress should come into your measures, I would Beg leave to mentioned to you Mr. Jonathan Rumford at Wilmington who is an active man and who, I am of opinion, will answer your expectation. You may be assured of every aid in my power—

423
From John Clowes, N. Waples, William Peery, and William Conwel

Sussex July 27th 1780.

We have reason to believe that Captains Nathaniel Hays and Rhoads Shankland have declined accepting the Commissions your Excellency were please to send them, appointing them to Command the two Companies of the 2nd Delaware Regiment of Militia raised in this County, now under Marching orders to join the Army under his Excellency Gen¹. Washington, both the Captaincies for this County will therefore be vacant.

The Men absolutely refused to March unless they were assured they should be Commanded by Captains from their Own County, and in order to give them satisfaction on that head we pledged ourselves to them that we would use our Interest with your Excellency to obtain Commissions for the Under named Gentlemen who we have every reason to believe will accept them:

We have therefore to request that your Excellency will be pleased to Commissionate Thomas Grove and George Smith as Captains to Command the two aforesaid Companies, who we conceive will be agreeable to the Men, and are worthy of the Confidence we desire to be placed in them.

424
To Colonel Evans

Dover July the 29th 1780.

I Just now received your letter of Yesterday. Major Mitchell set out from here Yesterday afternoon with orders to repair immediately to Wilmington and take Charge of the troops there. I have also order⁴ a Subaltern from one of the companies of this County to go up and assist the Major—The Companies from Kent & Sussex have all passed this place on their way to Wilmington and I Shall set out from home on Tuesday Morning to Review the Regiment and do What else may be Necessary.

425
From Ephraim Blaine

Kings Ferry August 3ᵈ 1780—

The Committee of Congress at Head Quarters having Called upon the States to furnish Supplies for Our Army (during the Campaign) which is In-

creasing fast, and makes the daily Consumption of Provisions very Considerable, and will Require every possible Exertion of the States to keep them supplied—your State is Requested to furnish five hundred barrels of flour, Seventy
One Thousand Six hundred & Seventy five pounds of Beef per Month and
five Thousand pounds of Bacon for the Summer. There is fourteen Brigades
assembled in this Neighbourhood, and Recruits hourly Comeing in, which
with the followers of the Army, now Consume One hundred barrels of flour
and Sixty five Beef Cattle daily—The Requisitions made by the Committee of
Congress upon the Respective States for Provisions were Calculated to Supply
Our Army, which is very shortly Expected in the field, and without a speedy
Complyance they cannot long subsist—have in the most pressing Terms to
beg your Excellency and Council to Urge your States Commissioners to Use
every possible means to facilitate their Respective Purchases, and Request your
Excellency not to Confine them to the Quantity Required. Whatever their
Purchases may Exceed your Quota, I shall take Care to have it settled in my
Continental Accounts and See you paid first Costs & Charges.

Your flour & Bacon must be delivered the Keeper of the Magazine at Philadelphia or Trenton, and your Beef Cattle to Capt John Little of Philada whom
I have appointed to superintend that Business, and forward them by Drover
to Head Quarters.

426
To Thomas Sim Lee[1]

Wilmington, August 5, 1780.

Two Days ago I received your Excellency's Letter of the 21st Ulto with a
Copy of an Embargo Act passed by the General Assembly of your State, and
now agreeable to your Request send you here[wit]h a [copy of the act] prohibiting the Exportation of Wheat, Flour &c. from this State.

427
To Samuel Huntington

Wilmington, August 9th 1780.

It may be necessary to advise your Excellency, that the Regiment raised from
the Militia of this State to reinforce the Army of the United States embarked
here this Morning for Philadelphia, on their Way to Camp. The Commanding Officer will call upon the Board of War for Arms and Accoutrements.

1 Governor of Maryland.

428

To John Holker

Wilmington August the 9th 1780

I received your letter of the 29th Ult?. at Wilmington Where I have been detained ever since on public business—I have inclosed you a Copy of an Act of the General Assembly of this State prohibiting the Exportation of Wheat, Flour &c. You will find by the last Clause in this Act That The President with the advice of the Privy-Council, by Proclamation, under his hand and The Great Seal of the State may Suspend the operation Thereof in part or in the Whole—I intend, on Sunday or Munday Next at farthest, to set out for Dover, in the neighbourhood of Which place the Members of the Privy-Council reside. I shall immediately call them together to consider of your application, and am so fully convinced they will concur with me in authorising your Agent in this State to purchase, That I have advised him to purchase but not to send the Flour out of the State until the proclamation Shall have passed the Seal. A proper person shall be appointed at the same time to inspect and Brand it.

I received a Letter this day from Mr. Robert Morris, with one from the Chevr. de La Luzerne, requesting permission to Load a Schooner, now lying at Wilmington, that will carry about 5 or 6 hundred barrels of Flour for the use of the French & Spanish Fleets in the West India's, and have wrote him That without your concurrance it cannot be permitted, as I would not wish Such Lycence to be extended to any but one public purchaser and that too for the sole purpose of supplying the Royal Marine of France, indeed I do not think the Privy-Council would agree to extend this indulgence to any more than one least it should interfer with the requisitions of Congress and You— Therefore if You would Wish the Vessel, at Wilmington, should be Loaded with Flour agreable to Mr. Morris's request I apprehend it would be better that you should direct your Agent in this State to do it with the Flour purchased on Your Account, and so accounted for by Mr. Morris with you—

429

To Henry Neill[1]

Wilmington, August 9 1780

You are immediately to proceed with the Regiment under your Command to the City of Philadelphia. Upon your Arrival at Philada. you are to apply to

1 Colonel commanding regiment of Delaware Militia.

the Honble the Board of War for Arms & Accoutrements for your Regiment, and when obtained to proceed without Loss of Time and join the Grand Army of the United States unless otherwise ordered by his Excellency General Washington.

You are to take with you to Philadelphia Herdman Anderson, Drum-Major of the Delaware Regiment, who deserted, as is said, from the Regiment at the Head of Elk—William Grace a Soldier in said Regiment and deserted on his way to Carolina—Benjamin Moody, a Soldier in the Delaware Regiment, reported that last winter to have deserted to the Enemy, but made his Escape from them when Kniphausen came out to Springfield in the Jersey, and gave himself up.

When you get to Philadelphia, you are to report these men to the Board of War, and if they approve of it, as the Delaware Regiment is now in Carolina, you are to take them with you to Camp, in order to do Duty in your Regiment, and when you return to report them again to the Board. If the Board of War do not approve of this, they are requested to take such other Order with respect to them as may be thought best. You are however to make known to me what shall be done in the Matter.

430
To Robert Morris[1]

Wilmington Augst the 10th 1780

Yesterday afternoon I received your letter of the 8th instant and am extreemly sorry that it is not in my power to Comply with your request—By a Clause in the Embargo Bill there is a power Vested in the President with the advice of the Privy-Council by Proclamation under the Great Seal, to suspend the operation of the Act in part or in the whole, but I cannot believe the Privy Council will think it prudent to grant this indulgence to any but Mr Holker the Consul of France who is intending to purchase by his agent within this State for the Royal Marine, and who has some time past applied to me for such indulgence, least it should interfer with the requisition of Congress and the Lycence intended Mr Holker—Therefore if you and Mr Holker have the same point in View, he may, when a Proclamation issues in his favour, permit his agent to load your vessel now at Wilmington—However this is a matter you and he are to settle—I have wrote to Mr Holker this day and shall write to him again when I get to Dover which I expect will be in a few days.

1 In July the French minister, Luzerne, had engaged Robert Morris as agent to procure flour for the use of the Spanish fleet in the West Indies. At the same time the French consul, Holker, was engaged through an agent in purchasing flour for the French navy.

431

From John Holker

Philadelphia August 10th 1780

Since I had the pleasure of writing last to your Excellency I am informed by Mr Rumford that he cannot purchase the 500 Barrels of best fresh Superfine Flour at the price of 90 per hundred, and the merchantable at 80. This Some what Surprises me, as I never authorised my agent here to give more for all that has been purchased in this City; in Mary-land I have obtained it at 70 & 75 the hundred; Notwithstanding, as it is prudent for me to Secure eight hundred Barrels of Superfine Flour, which Mr Rumford Says he can procure easily at 105. per %, I would consent to give that price for this Fine Flour Tendered at Philadelphia all charges included, Except the Commission, Rather than not to have it; but least I Should encure Censure, For So doing, without there being a necessity for it, I Beg leave to Sobmit the matter to your Excellency as much better informed With Respect to this Circumstance; Requesting you'll please to Instruct M Rumford as to this point & to authorise him to give the above Mentioned prices, if you Should think it necessary.

432

From John Jones

August 10th 1780

Notwithstanding the mildness of our government and the lenity and tenderness hitherto shown to the disaffected throughout this State and particularly to those of this County between two and three hundred of them for some time past have been ranging about the County disarming the well affected seizing the ammunition refusing to pay their taxes and in short openly avowing their intension of opposing the laws and threatening distruction to all that should oppose them.

Things thus being Circumstanced there was no time to be lost the general therefore gave immediate orders for the militia to hold themselves in rediness to march against those miscreants but previous to any movement being made no less than five different parties were sent out for the purpose of geting inteligence who were all taken prisoners it was then Judged necessary to send out a party of horse who were fired upon six of which were wounded one horse killed and Mr. Robert young taken prisoner. No doubt now remaining of their hostile intension the general was determined to march against them with what force he had Collected and after persuing them for three days and driving them from one Swamp into another have nearly dispersed them

433

From Solomon Maxwell[1]

Christiania Bridge. the 11th of Aug. 1780.

Having the honor of receiving 2 appointments from your Excellency in the Staff Dept. (for which I return you thanks) I am under the necessity of pointing out sundry inconveniences respecting my conducting the business, viz:

Col. Wades, Deputy, Quarter & Forrage Master still continue by his directions & think themselves entitled to pay & rations until discharged by him. I have hitherto occupied the wharves & stores at this Post as a Magazine for all Cont! Stores, Forrage &c. [for] which [it] is scarce sufficient. The owners of some part propose dispossessing me & taking them on private acct. If so, the provisions &c. will suffer, unless new ones are built.

The monthly expense at this Post is above 4000 dollars for Store-rent, Coopers & Fatigue men, exclusive of Clerk & Assistants. Sundry repairs is also wanted at the Forage-yard &c: in fact not less than 15000 dollars is immediately wanted to repair the premises. I should also wish to be informed the salary for Assistant &c. as the pay hitherto pr. month has not been half that of a common laborer, for which reason, I divided my own & also advanced considerably to them in order to have the business done. I have never pocketed one shilling for my services since the war commenced, but on the contrary, advanced 20 months expense at the post & after a depreciation of more than 10 to 1 have a Qr. Mr. Certificate yet unpaid. If your Ex^cy will please to order me a full list of directions under the new arrangement as also the late act of assembly respecting the public buildings, also advise me of whom & what manner the monthly expenditures of the post are to be drawn I shall then be enabled to conduct the business with more general satisfaction to all concerned.

434

From Peter White

Lewes Aug. the 12th 1780.

The supplies for this county have come in so very slow that I have only rec'd 300 bushels of corn from Lewis & Rehoboth—170 bushels of salt from Baltimore Hundred & as to purchasing it is in vain to attempt it as the people in general dislike the Certificates. One hundred bushels of corn is all I have got in that way & a few cattle. I am at a loss what to do with them. I do not believe

1 Superintendent of Stores.

in all the other hundred I have rec'd 100 bushels of corn & as for wheat we have none in our county & very little corn.

435
To Isaac Carty and William Millan[1]

Dover August the 22d 1780.

You will receive with this the Copy of Letter from Col!. Blaine, Commissary General of purchases, to the Honorable the Board of War, One from the Board of War to me, and one other from the Commissary General to me, all of them urging in the most pointed manner the Necessaty for your utmost Exertion in collecting and forwarding immediately, to the places therein directed, the Provisions required of this State—As I know you to have a Sincere and firm attachment to the freedom and Independence of America, I am well assured you will do every thing in your power to answer the expectations of the public, Especially when so much is Necessarily Expected from your department in order to bring about that great and most desirable purpose which we now have in full View—I wish you to turn your immediate attention prin[ci]pally to the Article of Flour, Meat, so far as it may be in your power, you Ought also to forward—With respect to Horses, Waggons &c I would not wish your attention to be taken from the other Articles for the sake of procuring them, especially as I have some reason to believe they are not now so much wanted as was at first Expected. However if I should receive any pressing call on that head, Shall immediately inform you—I hope you will write to me Shortly, and let me know as fully as possible, or at least so fully as that I may have an idea of what may be Expected and Wh[en?]

436
From John Collins

Sussex County August 22d, 1780

As I Have been present at the Examination of many of the Insurjints of this county, and some witnesses against them Before the Justices of peace—I shall now mention to your Excellency what appears Thereby—It appears that in June last, a Number of the insurjints associated to oppose the civil Law, and stand by each other—about the 15th of July about forty began to Train under one Batholomew Banum—the [?][2] of august There was embodied about 100

---

1 Receivers of Supplies for Kent and New Castle counties respectively.
2 Probably the fourth or fifth of August.

men. They then began to rob the inhabitants of their arms and accutrements—
with intent to Take what they caled the heads of the whigs, (the militia officers) and Carry them to the refugees on the 6th 7th 8th and 9th—upwards of
four hundred embodied at Different places, in the neighborhood—tho there
was but about 280 ranke file at there main Camp—Some of these ignorant
people were for opposing all law, others for establishing what they called the
King's Laws—and others for opposing the payment of Taxes—but generally
seem to have believed that all to the Southward of Cheseapeack Bay had laid
down their arms and submitted to the Kings Laws—and that They should
very easey make Sussex County dow the same—Some of their Leaders have
Submitted with Many others—much the grate number of which have given
up their armes and given Bail—Some of those that are out sent to me requesting me to meet them—in the woods and draw a petition to your Excellency to
pardon them—but on finding they did not intend to submitt, Till they ware
pardoned—I Lett them know you would receive no petition from them until
they submitted themselves—those that joined them From Maryland are sent to
Worcester goal—few of the armes took are brought in—

The taxes of all kinds are now paying very fast in this County—and I believe
will soon be fully Collected—the Barrer Capt. Smith being Just seting off—I
have not Time to coppy and abridge this therefore am obliged to Trouble your
Excellency with this rough draught—

437
From John Clowes

August 23rd 1780

Captain Smith has with his men Thomas Wells and John Wainwright who
have Entered in the Delaware Battalion for three years or during the War, and
Lowder Calaway, for only Two years, Mr Smith has their Inlistments.

I have given them no part of their Bounty Money, nor Administered the
oath to them—

Your Excellency will be able to Judge on hearing their particular Circumstances from Captain Smith, what part of the Bounty to pay them.

438
To the Board of War

Dover Aug.. 25th 1780.

Captain Smith of the Regiment Raised from the Militia of this State, has
with him 25 men collected since the others Marched, he has orders to call

upon the Board, have them Equiped, and then to Join the Regiment as soon as possible, Three of those men, towit, Thomas Wells, John Winright, & Lowder Calloway—have since they engaged to Serve in this, inlisted in the Delaware Regiment. Captain Smith has orders to report them as such to your Honors, so that when the Term of this Regiment is Expired they may be turned over to the Delaware's and also to report a certain John Stevens—a soldier lately deserted from the Delaware Regiment.—

439
From George Washington

Head Quarters near the Liberty Pole in Bergen County 27ʰ Augᵗ 1780.

The Honᵇˡᵉ the Committee of Cooperation having returned to Congress I am under the disagreeable necessity of informing your Excellency that the Army is again reduced to an extremity of distress for want of provision. The greater part of it had been without meat, from the 21ˢᵗ to the 26ᵗʰ. To endeavour to obtain some relief I moved down to this place with a view of stripping the lower parts of the County of the remainder of its Cattle, which after a most vigorous exaction is found to afford between two and three days supply only, and those consisting of Milch Cows and Calves of one or two years old—when this scanty pittance is consumed, I know not what will be our next resource, as the Commissary can give me no certain information of more than 120 head of Cattle expected from Pennsylvania and about 150 from Massachusetts. I mean in time to supply our immediate wants. Military coercion is no longer of any avail, as nothing further can possibly be collected from the Country in which we are obliged to take a position, without depriving the inhabitants of the last morsel. This mode of subsisting, supposing the desired end could be answered by it, besides being in the highest degree distressing to individuals, is attended with ruin to the morals and discipline of the Army—during the few days which we have been obliged to send out small parties to procure provision for themselves, the most enormous excesses have been committed.

It has been no inconsiderable support of our cause to have had in our power to contrast the conduct of our army with that of the enemy, and to convince the inhabitants that while their rights were wantonly violated by the British troops by ours they were respected. This distinction must unhappily now cease and we must assume the odious character of the plunderers instead of the protectors of the people, the direct consequence of which must be to alienate their minds from the army & [?] from the camp.

We have not yet been absolutely without Flour, but we have *this* day but *one* days supply in Camp, and I am not certain that there is a single Barrel between this place and Trenton. I shall be obliged therefore to draw down one or two hundred Barrels from a small Magazine which I have endeavoured to establish at West Point, for the security of the Garrison in case of a sudden investiture.

From the above State of facts it may be [guessed?] that this Army cannot possibly remain much longer together, unless very vigorous and immediate measures are taken by the States to comply with the requisitions made upon them. The Commy General has neither the means nor the power of procuring supplies—he is only to receive those from the several Agents. Without a speedy change of circumstances this dilemma will be involved; either the army must disband or what is, if possible, worse subsist upon the plunder of the people. I would fain flatter myself that a knowledge of our situation will produce the desired relief, not a relief of a few days as has generally heretofore been the case, but a supply equal to the establishment of Magazines for the Winter. If these are not formed before Roads are broken up by the Weather, we shall certainly experience the same difficulties and distresses the ensuing winter which we did the last. Altho' the troops have upon every occasion hitherto borne their wants with unparralled [*sic*] patience, it will be dangerous to trust too often to a repetition of the causes of discontent.

[On Reverse] Circular to States of New Hampshire, Massachusetts, Rhode Island, Connecticut, New York, New Jersey, Pennsylvania, Delaware, Maryland.

440

From William Millan

Cantwell's Bridge, the 28th of Aug. 1780.

I rec'd your Excy's favor of the 22nd *inst.* covering 3 copies of letters that urges the supplies for the army in pressing terms. I have for some time past been so well acquainted with the necessity for exertion in my Dept. that I have made use of every possible means to procure such a part of the supplies to be raised by this State as might be deemed sufficient for this county, but I am sorry to inform your Excy that my endeavors have not been attended with the wished-for success. The mode pointed out by our Legislature at their last session for raising supplies within this State will not, I am convinced, answer the purpose. I have been several times among the mills within this County & could not at any one time find more flour among them than would make up one month's supply of that article had I seized every barrel I met with &

the consequences attending such an event would effectually prevent any future suppl[i]es being got as the miller's absolutely declare they would immediately quit grinding, because they would expect the same Providence would be continued until [the] whole of the supplies were completed & the law do not authorize the receivers to seize wheat otherwise the millers quitting business would be no great inconvenience was there wheat to seize. I have got about 250 barrels of flour which the Millers made up voluntarily & which I will forward to Phila as soon as I can collect it. One half of the Mills with us are now idle for want of Water which will retard my sending it as soon as otherwise I would.

I have been very particular in my enquiries about wheat in this county & find the last crops were so exceedingly bad that very few farmers will have more than will serve them for seed & bread, after their tax in that article is paid. Many indeed will fall short of this. The Millers get most of their wheat from Maryland & as soon as the seizing act is put in execution, it will prevent any more coming from that State.

I am obliged to observe to your Excy that I can not think the gentlemen of the Assembly expected when they passed the last supply bill that it would be complied with. They might have judged their constituent[s'] circumstances by their own, they being all men of property & I can assure your Excy that not a member belonging to this County have offered me an article, but on the contrary refused, as they say they have nothing to spare. The first supply Bill which laid a Tax in produce on the inhabitants will, I hope, be attended with better success. People in general approve of it, tho' the collection of it will be tedious yet our principal dependence must be upon it. I wrote to Col. Blaine, acquainting him with some of these circumstances but not so particularly as I have to Your Excy I am concerned lest the army should suffer for want of Provisions & will continue to do all in my power to prevent so disagreeable a circumstance.

441

From Samuel Patterson

Xteen Septr. 1, 1780—

You have an accompt of a most disagreeable one, I said I never would send you such, but your and my feelings on so melancholly an accassion, duty prompted me to let you know, I believe it is too true, it is am well assurd. in the Maryland papers, it is gone up to congress, by General Gates aid.[1]

1 Patterson evidently means that the aide of General Gates was bringing to Congress the news of that General's defeat at Camden.

[P.S.] Intelligence Recd this Evening Xteen August 31, 1780 by Collo. White from Georgia. on the first of the Engagement with the British troops they were worsted and we kept the field and the[y] left one hundred and odd kil'd —being, the 16th August at Night. General Gates marchd. to Surprise General Cornwallis at Cambden, the Enemy also marchd. same night to surprise General Gates Each Armys discovered one another by the recounitring. Lay on their arms till day. Both armies, met within 8 miles of Cambden, when the whole engaged, wee drove the Enemy and took two field pieces, 900 of the Militia went of the field, when the enemy saw that, the[y] rallied, the enemy being much superior. then a most bloody ingagement came on with Bayonets. and our people in the confusion were surrounded. the Maryland line Cut all to pieces. General De Calb, seposd. kild Genl Smallwood Kild Genl Gist kild Collo Gunby kild. General Gates Safe. brot of by his aids with perswasion—said about 400 only Escapd besides the above Militia.

442

From Thomas Rodney[1]

Wilmington Sept: 1 1780

M: A. Montgomery left Philada last night and got down here early this morning—He Says he was informed by Sharp Delany and Several others Just before he left the City that General Gates had been Totally defeated near Camden and lost the greatest part of his Army Killed and Taken prisoners; That the enemy were forced to Action and Gates attacked to disadvantage by Too hasty a pursute, and the Malitia Giving way his Regulars were overpower'd. This account he says came by Express to Congress—Gates with The remainder of his Army has retreated to Hilsborough—If This account is True the Stroke is more Severe than that at Charles Town—Smallwood was killed but he could not learn any particulars respecting the Dalawares as only a general account of this matter had transpired tho Congress have the particulars—As M: Montgomerys immagination is fertile in painting I hope this affair will not Turn out altogether so bad but I fear Gates has Suffered considerably and has no doubt been Obliged to retreat but I cannot yet believe he has been Totally defeated as such accounts are always exaggerated in their first Transpiring—A Copper Bottom vessel belonging to McClannagin went up yesterday and brings account that the Dutch had permitted Two Brittish Frigates to Seize all the American Vessels at St Martins and the same was

---

1 Thomas Rodney had moved to Wilmington to be associated with Mr. Rumford in the exporting and importing business. Caesar Rodney seems to have been interested in the business also.

Hourly expected at Statia[1] when this vessel sailed. Capt.ns Montgomery & Bell are Arrived from France, Bell went up yesterday but we have not yet heard any news from them—The last news from the armiment ag.t Jamacia. they lay at Hispanola and were to make their Attack the first of August—It was reported yesterday in Philad.a that the second Division of the French were arrived—Our present hopes seem much to depend on this Armament & that in the West Indies

N.B. There is no doubt but our Main Army already Amounts to thirty thousand exclusive of the French force—so that no doubt New York will be invested as soon as the Second Division arrives.

P.S. Since writing the within Col. White past through this place from the Southward and give Some more particulars of The Action—He Says when Gen.l Gates drew near Camden Cornwallace Left it but fearing he Could not git of returned again That the same night Both Gates & Cornwallace formed a plan of surprizing each other. Of course both armies being in Motion Met near Camden a little before or about daylight; that after a smart action The Brittish were Obliged to retreat and being pursued too precipitately by the Malitia they got into disorder and the Brittish Taking advantage of this Circumstance returned to the Charge routed the Malitia and beat their whole force round our Regular Troops rushing upon them with fixed Bayonets where they were bravely opposed in the same manner Till over powered by numbers—Some of the Line forced their way through them and the Gen.l escaped with them—He adds That Gunby & Guist is killed but does not know any thing particular of our officers from whence I have hopes that none of them have fell or their names would have been mentioned—and it is not unlikely but some of them said to be dead are only prisoners—

We have Sent M.r Holker—747 barr.s of flower—

N.B. a very fine prize Ship just now past by up the river—2, OClock Capt.n Kain has Just now returned from Philad.a Says that one of Gen.l De-Calbs aids has arrived Express from Gen. Gates to Congress—Says Smallwood, and Gunby are killed that DeCalb being Wounded early in the Action was either killed or Taken Prisoner not known which, that the gen.l had no account of Gen.l Guest that he was on the left and all the above officers mentioned to be lost, on the Right, so that it is hoped the Left have fared better and that fortunately Guest may have made a retreat with the Left wing—The Malitia were in the Center and being Charged with the Horse were broke and the Horse wheeled to the right and left flanking our Troops while the Brittish line Charged in the front, but I expect from all accounts that the left may have fared much better than the right.

---

1 Probably St. Eustatius, an island in the Dutch West Indies.

443
To Thomas Rodney

Dover, Sept. 3d, 1780.

We have, within a few days past, had several very alarming accounts from the Southward, by way of Wilmington, Christiana Bridge—some that the whole of the Maryland and Delaware Line were cut off, others that a few escaped. Yesterday afternoon I received an account of this Matter from General Patterson in writing, it is the most favorable of any, and yet too shocking for an American ear. He thus relates it, "The sixteenth of August at night General Gates marched to surprise General Cornwallis at Camden. The enemy also marched the same night to surprise General Gates. The Armies by their scouts discovering each other, lay on their arms till day. That the two armies then met within eight miles of Camden, when the whole engaged; that our people drove the enemy and took two field-Pieces. That then, which I think is unlikely, nine hundred of our Militia went off the field, which the enemy seeing, Rallied, being then much superior, and a most bloody engagement came on with Bayonets. That our people in confusion were surrounded. The Maryland Line, which I suppose includes the Delawares, cut off all—General De Kalb supposed to be killed, General Smallwood killed—General Gist killed—Colonel Gunby killed—General Gates, with persuasion brought off by his aids—Said about four hundred only escaped, besides the above Militia." These accounts have filled the people in General here, who are friendly to the Cause, with deep concern, but it is impossible to paint the distress of those who have friends and connections in that little and brave Band of Officers.—I wish you would furnish me with the particulars of this affair as fully as possible—Indeavour to know whether Johnny Willson has fell or not—Sally is greatly distressed and I think she could not suffer much more if he certainly has. Your situation is such that I am disappointed in your not writing to me on a matter of such importance before now.

444
From Thomas Rodney

Wilmington Sept: 5th 1780.

I wrote you an Account of the Battle to the Southward as the inteligence came to hand, which was intended to be sent by Mr Hill who was at Dover about his wheat, but he went by without my seeing him, and the first Opertunity I had afterwards was by Mr Coakley, who (as I was inform'd by Mr

Baning & Pryor) did not git down Till yesterday tho he said he should be down the day before—The Accounts at that Time were very Uncertain & I waited with great Anxiety to git a more perfect account before I sent of my Letter Knowing very well that the friends and relations of the Dalawares would be greatly distressed on hearing the wild and extravagant reports then Circulating—Since I wrote last Col: Ramsey has been in this Town—Says he Saw Genl Gates letter to Congress—That it Contain'd only a very Uncertain Account of the Action for when our Line Charged the Enemy with fixed Baynets (which was done by the Line with Such Success that they got several pieces of the Enemies Artilery) the Malitia got into disorder and the Genl retiring to Rally them the Brittish Horse Took advantage of their confusion, broke through the line and Routed them & the Genl being thus Seperated from the Army in the heat of Action was pursued by a party of Horse 24 or 25 Miles, which was the reason he Could give no certain Account How it Terminated But expected from the Circumstances mentioned that they were Totally Routed. Some Gentlman (said to be one of the Engineers) has passed up since (but I did not see him) who says that there were only 900 of Our Regular Troops Engaged in the Action, that some where between four and five hundred of these were Killed and Taken prisoners, and that the rest made a safe retreat and that in Killed the Brittish suffered much more than Our Army. That the remainder of the Army which was the greater part, Baggage, Artilery, &c were in the rear 20 or 30 miles. I have some hope the Dalawares were among these but cannot learn particularly—These favourable Accounts are much increased in Credit by the Accounts Doctr or Parson Montgomery gives—He left the Army the 3d of August, 70 miles from Camden; and says that the whole of the Different Detatchments & the Main Army Consisted of Ten Thousand Men, that they had been scant of provisions but were then plentifully supply'd and in very High Spirits—That there was only three Brittish Regiments in Carolina—That one of them was in Charles Town and Two with Lord Cornwallace—the Rest of his force (Except some Cavalry) was Refugees and Tories. This I had from himself—That you may have all the intelegence that has come to hand at this Time I have inclosed you the Baltimore paper of the 29th Ult.—There is a Schooner here which arrived the end of last week in Seven weeks and five Days from Nants & L'Orient by which several packets and a great Number of Letters for Congress, The French Minister, Consul, and Commanders, as well as to Many Gentlemen and Merchants all of which we forwarded by Express on Saturday to, as afsd The passengers (several gentlemen) that Came in this Vessel inform us that the Brest part of the second Division of the French fleet with five thousand men On Board Sailed before they did, and were to be Joined in some Certain

Lattitude &c by the other 6 or 8 Ships of the Line from Toulon which had also Sailed, but they saw nothing of them on their Passage—The disturbances in England, Ireland and Scotland still rage in such a manner that the King has thought proper to Secure himself in the Castle of Winsor—And their was a report in France when this Vessel sailed that he had fled to Hanover—

Wednessday 6th

This day I shall set of To Philad? probably by Mr Baning. Shall have an Opertunity of writing you more particularly of the late Action.

P.S. I Just mention to You That Mr Montgomery Informs us that the Dalaware Officers have been greatly distressed for want of Cash, and we are now Seting afoot a Subscribtion in this place to Send them by way of Present (by Mr Montgomery as the first Safe Opertunity) an immediate Supply of Cash, I would ask that some Active Whigs would promote the Same thing in Kent & Communicat the same to Sussex—Mr Rumford & my self have subscribed Two thousand Dollars for this purpose and suppose others will follow in proportion &c—Robisson not come yet—

445
From Thomas Rodney

Wilmington Sept: 6th 1780

Since I closed my Letter to day Capt? Robisson Has arrived Safe in this port with a full Cargo Chiefly beat Sugars, in twenty Two days from Port Oprince[1] —He Sailed with Twenty Two Sail of the Line French and parted with them a few days ago in Latitude 38 bound for Rhode Island—I have nothing material to add at present—

N.B. I Omitted to inclose the Maryland paper as mentioned in My other Letter but have inclosed it in this—If you cant Come up you will Send directions what shall be done with your Share of Robissons Cargo—

446
To Timothy Pickering[2]

Dover Sep:. the 12th 1780

Some three or four days ago I received Your Letter of the 24th Ult?., informing me that you had appointed Donaldson Yates Esq:., of the Eastern Shore of Maryland to be deputy Quarter master for the States of Delaware and Maryland, and requesting the approbation of the executive Authority, so far as the

---

1 Port au Prince.   2 Quartermaster-General of the Continental Army.

appointment respected this State—In answer to that part of your Letter I have inclosed you a Copy, from the Minutes, of the President & Privy-Council's determination—I very much approve of Your plan with respect to the Transportation of Supplies from this State, therefore if his Excellency the Commander in Chief Shall Think proper to countermand his order as to the place of deposit, except the article of Wheat to be Manufactured into flour, and you will make that known to me, I will immediately give orders to the receivers to forward the Supplies to Trenton—I shall issue orders to the receivers concerning the Article of Horses.

447

To Thomas Rodney

Dover, Sept. the 12th, 1780.

The inteligence gained from the Southward by your late letters, has tended, almost totally, to remove the deep Concern the people here were under for the American Army in General and for their friends in particular, for certainly the first accounts of that Matter were dreadful. But our information, by those letters, of the arrival of so great a number Capital Ships has surpassed our most sanguine expectation, and lead us now to expect something Grand, Glorious and Decisive. We impatiently wait a confirmation of this, and that his Excellency the Commander in Chief has begun his Operations—With respect to my part of the St. Patrick's Cargo, as I cannot possibly go to Wilmington, would wish to have it sold and the money arising therefrom carried to my account with the Ship's husband, Mr. Rumford, so that I may have it ready to employ again in that or any other concern we may hereafter set on foot. I continue to be much afflicted with the Asthma, Crowded with public business and without either Secretary or Clerk. My love to Betsey and the Children and be pleased to make my Compliments to the gentlemen of Wilmington. I have experienced in most of them very striking marks of friendship and esteem.

448

From Thomas Rodney

Wilmington Sept: 12th 1780.

I wrote you at Philad? by M? Baning and then mentioned that the Dalawares were not in the Action to the Southerd which I was convinced of then by the best information I could git in Philad? but by the inclosed Copy of a Letter from Capt? Hugon of one of the Maryland Regiments it appears Other-

wise—Tho in other respects his Acct seem very inaccurate and uncertain—
He does not mention what persons are killed or wounded, nor who, nor what
number has escaped; and by his manner of expresseion it is Uncertain
Whether only one Captn or more are made prisoners, but I suppose only one;
and as he has mentioned the officers (at least the number) made prisoners I
should supposed he would have Mentioned those that were killed if he had
known of any—His Letter is dated the 22d and Governor Caswells the 23
whose account I Mentioned in my last—We make no doubt but in a few days
we Shall have a particular Account of this Matter from Some of Our Officers—

25 Baggs of Coffee—25 Baggs of Cocoa & 2 Baggs of Cotton of the Genl
Gates Cargo Came in by the St Patrick—Both Cargos were Divided to Day
among the Owners and your Share was Left in the hands of Mr Rumford and
he wishes to have your directions about it—

We are informed that a Certain Donaldson Yates of Maryland is appointed
A.Q.Master for this State as well as Maryland which (If I recollect the plan
of Congress) is inconsistant with it—And as the Citizens of this State git very
few appointments out of it I think it is but Just they Should have the benefit
of those in it unless no fit person Could be found—I believe There is Several
fit persons in the State that would accept of this appointment but I shall only
mention Captn Kain and would wish if this matter is not already Settled by
the Executive of this State in whose power it Chiefly is, that our own Citizens
might have a preference in this matter I have no doubt it is in your power to
do what you think best—as you know Captn Kain I shall only ad this that being a very Modest man he is Too backward to Apply himself—

It was reported here to day that you have recd a letter from Major Patton,
if its so we Shall be glad to hear what he writes—It is very healthy up here; as
Mr [?] Informs You are unwell and that it is sickly down there I would wish
you to come up and Stay a while—And if you Could git Molley to Keep House
Salley Could Come with You—We are Now Some better Settled and begin
to live as if residenters of the place—Hitherto our business has been done to
the Satisfaction of all Concerned and we have already made a Comm. of
£10,000, & business increasing—

449
From Thomas Rodney

Wilmington Tuesday Eveng Septr 12th 1780.

I wrote to you Yester[day] by Captn Caldwell—But just now have seen the
last paper in which is a full Acct of the unlucky Action to the Southward—It
Contains a letter from Genl Gates to Congress, a letter from Col. Sumpter,

a letter from Govenor Nash, and a letter to Gen! Washington from Gen! Gates with an Acc! of the Killed, Wounded, Missing and Prisoners, of the officers, which paper if the post Comes in Time I mean to send you by Capt! Stedham who I Expect will Carry this Tomorrow morning, but least the post Should not Come (the paper I saw belonged to a Maryland Gentleman) I shall inform you as to the Dalawares—They are in one respect very happy for there is not one officer among them Killed, wounded or Missing. But Eight of Them are Prisoners Viz. Col. Vaughan, Major Patton, Capt! Rhoads Capt! Larmouth, L! Duff, Skillington, Purvis & Ensign Roach; The Rest are among those who have fortunately escaped the perils of this disaster—Gen! De Calb, Capt! Williams & Duval, L! Coleman & Donovan of the Marylanders are Killed—Capt! Somerville, Gibson & Roun—L! Duval, Sears & En. Fickle of the same are wounded—and a Considerable number of Field officers &c (but no gen! officers) Taken Prisoners—Cornwallace had upward of five hundred Killed and Wounded Gen! Gates Says. Also that he Continue at Camden— That our army was increasing fast &c Several letters in the paper avow the French fleet (of Eighteen 18 Ships of the line beside frigates) are on our Coast Towit have passed by McTomkin &c by Capt! Steadham have sent you Seven doz limes part of a barrel Capt! Robisson made a present of to the Owners—

450
From Thomas Rodney

Wilmington Sept! 13th 1780.

The Owners of the S! Patrick are very desirous of Sending her Out again and therefore have requested that I would mention this matter to your self and some of the Gentlemen of the Council if necessary—The present imbargo it is well known was particularly required of this State by Congress; and that requisition complied with by the Legislature Contrary to their own Judgment, and therefore they Left Sufficient powers in the hands of the Executive to Mitigate the hardships of the imbargo whenever the reasons which induced Congress to ask it were done away—The reasons congress have generally avowed in favour of the imbargo is the fear of a Scarcity, and the fear of provisions falling into the hands of the Enemy—As to a Scarcity we know here that the millers are offering flower for sale that there is not money to purchase, and further that to great quantaties of wheat are offered them, that one of them said a few days ago he had been under the necessaty of refusing Eight thousand bushells for want of money—This is a Sign of general plenty however a scarcity may appear in any particular part—and as to its falling into the hands of the Enemy, this Concerns the owners nearly as well as the publick but they are very little apprehensive while the fleet of our Allies is superior to the Enemy—It is generally acknowledged that the riches and prosperity of our State in a peculiar manner greatly depends on Trade—Therefore the owners of the S.! Patrick think they may claim some favour in Consideration of their anxious endeavours to promote Trade and especially as they have been often unsuccesful and yet have Continued there endeavours—And shew'd by some little Successes how advantageous their endeavours are, not only to themselves but Hundreds of others—I might mentioned that this is the only Sea vessel belonging to the State—And that a Stranger Yea an Enemy, I mean the Bur-mudian, has lately recd as great favour of Congress itself, as these owners now ask, tho with submission in my opinion he very little deserved it—And it Also may be mentioned that the present imbargo is so Contrary to the Interests of the people of this State, that they sell under the rose great quantaties of flower down the River to the Outward bound Vessels—but as it is disgraceful to a people to make laws and brake them—the owners of this Vessel are desirous of Acting According to Law only—I would not have Troubled you with the mention of so many things which was previously known to you but that it Seems to be my peculiar duty from my situation in Governm't to be in a par-ticular manner the Patron of Trade and Commerce; And I believe there are very few Gentlemen of sense among us who are not well apprised of the ad-vantages arising from it to this State. And therefore I Trust when every thing is fully Considered by the Executive power they will see no impropriety in permiting the Owners of this Vessel to Load her out again agreeable to their petition—

N.B. If necessary you may shew this letter to the Council as I had not time to write to any of them on the matter—

P.S. Perhaps it may not be amiss to mention that in a few days we shall have Twenty thousand Dollars Subscribed here as a present to be sent immediately to the officers of the Dalaware Reg.! which will no doubt be subject to the dis-position of any Gen.! plan for their benefit

451
To Messrs. Adams, Clerk, and Rumford

Dover Sep.! the 15th 1780.

I this moment received by Express your application for a permission from the President and privy-Council to send out, with two hundred barrels of Flour, the Schooner S.! Patrick—I know your anxiety as well for the advantage of the State as for your own private emolument and do, as much as you possi-bly can, disapprove the scheme of embargoes—But as the General Assembly, knowing the disadvantage that this peice of policy laid the inhabitants of this State under, have, upon the requisition of Congress passed an Act for that purpose, I cannot think of voting for a suspension of the Act in favour of the owners of the St Patrick, or any other private purpose. More especially in a case Where I am personally Concerned—Therefore cannot see the propriety of calling the Privy [Council] to do an Act I disapprove myself tho interested— Be assured Gentle?. I shall always be ready to serve you and the State When I find it consistant with the duty of my Station, and am very sorry I cannot in this case think my self at Liberty to grant your request

452
From Samuel Huntington

Philad^a September 16, 1780.

Your Excellency will receive herewith enclosed an Act of Congress of the 15. Instant, requesting the several States therein mentioned to furnish Beef for supplying the Army in Proportion as expressed in the Act.

You will observe that three of the eastern States are requested to furnish one thousand Head of Cattle weekly. This will supply the Army through the present Campaign, after those Cattle shall begin to arrive at Camp; but in the mean Time for an immediate Supply, the State of Delaware is requested with all possible Despatch to furnish five Hundred & thirty Head of Cattle

The Army have been without Meat for several Days at different Times, a Situation too distressing & alarming in its Consequences to be again suffered to take Place

If the Requisitions contained in this Act be complied with by the several States, there will be no future Want of Meat for the Army this Campaign; but should they fail of a Compliance the most fatal Consequences must ensue

I am therefore to request in the strongest Terms that the Number of Beeves required from the Delaware State may be forwarded with as little Delay as possible, and flatter myself that from the pressing Necessity of the Case, that State will without Loss of Time comply with the present Requisition.

453
From Nicholas Van Dyke[1]

September 16th 1780

Your Excellency has or soon will receive an Application from Congress requesting an immediate supply of 500 Head of Beef Cattle; the same request

1 Member of Congress from Delaware.

has been made on Pennsylvania & Newjersey; the army at present is very near being without Meat, owing to the Change in the Quarter Master's Department having caused some Delay in forwarding Supplies of that Article from the Eastward; the wheels are now beginning to move & I hope our Army will not again be reduced to such distress, they have a tollerable supply of flour, but it will be very necessary that the Several States exert themselves in sending forward Flour, & short Forage while the Navigation is open & the Roads good; I informed Congress that our Assembly at their last Sessions, had in Compliance with the Requisition from Head Quarters made Provision for to supply the Cattle required, monthly—and under that it was probable some Cattle might soon be procured;—pray Sir urge the Purchasers or Collectors of Supplies in the respective Counties to an immediate Exertion, to procure the Cattle; and send them forward, even 1, or 200 in a Drove; could Mr Blane have Notice when any Number can be at Wilmington he would convey them from thence; under the Act of Assembly refered to, if my Memory serves me, Cattle were to be purchased & Certificates given for them, or seised, or to be Received in lieu of the Monthly Tax, it is necessary they be procured either one or other Ways, I shall endeavor to have the Expence of driving paid by Mr Blane or the Quarter Master as soon as possible—I can give you nothing New, I write in a hurry, the City is very sickly—but not so mortal as sickly—by late Accounts from the South'ard, our Force is more respectable than ever, and in a fair Way to drive & beat Cornwallis by defeating him, & not by being defeated, it is pretty clear that such another Victory would ruin his Lordship—

454

To Peter White[1]

Dover Septr. the 22d 1780.

Since sealing up the packet herewith sent, I had the Honor of Receiving your Letter of the 20th instant, with the inclosures by Captn. Warrington—I am Sorry to tell you that Coll. Pope has delivered up the Armed Vessel he commanded for the protection of our River Trade, so that the plan, so necessary to the Safe Transportation of the supplies from this State, Supplies without which the Army cannot do, Seems to be totally defeated by the Whim or obstinacy of some Gentlemen in your Town—However let them answer that matter to the General Assembly who I think wisely advised the Measure for protecting the Bay and River—Finding the Guns could not be had at Lewis I wrote by Col! Pope to the members of the Board of War on that head, Who

---

1 Receiver of Supplies for Sussex County.

Thought it necessary and would have furnished him with them had it been in their power, but as it was not, the Col! was under the Necessity of giving up the Vessel, as it would have been dangerous attempting to keep the Bay without them—Upon the Whole you are, in our present [situation?] . . . from time to time keeping in View the Act Constituting you[r] Authority— The call of the Army for the several Articles of Supply is so extreemly pressing that a failure in forwarding them is likely to be attended with the most dreadfull consequences, this you will find to be the case by the Copies of letters inclosed to you, therefore think it advisable to attempt the sending them forward at all events—Until further orders the supplies of Indian Corn and other Short forrage is to be delivered at Wilmington, to Donaldson Yeates Esq[uire] the deputy Quarter Master General, or to his deputy *there,* who will give Rects upon the delivery—The letters in the packet herewith sent will point out, in the Strong[est] Terms, the necessity for your immediately forwarding Beef-Cattle.

455
From William Moore[1]

In Council Sept.br 23. 1780

The Bearer hereof Mr Thomas Denton having engag'd a quantity of Wheat in Maryland to be ground into Flour in this State for the Use of the Army— I am to beg the favour of Your Permission for it's Passage through the Delaware State into this State for the Purposes aforesaid

456
To Thomas Rodney

Dover, Sept. the 25th, 1780.

I am much obliged by the letters lately received from you, more especially the one inclosed from Kirkwood[2] which has fully satisfied us with respect to the Delaware[s]. I wrote you a few days ago respecting my share of the St. Patrick's cargo, since when I am informed some of the articles are rather too low. If so, would have Mr. Rumford to delay the sale of such—however upon

1 Vice-President and later President of the Supreme Executive Council of Pennsylvania. He lived from 1735 to 1793.

2 When Lieutenant-Colonel Vaughan and Major Patten were captured by the British at the Battle of Camden, August 16, the Senior Captain of the Delaware Regiment, Robert Kirkwood, became the commanding officer of the remnants of that force and continued in active command until the end of the war He was brevetted Major, September 30, 1783

the whole would wish him to do what he thinks will be most for my advantage, whether it be to sell immediately or to delay the sale.

P.S.:—The first certain information you get of the arrival of the French fleet let me know it. My views are turned that way.

457

From Thomas Rodney

Wilmington 27th 1780[1]

Since I wrote you last I have had a very severe spell of sickness and am but just now got able to Crawl about again—By going [to] Philadª I got the fever —which has prevail[ed] so universally there that it has been almost like the plague only not so Mortal—Betsy too has had the Ague very severely, but one Comfort With us was that the Children have been very healthy—And as nobody here yet has take the French Fever as it is called, but Those Who have been at Philadª I hope it will not affect any of My family—You will conclude I have Not been in a situation to hear Much inteligence Indeed I was unable to Converse with numbers of gentlemen who Called to see Me Till yesterday —when I began to recover My Abilities a little—By Mr Gidder I am informed that Admiral Rodney with Ten ships of the line is arrived at New York. he says he saw a Captn Thomson who was a prisoner a while on board the Admirals ship, that he heard the Admiral declare he would either Loose his own fleet or Destroy that of the French. But the second Division of the French is not arrived yet and it is Conjectured by some they Only intendd to decoy Rodney here & then to fall on the Windward Islands in his Absence—Others think the French will perform but little—As to the Expedition against N. York it seems Given up—The Malitia are ordered home But The Genl and Army has Crossed North River and the Genl has Gone to Meet the French Commanders to Consult on future Operation. Whether they May be directed to the southward or where Uncertain—Our hopes has been in Activity because our Calamities require dispach. But the French policy seems grounding the war on Finance in hopes to ware Great Brittian Out with the Expence—But to our great distres Our Finances fails few tests

One of the Old. Delawares Who brought Genl DeCalbs Bagage at the late Action to the southward and passed by here yesterday to the board of War Called to let Me know that Captn Wilson to Whose Company he belonged, was very well when he left him at Salsburry but he had not pen Ink or paper to write. But was in as high spirits as a sodier without Money or Cloaths

---

1 The month was in all probability September

Could well be & so were they all, and seem'd happy as he says They expressed themselves, That they Brittish Could Take nothing more from them because they had it not to loose—To day a second mesenger Called on Me from the southern Army—says he left our officers all well, deliver'd me a letter from Col: Vaughan to his Wife which I hope you will have sent forward to her with Care—By these informants I learn that the force to the Southward was increasing very fast—That They had saved fourteen pieces of fine Artilery and a plenty of Amunision from the late disaster—That the North Carolina Malitia had turned Out And behaved with great Spirit since the late Action—That the greatest Vigalence and bravery seemed to inspire all the forces to recover their fortunes in that Quarter—

As Mr Mark McCall will perhaps hand you this with Col: Vaughans letter & One from the President of Congress I take this Opertunity of Mentioning to you that he has An Intention of Making Application to the State of Pensylvania for the Surveyor General Ship of that state and therefore desires a few lines of Recommendation from You to the President of that state which would no doubt be of Great service to him on this Application—I believe that No person of Equal abilities will apply for that office and he has some friends of Influence who will be in his favour. If he can git sufficient Recommendations from below to enable them to press the Matter in his favour—without which being a stranger and having No influence of his own in that state he will not Come in Competition with those who have.

You will see in Saturdays paper an insidious publication Trumped up by Mr Murry the Modian [?] and some wicked ones about this Town—with the pretence of Injuring Rumford but with a More Vilianous & insidious intention of injuring You & My self—Rumford has sued the [Modian?] on the occasion and a full investigation of this Matter will be made To find out those who are Concerned with him, who will not escape being Called to a Strict Account—There is No Conduct nor Merrits can avoid the Censures of the wicked—And especially the friends of America May always expect the Ill offices of Traitors & Enemies—But as to our business Which is much Grudged by some low lived Villians it has been transacted with the greatest integrity and so that No Exceptions can be Made & so shall be while I am Concerned—

This fever that I have had, has the dreadful Property of benuming as it were all the senses, and I feel My self so weak yet in that respect that I do not know whither I have wrote this Lettur so that you Can read it an understand it—

P.S. The day after I was Taken sick my Horse run of and have Not heard of him since. If he has got down below please to have him Taken Care of and send up by first opertunity

458

From Samuel Huntington

Philadª October 7, 1780.

I am directed by Congress to inform you that a Letter has been received from the Commander in Chief at Head Quarters, representing, that "the Army must again be reduced to Extremity for Want of Flour except a Supply should arrive in a few Days." As the Quota expected from the State of Delaware has not yet been forwarded, it is the earnest & most pressing Request of Congress that the same may be sent on with all possible Despatch.

459

From Thomas Rodney

Wilmington Octr 7th 1780

Since the last paper which Mr Brown Carried down, we have not hear'd any thing material here—Captⁿ McCannon[1] of the Dalaware Regiment has Come home to procure Cloathing for them, but I have not Seen him—It is likely, if he has not been already, that he will be with you next week—Captⁿ Bennet Informed me that he saw him on Munday but did not Learn any thing particular from him more than we had before except that he says the officers Take no notice of Gates—I forgot to send you by Brown a list of the members for this County—Viz. Councillor Doctr McDonagh assemblymen, Geo. Read, Nichs Vandike, Duff, Doctr Clayton, Lattimer, Wm Clark & Thos Montgomery, but it is probable you have had their names some other way before this—

We are all very well now but Betsy who cannot git quite Clear of the ague but is better—

I have not heard of my Horse yet and begin to fear he was stolen by some of the Straglers of the Maryland Regiment which went to the Southward about the time he went off—

N.B. the proffits on the Cargo of the schooner will neat about £80,000"0"0— after deductg the price of the Vessel, Cargo, & all Expences

---

1 William McKennan was promoted to Captain in 1781. In that year he enrolled recruits in Delaware for the Delaware Regiment, which troops were, however, ordered to Yorktown and participated in the siege of that town. Afterwards he led the troops to the southward where they joined the Delaware Battalion under Robert Kirkwood.

460
To Thomas Rodney

Dover, Oct. the 9ᵗʰ 1780.

My natural enemy, the Asthma has continued so close a seige ever since I left Wilmington & has acted so powerfully as to reduce me very low. However, from present appearances, I am led to believe you will see me at Wilmington on Monday next, at farthest & that to dinner. Mr. Magaw rides up with me & preaches at Appoquinimin next Sunday on his way there. This morn⁅ I rec'd your letter of the 7ᵗʰ inst. Capt. McKennan was with me on his way from the Southward & has given me a full acc't of the place—The battle & the present situation, temper & disposition of the troops as also of his arrant here. . . .

461
Commission of Nehemiah Tilton

Delaware State &c

To all whom it may Concern

Know Ye That I Caesar Rodney Esquire President, Commander in Chief &c of the Delaware State aforesaid Do hereby Nominate and appoint Nehemiah Tilton Esquire, Lt Coll in the Militia, Flag Officer to meet a Flag of Truce, now in Mispillion Creek, from New York, committed to the management of a certain Benjamin Galway. Trusting that said Nehemiah Tilton will inquire into the design and purport of the said Flag, and Do there in That Which of Right ought to be Done—

Given under my hand and Seal, at Dover, the Sixteenth day of October Anno Dom One Thousand, Seven hundred and Eighty.

CAESAR RODNEY

462
From Samuel Huntington

Philadelphia November 2. 1780

Your Excellency will receive herewith enclosed the Copy of an Act of Congress of the 25. Ulto, recommending to the respective States to exert their utmost Endeavours to furnish their Troops with Cloathing on the Terms formerly mentioned

463

From Silas Snow

Flat Bush long Island November 8th, 1780

Major Hodgson, and myself have again applyed to Your Excellency & Assembly for releaf, in our present distresses I hope You will not think us troublesome, when you have a particular account of our Sufferings from Captain Moor to whom I refer you and now must beg leave to trouble you with one request more, which is, that You would Give a Certificate directed to our Commissary General of prisoners acknowledging me to be a Captain taken in Actual service, provided you (from your knowledge of my services booth before and at the very time of my being taken) Should think it just, that I should be considered as in Service, such a Certificate would shortly effect my exchange, and put me on equal ground with Other prisoners, I am happy that I have to make this Request to a person so well acquainted with my services, principals, and conduct, and in whose Justice I have the greatest Confidence

464

From Ephraim Blaine

Philada 20th November 1780—

I take the liberty of addressing you upon the Subject of Supplies for our Army and am sorry to inform you I have been exceedingly disappointed in my Expectations from your State—The quantity of Provisions required is very small, and no State in the Union can furnish the requisitions of Congress with the same ease—Very little of the last Years Supplies have been furnish'd and I have been informed your Legislature have adjourn'd until the latter end of January next without doing any thing Effectual towards furnishing the Supplies due & preparing for the present—and that they have taken off the Embargo and given full liberty for exporting Flour, which will not only deprive yourselves but your neighbouring States from being able to procure their Quotas—

In the requisitions for the ensuing year a quantity of Salt Provisions is required from your State, and without the States are punctual in procuring the Salt Provisions in due Season the Army cannot be fed thro' the ensuing Summer—

I know it is your desire to see ample Provisions made for the Support of our Troops, and I beg & entreat your Excellency to adopt every possible measure to comply with the triffling demand made upon your State—your Salt

Provisions ought to be procured in the Season when Beef and Pork are plenty—

[Endorsement]
From the Commissary Gen!
dated Novem.br 1780. 20th
To be laid before the General
Assembly—
Urging the speedy furnishing of Supplies

465
From Mordecai Gist

Baltimore 20 Novemr 1780

I beg leave to Address your Excellency & thro' you sir, the General Assembly of your State, on the subject of General Green's requisition,[1] and in pursuance of my Orders to press its speedy & effectual execution. The General has further Instructed me to appoint places of rendezvous for the Troops to be raised in your State, and to acquaint Your Excellency therewith, that the Recruits may have directions where to Assemble. an Officer at each place will be appointed to Inspect them as they arrive, and I am particularly charg'd to give them positive directions not to receive any Recruits in the Service, whither by Draught, or voluntary Inlistment, unless they are above Five Feet Four Inches High, of a good sound Constitution perfect in their Limbs, and under Fifty Years of Age.

As the Stores under the direction of the Board of war, are incompetent to furnish the Necessary Clothing for your Troops, I beg leave to hint the Necessity of procuring them with all possible disspatch, that the March of the Troops (when raised) may not be impeded.

466
Addressee unknown

Dover Novr 28th 1780

I have with this wrote on one sheet of paper inclosed you the Copy of a Letter from his Excellency General Washington to Congress and Congress's

1 For recruits to fill up the depleted ranks of the Delaware Regiment as a result of the Battle of Camden, August 16, 1780 General Nathanael Greene had been sent south by Washington to take command of the southern department following the flight of General Gates from the battlefield of Camden.

Resolution thereon, A Copy of a Letter from the Honorable the Board of War and an Extract of one from the Commissary General of purchases, urging the necessity of forwarding Supplies for the use of the army, and of makeing proper & regular Return of them agreably to the directions of Congress and the General Assembly of this State—The above mentioned letters point out in so clear a manner the necessity of the utmost exertion on your part that nothing need be added, did not the dreadful consequences of a neglect impress me to it—Permit me therefore to beg you will no longer delay this most necessary business, and, as you value the Cause in which [we] are engaged, loose not moment of time that can be avoided—Let there be no more Cause of Complaint.

467
From David Hall[1]

Lewes, December 9th 1780

I have sent back Sergts Wilson & Edenfield as there is no necessity for detaining them at this post—

The Act of Assembly made for the relief of those concerned in the late Insurrection allows the married persons that inlist the Liberty of hiring a Substitute & have time given therein until the 10th of February for that purpose so that we cannot in Justice march them from this post agreeable to your Instructions. The number inlisted amounts to thirty six exceeding fine Recruits and I do not apprehend there will be near the danger of their deserting by detaining them here as if they were removed.

468
From O. H. Williams[2]

Camp Charlotte 18th Decemr 1780

I have the Honor to Inclose you an Abstract of Muster and Inspection of the Delaware Troops for the Month of November last

The Troops are very bare of Cloathing and there is no prospect of geting a Supply for them in this Country.

The long absence of Col Hall and the Capture of the other Field Officers is a real disadvantage to the Delaware Regiment

1 Although Colonel Hall never went south to join his regiment on account of old wounds received at the Battle of Germantown, he was active at Lewes in securing recruits.

2 Otho Holland Williams, Major, Stephenson's Maryland and Virginia rifle regiment; Colonel, 6th and 1st Maryland regiments; Deputy Adjutant-General, Southern Army, Brigadier-General and Assistant Inspector-General, Continental Army.

469

From Lewis Nicola[1]

Philadelphia, January 6th 1781

An Edward Delany, a recruit enlisted to serve in the corps raised by the Delaware State for four months,[2] & who deserted, applied to me to procure his discharge on repaying a thousand pounds bounty he had received. I informed Col Neil of the offer & he chose to accept it & sent me a discharge to be given to Delany on his paying the money to me, which has been done & notice thereof sent to the Colonel but as the money has not been called for I apprehend this transaction, which hapened in September last, has been forgot. I therefore think it proper to give your Excellency notice thereof & that the money is still in my hands at your disposal.

470

From Samuel Huntington

Philadelphia January 9. 1781

You will receive herewith enclosed, Copies of two Acts of Congress of the 5th & 8th Instant

By the former you will be informed that from the unwarrantable & cruel Treatment which our People who are Prisoners with the Enemy have received from them, in the Opinion of Congress an Exercise of the Law of [? is] recommended to the Executive of the States respectively to take effectual Measures for carrying into Execution the Acts of Congress of the 13th of January 1780 respecting Prisoners taken by the Citizens Troops or Ships of particular States

By the other (of the 8th Instant) it is earnestly recommended to the several States from New Hampshire to North Carolina inclusive to procure for the Use of the Officers in Captivity at New York & on Long Island, to be charged to the United States, their respective Quotas therein mentioned in Specie or Bills of Exchange on New York

It is presumed the Necessities of those Officers, the Distresses they have already suffered, & the more disagreable Situation they must yet be reduced to for want of the Means of Subsistence, unless those Supplies are obtained, [will] be sufficient to induce a Compliance with this Requisition as speedy as possible

1 Colonel, Invalid Regiment.
2 The Second Delaware Regiment which was stationed in Kent County, Maryland.

471

Message to the General Assembly[1]

Gentlemen of the General Assembly

Since your last adjournment divers acts of Congress and other papers which claim the attention of the Legislature of this State, have been transmitted to me. I have therefore directed the Secretary to lay them before your Honors for your Consideration, to wit, An Act of Congress, of the 30th of October last, containing the appointment of Major General Green to the Command of the Southern Department and asurtaining the powers vested in him by Congress with a recommendation to the several States from Delaware to Georgia inclusive to afford him all necessary aid & assistance—a Letter from General Green of the 10th of November last, with a requisition for aids of men and money from this State and also for Supplies of Provisions, for the Southern Army, together with a Letter from General Gist of the 20th following on the same subject—An Act of Congress, of the 25th of October last, recommending to the several States to furnish their Quota of Troops with Clothing on the Terms expressed in former Resolutions of Congress on this Subject—A circular Letter from Congress of the 9th of November, with an Act of the 4th preceeding, recommending to the several States to Levy their several proportions of a Tax Equal in value to six millions of Silver Dollars to be paid partly in the specific article therein enumerated and the residue in Gold or Silver or Bills of Credit emitted pursuant to the Resolution of the 18th of March last— And also an extract of a Letter from General Washington, and an Act of Congress, of the 14th of November, urging, that the Quotas of Provisions assigned to the States of Pensylvania, Delaware and Maryland, or as great a Proportion thereof as can be quickly procured, be forwarded, without loss of time, for the use of the Army—together with a Letter from the Commissary General of Provisions on the same Subject—And also an Act of Congress, of the 22d Ult? communicating extracts of two Letters, one from General Washington, and the other from Europe, and earnestly requesting, That effectual measures be speedily taken for recruiting the Army to its full compliment with the strictest punctuality, and for furnishing the supplies of Provisions & money assigned for their Support.

The several Requisitions herein before specified having in view the attainment of the grand objects of the Federal Union, I have no Doubt but your Honors will give them your most serious attention, and afford every aid in

---

1 The General Assembly met in New Castle from January 4 to February 13, 1781.

Compliance therewith, which the Abilities and Circumstances of the State will admit.

CAESAR RODNEY

New Castle 12th Jany 1781.

472
From Samuel Huntington

Philadelphia January 13. 1781

Your Excellency will receive herewith enclosed, the Copy of an Act of Congress regulating the additional Pay of Aids de Camp, Brigade Majors, Adjutants & Regimental Pay Masters—also Regimental Pay Master & Clothier.

473
From Peter White

Lewes January the 14 1781

I have inclosed you the Returns of the supplies that I have Received the three month past Which is very Trifling I expect in a month or two to have the Stores full I should be glad to no what is to be don with the Supplies on Nanticok and Broad Creek which is Taking a grat deal of Damage as the Stores are full

474
Message to the General Assembly

Gentlemen of the Assembly

In answer to your Message of the 13th instant, I beg leave to acquaint your Honors that the Receivers[1] have sent me no returns since their several appointments, except one from the Receiver of Sussex County which will be laid before you herewith, tho' strictly injoined to it by my instructions as well as by the Acts of Assembly referred to, and Therefore it is not in my power to give the House That information they wish to have relative to the collection and delivery of supplies—I believe they have collected considerable Quantities but have been much interrupted in the Transportation thereof from the Counties of Kent and Sussex by the Refugee armed Boats—The Receiver for

1 Receivers of Supplies for the army.

Newcastle County informs me that for some time past he has not been able to carry on his business for want of a supply of money.

CAESAR RODNEY

Newcastle Jan? 15th 1781

475
From Ephraim Blaine

Head Quarters New Windsor[1] 18th Jan? 1781.

I presume your Excellency has received the requisitions of Congress a considerable time ago for the Supplies of our Army this year—and that means have been adopted by your Legislature to procure them in due time—Congress have pointed out the proportions of delivery, and his Excellency General Washington the places of deposit.—The quantity of Provisions required from your State is very small and may be easily furnish'd if power is given your Agent to execute—

I need not mention to your Excellency the great punctuality there ought to be observed by these States in procuring and delivering the supplies required, and the uneasiness the want of one days provisions occasions with the soldiery, *to prevent which* I beg your Executive & Legislature to adopt such means as will fully afford the Supplies required—without which it will be impossible for me to attempt to feed the Army—the requisitions of Congress were barely calculated to support the Troops they have reason to expect in the field next campaign, from the present prospects of State supplies I dread the most fatal Consequences—the Garrison at West Point, and the Troops cantoon'd in this Neighborhood have been several days upon half allowance of Bread and have but a very temporary supply of Beef, if our Situation is such in the most plentifull season of the year and when the Army is much reduc'd—I leave you to judge what it must be next summer with twenty or thirty thousand men in the field operating against the Enemy—the consequences must undoubtedly be then disolution for want of Subsistance, without the States use tenfold exertions in procuring the Supplies.

Congress have ordered me to make monthly returns of all State supplies and for that purpose to call upon the executive of each State, have therefore to request your Excellency to give express orders to your Agent to furnish me with an accurate Return of all Supplies obtain'd from your State in the year Eighty and to whom delivered—and to make proper Monthly returns in future to my Office in Philadelphia—

1 Washington's headquarters on the Hudson, south of West Point.

When I settle the Accts of the Agent who acted for me in your State last year, I shall afford you a return of all provisions purchased on Continental Account—let no cause whatever prevent you from furnishing the Supplies demanded by Congress—

476
Message to the General Assembly

Gentlemen of the General Assembly

The Secretary will lay before your Honors for consideration, a Letter from the President of Congress dated the 9th instant with an Act of the 5th relative to the Treatment of Prisoners, and one other of the 8th Recommending it to the several States from New Hampshire to North Carolina inclusive to procure, for the use of the officers in Captivity at New York and on Long Island, their respective Quotas therein mentioned in Specie of Bills of Exchange on New-York—A Letter of the 13th instant with an Act of the 12th regulating the additional pay of the several officers therein mentioned—The Secretary will [lay] also before you a Petition from Robert Hodgson and Silas Snow prisoners on Long-Island, a Letter of the 12th Ult? from Timothy Pickering Esquire Quartermaster General, with a Resolution of Congress inclosed, and a Letter of the 20th instant from the President of Congress, requesting that this State's Quota of Flour may be forwarded to Trenton with a Resolution of Congress of the same date in Consequence of which the Letter was wrote.

CAESAR RODNEY

Newcastle January
the 25th 1781.

477
From Mordecai Gist

Baltimore 29 January 1781

My last Letter to you on the Subject of General Greenes requisition remains unanswered, from whence I conclude that the General Assembly of Your State have not yet adopted the necessary measures for granting the supplies call'd for, and as this Subject will probably engage part of their attention thro' the course of the present sessions I beg leave to hint the necessity of drawing their deliberations to a speedy & conclusive point. I am just Favor'd with a letter from General Greene wherein he directs me to inform You that the enervated State of our army in the Southern department requires your immediate assistance, and renders it indispensably necessary that some mode should be adopted for the completion of your quota of Troops and Supplies as soon as possible.

As I am order'd to remain in this department to Inspect the recruits and forward the Supplies from Delaware and Maryland, I beg Your Excellency will inform me what may be expected from Your State. I cannot doubt but the Legislature of Delaware in conjunction with those other States that compose the Southern Army will exert every power to remove that source of disappointment which has so often clog'd the operations of the American Army, & Clouded with misfortunes the Characters of her Officers.

478

Message to the General Assembly

Gentlemen of the General Assembly

I have just now received a Letter of the 18th of December last from the Assistant Inspector General of the Southern Army with a Return of the Officers belonging to the Delaware Regiment, and a Return of Clothing, Arms, Accoutrements Ammunition, &c., and have directed the Secretary to lay them before your Honors, with a Letter of the 19th from the Same person inclosing a General return of the Regiment, and a Letter of the 18th January from the Commissary General of Purchases—The Secretary will Also lay before you a Petition signed by Mrs. Elizabeth Gordon and addressed to your Honors praying that permission may be Granted to her husband, Charles Gordon, to return to his Family, and be received as a Citizen of this State, with a Letter from Joseph Nicholson Esquire, in the State of Maryland, addressed to me, to the purpose of the above mentioned Petition.

CAESAR RODNEY

Newcastle February the
    1st 1781

479

From Peter Wade

Christeen Bridge 6th Feby 1781

The Necessity of Geting in Supplies & Taking care of General Washingtons Baggage Horses are the causes of my Being thus far Troublesome.—

Donaldson Yeates Esqr D Q M has told me repeatedly that he had promises both from the Gentlemen of the Council & Assembley to have the Supplies of this State Sent in Imediately to the places of deposit. Wilmington is the Chief Magazine for that purpose, & for want of hay & Short food there, I am Obliged to Take his Excellys horses from that [place] to this, Tho' here I can not support them a day longer, Therefore Sir if you'l pleas to give me an Order on the Receiver of Supplies in Kent County to Issue Forage for use of these Horses, i'l send them down, Otherways Know not what to do.

480
To Samuel Huntington

NewCastle 15th Feb. 1781.

The General Assembly of this State, which have been sitting here about a Month past, having now adjourned to the 28th Day of May next, I deem it necessary to inform Congress of the Result of their Deliberations. The several Resolutions of Congress which have been transmitted to me from Time to Time, I have laid before them, and on Monday Evening they rose, having passed the two following Acts relative to the Business recommended by Congress—one for cancelling the present circulating Bills of Credit, and for emitting and funding new Bills according to the Resolutions of the 18th of March —and the other for recruiting the Regiment of this State; Copies of which I shall transmit you when they are printed.

The last Resolutions that were transmitted to me, recommending to the several States to pass Laws vesting Congress with Powers to levy an Impost of five per Cent on Articles imported &c. were laid before the General Assembly as soon as they were received, which they have not acted upon, but have deferred this, with other Business, to the Time to which they stand adjourned.

481
From David Hall

Lewes Feby 19th 1781—

The Receiver at this post Captain White upon application to him for provisions replied that he could not furnish any, being without money & no person would sell without having a most exorbitant price in Certificates, and our provision being by that means very scanty I have been under the necessity of permitting the Recruits to go to their respective homes & collect them every fortnight at this place, fourteen have deserted.

As the Recruits cannot remain here without provisions you will send your Instructions what shall be done with them, the Fees being undischarged I cannot make myself liable by marching them off—

If your Excellency should write to the Southward I should be glad you would communicate to the commanding officer the reason for my not joining the Regiment having remained since my leaving the Army in a bad state of Health until these few months past & since that detained by want of Cash & clothing—as I intend setting off at farthest by the first of April for the Army or sooner if I can be provided with money & clothing both of which I cannot do without, you would much oblige if you could point out to me what Method I shall take to procure the money—having received no pay for these eight or ten months past my finances are run very low and I dont know but I should get into Tortar Limbo if I should attempt to leave this place without discharging.

482

From James Booth

New Castle, 23ᵈ Feb. 1781.—

Mʳ Bedford will deliver your Excellency one hundred Copies of the act for recruiting the Regiment, which are as many as he can carry, with Convenience, of the Quotas of Kent and Sussex. Copies of the other Acts are not yet completed, nor indeed is the Transcribing of them perfected, which is the Reason why I have not transmitted those Laws, and the Commissions. This Delay I hope will not be attended with any injurious Consequences especially as you are furnished with Copies of such Laws as call your immediate Attention; and I am persuaded your Excellency will the more readily excuse it, when you are pleased to reflect that this is our Court Week, and to make it still more busy we have a Orphans Court in addition to those appointed by Law to be held now.

I have no news to communicate, unless it be the Arrival of Paul Jones at Philadᵃ, which you have no doubt heard.

483

To Samuel Huntington

Dover February the 24th 1781

I beg leave to inform Congress That, in Virtue of An Act passed the last Sitting of the General Assembly, for calling out of Circulation and cancelling the Quota of this State, according to the present apportionment, of all the Bills of Credit emitted by Congress, and for Emitting and funding new Bills according to the Resolution of Congress of the Eighteenth of March last, and for other purposes, I have, with the advice of the Privy-Council, appointed Gunning Bedford, George Lattimer, Thomas Duff, and Jacob Broom Esquires, residenters of Newcastle County, to sign and number the above mentioned new Bills—When the Act is printed, a Copy shall be sent to Congress

484
From Samuel Patterson

Xteen[1] March 1, 1781

Your favour recd by Mr John Battell. am sorry our public funds are run out. but hopes soon to be repaird and wishes Mr Battle had been paid. I am now foreclosd by a line chalkd out by the General Assbl to me to pay the supplies first for our Regmt

when that is done Mr Battell comes in. he must rest with patience, and try to bear a little with the times

Glorious news. I now send you the paper. at this place all confusion and hurry. this day is expected the Marquis de la Fayett with 1500 Troops. heavy cannon Bagage &c No provision here, pressing of Teams &c &c only 3 days Notice Bound for to seize Traytor Arnold[2]

as Mr Battell does not return directly have sent this forward to chance, which I hope will arrive before him.

[P.S.] with this I have sent a paper the French is left Virginia

485
From Samuel Huntington

Philadelphia March 2. 1781

By the Act of Congress herewith enclosed your Excellency will be informed, that the Articles of Confederation & perpetual Union between the thirteen United States are formally & finally ratified by all the States.[3]

We are happy to congratulate our Constituents on this important Event, desired by our Friends but dreaded by our Enemies—

(ENCLOSURE)

IN CONGRESS March 1st 1781.

ACCORDING to the order of the Day, the honble John Hanson and Daniel

1 Christiana Bridge.

2 Benedict Arnold was ravaging Virginia with a British force and Lafayette was sent by Washington to attempt his capture.

3 The Articles of Confederation were adopted by Congress at York, Pennsylvania, November 15, 1777, but went into effect only when the thirteenth state (Maryland) ratified them. Delaware was the twelfth state to ratify.

Carrol two of the Delegates for the State of Maryland, In pursuance of the Act of Legislature of that State, entitled "An Act to empower the Delegates of this State in Congress to subscribe and ratify the Articles of Confederation." which was read in Congress the twelfth of February last, and a Copy thereof entered upon the Minutes, did in behalf of the said State of Maryland, sign and ratify the said Articles of Confederation; By which Act the Confederation of the United States of America was compleated, each and every of the thirteen united States, from New Hampshire to Georgia, both included, having adopted and confirmed, and by their Delegates in Congress, ratified the same.

> Extract from the Minutes
> Chas Thomson jnr

486
From Thomas Rodney

Philadᵃ March 2ᵈ 1781—

Mr Pryor intending to set of in the morning have set down to mention some news that Came to hand to day—The minister of France informed Congress this afternoon That the America a 64 Gun Brittish Ship which having been blown of in the late Storm being returned To her Station in Guardners bay, & by that means the Brittish having a Superiority to the French fleet at Rhode Island it had been thought necessary to Order the Squadron back from Virgina—which he informed had Taken Six prizes one the Romulus of 44 Guns & 500 men and Two Strong Privateers from New York—By advices also recd: To say it appears that Cornwallace had passed the Roanoke River—That Col: Lee Had made an attack on a party of his Cavalry and killed 13, & taken 30 prisoners and Totaly defeated the Party—That Genl Green was Joined by 1300 malitia & 800 Rifle-men—So that great things probably may be accomplished there in a few days—I have Given my attendance all this week in Congress and have had an Opertunity of seeing how essential it is for every State to keep up their representation there—Our State will find it much more to their Interest To give Such a reasonable allowance as will enable their Delligates To Stay here, than to be un[r]epresented—Upon the Confederati[on] being Confirmed New Hamshire & Rhode Island having each but one member— therefore became unrepresented; they thought it so essential that they moved Congress to adjourn appointing a Committee of the States to Sit Till they Could be represented—I do not mention this because I wish them To enable me to stay, but because I think they ought to make it an essential point to be represented and that they may enable others to attend that I may attend my own interests at home for nothing that I would wish them to give would Compensate for my Staying. Yet I think it so necessary for the Interests of the State that I intend to give all the attendance in my power Till they git better Supplied—

Yesterday the Confederation was finally rattified and Confirmed,—At Two OClock we had a Colation at the President of Congress's—At five I Dined at Mr McKeans with the President & Vice President and Sundry members of assembly to this State and Sundry members of Congress & others—Thus you hear this Situation is not without the flattering inducements of Good Company & Good Living—But as have not yet had it in my power to git lodgings to my mind, have not yet been waited on by the Minister of France whose Custom it is to wait on every member of Congress as soon as he Takes lodgings.

As I may often Communicate to you many things which ought not to be publick I shall only request that you will always attend to such things as your own Judgment points out to be of that nature which may save me the Trouble of particularising them

N.B. I am much pleased to find that all your old acquaintances in Congress Still profess the warmest Esteem for you.[1]

487
From Peter Wade

Christeen Bridge 6th March 1781

I have found it a very Difficult Task to furnish means to forward the Troops & Stores &c for the division under the Command of the Marquis De lafayat to the Head of Elk; & the Stores are not all got over yet for want of waggons, which Delays the Troops at Head of Elk. My reason therefore for Troubling your Excellency with this is to inform you That I expect a Number of Troops this way Shortly, & find it all together Necessary to Apply to the Govenor of this State for his aid & Influence over some of the people who I find from Experience Cloak Themselves with the laws of the state, to prevent them from doing Voluntary Service in forwarding the Troops. Therefore hope Sir That if Consistant you! pleas to Clothe some person here with power to Obtain the Necessary means, for forwarding the Troops, by force of your Authority if milder Applic[a]t[i]on will not do—as undoubtedly Sir you know the Absolute Necessity there is for forwarding the Troops &c.

1 Thomas Rodney was elected a delegate to Congress together with Thomas McKean and Nicholas Van Dyke on February 10, 1781, by the General Assembly sitting at New Castle.

488
From Samuel Huntington

Philadelphia March 7. 1781

By the Act of Congress herewith enclosed your Excellency will be informed that Samuel Patterson & John Thompson—Esquires are appointed Commissioners on the Part of the United States, to endorse the Bills that shall be emitted by the State of Delaware pursuant to the Act of Congress of the 18th of March last

(ENCLOSURE)

BY

The United States in Congress Assembled.—
    March 6th 1781
RESOLVED, that Samuel Patterson and John Thompson Esqrs be appointed Commissioners on the part of the United States of America, either of them to endorse the Bills that shall be emitted by the State of Delaware pursuant to the Act of Congress of the 18th day of March 1780.

Extract from the Minutes
Chas Thomson jnr

489
From Thomas Rodney

Wilmington March 13th 1781—

The last I wrote was by Mr Pryor. This will go by Captn Kain who Goes down Tomorrow morning about provisions for the new recruits there being none of the meat kind here—

The last dispatches from the Southern Army were very favourable Ten Thousand malitia having Turned out to Support Genl Green and they kept Cornwallace So Close that no party dare venture [out from the] main body beyond his Piquets—And both [regulars and] malitia were in the highest spirits . . . had also Collected 1500 men in Corn[wallace] . . . and had been within 20 miles of . . . and destroyed great quantities of [their] Supplies & Cut of their Convoys—This was the Intelligence when I left Philada on Sunday but on my way down I meat a gentleman from Richmond (Virginia) who informed me that an express had arrived there just before he set off informing that Cornwallace had made a Shew of prepairing Timber and boats as if he intended to pass the Dan River, and leaving his Cavalry to keep up

that appearance, decamped in the night and made so rapid a retreat, with his
main body that he had got almost to Hillsborrough before our Army who were
preparing to oppose his Crossing the River discovered he was gone; but that
they had pursued him with all speed and pressed him so hard that he passed
Hilsborrow without Halting & Took a Circuitious route to avoid Marion least
his retreat should be interupted by him—For Marion after distroying the
Stores Toward Charles Town was pursuing Cornwallace as he advanced—

I informed you in my last that the French Squadron had returned from Virginia to Rhode Island again—but the . . . man Came here last night . . .
Says that there is another . . . that Arnold is now blocked . . . also brought
[aw]ay from . . .

A strong report has prev . . . past that all the American Vessel[s] . . . out
of S! Eustatia, and there are some reasons to give it credit yet many think that
it is only a finese of the merchants to raise the price of goods—If it be true it
is no publick disadvantage

The Completion of the Confederation I believe will ad greatly to the Vigor
of the exertions both of the Union and Alliance—Congress are well disposed
to be active in providing ways & means to carry on the war with Spirit,—They
find from the information of their officers that the Tender of the new money
at the same value of Specie, is a great hindrance to that Credit They could
otherwise git in purchasing Supplies and it is the general wish that they were
out of the way for it was not their desire by the Resolution of the 18th of
March that the money should be made a Lawfull Tender, at the Value of
Specie but that the States Should have Convinced the people of its value by
the Certain security of redemption—And in Connecticut where it is not a legal
Tender it is in better Credit than in Pensylvania so that you see the moderation
of Our Law will not meet the disapprobation of Congress—

I left Congress on Sunda[y] . . .

490

From Samuel Huntington

Philadelphia March 23. 1781

Your Excellency will receive herewith enclosed, two Acts of Congress of
the 16th & 23d Instant, directing that all Debts liquidated in or contracted for
Specie Value shall be paid in Specie or other Money equivalent according to
the current Exchange compared with Specie

Also recommending to the several States to amend their Laws making the
Bills of Credit emitted under the Authority of Congress a legal Tender, so

that such Bills shall not be a legal Tender in any other Manner than at their current Value compared with Gold & Silver

But, what will more particularly claim the Attention of your Legislature as of great Importance is, the Requisition for six Millions of Dollars, that is, one Million & an half of Dollars to be paid quarterly, the first quarterly Payment to be made on the first Day of June next, the Quota of each State being apportioned in the enclosed Act; and Payment to be made on this Requisition as also the several others therein referred to, in Gold or Silver or Bills emitted by any of the States whatever in Pursuance of the Resolutions of the 18th of March 1780

This Assessment is not to be considered as the Proportion of any State, but, being paid, is to be adjusted & settled with Interest in Future upon equitable Principles, in the Manner expressed in the Act

It is with Reluctance that Congress are compelled to make this Requisition, but the absolute Necessity of the Case will appear so obvious, that we presume the respective States will yield a ready & cheerful Compliance therewith to the utmost of their Power—

491

To Thomas Rodney

Dover April the 13th, 1781

I have received a Recommendation of Congress to the Executives of Delaware, Maryland and Virginia, to remove the Provisions and Forage within the Peninsula, so that they may not fall into the hands of our enemies.—If the Embarkation mentioned should take place the Enemy doubtless will have the possession of the waters of Delaware and Chesepeak and therefore have the Stores in their power unless removed to the northward of Christiana River towards the State of Pennsylvania. You and the other Delegates from this State well know the difficulty attending such a Step, in short, you know it is impossible—There is a great Quantity of Flour and Indian Corn in the Stores convenient to the Delaware, There is no doubt but that these Articles are much wanted for the use of our Army and might be soon removed by our River Vessels could they be protected against the Refugees, but Sir you know that this State can immediately, afford no such protection, nor have I in View any public Body from whom such immediate necessary Aid can be Afforded as from Congress—All that can be expected to be done by the Executive of this State will be done, but the public cannot reasonably expect impossibilities, if they do they will be deceived—Whether the Embarkation mentioned takes place or not, the Flour and Corn, I apprehend, are articles that our Army stands in great need of, and therefore worthy the greatest attention. The Receivers are oblidged to stop taking in Grain for want of Stores, such as they could procure being full—You will be pleased to communicate the contents of this Letter to the other Delegates for this State, and Act as you all shall think best for the public good.—I am in tolerable good Health and wish to hear from you often.

492

From Samuel Huntington

Philadelphia April 19. 1781.

Your Excellency will receive herewith enclosed, an Ordinance for establishing Courts for the Trial of Piracies and Felonies committed upon the high Seas, passed in Conformity to Articles of Confederation—

493

To David Hall

Dover April the 20th 1781

You will find by General Smallwood's letter addressed to me and sent to you by Captain James Moore for your perusal, The pressing necessity there is for immediately filling and Convening at a proper place, the Delaware Regiment so that they may be marched to the Southward where it is intended they shall Act—As Captain Moor is the oldest officer now in this State and belonging to the Regiment, except yourself, I have sent him to you to know whether you mean immediately to take an active part in this most important business and inform me of it, so that I may know to whom I am to issue my orders from time to time as occasion may require—My present orders are that all the soldiers belonging to the Delaware Regiment, as well those who were formerly inlisted for the war, as those inlisted in virtue of the late Act of Assembly, shall be as soon as possible convened at Christiana Bridge and there wait my orders for marching agreably to the Act. Those that hereafter may be got by the recruiting officers for the different Counties are also to be forwarded to the same place without the least delay—I am persuaded that your Attachment to the Cause and inclination to discharge your Duty will be sufficient inducements for you immediately to set about this business or commit it to such of your officers as will do it, in which from their former attachment to, and activity in this best of Causes, I may venture to say you cannot go amiss. You will be pleased to let me hear from you by Captain Moore,

494
From Thomas Rodney

Wilmington Ap! 22 [1781]

On Friday an Express boat arriv[ed from] S! Croix with the important and agreeable [news] that the Cork Fleet Consisting of One hun[dred] and thirty sails of Transports Convoy'd by three [ships of] the Line & several Frigates was Captured by a French and Spa[nish] Fleet—This acc! is brought to S! Lucia by [a ship] that says she sail[ed] with the fleet from Cork—[That] 400 leagues to the Ea[s]tward they fell in with 14 French & Spannish Ships of the Line that [the] greatest part of the Cork fleet was Captured be[fore] she Could git away, that it was with great difficulty she escaped & supposed none of the rest of the fleet unless a Chance Vessel could escape

This hapening at this Critical Time is the greatest Blow the Brittish has yet recd: and in its consiquences must cut up all their opperations in America by the roots—being in haste have nothing else of importance to mention at present—I have sent by Cole a book Containing the Constitutions of the States &? & the last papers—I must return to Congress Tomorrow—& came down but yesterday—

495
From William Livingston

Trenton 24th: April 1781

I have the honour of your Favour of the 14th instant; and am much obliged to you for those Laws of your State which it inclosed. The Act for the protection of the trade of your State on the River & Bay of Delaware, will certainly have *my more immediate attention,* as it may considerably affect New Jersey. You have taken us by the right handle, in making it our interest to protect your coast as well as our own. I hope our Legislature will not hesitate to bring our Citizens within the exemption of Salvage provisionally specified by your Law for us & Pennsylvania. The expence is trifling, & the Utility important. Indeed, abstracted from every other consideration, I think we owe it to our three most southern Counties, which are as much exposed to the armed Vessels of the Enemy, as is your State: And I have been not a little mortified that those dirty Piccaroons should hitherto have defied with impunity all the States reached by that River; and in mimickry of the Tyrant their master, who blasphemously claims the Sovereignty of the Ocean, so long have rode triumphant on the Delaware.

If you, my dear Sir, entertain a *pleasing remembrance of the many happy hours we have spent together,* I can assure you that I have not forgotten them, and among the many other reasons I have for wishing the British Plunderers to *the place from whence they came,* I rank the one of being thereby enabled to see some of my old acquaintances, & particularly of having an opportunity by a personal interview to shew you with how much attachment I am

496
From Samuel Huntington

Philadelphia April 29. 1781

Your Excellency will receive enclosed a Resolve of Congress of the 20th Instant, recommending to the several States therein named to make good the Depreciation of the monthly Pay to the Officers & Soldiers belonging to Colonel Moses Hazens Regiment, that are considered as Part of those States Quotas, in the same Manner they have made good the Depreciation to the Officers & Soldiers in the Battallions belonging to the Line of those States respectively—

497
From Samuel Huntington

Philadelphia May 19. 1781

Your Excellency will receive enclosed the Copy of a Resolve of the 17th Instant, recommending to the several Legislatures to enact Laws making further Provision (as specified in the Resolve) to guard against the Abuses & deceitful Practices of the British by making Use of Papers and Clearances they may take in American Vessels.

The Measures recommended in this, and the former Resolve of the 11th of November 1780 become the more necessary, as our Allies have not only suffered by the Deception of the British, but in several Instances our own People in the West Indies have also suffered from the French, under the Apprehension that they were British, for Want of Evidence & proper Documents to evince the contrary—

498
From Samuel Huntington

Philadelphia May 24. 1781

Your Excellency will receive enclosed, several Resolves of Congress of the 22d Instant, upon the Report of a Committee appointed to devise further Ways and Means to carry on the present Campaign

As the Measures proposed in these Resolves are the Result of Necessity after due Deliberation, it is expected the Necessity as well as the Importance of those Measures will have a suitable Impression upon the States universally, and excite them to a vigorous and punctual Compliance—

499
Message to the General Assembly[1]

Gentlemen of the General Assembly,

Since your last Sitting the following Acts of Congress, which merit your Attention, having been transmitted to me, accompanied with Letters from the President, I have directed the Secretary to lay them before your Honors, to wit, one, of the first of March last, announcing the Completion and final Ratification of the Articles of Confederation—an ordinance of the 5th of April last, establishing Courts for the Trial of Piracies and Felonies committed on the high Seas—an Act of the 20th of the same month, for making good the Depriciation in the Monthly Pay of the Officers and Privates of Col. Hazen's Regiment that are considered as Part of the Quota of the States respectively &c.—Proceedings of Congress of the 18th containing a Representation of their National affairs, the amount of the Public Debts against the United States, and the Estimates for the Current Year—One of the 18th May, recommending that Measures be taken to guard against Abuses by the British of the Papers and Clearances of American Vessels—two, of the 16th March and 22d May, on the Subject of Finance.—

The Secretary will also lay before your Honors an Act of Congress of the 16th of March appointing Commissioners to sign and number the new Bills of Credit of this State, and also a Letter from the Board of War of the 13th on the Subject of Clothing for the Recruits lately raised in this State.

CAESAR RODNEY

Dover, 28th May 1781

500
From Thomas Rodney

Wilmington May 31st 1781—

Since I returned to Wilmington there has been no news Stirring that would bare Transmitting Till lately. You will see in the paper (Carried by Col. Hall) under the London head That near five thousand Troops is said to have been ready to imbark for America—A Vessel arrived in this port the day before

---

1 The General Assembly met at Lewes from May 28 to June 19, 1781.

yesterday which left Cadis (40 miles N.W. of Gilbraltar) on the 15th of Aprill. The Capt? says that the Brittish Fleet Consisting of 27 Sail of the Line had passed by Cadis and releeved Gibraltar before he sailed—That the Spanish Fleet consisting of 32 Sail of the Line were in that part when the Brittish passed by, but as the Brittish had a greater number of heavy Ships they were a fraid To Turn out 'Till the arrival of the French which they expected—As the Capt? brought no dispatches or letters for Philad? I Sent this account to Congress—

This is the Sum of the adverse news at present—General Green's Letter and other Accounts in the paper will inform you how affairs are to the Southward.

It is now believed at Camp that the Brittish are Serious in their intention of Totally evacuating New York as it is impossible for them to hold that place, after the arrival of the Second Division without giving up all their expectations to the Southward, which They Cannot do as the fate of their navy in a great measure depends on the fate of the Carolina's—I expect To go to Congress next week from whence you will hear by the first opertunity—As much depends at this time on the Spirited exirtions of the States I hope our State will do every thing in their power

501

From James Booth

Lewes, June 6, 1781.

Whether you are engaged in Business or in Pleasure I hope you'll excuse me in obtruding one Moment on your Time in giving you an Acco! of the Session. When I came down from my Information you were expected To Day; but the Gentlemen from Kent, who arrived here on Monday, acquainted us that you would not set out 'till the last of this week. Should this be your Intention I am apprehensive your Ride will be useless, because from the present Aspect of the Business and the Disposition of the Members, every one seems convinced that the Session will end on Saturday Evening. Indeed, Necessity will compel them to compleat the Business by that Time; for I am very well assured that, unless they do, several members will assume the Power of proroguing the Legislature, I mean by running away and leaving them without a sufficient Number to compose a House. No Urgency or Importance of any Business can, I believe induce them to continue here longer than this Week. The matters they have taken up and intend to finish are these two only —An Act for supplying the Army by raising 45,000 Specie Dollars or an Equivalent in Supplies, by Tax.—And a Supplemt? Act to the Finance Law; the general Tenor of which is to make the new Bill a legal Tender only at their current Value. This Business I think they may compleat.

As to News I can have none to communicate from this Place—We are se-
cluded here from all the world; and every Person seems to have as great a
Depression of Spirits as if he was alone. I wish you were here, for at the Sessions last Spring Cheerfulness and Mirth seem'd to reign where nothing now
appears but Dulness and Dissatisfaction. Every Man looks as if he was con-
templating himself or the great Expanse of Waters before him, and some
Times commenting on the poor sandy Soil of Sussex; but when the Proportion of the Specie Doll.ᵣˢ comes to be fixed for each County, I think we shall
hear many Eulogiums on the Fertility of these same sandy Lands.

Last Night we expected an Alarm—a Refugee Boat came round the Cape in
the Afternoon and was proceeding up the Bay at a considerable Distance
from the Land, that she might, as it was thought, remain undiscovered; but
a little while before Night she was observed to alter her course and make
towards Lewes Creek. We have since heard nothing of her.—

502

From Samuel Huntington

Philadelphia June 6. 1781.

Your Excellency will receive enclosed, a Resolve of Congress of the 2d Instant, directing, that all Bills which are issued in the respective States in Pursuance of the Resolution of the 18th of March 1780, after the Expiration of one
Year from the Time the Interest on such Bills begins to be completed, be
stamped with the Words or Characters Int. pd one, (or 1) Year.

And that such of the said Bills as have already issued, whenever the Interest
is paid, be stamped in like Manner, to prevent the Necessity & Expence of exchanging them

It is also the Sense of Congress that the several States suspend, as far as
possible, the Issuing of such Part of their respective Quotas of said Bills as
remain to be issued—

503

To John Dickinson and George Read

Dover June the 6th 1781.

I have this moment received a packet from the President of Congress.
Which makes me Anxious to see you both on your way to Lewis—I think
when you see the Contents you will both be of opinion that you Ought to go
and the sooner the better—If you do not come to Town tomorrow morning

by Eleven OClock I must send the Packet to the General Assembly by Express —By a number of Letters in Yesterdays paper the Count De Grass has Arived in the West India's with 25 Ships of the line and 152 Transports. He Engaged the British Fleet off Martinic and beat them—The Fleet was but 37 days from Brest. Five other Ships of the Line parted them in a certain Latitude bound for the Fleet at Rode Island—

504

Message to the General Assembly

Gentlemen of the General Assembly

An Act of Congress of the 31st Ulto a Letter from the President of Congress of the first Instant, and two others of the second, merit your most serious attention. I have therefore sent them to the Secretary and directed him to lay them before your Honors for immediate Consideration.

CAESAR RODNEY

Dover June the 7th 1781.

505

From Thomas Rodney

Wilmington June 9th 1781—

I Set down to give some intelligence but as there is no direct opertunities to Lewis know not when you may receive it—The Count De Grasse sailed from Brest with Thirty Ships of the Line—five he sent of[f] to the East Indies and five more off the western Islands with forty Transports and 14 Regiments he sent to us but they have not arrived yet—with the Rest he arrived with a very large Convoy in 37 days at Martinees[1]—off this Island he fell in with the Brittish Fleet Consisting of 17 ships of the Line and gave them a Severe drubing and cleared the Sea of them after which 7000 Troops were immediately imbarqued & Landed at St Lucy[2] which Island it is expected is by this Time in the Hands of Our Allies—The whole French Fleet Consists of One ship of 100 guns, 4 of 80, 16 of 74—3 of 64 and 3 Flutes & Six frigates at Martinees including what was there before—We have an acct from the southward by water & by Land that Lord Rawdon having evacuated Camden was on his retreat to Charles Town That he was overtaken within 20 miles of Charles Town by Genl Green & Totally defeated and it is expected Green is in possession of Charles Town Cornwallace joined Arnold about the 20th Ult. at Peters-

---

1 Martinique. 2 St. Lucia.

bourgh[1] Virginia—The Marquis[2] at the head of 1000 Regulars & 4000 malitia is giving them all the opposition he can—Gen! Wain[3] will join him in a few days and the malitia being now well armed are Turning out with great Spirit —a Letter from Virginia says a detachment of 2000 Troops from N.Y. is arrived at Portsmouth to Reinforce Cornwallace—Rivington Confesses the disableing three Ships in the action at Martinees but says there was no more in the action and salves it up by ading that Admiral Rodney is prepairing to avenge the injury but other accounts say he is so heavy Laden with the Plunder of St Ustatius[4] he cannot move to the assistance of Admiral Hood who commanded in the late Action—all Rivington has to say for his friends to the Southward is that Lord Rawdon is reinforced with one Regiment and that Cornwallace & Arnold is distroying a great deal of Tobacco on James River &c—Being necessarily detained at home this week I expect to move toward Congress To morrow—

506
Message to the General Assembly

An Act of Congress [of the?] instant relative to the [?] of Credit issued or to be issued in conformity to the Resolutions of the 18th March 1780, having been transmitted to me by the President of Congress, I have directed the Secretary to lay the same before your Honors; together with a Letter from the Board of War of the 30th Ult? inclosing copies of two Acts of Congress respecting specific Supplies directed to be raised for the last Campaign; and also a Return by Cap! Kean, appt'd Recruiting Officer for New Castle County, of Men inlisted for recruiting the Regiment of this State. I also beg leave to inform your Honors that the Receivers of Supplies in the several Counties of this State have made me no Return of Supplies by them received since the last Sitting of the General Assembly.

C. RODNEY

Lewis June 13th 1781.

507
From Thomas Rodney

[Philadelphia, June 14, 1781]

[You will find by the contents of this, that it is a][5] Confidential Letter, conveying you very important and pleasing intelligence.

1 South of Richmond   2 Lafayette.   3 Anthony Wayne.   4 St Eustatius.
5 Parts of letter, appearing within brackets, were copied from Niles' *Principles and Acts of the Revolution*, being illegible in original letter.

Congress has received a Letter from the King of France and are also other-wise officially informed by his minister here—That the Empress of Russia threw out an invitation for the Belligerent powers to apply for her mediation at which the Court of London eagerly caut and mentioned the emperor of Germany as another mediator and a Congress was proposed to be opened at Viena for the purpose of Settling a general Peace—The answer of the Court of France was that they could send no plenip? to said Congress till they had Consulted their Allies, but as the mediators are such respectable Powers and may be so fully relied on for justice, the King presses the United States to Submit to the mediation and that the first prelimanary he will insist on, pre-vious to any other negociations, shall be the Independance of the United States in full, and upon obtaining this, request that the States may be as moderate in all other demands as possible, that the mediating powers may thereby re-ceive favourable impressions of our Equity and Justice—The same mediating application was made to the Court of Spain and their answer was that they Could not do any thing but in conjunction with their Ally the King of France —So that the Congress of mediation is likely to be delayed 'Till our dispatches reach France—However the King says that if he is so pressed that he Cannot decently delay sending a plenipo. 'Till that Time, he shall insist on the pre-liminary before mentioned, and then only proceed in the negotiation so as to have it in such forwardness as will not injure America against their Plenipo. & instructions [arrived. The King of France thinks that very equitable terms of peace may be obtained through this mediation, but urges us strongly] to exert [ourselves this campaign—as the wresting the Southern States out of] the hands of the [British, will contribute] greatly to Lessen their [demands] and make them more readily inclined to Equitable Terms of peace; and that our exertions ought to be Quick and Vigirous, least a Truce should take place and to ensure the Success of this mediation we ought to make the most ample and Vigirous Prepairations for carrying on the war—Brittain made an at-tempt through a M⸢ Cumberland to negotiate a Seperate treaty with Spain, but this has fail'd tho M⸢ Cumberland is Still at Madrid. Spain would not Treat but in Conjunction with France, and France Cannot treat but in Con-junction with America thus are we linked together so that the Independance of America now stands on prosperous ground and no further doubt need to remain about it—For this much is certain all the powers of europe (Brittain excepted) wish u[s] to [be] Independant—Thus far in Confidence with this addition that [Con]gress have appointed Doct⸢ Franklin, J. Adams, J. Jay, H. Laurence, and Gover[nor] Jefferson their principas[1] for settling the peace —They first agreed to app[oint] but one, & Adams was appointed before I

1 Principals, i.e., plenipotentiaries.

came up—they then agreed to add Two men, Then Jay was appointed—then Jefferson had five votes, Franklin four & Lawrence one—The States voted the same way three times—Th[en] I proposed to the members of Virginia & Pensylvania that we s[hould] appoint them both which being generally agreed to this da[y] was appointed for the purpose & then Lawrence was included also—The appointment now Consists of five—New hamshire Pensylvania, Dalaware and Maryland were for Franklin, South Carolina for Lawrence and Masichusets, Conecticut, Jersy, Virgina & N. Carolina for Jefferson—Rhode Island and N.York u[n]represented, Georgia absent—M̃ McKean wanted to alter in favour of Jefferson and leave Franklin out which upon Georgias coming in [would have carried him; but I would not give up Franklin, and by the manner of proposing to appoint them both, got him appointed—though this was exceedingly against the grain of several members. He will now be put at the head of the Commission. His abilities, character and influence are what will be of most use to us in] Europe—J. Adams is not much liked at the F. Court—I shall say no more on this head till I see you. I wish you may find an inclination to come up to Wilmington as soon as the assembly rises—I have an expectation that the President of Congress & his Lady will spend a few days with us about that Time and he is very desirous to see you—

Green has Taken Camden and Two other posts and we make no doubt but the Brittish have lost every post in Georgia & the Carolinas by this Time except Savannah, Charles Town and Wilmington—Green has had a rapid Seerres of success—

Pensylvania is Determined to be Vigirous in giving Afectual aid against Cornwallace and there is no doubt but Maryland will do the same. I hope our State will not be behind them, a bold push now obtains us every thing we have no account of any reenforcements arrived yet to the Brittish from the other side the water—M̃ Morris[1] is gitting our Finances into a better Train and all things now begin to favour us—

508

From Thomas Rodney

Philadã June 15th 1781—

Yesterday I wrote you respecting the Congress of mediation but when I shall have an opertunity by which I may safely trust the conveyance of such

---

1 Robert Morris assumed the office of Superintendent of Finance on May 14, 1781.

intelligence is uncertain—This important business has chiefly Taken up the time of Congress since I last came up and is now Completed.

It was closed by the decision of an important article in the instructions to Our Commissioners which requires them after having obtained our Independence in all things else to be Ultimately Governed by the advice of the French Court or minister—It was moved to reconsider this Clause and to Strike it out as being too Abject and Humiliating—It was argued some hours and at last rejected so that the Clause stands and the French Court is thereby in possession of full and Sufficient powers to make a peace, for there is not the least doubt but the mediating powers will readily Consent to our Independence provided they may make it as Simple as possible and it will be even the Interests of France that they should do this least we should at a future day form an alliance with great Brittain—I was against this Clause because I think it must convince even the French Court that we are reduced to a weak and abject State and that we have lost all that Spirit and dignity which once appeared in the proceedings of Congress and considering our selves unable to Carry on the war any longer we are ready To Accept of peace on any Terms; and we may be sure they will not hisitate about granting any thing the mediating powers may require respecting us after they Consent to our Independance so that there need be no longer doubt about the Certainty of peace—I am far from thinking we are reduced to a State of such necessaty—Yet what is done for ought I know may be best, we have much relyance on its being the Interests of all the powers Concerned to place us in such a respectable situation that we may not fall a prey to any one of them, and that they may all have an equal opertunity of enjoying the benefit of Our Commerce—and there was some fear that our Plenepotentiaries might make such extravigant demands as would preclude an equitable peace and in this Case that France would not be obliged to procecute the war with the direct Object of the Alliance being Simply Independance—And Genl Washington strongly presses the making Peace on the best Terms that can be Obtained—Indeed all the powers of Europe seem so eager to have great Brittain reduced to a Level with themselves that no danger may arise perhaps from this unlimited confidence which we have placed in the Court of France and indeed where there own interests is not materially in view perhaps she may do better for us than we could for our selves for we may suppose that as a new System of Policy is now to be Settled that all the ablest negociaters in Europe will be sent to this Congress and our Plenepo. not being so well versed in the refined art of negociation might by them be overeached or mislead more easily than the French who are much better acquainted with the Interests of Europe and inferior to none of them in the Arts of negociation—In a word if they give us our rank among the nations our Own natural advantages will soon Lift us above them all—Yet I could not help observing on this occasion a little geeringly to M. Smith of Virginia "That the great Virginians who alone Talked of Conquering Brittain, were now reduced to the sad necessaty of owning that they were on their knees at the feet and mercy of the French Monarch and had nothing to expect but pra[y] his benevolence" for such expressions were made use of by M.ʳ Maddiso[n of that] State; and all there members were on that side of the question except Col. [?]

Every thing respecting this Treaty is required to be kept [secret by] Congress and they are such excellent hands at doing this that I h[eard] about it almost, by common report before I came up, yet I wo[uld not] have any thing transpire through me—I expect to go home [next] week and wish your business would permit you to be at Wilmin[gton] then—
Saturday June 16th

We have an acc.ᵗ by an officer from the Eastward that a 50 gun Ship Two frigates and Two flutes with some store ships & 1200, Men are arrived at Boston fro[m] France and that the Alliance & a number of American Vessels are also arrived with them—

The operations against new York may be Expected to Commence Shortly —The last Intelligence from Virginia (8th Inst.) says Wain had joined the marquis—That Lessely with 1000, men ha[d] landed up Patomack—Tarlton had advanced toward the he[ad] of James River to Distroy a large quantity of Stores which were Guarded by the Barron Stuben, and Tarlton being Too week to Effect it Cornwallace was moving that way with his whole Army but the Virginians think that Greens Successes to the Southward will oblige him to Continue his Rout Toward Carolina—

509

To Samuel Huntington

Dover, 22.ᵈ June 1781

The several Acts of Congress which have been transmitted to me since the last Sitting of the Legislature have been laid before the General Assembly of this State at their late Session which concluded on the 20.ᵗʰ Instant. They now stand adjourned to the 3.ᵈ of September next, having passed the following Laws in consequence of the Acts of Congress which have been communicated to them—An Act for raising Twenty one Thousand Dollars in Specie—and an Act for expediting the march of the Recruits raised for the Delaware Regiment. When the Laws are printed I shall transmit them to Congress.

510
To the Board of War

Dover, 22ᵈ June 1781

Agreeably to the inclosed Resolution of the General Assembly I am to inform your Honors that this State being unable to arm, equip and accoutre the Regᵗ of Militia required of them by the Act of Congress of the 31ˢᵗ of May, have requested my Application to the Board for the Loan of as many Arms & Accoutrements as will be necessary to equip Five Hundred of the Militia.

511
Addressee unknown

Dover, 23ᵈ June 1781

In order to expedite the march of the Recruits raised for the Delaware Regiment, the General Assembly have passed a Law to appropriate a Part of the Bounty-Money that now is or may come into your Hands, and which is not expended in Bounties to Recruits already inlisted to the Purpose of purchasing such Necessary clothing as they immediately want, and also for furnishing a certain sum to the officers who are to march with them. The Money thus appropriated is by the said Law made subject to my Draught on the respective Recruiting Officers, and is to be replaced by the like sum from the Treasury when the same shall be collected: And as it is essentially necessary, that those Recruits march with all possible Dispatch to the Regᵗ and probably a Part of the Boun[ty] Monies afsᵈ may be uncollected, I do earn[estly] enjoin you to procure the same without Delay, so that the Troops may be immediately forwarded. *The Clothier-General may shortly receive a Part of the same upon my Order, and enable the Recruits to be sent forward, with the clothing which is absolutely necessary for them.*

512
From Henry Neill[1]

Lewes Town June 27th 1781

Your offering me the Command of this Regiment to be rais'd does me great honor and wou'd my health permit I wou'd except of it with chearfullness but

---

1 Neill having commanded the Second Delaware Regiment of the Continental Line as Lieutenant-Colonel the previous year, which regiment, after service in Kent County, Maryland, had been discharged October 28, 1780, President Rodney offered him the command of a militia regiment requested by Congress, May 31, 1781, and authorized by a resolution of the General Assembly at Lewes, June 18. This regiment was to be subject to the orders of the Commander-in-Chief, George Washington.

the least fatigue has such an affect on me it wou'd render me incapable of Military duty. I shall do everything in my power to forward the expedition from this County.

513
From Samuel Patterson

Xteen Bridge. June 28th 1781.

I rec.d your Ex.cys letter last Eve.g of the 22.nd inst. dated at Dover. I observe the contents & shall acct agreeable thereto. In yours, you say "agreeable to an act passed, the 21st day of June 1780 specifying the number of men which each of the companies of militia should furnish." I know of no such law. I rather think there is a mistake & it must be 1781. I wish if so, your Ex.cy would transmit the extracts of the law as I shall be much at a loss without. However, I shall go on with your orders by the old law. I would have sent you a paper, if I had a sure conveyance—There is but a little in it—It is only the Dutch declaration of war & their reasons that induced them & the baseness of Britain.

By the last acct.s, I see that Cornwallis is at Richmond still. A battle is expected by the marquis.

514
From Robert Morris

Philadelphia 6th July 1781—

I do myself the honour to enclose the copy of an Act of Congress of the 28th of June 1781, from which your excellency will perceive, that I am directed to press a Compliance with the several requisitions of Congress, upon your State, Immediatly upon the Receipt of this Resolution, I wrote to the Treasury Board, the Commissary General and the Quarter Master General for Returns, by which to determine the several Balances due, whenever I shall have received them, I will do myself the honour of addressing your Excellency again On the Subject, and am to pray that in the Interim Measures may be taken within your State, to Comply with these several Requisitions, as far as they may hitherto have been Uncomplied with, the Object of my Present Letter is to give you early Notice of that Resolution, and further to inform you as the Balance of these Requisitions is the Only Fund from which the expenditures of the Campaign are to be drawn I must Urge the most Speedy and punctual compliance on the part of the several States, Your Excellencys Good Sense will render it Unnecessary for me to dwell on this Subject and your regard for the Publick Interest will I am Confident interest you most deeply in facilitating a Compliance with this Essential demand—

515
From Thomas Rodney

Philad? July 10th 1781—

We recd. a Letter this morning from the Comm. in Chief Giving an account of an action near Kings Bridge

He had lay'd a plan for the Duke De lazon with his legion consisting of 600 Horse to surprize a post of Refugees at Morrisene and Gen! Lincoln to make a Diversion in his favour moved down the north River with 800 men in boats while our Army moved down to Take advantage of Circumstances—Gen! Roshambeau Also moved forward to be ready to support the Legion—Gen! Lincoln Landed near where fort Independance stood about four miles from Kings Bridge—And before the Duke arrived at the post of surprize an action Commenced with the Brittish and Gen! Lincoln near Hearlam which Gave the alarm and the Duke finding himself thus disappointed pushed Down to the assistance of Lincoln who endeavourd to Draw the Enemy of so that the Duke might Turn their Flank But they warrely Crossed the Harleam in Boats a party of our Army having Cut them of from the Bridge—This Gave the Comm. in Chief & his Chief Engineer Duportail an opertunity of Approaching so near as to reconnitre the Enemie's works in that Quarter after which the army retired undisturbed—We had 7. killed & 20 wounded—The French army was to join ours on the 7th—

P.S. Congress has been endeavouring some time past to elect a new President M! Huntington[1] having often applied for leave to go Home on account of his health and private affairs, and Yesterday M! Johnson of N. Carolina was appointed but he declined it on Account of his Bad state of health, and to day M! McKean[2] was appointed and prevailed on to serve Till October next at which time he says he is determined to decline serving in Congress any longer—

516
From Robert Morris

Philadelphia July 16" 1781—

I had the honour to inform your Excellency On the 6" inst. of an Act of Congress of the 28" June last directing me to press a Compliance with the

1 Samuel Huntington could have remained President of Congress for one year from March 1, 1781, according to the provisions of the Articles of Confederation.

2 Thomas McKean of Delaware, who was elected President of Congress on July 10, could have continued holding that office until July 10, 1782, but resigning in October, he served only until November 5, 1781, when he was succeeded by John Hanson of Maryland.

several Requisitions of Congress on your State, I am not yet in Condition to state the Account of Specefic Supplies, but I enclose you a Certified Copy of the Acco^t of your State for Money, by which it appears that there is due to the United States 2428000-- dollars of the Old Emiss^n. and 153.148 $\underline{60}$ of the new exclusive of the 4/10 due by the Resolution of the 18" March 1780. Your Excellency will be able to determine how much has been paid as also how much of the Specific Supplies has been furnished, the Remainder of those Supplies forms an additional balance due to the United States which it is my duty to urge the Payment of, I am therefore to request that you will be pleased to lay these Matters before the Legislature of Your State and intreat their Compliance with the Requisition of Congress, Your Excellency must be Sensible of the Impracticability of carrying on the War unless the States will Cheerfully furnish the Means. Whatever they grant will I trust be faithfully applied so as to produce the greatest good to the whole, but if the Means be withheld those and those only who are instrumental in it must be chargeable with the Consequence

Having the most thorough Reliance on your Excellencys Disposition to promote the Publick Cause—I earnestly recommend to you this very Important Object—

517
From Edward Tilghman[1]

Wye [Maryland] 17.th July 1781

Politics which separate so many having form'd some little Connection between you and myself I am encourag'd to present to your Notice my Son Matthew (who purposes spending some Time in his Brother's Office) In Hope that his Conduct may merit the Advantages of your Countenance and Influence.

Your Sand I am told seems nearly run out, mine is very nearly—far different are my Feelings from what they were when I gave my last Farewel to Brigadier Gen! president Ruggles—Permit me Sir to congratulate you on the advancement of our Friend your former Collegue to the Presidency in Congress[2]—An Idea which I fancy did not strike him while he and my old Friend Gadsden were sparring about the Dress of the Bratt he introduced into our former Congress but I am growing tiresome to you as well as myself and therefore (as the saying is) conclude—

1 Edward Tilghman, member of the Stamp Act Congress in 1765 from Maryland.
2 Thomas McKean.

518

From Robert Morris

Philadelphia 25th July 1781.—

I had the honor to write to you on the 16th Instant, inclosing a Certified Copy of the Account of your State as it stands in the Treasury Books of the United States. I now pray leave to recall your Attention to it. It gives me very great pain to learn that there is a pernicious Idea prevalent among some of the States that their Accounts are not to be adjusted with the Continent. Such an Idea cannot fail to spead listless Languor over all our Operations. To suppose this expensive War can be carried on without joint and strenuous Efforts is beneath the wisdom of those who are called to the high offices of Legislation. Those who inculcate maxims which tend to relax these Efforts most certainly injure the common Cause whatever may be the Motives which inspire their Conduct. If once an opinion is admitted, that those States who do least and charge most will derive the greatest benefit, and endure the smallest Evils, Your Excellency will perceive, that shameless Inactivity must take place of that noble Emulation which ought to pervade and animate the whole Union. It is my particular duty Sir, while I remind my fellow Citizens of those Tasks which it is incumbent on them to perform to remove if I can every Impediment which lies in the way, or which may have been raised by disaffection, self Interest or Mistake. I take therefore this early opportunity to assure you, that all the accounts of the several States shall be speedily liquidated, if I can possibly effect it, and my Efforts for that purpose shall be unceasing. I make this assurance in the most solemn Manner, and I intreat that the Consequences of a contrary assertion may be most seriously weighed and considered, before it is made or believed.—

These accounts naturally divide themselves into two considerable branches, viz. those which are previous and those which are Subsequent to the Resolutions of Congress of the 18th March 1780. The former must be adjusted as soon as proper officers can be found and appointed for the purpose, and proper principles Established so as that they may be liquidated in an equitable Manner, for I am determined that Justice shall be the Rule of my Conduct, as far as the measure of abilities which the almighty has been pleased to bestow shall enable me to distinguish between Right and wrong. I shall never permit a doubt that the States will do what is right; neither will I ever believe that any one of them can expect to derive advantage from doing what is wrong. It is by being just to Individuals, to each other, to the Union, to All; by generous grants of Soled Revennue, and by adopting energetic Methods to collect that Revenue; And not by complainings, Vauntings or Recriminations, that these

States must expect to establish their Independence, and rise into power, Consequence and Grandeur.

I speak to your Excellency with Freedom, because it is my duty so to speak, and because I am Convinced that the Language of plain Sincerity is the only proper Language to the first Magistrate of a free Community.—The accounts I have mention'd, as Subsequent to the Resolutions of the 18th March 1780, admit of an immediate Settlement. The several States have all the necessary Materials. One side of this account consists of demands made by Resolutions of Congress, long since forwarded—the other must consist of the compliances with those demands. This latter part I am not in Capacity to State, and for that reason I am to request the earliest Information which the nature of things will permit, of the Monies Supplies, Transportation & which have been paid, advanced, or furnished by your State in order that I may know what remains due. The sooner full information can be obtain'd the sooner shall we know what to rely on, and how to do equal Justice to those who have Contributed, and those who have not, To those who have Contributed at one period, and those who have contributed at another.—I inclose an account of the Specific Supplies demanded of your State, as extracted from the Journals of Congress, tho without any mention of what has been done in Consequence of those Resolutions, because as I have already observed, Your Excellency will be able to discover the ballance much better than I can.—

I am further to intreat Sir, that I may be favoured with Copies of the several Acts passed in your State since the 18th March 1780. for the collection of Taxes, and furnishing Supplies or other Aids, to the United States; The manner in which such Acts have been executed; The times which may have been necessary for them to operate; and the Consequences of their Operation. I must also pray to be informed of so much of the Internal Police of your State as relates to the laying, assessing, levying and collecting of Taxes.—I beg leave to assure your Excellency that I am not prompted either by Idle Curiosity, or by a Wish to discover what prudence would dictate to Conceal.—It is necessary that I should be informed of these things, and I take the plain, open, candid Method of acquiring Information. To palliate or Conceal any Evils or Disorders in our Situation, can answer no good purpose. They must be known before they can be cured. We must also know what Resources can be brought forth, that we may proportion our Efforts to our Means, and our demands to both. It is necessary that we should be in Condition to prosecute the War with Ease before we can expect to lay down our Arms with Security, before we can treat of Peace honorably, and before we can conclude it with advantage. I feel myself fettered at every Moment and embarassed in every Operation from my Ignorance of our Actual State, and of what is reasonably to be asked or expected. Yet when I consider our real Wealth and numbers, and when I compare them with those of other Countries, I feel a thorough Conviction that we may do much more than we have yet done and with more Ease to ourselves than we have yet felt, provided we adopt the proper Modes of Revennue and Expenditure.—

Your Excellencys good Sense will Anticipate my observation on the Necessity of being inform'd what Monies are in your Treasury, and what Sums you expect to have there, as also the times by which they must probably be brought in. In addition to this I must pray you to Communicate the several appropriations.—A misfortune peculiar to America requires that I intreat your Excellency to undertake one more Task which perhaps is far from being the least difficult. It is Sir that you will write very fully as to the amount of the several Paper Currencies now Circulating in your State, the probable increase or decrease of each and the respective Rates of Depreciation.—

Having now Stated the several Communications which are most Indispensible let me intreat of your Excellencys goodness that they may be made as speedily as possible, to the End that I may be early prepared with those propositions which, from a View of all Circumstances may be most likely to extricate us from our present difficulties.—I am also to intreat that you will inform me when your Legislature is to meet. My reason for making this request is, that any proposals to be made to them may arrive in Season for their attentive deliberation.—I know that I give you much trouble, but I also know that it will be pleasing to you, because the Time and Labour will be expended in the Service of your Country—If Sir my feeble but honest Efforts, should open to us the prospect of American Glory, If we should be enabled to look forward to a period when supported by Solid Revenue and Resource this War should have no other duration than the Wisdom of Congress might allow, and when its object should be the honour and not the Independance of our Country. If with these fair views the States should be roused, existed Animated in the pursuit, and unitedly determining to be in that happy Situation, find themselves placed there by the very determination. If Sir these things should happen; and what is more if they should happen soon, The reflection that your Industry has principally Contributed to effect them would be the rich reward of your Toils, and give to your best Feelings, their amplest Gratification.—

519

To Thomas Rodney

Dover Aug 16. 1781.

Mr. Millan informs me that Jacob Boulden & others, have a mind voluntarily to fit out a parcel of vessels & go in pursuit of the Refugee Boats now in our Bay & River. & has requested my consent to their taking into that service the state schooner, now at Wilmington. They purpose also as Mr Millan tells me to take Continental commissions from you—if this be the case, it is my advice, that the state schooner aforesaid be put into the possession of the person you may think proper to commissionate for the purpose above mentioned, & then to be returned to the care of the person who now hath her. I am much in the same state of Health as when I left Wilmington.

520

From Donaldson Yates[1]

Elk [Maryland] 16th Augt 1781—

Viewing it to be a most Interesting matter to the peace and good order of the inhabitants of a State Joined with the Beneficies to the United Interests, to have the public posts supplied with means of business,—permit me to adress you on the situation of the post at Xteen,[2] and to crave the exertion of the State, thro' your notice for every Aid that can be reasonably afforded at this distressed Crisis of our public finances, at present I know of no other resourses —The present State of the post, we have not provisions to subsist troops, or forage to pass teams or support any at the post, a waggon or two is wanted to march the state troops which will be required with them during the Campaign, believe me thro' every period of the post business, I have been under the utmost dificulties owing to the supplies not being made agreable to the Stipulations which appeard to me to be made on the part of the State, I have been informed money have been called from the people in lieu of some of the specific articles granted by the Legislature for the support of the post, when at the same time we were destitute of any such article of supply, I am of oppinion from the present order of business, all supplies made by the State are to be regularly delivered, in order to meet a due and regular Credit, and enable us to make monthly returns that a true State of [the] magazines may appear at all ti[mes a] matter mo[st esse]ntial while we are under the [necessity] of suppor[ting ar]mys, probably an enquiry may [be] necessary, [and ap]prehend some supplies of stores [?] early by the [?] is yet in bulk at Xteen, I have reason to expect the passage of troops soon thro' the state this happening in our present situation, it would not be in my power to give regular assistance, necessity in this case would tend to disorder and distress to individuals these

1 Deputy Quartermaster for Maryland and Delaware.
2 Christiana Bridge.

considerations prompts me to pray your order and directions to any timely aid you think can be obtained, the Gent? who waits on you with this superintends the business of this post and will give you every other information in his power

521

From Nathanael Greene[1]

Camp High Hills, Santee, August 21st 1781

I do myself the honor to enclose you a return of the Delaware Regiment by which you will see they have thin ranks. What the State is doing or what she has done for filling her regiment up to the establishment agreeable to the requisition of Congress I am not advisd. The deplorable situation of the Southern States and the peculiar state of politicks in Europe I perswade [myself] are stronger arguments to induce the State to fill their regiment than I can make use of—But be assurd Sir however pressing our difficulties have been in this quarter the past season they will in all probability increase on our hands at the close of this campaign if there can be said to be any close to a campaign that goes on summer and winter.

I have the pleasure to assure you that your troops without exception have behaved well upon all occasions and for their zeal and fidelity deserve the highest applause.

522

From Robert Morris

Office of Finance 22nd. August 1781.—

I have already in a former Letter forwarded to your Excellency an Account of the Specific Supplies which Congress had demanded from your State. It now becomes my duty again to press for a Compliance with those demands. The Exigencies of the Service require immediate attention. We are on the Eve of the most active Operations, and should they be in any wise retarded by the want of necessary Supplies, the most unhappy Consequences may follow. Those who may be justly chargeable with neglect will have to answer for it to their Country, to their Allies, to the present Generation, and to all posterity. I hope, intreat, expect the utmost possible Efforts on the part of your State, and I confide in your Excellency's prudence and Vigour to render those Efforts effectual. I beg to know most Speedily Sir, what Supplies are collected, and at

1 General in command of the Continental Army in the Southern Department.

what places, as also the times and places at which the remainder are to be expected. I cannot express to you my Solicitude on this Occasion.—

My declaration to Congress when I entered upon Administration will prevent the blame of ill Accidents from lighting upon me, even if I were less attentive than I am; but it is impossible not to feel most deeply on Occasions, where the greatest Objects may be impaired or destroyed by Indolence or Neglect. I must therefore again reiterate my requests; and while I assure you that nothing but the urgency of our affairs would render me thus Importunate. I must also assure you that while those affairs continue so Urgent I must continue to importune—

523

To Thomas Rodney

Dover, Aug. the 30th 1781.

I have enclosed you a copy of the lease you wrote for. I have filled up Commissions for Capt. Pope & Capt. Brown, which came in the old channel as you was apprehensive they would. I have no lower County news worth communicating—but am extremely anxious for the event of this Campaign as from public authority I have reason to expect that we are upon the eve of the most active operations upon our part. I am sorry that we are so illy provided as to the state of supplies especially at this time & do most sincerely wish the General Assembly had if they could done more & on this or such like occasions had vested me as Commander in chief with more power. The State of Affairs seems to require it & it might have been attended with less inconveniency & even damage to individuals by the marching of the Troops.

524

From John Jones

September 1st 1781.

The Major's place having been vacant for some time past by the death of James Mitchell; and Capt John Mitchell being the oldest captain in the Battalion: I take the liberty to mention him as a person that would be agreeable to the officers of the Regiment. And Jacob Irons, as second Lieutenant, and James Miller, as ensign; both in Captain Godwins Compy there are several other Vacencies which Col. Kollock promises to acquaint you with. I should be much obliged to your Excellency for ordering the Commissions to be made out in time for Col. Kollock to bring down with him.

525

From Robert Morris

Office of Finance September 18th. 1781.—

The Commissary General of Purchases, in a Letter of the 15th Instant mentions to me that he shall want a considerable Quantity of Salt at the Head of Elk. As this is very convenient for the State of Delaware, and there is now an existing Demand by the Requisitions of Congress for five hundred Bushels of Salt, I have directed applications to you which I hope will be complied with.—

526

From Ephraim Blaine

Choptank River Oxford Landing [Maryland] 4th October 1781—

I am upon this Shore ordering the Supplies of Provisions Forward to our Army in Virginia—the French Army & Navy with our Continental Troops and Militia consume Sixty thousand Rations per day—we have no Magazine established and are only feeding them from day to day—and I fear it will be impossible to keep up a regular Supply without the utmost Exertion of this State and yours in forwarding to the most convenient Landings upon the Chesepeak the Supplies required by Congress—have therefore in the most pressing terms to request your Excellency to order the Exertions in your Agents and a punctual compliance in procuring those Supplies and delivering the same at the places of deposit to Donaldson Yeates Esquire State Quarter Master who will adopt proper measures to have them forwarded to the Army with the utmost dispatch—Choptank Bridge and the other Landings which lead to Chesepeack Bay would be very convenient places to receive your Supplies.

Our Army have invested Lord Cornwallis and his Army in the Town of York and last Sunday, which was the day I left our Army they had taken possession of all his out Works and redoubts. On Monday all our heavy Artillery would be brought from Burwells ferry on James River, and our Engineers was to have run a line Circumvalation at more than five hundred yards from the Enemy's Works which inclose the town from which Line, our Army will advance by regular Approaches until they Subdue his Lordship with an Army of Seven thousand men which I have not the least doubt will be accomplished in the course of twenty Days—Men who are day & night upon fatigue and exposed to the greatest Danger ought to be regularly Supplied with Provisions and every refreshment they are entitled to—for God sake give me every Assistance and let no excuse prevent the Commissioners from doing their duty

527
From Thomas Rodney

Wilmington Oct. 19th 1781—

When I was down I intended to have advised with you about the offices but coming away sooner than expected it did not occur—If I thought they would be granted at a future day contrary to our wishes I shuld prefer giving them up at this time while you have it in your power to do otherwise. But if it was safe in this respect to hold them longer, the proffits tho small which comes to me would be some inducement for my letting them be, as the publick service lays me under the necessaty of spending a good-deal of my own money for which there does not seem much probability of gitting any other satisfaction than the proffits of those offices which they have been pleased to give me which in deed is much less than the expence I am at in their service—However upon the whole I shall refer the matter to your judgment—You were inclined I know that they should go to Simon and I wanted him when I came up here to administer them by deputation that he might in that Caracter under my Direction & yours to which I should have refered him, have fitted himself to accept of them with Credit to the giver—But this he declind and laid me under the necessaty of Applying to M. Tilton who out of friendship undertook —I communicated to him at the Time your desire relative to Simon that the way might Still be left open—Yet as he has given himself the Trouble of this Charge and fitting himself for it he might think it a little hard to be deprived of them so soon and as he is a particular and deserving friend whom I greatly esteem I would not wish to offend him or even give him any uneasiness on the Occasion tho I at the same time wish to serve Simon who is very deserving—You will consider these circumstances and determine whether it may not be best to wait a more favourable time to dispose of them.

It is true it [is] very doubtful and uncertain who our next President may be[1] —and indeed I think it likely that the difficulty of gitting one that will meet with the general approbation, probably will make it some time before any is Elected—in this Case I think it is likely that the government will again devolve on you—Viz. M. Dickenson will probably be appointed Speaker of the Council—and yourself Speaker of the Assembly in which case as he will not make any stay in the State, the government by the Constitution will devolve on you

1 Caesar Rodney having assumed the Presidency of the Delaware State in April 1778, the constitutional term of three years had expired the previous spring.

untill a new President is Elected—So that if the matter of office should be put of at present, it may still remain in your power to dispose of them in the best manner. However without saying more I shall submit the matter intirely to your judgment to do as you think best—

I have not mentioned this matter to Mr Tilton since he has been here because I did not know what to say to him without having advised with you— I understand that John Clark having taken a parole has [?] himself from acting as Chief Justice of the Commonple[as, in which] Case I think it will be well to press the filling that Post and Mr Collins will not Accept to appoint Tilton who it appears to me will fill the office with more Credit than any other in your power if Collins refuses—This too would leave the matter of the offices altogether open—If Collins refuses this appointment I wish the Assembly to put him in Congress—for you may be assured that State interest prevails so much in that Council at present that you want members whose particular and strong attachment to this State will not let them be carried away by Junto's or parties—By this I do not mean the lea[s]t insinuation against either of my worthy Colleagues for both of whom I have a particular Esteem, and whose conduct when I have been present has, generally met with my intire approbation. But as it is likely Mr McKean will not serve any longer it will be necessary to appoint another at least—

I wish the Legislature would consider seriously the importance of keeping up a well regulated malitia—And that they have solemnly pledged their faith to the United States in the Confederation that they will keep up such a malitia —This is not only necessary for our safety at present, but in future, least the neighbouring States seeing us weak and feble may hereafter be tempted to invade our Liberties contrary to the Confederation—The malitia will never be of any consiquence untill they are established agreeable to a system of pure military principles unmixt by Civil imbarrasments except their being subject to their supreme Direction and Controle—And the malitia being the same people who Compose the Civil government there never can be any danger of their Acting upon military principles as Malitia when the Safety of their Civil polity absolutely requires it—A Constant view to the incouragement of Commerce and Agriculture is Absolutely necessary to enable us to make those exirtions in the present war which is Our duty[1]—Therefore I hope effectual measures will be Taken to prevent the Refugees from harrassing our Bay next summer—

These things I know will not escape your attention yet the mention of them can do [no] injury—We are all pretty well at present and hope to be down about the November Court—

1 This letter was written on the day Cornwallis surrendered at Yorktown.

528

Message to the General Assembly

Gentlemen of the General Assembly,[1]

The repeated and pressing applications made to me since the Sitting of the last General Assembly relative to the Supplies which have been required by Congress from this State, induces me to intreat the Attention of your Honors to this Subject. The Aids thus sollicited seem to be particularly of Provisions, and it may be remembered, that no specific Supplies have been granted by this State for the Service of the present year. Of the last Grant of Money made by the Legislature, by which those Supplies could be procured, if it was to be so appropriated, none has yet, I believe, been brought into the Treasury.

I must also request your attention to the Act of Congress, of the 3d. of February last, for levying an Impost of five per Cent. on articles of Merchandize imported and on Prizes and Prize-Goods.

The Secretary will lay before your Honors the several Applications which have been made to me on these Subjects; and also all other Public Papers that have been received by me, among these are, a Memorial and Letter from the Consul of France, complaining of the injurious and illegal Conduct of the Inhabitants of Lewes Town, towards the Sieur Heguy, and the other Officers and Crew of a French vessel that was wrecked near that Place, on the 29th of April last, and solliciting the Interference of the Authority of this State for Reparation and Satisfaction for the Injury sustained.

I must also request your Honors to make Provision for the Payment of a Fee to James Wilson Esqr. of Philadelphia, who was employed to defend the Claim of this State to the Schooner Fortune, upon an appeal from a Decree of the Court of Admiralty here to the Court of Appeals of the United States.

CAESAR RODNEY

Dover, Octr. 25th, 1781.

529

Addressee unknown

The concern you express for my Welfare, and your inquiry with re[s]pect to the State of that Horrid and most obstinate disorder, the Cancer, which I now Labour under and am Endeavouring to have cured,[2] adds to the many Proofs

---

1 The General Assembly met in Dover from October 20 to November 14, 1781.

2 It was in the year 1768 that Caesar Rodney had first sought a cure in Philadelphia of the cancer on his face. During the intervening fourteen years, while living through the strenuous years of the Revolution, this serious ailment had sapped his vitality to such an extent that now, upon his

you have hitherto given of your friendship for me, and be assured that Duty
as well as inclination leads me to give to so friendly a correspondant the most
satisfactory answer in my power, especially on that head—It is now four weeks
since the Doctor first dressed me, which he has continued to do twice a day
ever since. The Doct! declares with the greatest confidence that he shall perfect
a cure. Many of those who have been under his hands, with similar complaints, but not half so bad, have been to Visit me, and are of opinion with the
Doct^r, in short they don't seem to have a single doubt, and my inclination and
wishes to be relieved from so intolerable a disorder leads me to hope they are
right—but was I left to form a Judgement from my own feelings I should not
be verry sanguine, I have doubts; However, be this as it may, I am determined
to persevere, it is a matter of the first consequence to me in this world, no
less than Life or Death. The Issue is Joined and must now be Tryed. The
Doctor must conquer the Cancer, or the Cancer will conquer me—You are
pleased to speak respectfully of my conduct in public matters—I am much
oblidged to you for your good opinion, and honestly confess that few things
afford me more real satisfaction than that my conduct especially in the public walks of life should meet the approbation of Good men—When the contest between Great Britain and America first commenced, I stept forth among
others in order to obtain a redress of Greivances. This and no other was my
aim until absolutely refused. The Question then was Independence or the
Bayonet, I was at no loss in determining which to chuse. Independence then
necessarily become the American Cause, to this Cause I have Strictly adhered,
and hope it will ere long be established, but Sir I always kept in View the good
order well Being and Happiness of the people, more especially those over
whom I had lately the Honor to preside, and Trust That none who know
me believe otherwise—If I should get the better of this Complaint before mentioned verry lettle Service can be expected of me in future, my constitution, I
find, is too much unhinged for me to discharge the duties in a public Station
of any considerable importance agreably to the people's expectation, or my
whishes, in short my constitution requires Rest and my wish is to indulge it.
—The inteligence we have received from the other side of the water lead us to
suppose the enemy intend a Vigorous campaign. This is no more than I expected, for they are not in a scituation to propose terms of Peace in a direct
manner, Their affairs are too embarrassed. They must keep up appearances,
until they can bring it about in some other way, either by withdrawing their
Troops from America and bringing their whole force to act against France and
Spain, or by procuring a Peace through the mediation of Some of the Nut[r]al

relinquishing the cares of a war governor, his life was fast approaching its end. The undated letter
is endorsed: "Winter 1782 by C. R. when he went to Phila^d to Dr. Martin."

Powers—Upon the whole I think we shall have Peace or at least a cessation of arms before it be long, and that finally it will be crowned with the Independence of the United States.

Sir

When I left home I expected to have gone no further [than] Wilmington and there been attended by the Doctor for the cure of my Cancerous complaint, but on seeing him found I was under the disagreable necessity of repairing to Philadelphia where I have been between five and six weeks and where it is most likely I shall be detained many weeks more—I am necessarily at a verry considerable expence, my cash is running verry low, and, by means of the refugees, all communication between that part of the State where I live, and the market here is intirely cut off—Now Sir being thus circumstanced, if there is any money due to me which ought to come through your hands, you will oblidge me exceedingly by procuring and transmitting it to me, or any part thereof, that you have or may receive, as soon as possible—You will be pleased on the rect. of this letter to write to me concerning this business—I now begin to have some hopes that the Doctor will perfect a cure, but the disorder is extremely obstinate and therefore you may readily suppose it will be a tedious as well as painfull business—However as it is a matter of the first consequence to me I am determined to persevere—We have no news worth communicating but are in expectation every day of something important from several different Quarters

530
From Thomas Rodney

Wilmington Feby 9th 1782

Lysha got safe home Yesterday about five OClock By him I recd your letter and the papers (and one in the morning before he Came)—also my Cloaths—I intend to Set of to Dover tomorrow and shall endeavour to rent your place if posible before my return.

Col. G. Lattimer come to my house since dusk & has just gone away he informs me that the Assembly has passed or had ready when he left them seven acts one for the protection of the bay, one for the preventing taking Vessels out of the harbours of this State, one a Malitia Law and one for remedying some defects in a former Law &c That yourself Mr McKean, Phill. Dickerson and Sam Wharton are appointed Deligates the Col Observed that the appointment was made after he left the assembly and that he shou'd not have voted for either of the Two last That the appointment was very Supprizing and

Especially the Latter. and in my opinion it is very Extraordanary indeed to appoint a man who has been all the war and long before residing in England intimate with ministerial and political men, and has no knowledge of or connection with the affairs of this State, and perhaps hardly an acquaintance in it except with G. Read—but this is a Sample of a new system of Politics now Established no privey Concil (or any juges or justices for Kent) are appointed.

Col: Lattimer Says he left the President at OFlins when he came up here—that he is on his way to Philadᵃ—

I had a letter from Simon to day and I suppose all are well as he has not mentioned the Contrary—He writes that the C. justice has threatened them very much about the Brig, that they mean to keep possession Till advised otherwise—A prohibition was presented to me the day before yesterday, and a Copy to the Marshall &c and tho I am clearly convinced that it is Granted without proper authority, yet as it is likely the other judges when the Court sits may be govern'd by the conduct of the C. Justice, to save the parties the Expence of Appeals &c I have advised the marshall to deliver the Brig to the Libels and advise them to apply to Two Majistrates under the Act of Assembly—

By the Solemn opinion of all the Judges of the Common Law as reported in Lord Cook they never Issued a prohibition but in Term Time in open Court and never at any time in the Vacation and the marshall says he was present and heard the pleadings & that nothing contrary to this was Shewn—and tho this matter will now go of as I have advised, I shall be glad when an opertunity offers, to hear Mr McKeans opinion respecting this affair.—There is no doubt but the Conduct of the Chief Justice in this affair will licence a general Trade to New York— . . .

531

To Thomas Rodney

Philadᵃ Febʸ ye 21st 1782

I recd your Letter by Coll Pope, dated the 18th. I think it was on that day, not expecting you would return so soon from Kent, That I wrote to Betsey, since when I am inclining to be of opinion with the Doctr. that my disorder is mending, and therefore as the compleating a Cure of it, is a matter to me of the first consequence I have concluded to stay here the whole of next week in order to see what change may be made in that time. so that you need not think of coming up sooner, unless you should have some other inducement—The British hold forth the appearance of another Vigorous Campaign. This I expected, as they are certainly not in a scituation to propose a Peace in any direct manner, but they certainly must adopt some method to bring it about either by withdrawing the Troops from America and thereby change the mode of opposition and endeavouring to obtain the mediation of some of the Neutral powers—in short I think their affairs are so circumstanced that it must finally end in the Independence of America, and that we may, either by the withdrawing the Troops, or by a cessation of Arms, soon feel the good effects of that Independence—I don't know certainly how this Letter may get to your hands or I would send you the last papers, but don't doubt you have seen them by this time—Since Elisha left this I have discovered your powder-Bag—Pomatum &c and they are safe.

532

From Thomas Rodney

Wilmington Feby 27th 1782—

I wrote by Captⁿ Moore a day or two ago and therefore have but little to say at this Time, but as the barer Captⁿ Prole will be down again in a day or two it will give you an opertunity of writing by him—A small Vessel from the west Indies and laden chiefly with rum was Taken a few days ago in our Bay by the Refugees and the Captⁿ and officers wounded and ill treated after surrender, several men were killed in the Contests—The officers as we are informed are at Dover— . . .

533

To Thomas Rodney

Philadelphia March 18th 1782.

I have sent you with this Letter the Pensylvania Packet of Saturday last wherein you will see in Lord North's Speech upon Sir James Lowther's motion, that he is oblidged to declare and promise that Ministry will not prosecute the War in America offensively, in short they don't seem to have an Idea of maintaining any Post here except New-York. It appears clearly that if he had not made this declaration early in the debate that the motion of Sir James would have been carried by a considerable majority, and even with this declaration He carried a Vote for postponing that motion and taking up the order of the day, by a majority of no more than forty one, when there were present four hundred members including the Speaker. There are great Bett's in this City, That Charles-Town was evacuated on or before the Thirteenth of this month[1]—Yesterday we received certain accounts That the Island of St. Kitts

1 Charleston was evacuated by the British December 14, 1782.

is totally in possession of the French & that the British Troops Killed & taken Prisoners, amount to upward of Two Thousand five hundred. A gentleman informed me last evening, that the articles of capitulation were in Town, I have not as yet seen them—Mr. McKean informs me that Mr. Matlack the Secretary received a Letter yesterday from new-York or from some person who had Just left that place, informing him that a packet had Just arrived there with the following accounts, That a Peace was concluded between Great Britain and the States of Holland, and that a Total change in the Ministry had taken Place, That Lord Shelburn was at the head of the Treasury, Lord How at the head of the Admiralty, Coll. Barry Secretary for American affairs &c.[1]—If these accounts be True, which is not verry improbable, it is most likely that Sir James's [motion] has been taken up again and carried—I make no doubt that the Ministry might have maintained their majority in Parliament for carrying the American War in the manner they would wish but an inflamitary [Disorder] has seized the People which Ministry cannot cure. This Disorder was carried from Virginia, broke out in the Cities of London & Westminster and will probably run throughout the whole Island—It is clear that the British have shifted their Ground, and if they do not succeed [in] this Campaign beyond even their own most sanguine expectations, they must, in my opinion sue for a Peace on such Terms as they may be most likely to obtain it, be them what they may. . . .

534
To Thomas Rodney

Philadelphia. March 19. 1782.

Together with my other letter & the paper of Saturday, Mr. Danl Freeman will deliver you this letter & this day's paper, in which you find but little news Except the capitulation of St. Kitts. The paper of this day makes no mention of a change in the Ministry, but I am nevertheless satisfied it is true—& my opinion is founded on information rec'd this morng from good authority, that a certain person in this city who would not wish his name should be made use of, has rec'd a late New-York News-paper on which is wrote by a person formerly of distinction in this place, the account & names of the persons now in place. I have not heard as yet who they are, except those mentioned in my other letter.

A Congressional gentleman told me this morng & that I might rely on it, that Charles-town was actually evacuated, & as well as he could remember on

---

1 Lord North, the Prime Minister, resigned on March 20 A motion urging the King to end the war had passed the House of Commons on February 27.

the 24th of February, & that an Express from that Quarter is Every day expected. In all probability we shall hear more of these important matters in a
few days. I wish you health & success in the prosecution of the business you
went to Kent about. I am astonished at not seeing your advertisement in this
day's paper, & shall send for Miers to Know why he has neglected it.

535
To Thomas Rodney

Philada. March 25th 1782—

. . . The merchants here have bought the Hyder-Alley of sixteen Six
pounders as a Guarda Costa. She is now down the Bay and is, or is to be commanded by Captn. Barny who maried a sister of Wilmington Bedford—I am
informed they are carrying on Coll. Popes Vessel with Spirit, and the Assembly here have appropriated certain of their funds, for fitting out one similar to that of Pope's. When these things are compleated Grain will be of more
value below—

, Mr. McKean told me last evening, That the captain of a Vessel who was
taken down the Bay some time ago by one Jones a refugee Captain and had
had his nose cut by him after he had surrendered, was come to this City, and
as he was walking out Yesterday somewhere about the water side to his great
surprise saw this same refugee Captain Jones and knew him whereupon he
immediately had him apprehended and sent to Prison—Mr. McKean says he
had notice of it Yesterday, and they were to be brought before him this morning for examination. I have not heard since what had passed on the examination—This fellow must have come here in order to inform himself what Vessels were going out, when they were to go, and what strength they were of—It
was a bold undertaking for which I hope he will be hanged—My hopes of
succeeding with respect to my complaint increases almost every day, but my
patience is almost wore out, my anxiety to get home is verry great and increases daily—

536
To Thomas Rodney

Philadelphia April 2d 1782.

As I have not heard from you since your Letter of the 19th Ulto. at Dover,
and as we have verry little news worth communicating, I am not well furnished with subject matter for this Letter—I packed up a number of News-

papers yesterday and committed them to the care of Mr. Sykes, together with
a Letter dated the day before, who promised to deliver them to you at Wilmington, Where, as I stand informed by Mr. John Vining, You arrived on
fryday last from Kent—There is a report prevailing here, in which I do not
verry much confide, That the British Fleet under the command of Sir Saml.
Hood, is blocked up at Antigua by the French Fleet, which is greatly superior
to that of the British, That the French have Landed six Thousand Land-Forces
on the Island, That admiral Rodney [?] arrive with Twelve Ships of the Line,
and cannot form a Junction with Sir Saml.—This account, it seems, comes by
a vessel from St. Thomas's to Baltimore—but a circumstance which gives it
more credit than it otherwise would have had is, That some of the disaffected
here, were whispering it about, with some degree of concern, several days before the account came from Baltimore—Missrs. Faress of your Town, with two
children of which she had been delivered, was buried here Yesterday—I begin
to be verry Sanguine in my expectation that a cure of my disorder will be
perfected but it is so obstinate and there is so much to do, That I am convinced
it will take many months yet to compleat the business. I have therefore meditated a retreat for about two weeks, to take place some two or three weeks
hence, but then to return to the charge—The scituation of my affairs seems to
make this step necessary, and I am in great hopes that about three weeks from
this time I may venture to take this step without danger—however shall write
further about it—

537

To Thomas Rodney

Philadelphia May 11th 1782.

Mr. Moses Levy will deliver you this Letter and the news-papers of this day
& Wednesday last, by the papers you'l find that the former minority men have
carried the principal point they had in view which was a change of the Ministry and then have taken up the old Plan of sending Commissioners to treat
with the States Generally as individually. However, bitter as the *Pill* is they
must swallow it before long—Their present view is to unite Great Britain and
America and under a total change in Ministry they flatter themselves they shall
succeed, supposing we looked upon those former Minority-men to be our
friends, but I should suppose no good man ever did or ever will believe that
any of them had the least friendship for us, but on the other hand wished
unanimusly to subjugate us and will consider the Step they have now taken in
that point of View— . . .

538
To Thomas Rodney

Wilmington Sepr. 11th 1782.

On Sunday last about three hours before I received your Letter, Captn. John Willson set out for Philadelphia upon your old Gray Horse under a promise of returning him the next day by Lieut. Kidd, however the Horse did not return till this evening which put it out of my power to send him off for Kent before tomorrow morning—I have not been able to procure you either yesterdays or this days paper. They give an account, received by a packet arrived in Six weeks from Falmouth, of another considerable change in the Ministry of Great Britain Marquis of Rockingham dead, Earl of Shelburn first Lord of the Treasury & prime Minister, Temple & Pitt Secretaries of State,—Keppel, Fox, Burk & five or six others resigned—This change is not accounted for as yet—Mr. Dickinson, the President,[1] who was to see me to day, is of opinion with my self that it has arose from some disturbance among themselves, This ministry being made up of two parties Jumbled together, The Rockingham & the Bedford.

The papers have also the Kings Speech, very mild and good natured—There is also an account of the French Fleet in the East Indias having beat the British Fleet there and captured four or six of them all of the Line, and gained many other advantages—

539
From John Rodney

[No date. 1780–82?]

By the Constitution of this State it appears that the President and Privy Council are vested with a power, of nominating & appointing most of the Ministerial Officers; and it seems to have been the intention of the Convention, that they shou'd not continue in their respective Offices, longer than five years if other proper persons could be found; at the same time it is implied, that a discretionary power is given to the President to continue such, if that should not be the case.—

Upon the Death of Mr Holt, the Justices of the Peace here nominated Jacob Kollock ju., David Hall & my self, for the Office of Clerk of the Peace; that office as well as the prothonotary's became vacant by Mr Holt's death—*they*

---

1 John Dickinson succeeded Caesar Rodney as President of Delaware.

made such Interest with Governor Hamilton, that he gave the prothonotary's to M! Kollock, and the Clk: of the Peace to M! Hall, who continued in those Offices 'till the year 1777, when a new Commission came to each of them for the said respective Offices—but M! Kollock refusing to accept his Commission, the prothonotary's office was also added to Coll. Hall; and about two years ago my Term as Trustee of the Loan Office espiring the Assembly saw fit to Confer that Office likewise on Coll. Hall.

We have little Trade here being as it were blocked up with the Refugees & privateers—I hold no Office except Clerk of the Supreme Court, which commenced in June 1778.—And as I Officiated in the above mentioned offices in M! Holt's Time for several years, of consequence must be in some measure acquainted with the business: Therefore if his Excellency the President & the Council should think proper to change those Offices, I should be exceedingly Obliged to them to favour me with the prothonotary's if they should not see meet to grant both.

But the misfortune is, I have very little acquaintance with either the President or Council, which lays me under the necessity of requesting your good offices in my behalf, which I make no doubt you'l be good enough to do, and from your Intimacy with his Excellency, & acquaintance with the members of the Council, I apprehend a word from you in my behalf, will have more weight, than anything I could say on the Occasion, were I personally present.—

540

From Eleazar McComb[1]

Philadelphia 12th March 1783.

I sit down to mention the news of the day, which you will be pleased to communicate to our friends in Dover.

Captain Barney arrived this day from France, under the protection of a passport signed by the British King, and brought the Preliminary Articles of Peace, signed by the Commissioners on the part of Great Britain and the United States of America, on the 30th November last. The Preamble sets forth that they are not to take effect 'till a Peace with France is concluded, and that they are to be included in, and make part of, the definitive Treaty.

By the 1st Article the King of G. Britain acknowledges the United States of America to be free, independant and sovereign States, and for himself, his

---

1 Delegate in Congress from Delaware.

heirs and Successors, forever relinquishes all right and title to them. By the 2d the boundaries are fixed, to begin at the North West angle of Nova Scotia, and run to the North West head of Connecticut River—then down the River to the 45th degree of North Latitude—then thro' the Lakes Ontario, Erie, Huron, Superiour, long Lake, and Lake of the Woods; and from the North West end of the latter a due West Course to the river Mississipi—Then down that river to the 31st degree of North Latitude,—then to the river Apalachicola,—from thence to the flint river—from thence to St. Mary's river, and down that river to the Atlantic Ocean. The line between New England and Nova Scotia to begin at the Mouth of the river St Croix, which empties into the Bay of Fundy, and run from thence to the first place of beginning, including all Islands within 20 leagues of the Land, except such as were formerly known to belong to Nova Scotia. By the 3d we have a right to fish on the Banks of Newfoundland, and to cure the fish on certain uninhabited islands. By the 4th Creditors in either Country are to be allowed to recover their just debts contracted before the year 1775. By the 5th Congress is to recommend to the Several States to restore confiscated property to real British subjects, and also to Persons resident within the British lines who have not borne Arms against the United States; and to suffer others of different descriptions to go into any of the States and remain 12 Months in order to endeavour to recover their property—to revise their Laws for Confiscation, so that the estates which have been sold may be restored to the former owners, they refunding the real value of the sums actually paid for such estates. By the 6th there are to be no confiscations in future, nor any prosecutions for past offences. By the 7th Firm friendship is to be established—all Hostilities to cease—all prisoners set at liberty, and the British troops withdrawn as soon as possible, without destroying or carrying off property. American artillery to be left behind, and all Records which have fallen into the hands of their officers to be restored. By the 8th the Navigation of the river Mississippi is to be free to both Countries. By the 9th it is agreed that if any place should be conquer'd by either party from the other before the arrival of the articles the same shall be restored.

This account is taken from short Notes Made in Congress during the reading of the articles, and therefore cannot be supposed to be very Accurate. I write it in haste in hopes of meetting with a conveyance this evening—if it should not go before to-morrow it may be accompanied with a News Paper.

Please to present my Compliments to Dr Tilton, and inform him that the Commutation of the officers half-pay was agitated in Congress on Monday last, and the question lost by the division of Connecticut. I think it probable it will be brought on again in a few days.

541

To James Newman et al.

Delaware State

In the Legislative Council at Dover

October the 28th 1783—

To James Newnam Sergeant at arms and to all other officers within the County of Sussex in the said State—

You are hereby strictly charged and commanded to Summon John Wiltbank and John Laws Esquires both of the said County of Sussex to be and appear before the Honourable the Legislative Council on Thursday the sixth day of November next ensuing at ten of the Clock in the morning of the same day then and there to testify all and singular those things which they shall know or be examined in concerning the conducting and carrying on of the last General Election held at Lewis Town for the said County of Sussex on the first day of this present month of October: Hereof fail not at your Peril—

Given by order of the Honourable the Legislative Council aforesaid at Dover the twenty eighth day of October in the year of our Lord one thousand seven hundred and eighty three and in the Eighth year of our Independency—

Caesar Rodney Speaker[1]

Attest.

James Sykes Clk

542

Foreword in Thomas Rodney's Account Book as Executor of Caesar Rodney's Estate

Be it Remembered that the Hon Caesar Rodney Esq Speaker of the Legislative Council and Member of Congress, and President, Capt[n] General & Commander in Chief of the Delaware State—Died at Poplar Grove near Dover and on the west side the Dover River, his then place of Residence in the 57th year of his age on Saturday the twenty sixth day of June about Seven Oclock in the evening 1784

He left his last will and Testament in writing under his hand and Seal which Will was proved before the President of the State on the 13th day of

1 As Speaker of the Upper House of the General Assembly (Legislative Council) Caesar Rodney was also Vice-President of the State.

July following—And by the said will he made his brother Thomas Rodney sole Executor during his life and his brother William to succeed.[1]

THOMAS RODNEY

543

To John Baning

Sir

It is particularly requested that the Council, should attend the funeral of the Honbl. Caesar Rodney, at his late Dwelling place, on Monday Morning,[2] Eight oClock.

Saturday Evening

[1] The book contains a full account of the administration by Thomas Rodney of Caesar Rodney's estate.

[2] June 28, 1784.

APPENDIX

NOTE ON CAESAR RODNEY'S GENEALOGY

THE name Rodney, spelled however Rodeney until the time of Caesar Rodney the Signer, comes down through the centuries in England a very distinguished one. The first Rodney of whom there is any record was one Sir Walter Rodeney who, it is recorded, came into England from France with the Empress Maud in 1095, that is, about twenty-nine years after William the Conqueror defeated King Harold at Hastings. Sir John Rodeney (born 1551, died 1612) of Morelinch Parish, Somersetshire, represented the seventeenth generation from Sir Walter, all generations from Sir Walter to Sir John save four having been knighted by the crown.

Sir John Rodeney married Jane Seymour, who was the daughter of Sir Henry Seymour; and thus the niece of Edward Seymour, Duke of Somerset, of Queen Jane Seymour, third wife of Henry VIII of England, and of Baron Thomas Seymour, husband of Catherine Parr, widow of Henry VIII.

The third son of Sir John Rodeney and Jane Seymour was William Rodeney (born in 1600), who married Alice Caesar, the daughter of Sir Thomas Caesar and his third wife, Susanna Ryther, a daughter of Sir William Ryther. Sir Thomas Caesar and his brothers, Sir Julius Caesar and the Rev. Henry Caesar, D.D., were sons of Dr. Caesar Adelmare, physician to Queen Mary, who came to England from Italy in 1550, and of his wife, Margaret Perin, daughter of Martin Perin. Dr. Caesar Adelmare was the son of Peter Maria Adelmare of Treviso, Italy, and his wife, Paola de Paolo Caesarino.

William Rodeney and Alice Caesar had two sons, named William and Caesar. The latter married a woman whose first name was Sarah, some time before 1666, and later emigrated to the island of Antigua in the British West Indies. The first son of William Rodeney and Alice Caesar married a woman whose first name was Rachel. She is mentioned in the will of William Rodeney, the emigrant to America, as "mother," and as living in Bristol, England, with two of his sisters, Elizabeth Rodeney and Rachel Curtis.

William Rodeney the emigrant, son of William Rodeney and Rachel, and grandson of William Rodeney and Alice Caesar, was born in 1652, died September 8, 1708, and was buried on Byfield Plantation near Dover, Kent County, Delaware.[1] Having come to America from Bristol, probably in 1681, William Rodeney seems to have landed at some point on the Eastern Shore of Maryland and later gone thence to Philadelphia. From Philadelphia he went

1 His will was dated May 1, 1708, and probated October 4, 1708. (See Will Book B 1–65 in Kent County Register of Wills Office, Dover, Delaware)

to Sussex County to live, and later became a resident of Kent County. He married twice. His first wife was Mary Hollyman, by whom were born three children, William (died 1732), Rachel (died 1695), and Thomas (died 1709). William Rodeney, the first son of William Rodeney the emigrant, married Ruth Curtis, who gave birth to five children, one daughter and two sons dying in infancy, the oldest child, Penelope, marrying James Gorrel, and the youngest, John (born 1723, died 1792), who first married Sarah Paynter, by whom there was no issue, and later, Ruth Hunn. John became by his second wife the progenitor of the Lewes and New Castle lines of Rodneys which have many distinguished members on their rolls, the former including Daniel Rodney, Governor, Member of Congress, and United States Senator; the latter including George B. Rodney, Member of Congress.

William Rodeney the emigrant married his second wife, Sarah Jones, on February 20, 1693. She was the daughter of a well-to-do landowner in Kent County named Daniel Jones. By her he had six children: Daniel (died 1744), John (died 1708), Anthony (died 1720), George (died 1725), Sarah (died 1727), and Caesar, who was born October 12, 1707, and who died May 3, 1745. William Rodeney the emigrant became quite a prominent political figure in the Government of the Three Lower Counties, the principal honor coming to him being his election as the first Speaker of the Assembly after the legislative secession in 1704. On the occasion of William Rodeney's death in 1708, James Logan, the well-known secretary to William Penn, referred to his passing as a serious loss to the Government.

Caesar, the youngest child of William Rodeney the emigrant, inherited his father's entire estate. He married Elizabeth Crawford, the daughter of the Rev. Thomas Crawford, an Episcopal clergyman, on October 13, 1727. By her there were born eight children, five sons and three daughters: Caesar Rodney, the Signer of the Declaration of Independence (born October 7, 1728, died a bachelor June 26, 1784), Elizabeth (born 1730, died 1765), George (born 1731/2, died 1750), Sarah (born 1733/4, died 1734), Mary (born 1735, married Joshua Gordon, died 1782), William (born 1738, married Lydia Paradee, 1762, died 1787), Daniel (born 1741, died 1764), and Thomas (born 1744, married Elizabeth Fisher, 1771, and died in Mississippi Territory in 1811).

Upon the death of Caesar Rodney the elder, his widow, Elizabeth Crawford Rodeney, married the second time a man named Thomas Wilson, by whom she had two more children named Sarah and John, the former of whom is always referred to in Caesar Rodney's letters as Sally, and who seems to have presided over his household although married to one Simon Wilmer Wilson. There were two children of this union, namely, Caesar Rodney Wilson and Elizabeth Wilson.

Caesar Rodney's sister Mary had five children by Joshua Gordon: Elizabeth (married Dr. John Brinckle), Sarah (married one Pleasanton), Samuel, Mary, and Letitia (the last three dying young); and his brother Daniel had a daughter named Sarah, who married one John Ferguson. His brother Thomas and Elizabeth Fisher had two children, Caesar Augustus Rodney, who married Susan Hunn of Philadelphia, and Lavinia, who married one John Fisher. Caesar Rodney's brother William had by his wife, Lydia Paradee, five children: Letitia (married Dr. John Laws), Elizabeth, Lydia, Mary, and John (the last four dying young).[1]

In his will and codicil of January 20, 1784, and March 27, 1784,[2] respectively, Caesar Rodney the Signer bequeathed personal property to the following: William Rodney, his brother; Sarah Wilson, his half sister; Lavinia Rodney, his niece (daughter of his brother Thomas); John Wilson, his half brother; Caesar Augustus Rodney, his nephew (son of his brother Thomas); Caesar Rodney Wilson, son of his half sister Sarah Wilson; Letitia Rodney, his niece (daughter of his brother William); Elizabeth Gordon, his niece (daughter of his sister Mary Gordon); Sarah Rodney, his niece (daughter of his brother Daniel). Most of his real estate he devised to his nephew, Caesar Augustus Rodney.

The Caesar Rodney letters came into the possession of his executor, his brother Thomas, and from him they were inherited by his son, Caesar Augustus Rodney, who in turn bequeathed them to his son, Thomas McKean Rodney of Wilmington. They were successively owned by Thomas McKean Rodney's sons, Caesar Augustus Rodney, who died in 1884, and John M. Clayton Rodney, who died in 1918. A sister, Mrs. H. N. Twells of Woodbury, New Jersey, inherited them from her brother, and after her death, they were sold by Mr. Twells in 1919 at auction in Philadelphia, and are now owned principally by the Historical Society of Delaware, the Delaware Public Archives Commission, the Genealogical Society of Pennsylvania, the Library of Congress, the New York Public Library, and Mr. Frank H. Stewart of Woodbury, New Jersey.[3]

---

1 The authority for the principal part of the genealogical account is a blueprint chart compiled by W. Nelson Mayhew of Philadelphia in 1909 and deposited in the Historical Society of Pennsylvania Certain additions have been made upon the authority of entries in the Rodney Bible in the possession of Hon. Richard S Rodney, New Castle, Delaware

2 Caesar Rodney's original will and codicil are deposited in the Delaware Public Archives; copies are owned by the Historical Society of Delaware The account book of Thomas Rodney, the administrator of the estate, is owned by Mr. Frank H. Stewart, President of the Gloucester County (New Jersey) Historical Society.

3 See Stan V. Henkel's catalogues nos. 1236 and 1238.

SOURCES OF MATERIAL

Ownership of the originals of the letters and documents printed in this volume is as follows:

(The letters "o.d." refer to an original draft, which was usually retained by the writer for his own files, a clean copy being sent to the addressee.)

HISTORICAL SOCIETY OF DELAWARE, WILMINGTON, DEL.

2, 3, 4, 6 (*o.d.*), 7, 8, 11, 14, 15, 16, 17, 19, 21, 22, 24, 25, 26 (*o.d.*), 31, 35, 36, 38, 39, 56, 61, 63, 67, 68, 74, 76, 79, 85, 88, 95, 99, 102, 103, 104, 107, 108, 111, 113, 114, 118, 120, 121, 122, 126, 129, 133, 135, 138, 139, 140, 142, 144, 145, 146, 151 (*o.d.*), 152, 153, 154, 155 (*o.d.*), 158, 163, 170, 174, 180 (*o.d.*), 188, 212 (*o.d.*), 216, 217, 220 (*o.d.*), 229, 231, 234, 239, 243, 261, 262, 268 (*o.d.*), 280, 284 (*o.d.*), 291 (*o.d.*), 293 (*o.d.*), 296 (*o.d.*), 297, 300, 301, 304, 305, 313, 314, 321, 323, 324, 326, 328, 329, 333, 334, 337, 340, 348, 352, 353, 356, 362, 365, 366, 374, 376, 379, 383, 387, 394, 396 (*o.d.*), 397 (*o.d.*), 398 (*o d.*), 404 (*o.d.*), 407, 410, 415, 418 (*o.d.*), 422 (*o.d.*), 428, 435 (*o.d.*), 438 (*o.d.*), 442, 444, 445, 446 (*o.d.*), 448, 449, 450, 451 (*o.d.*), 454 (*o.d.*), 459, 479, 482, 483 (*o.d.*), 486, 487, 489, 491 (*o.d.*), 494, 500, 501, 505, 507, 508, 515, 520, 524, 527, 530, 532, 539.

DELAWARE PUBLIC ARCHIVES, DOVER, DEL.

64, 69, 78, 81, 83, 86, 90, 92 (*typewritten copy*), 105, 130, 131, 148, 150 (*o.d.*), 167, 175, 178, 182 (*photostat*), 183 (*o.d.*), 185, 187 (*o.d.*), 189, 191 (*o.d.*), 193 (*o.d.*), 196, 199, 201, 202, 203, 205, 208, 233, 237, 238, 245, 246, 247, 254, 256 (*o.d.*), 260, 271, 272, 283 (*o.d.*), 298 (*o.d.*), 315 (*o.d.*), 318, 319, 327, 331, 336 (*o.d.*), 367, 375, 377 (*o.d.*), 380, 389, 391 (*o.d.*), 401, 403, 424, 426, 429 (*o.d.*), 435, 437, 462, 463, 464, 465, 467, 470, 472, 473, 475, 481, 485, 488, 490, 492, 496, 497, 498, 502, 514, 516, 518, 522, 525, 526, 543.

LIBRARY OF CONGRESS, WASHINGTON, D.C.

47, 51, 159 (*o.d.*), 209 (*o.d.*), 211, 214 (*o.d.*), 250, 251 (*o.d.*), 286, 288, 303, 307, 317, 322, 325, 341, 343 (*o.d.*), 344 (*o.d.*), 345, 347, 357 (*o.d.*), 360, 364, 368, 392, 398, 408, 409, 411, 417, 419 (*o.d.*), 425, 426 (*o.d.*), 427, 430 (*o.d.*), 439 (*o.d.*), 457, 466 (*o.d.*), 471, 474, 476, 480, 499, 504, 506, 509 (*o.d.*), 510 (*o.d.*), 511 (*o.d.*).

——*Rodney MSS*, 26, 278, 282.

——*Papers of the Continental Congress*, Vol. 70, 257 (*fol.* 647), 258 (*fol.* 651), 291 (*fol.* 675), 293 (*fol.* 679), 294 (*fol.* 683), 296 (*fol.* 687), 308 (*fol.* 695), 384 (*fol.* 723), 388 (*fol.* 727), 396 (*fol.* 737), 404 (*fol.* 741), 418 (*fol.* 757), 509 (*fol.* 769); Vol. 78, 186 (*fol.* 101).

——*Washington Papers*, 210, 212.

——*Presidents' Letter Book*, Vol. II, 292, 295, 370, 452, 458.

——*Force Transcripts,* 41, 57, 71, 73, 162, 166, 171, 172, 173, 177, 179, 181, 192, 194, 195, 198, 213, 215, 219, 242, 249, 277, 281, 285, 302, 309, 312, 320, 335, 349, 354, 355, 361, 383, 393, 399, 405, 406, 412, 414, 416, 433, 434, 440, 460, 513, 519, 523, 534.

GENEALOGICAL SOCIETY OF PENNSYLVANIA, PHILADELPHIA, PA.
18, 30, 32, 33, 37, 43, 45, 62, 75, 77, 82, 94, 101, 110, 119, 124, 160, 164, 165, 168, 218, 221, 223, 225, 232, 236, 241, 244, 251, 255, 267, 268, 274, 290, 308 (*o.d.*), 316, 330, 332, 342, 369, 371, 372, 373, 385, 390, 453, 455, 484, 493, 517, 540.

NEW YORK PUBLIC LIBRARY, NEW YORK, N.Y.
9, 29 (*Emmett Coll.*), 52, 70, 109 (*o.d., Bancroft Coll.,* I, 207), 112 (*same,* 215), 117 (*Emmett Coll.*), 132, 157, 161, 169, 184, 190, 204, 210 (*o.d.*), 226, 252, 294 (*o.d.*), 311, 350, 359, 382, 402, 421, 431, 535 (*Emmett Coll.*), 538.

AMERICAN ANTIQUARIAN SOCIETY, WORCESTER, MASS.
80, 248.

CHICAGO HISTORICAL SOCIETY, CHICAGO, ILL.
240.

ILLINOIS STATE HISTORICAL SOCIETY, SPRINGFIELD, ILL.
264, 265.

MAINE HISTORICAL SOCIETY, PORTLAND, ME.
93.

NEW YORK HISTORICAL SOCIETY, NEW YORK, N.Y.
97, 275, 287, 338, 346, 378 (*McLane Papers,* Vol. I), 413, 477.

HISTORICAL SOCIETY OF PENNSYLVANIA, PHILADELPHIA, PA.
40 (*Misc. Papers, 1655–1805, Three Lower Counties, Del.*), 44 (*same*), 60 (*same*), 269 (*Dreer Coll.,* II, 40), 503.

WISCONSIN HISTORICAL SOCIETY, MADISON, WIS.
339.

COMMONWEALTH OF MASSACHUSETTS ARCHIVES, BOSTON, MASS.
310.

COMMONWEALTH OF PENNSYLVANIA ARCHIVES, HARRISBURG, PA.
363, 533.

HAVERFORD COLLEGE LIBRARY (*Roberts Collection*), HAVERFORD, PA.
50, 298, 299, 478, 491, 528.

UNIVERSITY OF PENNSYLVANIA LIBRARY, PHILADELPHIA, PA.
531.

YALE UNIVERSITY LIBRARY, NEW HAVEN, CONN.
46, 395.

WILLIAM L. CLEMENS LIBRARY, ANN ARBOR, MICH.
521 (*Nathanael Greene Papers*).

HENRY E. HUNTINGTON LIBRARY, SAN MARINO, CAL.
115.

J. P. MORGAN LIBRARY, NEW YORK, N.Y.
155, 266, 276, 537.

GEORGE A. BALL, MUNCIE, IND.
54, 96.

J. DANFORTH BUSH, WILMINGTON, DEL.
28.

HON. JOHN W. GARRETT, BALTIMORE, MD.
23 (*o.d.*), 147.

GOODSPEED'S BOOK SHOP, BOSTON, MASS.
206.

JOHN GRIBBEL, PHILADELPHIA, PA.
49, 53, 443, 447.

J. STUART GROVES, WILMINGTON, DEL.
48, 224, 263, 273, 279, 358, 420, 456.

MRS. FLORENCE BAYARD HILLES, WILMINGTON, DEL.
351 (*o.d.*), 386 (*o.d.*).

MRS. ANNE READ JANVIER, NEW CASTLE, DEL.
10.

JAMES G. LONGFELLOW, WILMINGTON, DEL.
461.

WILLARD S. MORSE, SANTA MONICA, CAL.
34 (*photostat*), 42, 235, 244 (*o.d.*), 253, 400, 436, 441, 512, 529, 536, 541.

R. C. NORTON, CLEVELAND, OHIO.
230.

FREDERICK S. PECK, PROVIDENCE, R.I.
65, 89, 176, 423, 468, 469, 495.

HON. RICHARD S. RODNEY, NEW CASTLE, DEL.
1, 27, 58, 106, 109, 116, 134, 137, 149.

DR. A. S. W. ROSENBACH, PHILADELPHIA, PA.
23, 87, 91, 156, 207, 227, 270.

FRANK H. STEWART, WOODBURY, N.J.
5, 6, 12, 13, 20, 542.

Rev. Roderick Terry, Newport, R.I.
    127.

Gabriel Wells, New York, N.Y.
    71 (*o.d.*).

The following letters and documents were copied from printed sources:

American Archives, Peter Force, Editor.
    98 (*5th series,* I, 944), 100 (*same,* p. 1092), 123 (*5th series,* II, 510), 125 (*same,* p. 840), 128 (*same,* p. 918), 136 (*5th series,* III, 653), 141 (*same,* p. 1370), 143 (*same,* p. 1446).

Journals of the Continental Congress, Worthington C. Ford, Editor, XIII, 186–188.
    306.

Letters of Members of the Continental Congress, Edmund C. Burnett, Editor.
    72 (I, 455. Original said to be owned by Wm. D. Ely, Providence, R.I.), 259 (III, 197).

Autograph Letters and Autographs of the Signers of the Declaration of Independence in the possession of George C. Thomas.
    228.

Delaware Register, William Huffington, Editor, I, 101.
    66.

Principles and Acts of the Revolution, Hezekiah Niles, p. 250.
    222.

Pennsylvania Journal and Weekly Advertiser, June 19, 1776.
    84.

Pennsylvania Magazine of History and Biography, XXXIX, 109.
    432.

Stan V. Henkels, *Catalogue,* No. 1236.
    55 (p. 16, item 42), 59 (p. 17, item 43).

Unidentified Catalogue Clippings.
    200, 289.

INDEX

INDEX

Names in the Preface are not indexed, and those of persons in the Rodney family previous to Rodney the emigrant and of persons dying in infancy are not included; all others are intended to appear, with the exception of Caesar Rodney the Signer himself, and unidentified names in very contracted form. It is thought unnecessary to list under his name the varied references to our Caesar Rodney's life and activities, since a résumé is given in the Biographical Sketch, pages 3–17, and the chronological order is followed in the letters. His incumbency of several offices is cited under the names of those offices and organizations, or under the word Commission, or both. Certain of the personal aspects of his life will be found under the words Birth, Education, Property, Travel, Health, Death, Grave, Will. A genealogy of the Rodneys is given on pages 445–447. Letters to and from Thomas Rodney are not usually found indexed under his name, owing to their frequency. Likewise, letters to or from Dover, Philadelphia, and Wilmington, etc., are not indexed as such under those names. A number of entries of related significance are grouped under such headings as Armies, Arms, Assembly, Clothing, Commissions, Congress, Courts, Forage, Live Stock, Naval, Navies, News, Provisions, Supplies, etc.

Guy, *Mr.*, "Mr. Guy's medicines," 31

Habeas corpus, 258, 262, 264
Haddonfield, N.J., 181
Hall, *Col.* David, 55, 89, 191, 195, 203–204,
    206, 210, 255, 257, 258, 259, 275, 306,
    337, 350, 390, 397–398, 405, 408, 438–439
——, John, 57
——, *Dr.* Joseph, 253
Hall of fame, Caesar Rodney in, 17
Hambleton (Hamilton?), *Capt.*, 130
Hamburgh, Del., 234
Hamilton, *Capt.*, 160
——, Andrew, 36
——, *Gov.* James, 29–30, 31, 439
Hancock, John, 58, 79, 95, 144, 201
Handy or Handley, *Col.*, 311
Hanson, John, 399–400, 419
——, Thomas, 51
Hardy, *Admiral Sir* Charles, 326
Harlem, N.Y., 121–122
Harlem River, 121–122
Harney, *Lieut.* Genethan or Jonathan, 109, 110,
    131 (Harvey)
Harrison, *Major*, 212
——, *Gov.* Benjamin, 9
Harvey, *Lieut.* See Harney, *Lieut.* Genethan
Haslet, *Col.* John, 5, 9, 51, 64, 70, 73, 74, 77,
    78, 79, 82, 84, 86, 88, 93, 94, 95, 98, 102,
    106, 108, 109, 110, 111, 114, 115–117,
    122, 123, 125, 126, 131, 132, 133, 136,
    137, 139, 140, 142–143, 146, 152, 171,
    172, 191
——, *Mrs.* John, 109, 113, 115–116, 117, 132,
    146, 153, 179
Haughey, Robert, 224, 233
Hawkley. See Hockley
Hayett, Peter. See Hyatt, Peter
Hays, *Capt.* Nathaniel, 361
Hazel, Benjamin, 138, 158
Hazen, *Col.* Moses, 407, 408
Hazlet, John.. See Haslet, *Col.* John
Head of Elk. See Elk, Md.
Health of Caesar Rodney, 16, 28–31, 430–432,
    433, 436, 437
Heath, *Gen.* William, 153
Heguy, *Sieur*, 430
Hell Gate, N.Y., 139

"Hen and Chickens," 203
Henly (Henley), *Maj.* Thomas, 138
Henry, *Capt.*, 150
——, Matthew, shallopman, 49, 53
Hessians. See Mercenaries, Hessians
Hill, ——, 374
Hillegas, Michael, Treasurer, 107
Hillmer, *Col.*, 166
Hillsboro, N.C., 372, 403
Hitchcock (Hitchcocks), *Col.* Daniel, 154
Hockley (Hawkley), ——, 36, 49, 52
Hodgden, ——, 111
Hodgson, *Lieut.-Col.* (*Maj.*) Robert, 30, 104,
    135, 282, 298, 330, 388, 395
Hogs. See Live stock
Holes, John, 278
Holker, John (French consul), 357, 360, 363,
    364, 365, 373
Holland, *Capt.* (*Ensign, Adjutant, Lieut.*),
    Thomas, 73, 74, 153
Holliday (Holladay), Robert, 53, 58, 64
Hollingsworth, *Col.* Henry, 338
——, Jacob, 223
Hollyman, Mary. See Rodney, Mary (Holly-
    man) (*Mrs.* William Rodeney)
Holt, Ryves, 438
Homes, *Lieut.-Col.*, 167
Hood, *Admiral Sir* Samuel (first Viscount
    Hood), 412, 437
Hooper, *Col.*, 178
——, William, 69, 251–252
Hopkins, Esek, Commander of the fleet, 352
Hopkinson, Francis, Treasurer, 297
Hornshook, N.Y., 121
Horse (Light horse, etc.), 61, 62, 69, 143, 147,
    153, 156, 173, 207–209, 212–214, 221,
    229, 230, 231, 232, 235, 237, 242, 248,
    253, 256, 289, 293, 331, 373, 377, 400
Horses, 144, 167, 171, 177, 212, 213, 218, 347,
    349, 352, 367, 397, 419
Horse racing, 146, 349
Horsey, William, 125
Hosman, *Lieut.* Joseph, 306
Hospital, General, 106
Hospitals for poor, 36
House of Assembly. See Assembly
House of Commons. See Parliament
House of Lords. See Parliament

CPSIA information can be obtained
at www.ICGtesting.com
Printed in the USA
BVHW051407141021
618837BV00005B/52